BOOKS BY GEORGE VECSEY

Coal Miner's Daughter (with Loretta Lynn)

Martina (with Martina Navratilova)

Five O'Clock Comes Early: A Young Man's Battle with Alcoholism
(with Bob Welch)

One Sunset a Week: The Story of a Coal Miner

Getting Off the Ground: The Pioneers of Aviation Speak for Themselves
(with George C. Dade)

*Joy in Mudville: Being a Complete Account of the Unparalleled History
of the New York Mets*

The Way It Was: Great Sports Events from the Past (editor)

A Year in the Sun

A YEAR IN THE SUN

The Games, the Players,
the Pleasure of Sports

GEORGE VECSEY

𝕿imes BOOKS

Grateful acknowledgment is made to the following for permission to reprint previously
published material:

CPP/Belwin, Inc. and International Music Publications: Excerpt from the lyrics of
"City of New Orleans" by Steve Goodman. Copyright © 1970, 1971 by Buddah Music
Inc. and Turnpike Tom Music. Rights assigned to CBS Catalogue Partnership. All rights
controlled and administered by CBS U Catalog Inc. Used by permission. International
Copyright Secured. Made in U.S.A. All Rights Reserved.

The New York Times Company: Excerpts from George Vecsey's columns. Copyright ©
1986 by The New York Times Company. Reprinted by permission. All rights reserved.

LIBRARY OF CONGRESS CATALOGING-IN-PUBLICATION DATA
Vecsey, George.
A year in the sun / by George Vecsey.
  p. cm.
ISBN 0-8129-1678-6 : $18.95
1. Vecsey, George.   2. Sportswriters—United States—Biography.
I. Title.
GV742.42.V43A3 1989
070.4'49796'0924—dc19
[B]

Manufactured in the United States of America
Designed by Beth Tondreau Design/Jane Treuhaft
9 8 7 6 5 4 3 2
First Edition

To May Spencer Vecsey,
For All the Love and Attention

ACKNOWLEDGMENTS

There has never been an acknowledgments page that did not thank somebody for "getting me through" or "putting up with my neuroses." I've written the line more than a few times myself, always for the same person: my wife, Marianne Graham Vecsey. This time she outdid herself. While running what became a nursing home, boardinghouse, and furniture clearance center at times, out of necessity she put aside her own career as an artist to enable me to pursue my self-involvement in this book. (She says Georgia O'Keeffe had a few nonproductive years, too.) She has been a friend, counselor, editor, and valet for a long time, and without her, there would be no career, no book.

I also want to thank:

Our children, for growing up and staying close. In this diary of 1986, David has a featured role because he was the last child home, but our love and aspirations for Laura and Corinna remain constant.

Jonathan B. Segal, the vice-president and editorial director of Times Books, for keeping after me all these years.

Esther Newberg, for finding room for one more client.

Howard Angione and Gordon Thompson, for helping me cope with the computer age.

Sam Freedman, for the double compliment of praise and prodding. Jessica Siegal, for suggesting the added chapter.

Our friends around the world, who make it fun to keep going.

Everybody at *The New York Times,* for making me proud to be a lifer.

PROLOGUE

My father took me to a baseball game when I was seven. A lot of parents take their children to ball games, but this was different. Using his press pass, he escorted me into the press room, where I learned that the game of baseball was played not only on the field. I can remember the beery laughter, the knowing voices, the gruff attendant who slid a soda across the bar to me. I can also remember Dixie Walker hitting a home run over the tall screen in right field, and I can remember the Brooklyn Dodgers beating the Cincinnati Reds by a score of 5–3.

Afterward, my father took me to a fence alongside the Dodger clubhouse, where the last straggling players clumped down the runway. He pointed out some of the reporters, visiting the clubhouse—"for quotes." The next day, he said, their stories would be in the papers. The *Daily News. PM. The New York Times.* The *Tribune.*

As we took the subway home, I thought about the world my father had shown me—outside in the daytime, beyond the bounds of office and school, watching the games, meeting the players, getting to write stories and seeing them in print the next day.

While my classmates were in school, while my mom was home running a house full of children, while my father would normally be in the office editing copy, these reporters were off on a permanent case of hookey. Sounded pretty good to me.

Since that afternoon in 1946, I have pursued my childhood vision of journalism as truancy, journalism as escapism, journalism as adventure, journalism as experience. I had to leave sports for ten years to keep the thrills coming.

I have covered the World Series and the Olympics, and also the death of a hundred people in a narrow coal valley in West Virginia. I have covered the final matches of Joe Frazier and Muhammad Ali, and also covered a papal conclave in Rome and followed Pope John Paul II on his first trips to Mexico and the United States.

I am the only journalist I know who has interviewed Casey Stengel, Loretta Lynn, and the Dalai Lama. What scared me was, I thought I understood all three of them.

Somehow I wound up back in sports, as a columnist for *The New York Times,* and the real adventure began to be internal, a search within. At first I thought a sports column was merely a "bully pulpit" for venting all the things you knew, all the opinions you held, but it became much more than that.

Because a sports column is personal, opinionated, and free-wheeling, it can become a Freudian expression—fifty minutes at the word processor instead of on the couch. Why do I sometimes write in the first person? Why do I write so many columns about female athletes? Why do I think boxing should be abolished? How do I get my ideas? Where do they come from? They pay you to take a Rorschach test.

On the one day for which they were written, those columns were the most important thing in my working life, close to a compulsion. They were formed by events, shaped by odd workings of my mind, framed by time, limited by my finite ability, built on facts and opinions that may or may not have been correct, and colored by everything that had happened in my life up to then.

The column never goes away. When I was a reporter, I could finish an assignment, take the phone off the hook, and not feel guilty. As a columnist, I know there is always a space reserved for me that day or the next. One suspects they could find somebody else to fill that space, but one really doesn't want to find out.

As a columnist, writing four times a week, I feel a kinship with Sisyphus, the legendary king of Corinth who was sentenced to push a huge rock up a hill for eternity. When he reached the summit, the rock would tumble downhill, and Sisyphus would have to start all over again. Albert Camus once said that he liked to think Sisyphus enjoyed what he was doing.

* * *

In 1986, while I was covering the Goodwill Games in Moscow, my wife and I stood on a balcony of our hotel suite, staring straight into the fantastic striped onion domes of St. Basil's. It occurred to me that the seven-year-old standing outside the Dodger clubhouse in 1946 would not have dared to dream of a suite overlooking Red Square, but this was part of that vision—the continued adventure, the long escape.

At the end of the year, when I prepared my annual "Postcards" column, I realized I had more to say about my assignments in Mexico and the Soviet Union, the Mets winning the World Series, athletes dying from drugs, the Giants flexing their muscles toward the Super Bowl, and Dwight Gooden getting into a scrape with police officers in Tampa.

I wanted to write not only about sports, not only about athletes, but about journalism, about writing a column, about curiosity, about creativity, about listening to the inner ear—why I wrote those columns, why I went to those events, what my options had been. As the book evolved, it also included my parents, my family, my friends, all the people who shaped me, all the places I had been, the books I had read, the songs I had heard.

In writing about 1986, I tried to limit myself to what I knew, how I felt, at the moment the column was being formed. A few times I have added italicized comments, mostly to let the reader know I am aware that life kept moving. Nobody knows that more than a journalist—even one who has been at the ballpark, one way or the other, for more than forty years.

A YEAR
IN THE SUN

JANUARY

MIAMI, JANUARY 1

We are caught in a traffic jam, half a mile from the Orange Bowl. I look out the bus window and see people with blue cat's-paws painted on their faces, other people with red stripes painted on their faces. They are in different cars, waving pennants and honking horns, fans of the Penn State Nittany Lions and the Oklahoma Sooners showing their school colors.

In the press bus, we run the style gamut from T-shirts to jackets and ties, but no cat's-paws, no stripes.

Tonight's Orange Bowl will decide the national championship. Most of us have been working on the morality-play angle, pitting Joe Paterno, the high-minded coach of Penn State, against Barry Switzer, the rule-bending coach of Oklahoma—two schools and two states locked into stereotypes, good versus evil, unless you happen to live in Oklahoma.

There will not be one writer in the press box tonight who has not, at least once in the past week, revived Paterno's offhand remark, six years ago, that he was not ready to retire and leave coaching to "the Barry Switzers and Jackie Sherrills of the world." Paterno has been downplaying the remark ever since, while Switzer has been trying to show the world that he's not such a bad fellow.

Switzer has the juicier role in this script. What actor would not prefer to play the swaggering bad guy than the righteous civic father? He reminds me of Rod Steiger in the movie *No Way to Treat a Lady*. When somebody discovers Steiger is a sadist, Steiger cocks his hip, flips his wrist, and lisps, "That's doesn't mean I'm not a nice person." Switzer is the son of a bootlegger, ran some hootch and packed a weapon before he ever got to college, and has been involved in stock scandal and divorce between national championships. He drinks hard and recruits hard. That doesn't mean he's not a nice person, maybe.

Like Spencer Tracy playing yet another honest district attorney, Paterno supports ethical recruiting, endows his university with money, and makes sure his players earn their degrees.

Of course, I respect Joe Paterno more than Barry Switzer. Of course. But when I see two huge squads representing two huge universities playing on national television on New Year's night, I have trouble separating the two schools and even the two coaches. I see them as part of the same system.

When the bus arrives at the decaying old bowl, it is already dark out, the air muggy, the noise intense. Friends and family of the players are lined up at the reservation windows, waiting for their passes. Fathers, mothers, little brothers, big sisters, girlfriends. This tropical evening is the biggest night of their lives. I must remember, this game is for them, not for us.

As I pass two young black girls, maybe twelve years old, one of them giggles and says, "Hi, Abe." I smile at her. With my reddish square-cut beard with no mustache, a thin frame and a long, serious face, I seem Lincolnesque to some people. My standard line is, "Hey, it's better than looking like Nixon or Reagan."

I take the elevator to the press box, already crowded with reporters and columnists from around the country. I recognize more than half of them, the familiar faces, the old war-horses, from the World Series, the Super Bowl, the Kentucky Derby, along with regional football specialists I don't recognize.

"You're still on the beat," I say to a very large, very handsome man, standing with a soda in his hand.

John Ed Bradley played center for Louisiana State University in three different bowl games. Only a few years later, he is writing sports for the *Washington Post,* under orders from a large coterie of editors, agents, friends, family, and other admirers to write that first novel, get out of this business. The good ones leave younger and younger these days.

"How's the novel?" I ask.

"Comin' along," John Ed says. From a southern man, that could mean anything. We make a date for dinner tomorrow night. My wife will enjoy hectoring him to write that novel.

I glance at the teams warming up on the field, all those mysterious formations. After all my years in sports, football is still foreign territory to me. Growing up in Queens with a sports journalist for a father, I had a dream of walking through the press gate, through a dark tunnel, up to the batting cage of Ebbets Field, standing on grass in the noon sunlight, watching the Brooklyn Dodgers take batting practice. I reached most of that dream when I was twenty-one; I still live it when I check into any ballpark.

The two *Times* seats are high above the fifty-yard line, as *Times* seats tend to be. I squeeze alongside Malcolm Moran, a huge teddy bear of a man who seems even bigger with his telephone, his bulky Teleram computer, his tiny television, his binoculars, and his press guides and notebook spread around him. He's writing on deadline and needs every one of his tools. Because of the late start, I am not writing a column tonight, but will comment on the national championship for the Friday paper.

"I'll cover one locker room for you," I tell Malcolm.

I take out my headset and listen to my Jacques Brel cassette, French in my ears, passion in my heart, in a football press box. Some of my colleagues think I am antisocial because I listen to cassettes in press boxes, but everybody has his own way to prepare to work.

My hero in this regard is Rich Gossage, the country hardball pitcher who used to be with the Yankees. Before a game, the Goose liked to sit in his locker and sing "Blue Eyes Crying in the Rain." Goose found out I am part country boy, and sometimes he invited me to sit and croon along with Willie Nelson.

Goose's teammates did not say, "Goose, why don't you be more sociable?" For one thing, Goose is somewhat big and has something of a temper. For another thing, they knew Goose had his own timetable. He would yawn and close his eyes and sing along with Willie, and sometime around the first inning he would amble out to the bullpen, and sometime around the sixth inning he would ingest a cup of black coffee and his eyes would widen, and when the Yankees' manager-of-the-week got on the telephone, Goose's right arm was tingling. Goose knew how to pace himself.

With Jacques Brel taking me to the cafés of Brussels and Paris, I study the names and the numbers on the program. Lindsey Nelson, the grand master of college football broadcasters, once told me he could come into town on Friday night, memorize two complete rosters, including pronunciations, by Saturday afternoon, and totally forget them by the time his plane took off Saturday night.

Finally, the game starts, seemingly miles below us, on the other side of thick glass windows. The players are like chess pieces down there; we squirm to watch the overhead television monitors for every replay. The fans at home see and hear more of a football game than a reporter does.

A few years ago, I got home from a Giants game, and on the eleven o'clock news I saw a player cut inside right tackle for the touchdown, which was interesting, since I had described him cutting inside left tackle. Fixed it for the second edition, I did.

Tonight, Penn State gives up a few interceptions and Paterno changes quarterbacks, but nothing helps. Oklahoma—the bad guys, the black hats—will be the national champion.

In the final minutes, many of us take the press elevator and rush through the tunnel toward the field. The noise of the crowd surprises me with its concussion. Every time the ball is moved, a huge wave of sound bellows from the stands, mass moans, mass sighs, mass cheers.

We stand right on the sidelines, watching players with dirt and blood and grass stains all over their uniforms, with bruised faces and cut forearms, still hitting each other. The impact of their helmets and their shoulder pads goes "chunk-chunk-chunk," and you can hear them grunt when they block one another. This is a different game from what we were watching behind thick glass.

When the gun goes off, the Oklahoma players dance on the field, celebrating their 25–10 victory. The reporters wait under the stands, watching the Penn State players funnel toward their locker room. With their helmets off, the players look younger than they appear on television, baby-faced kids of eighteen and nineteen, a few of them crying.

"Heads up, heads up," shouts Rogers Alexander, a burly black senior linebacker. The players brace themselves, their eyes hard again as they walk through the gauntlet of reporters. If this were President Reagan rushing off from the White House, we would be shouting questions at him over the roar of the helicopter engines, but the ritual of sports reporting is to wait until the formal press conference.

As long as I have been in sports, I have discovered that losers are often more interesting than winners. Also, there is usually less of a crowd around losing teams.

After a while, Joe Paterno comes out and stands in front of a microphone, facing the television cameras and the lights, his eyes blinking behind his thick glasses. In his enduring Brooklyn accent, Paterno says, "We got beaten by a better team. We did not play well enough to win, but we can still hold our heads up."

Paterno makes his regular pitch for an official national-championship game rather than leaving it to the dubious wisdom of the polls, but he knows Oklahoma is the champion this year.

I don't bother rushing to the Oklahoma side to hear what Barry Switzer has to say. The winning coach must put in an appearance at a press conference tomorrow morning—later today, by now. As long as I have been in sports, I cannot get over the feeling it is not natural to be awake after midnight. Being a morning person is something of a professional disadvantage to a sports journalist, but I make do.

The press elevator is running slow because television technicians have commandeered it to dismantle their elaborate equipment. One thing you learn quickly in this business is who is important and who is not. After a long delay, I deliver the Penn State quotes to Malcolm, who is finishing his sub story for the last few thousand papers, writing for the archives.

Because it is not my night to write, my Goose Gossage adrenaline never kicked in. I go out in the street, littered with drunken fans, and find a cab back to the hotel. Marianne is already asleep, so I crawl into bed thinking about my lead for tomorrow.

MIAMI, JANUARY 2

Barry Switzer seems amazingly refreshed on an hour and a half of sleep, smirking like Rod Steiger playing comedy. He's reformed a bit in his old age—"not trying to be all-hospitality room anymore," he says with a wink.

He gives credit to the players, although he does admit he is one terrific recruiter, charming moms and dads at kitchen tables all over the Southwest.

"Those players in Norman, Oklahoma, didn't just fall out of the sky," he concedes.

We are all a little numb from working late last night, and are grateful for a little good-old-boy humor in our notepads.

After listening to Joe Paterno last night, talking up a national-championship play-off, I started thinking about writing a column defending the current system of coaches and football writers voting in two different polls.

I kind of like the crassness of the bowl system—the syrupy southern committee members coming around to college games in their tomato-red and lox-pink sports jackets, calling everybody "Hoss" and "Buddy," trying to snag the best teams available.

The bowl system is also a boon to a sports columnist. You can write about the ratings, the accusations, the regional prejudices, the hurt feelings, the deals, the lack of clear-cut winners, the feuds and disagreements, for years on end.

I find it incongruous that Joe Paterno, as played by Spencer Tracy, with a reputation for academic soundness, wants to extend the college season a few more weeks. Switzer, who knows about skulduggery, admits there is going to be skulduggery in any system.

"There are certain schools that will never win the national title with a play-off. There just aren't enough positions for them," he says. Referring to another football coach, he adds, "Lou Holtz said to put the four top teams into a computer, but I don't know if that's feasible, either. Who feeds the computer?"

Paterno's annoyance with the system dates back to 1969, when Penn State won all eleven games but was outpointed by undefeated Texas in both polls. Paterno was particularly unhappy when a public servant named Richard Milhous Nixon attended the Texas-Arkansas game and declared on national television that the winner of that game would be the national champion.

At the Penn State graduation in 1973, while the same Mr. Nixon was in a bit of legal trouble, Paterno told the audience, "I don't understand how Richard Nixon could know so much about college football in 1969 and so little about Watergate in 1973."

In the interests of fair journalism, I restrain myself from resurrecting Paterno's Nixon quote any more than, oh, twice a year. And today is one of those days.

Last night while falling asleep, I thought about the adage we used to repeat in the picturesque coal hollers of central Queens: "If it ain't broke, don't fix it." With that theme, my column is about halfway written.

KEY WEST, JANUARY 3

I am walking the tropical streets with my wife, looking for the perfect conch-chowder restaurant. Just to help out the paper, I volunteered to stay behind in Florida to write about the Browns-Dolphins game tomorrow, before heading up to Chicago for the Giants-Bears play-off on Sunday. It just happened that I had a day off to take my honey to Key West.

Being out in the middle of the day still feels like hookey to me. The palm trees and bright sun remind me of our first trip to Florida in March of 1961. I was just out of college, writing high-school sports for *Newsday,* dreaming of being Jimmy Cannon or Dick Young. Marianne and I had been married six months; we went to jai-alai games and got burned at the beach and ran low on cash and ate in cheap restaurants, the things kids do on spring break.

On our way through St. Petersburg, by some mysterious coincidence, I parked outside Al Lang Field, where the St. Louis Cardinals train.

Five minutes later, I spotted two men carrying duffel bags—freckle-faced Red Schoendienst and Stan Musial, the laughing warrior who had terrorized my Brooklyn Dodgers back in the old days.

I poked Marianne and said, "Look, look, that's Stan Musial and Red Schoendienst," and Marianne said, "Umm, that's nice." We didn't stay for the game—group decision—but I had taken a glimpse of spring training. I would remember my way back.

A few days later, we stopped in downtown Miami to drink papaya juice and let me practice my Spanish. When people sensed the young gringo spoke a few words of Spanish, they dropped their voices. I was hardly trying to play Mr. Trench Coat, but it seemed pretty clear that something was going on in Flagler Street in March of 1961. People were buzzing in and out of stores, pointing and staring. After we got home, in April, the papers were full of the Bay of Pigs invasion. I felt a rush of journalistic pride that I had sensed something in the papaya-juice stand.

The wanderlust sustained me in the next few years, as I was traveling around the country with the Mets and Yankees, achieving all my goals by the time I was twenty-five.

Marianne Graham was surprised to find herself married to a baseball writer. We had been co-editors of two yearbooks at Hofstra College, and somehow decided to collaborate on a marriage, too. On our wedding night, she discovered what kind of suave husband I was going to be when I registered only myself at the Plaza Hotel, despite the desk clerk clearing his throat and nodding toward the young girl in the white dress standing behind me. On our way back from a late supper, I bought the early edition of *The Times* to catch up on the baseball scores.

It's been that way ever since, newsprint on my fingers, scores on the radio, telephone calls at odd hours, dinners with the chattering Chipmunks of the press box, long waits outside the press-box door, confusing explanations as to why I wouldn't be home on our anniversary, October 1.

My wanderlust took me out of sports in 1970, turned me into a national news reporter. Marianne was thrilled, because she got to meet activists and writers, artists and politicians, helped me cover the assassination of the governor of Bermuda, helped me cover the funeral of Pope Paul VI in Rome, wrote a children's book with me about the Bermuda Triangle, and evoked some great conversations with Loretta Lynn while I was writing *Coal Miner's Daughter*.

While serving as my eyes and ears and conscience, Marianne has sold more than a hundred of her paintings, geometric color progressions in watercolor. One patron hung Marianne's painting opposite a Wyeth in his living room—"I like the Vecsey better," he says.

It was hard for her to accept my going back to sports in 1980, to make small talk with people who ask whether the Giants will win the Super Bowl or why my brother Pete wrote that nasty crack about Bernard King in the *Post*. But the artist in her realized the challenge of writing a column, and she could see the benefits, too.

We are starting off the new year in a warm place, a free day in Key West. In a few weeks, I'll go to the Super Bowl in New Orleans. This summer Marianne will go with me to Mexico for the World Cup of soccer, and immediately after that I will cover the Goodwill Games in Moscow, and then it will be time for the baseball pennant race and the World Series, the childhood dream, over and over again.

The dream has shifted a bit since I was seven. It is not enough just to go out to the arena anymore. Now I respond only to the new story, the new location, the new feeling, the new character, like being on Flagler Street in March of 1961 and knowing that something is happening. Will there be enough of that in this new year?

MIAMI, JANUARY 4

When I got back from my day off in Key West, the red light was flashing on my telephone. *Call your office. "Where have you been? We've been trying to get you all day." The guilt that keeps a journalist hopping.* Dave DeBusschere, the general manager of the Knicks, has just been fired. Can you switch from a column about the football play-offs to the firing of a sports deity? No problem.

When I switched from covering religion back to sports, people asked whether there was a culture shock. Actually, I told them, religion and sports have a lot in common. They both take place on weekends. They both involve large gatherings. They both use music and pageantry. They both command great loyalty from the true believers. They both have their holy places, their shrines. They both have their divinities and their fallen angels, their saints and their sinners.

The deities are always with us. Reggie Jackson, Chris Evert, Julius Erving, Steve Garvey, Bill Bradley. The fans see them performing on the field and performing in the postgame interviews, but the sports reporters see them in more informal settings, where there is a chance for a series of questions, an unguarded response.

When the news was delivered to me in my hotel room, I had no clippings, no press guides, and there was no answer at DeBusschere's home on Long Island. I'll write this column off the top of my head, which is what sports columnists sometimes do. We store up images and quotes, never knowing when we will have to write about our deities.

The last time I saw DeBusschere was in his office a month ago. He was forcing a smile and insisting everything would turn out fine, but he did not look very confident. His uniform number, 22, hangs from the rafters of Madison Square Garden to honor the purposeful way he moved in satin shorts, but he seemed nervous as a sports executive, lacking the innate capacity for small talk, long hours, details, and intrigue.

As we sat in his office a month ago, he was under fire from fans and the tabloid press, particularly my brother Peter, the basketball columnist at the *New York Post*. The Knick players were not recuperating from injuries, they were having contract problems, trades were not working out.

DeBusschere and I have known each other casually for eighteen years, but we had never really sat down alone. I tried to make him comfortable with a little small talk about Garden City, where he lives and where my son goes to private school.

He told me how hard it was for his children because of his name, how other children pick up the viciousness from the fans and the tabloid press. He said some children would say, "The Knicks stink," or "Your father stinks," to his children.

Was he referring obliquely to the criticisms in Pete's columns? Am I my brother's keeper? Did he raise the issue as a device for sympathy? He did not seem that manipulative, but I could not be sure. While we sat around, a couple of suburban fathers talking about schools, I thought to myself, Oh, damn, why did he tell me that?

Sometimes we are co-opted in some slight, human way just by getting to know our subject. I was once invited to supper by a strip-mine operator who was notorious for gouging the mountainsides of eastern Kentucky. As I sat down with his family, we all paused to say grace, and I thought to myself, Oh, damn, I'm holding hands with a strip-mine operator. I'm sure my article was 5 percent kinder after I had prayed with the man. I'll never know if he planned it that way.

DeBusschere seemed to squirm when I asked him what it was like to work for Gulf and Western, the giant conglomerate that owns the Knickerbockers. I probably should have pressed it.

I wrote a column saying it was not DeBusschere's fault that his players kept getting injured, but that DeBusschere would not have endless time, not in New York, not working for the sharks from Gulf and Western. Things were not working out for this New York deity.

I'm not one of those sports columnists who will claim to be good friends with most of the sports deities. The few athletes who became my friends tended to be struggling players like Bill Robinson, Steve Hamilton, Ruben Amaro, and Jim Bouton with the Yankees, Ed Charles and Larry Bearnarth with the Mets. Recently, I have become close to two superior athletes, Bob Welch, the Dodger pitcher, after helping him write a book about his alcoholism, and Martina Navratilova, after writing her autobiography.

The biggest sports deities have more than enough people wanting to be their friends without needing reporters. And the very act of our writing about them so often tends to discourage friendship. We know them, but we don't know them.

When I was a baseball reporter in the sixties, it used to drive me crazy to have somebody ask, "But what is Mickey Mantle really like?" I always thought I had settled that once and for all in my most recent article.

"He's a courageous athlete who's good to his friends, but who does not take care of his body," I would say. "He usually burps and glares and says, 'Fuuuuck,' whenever a reporter comes over to his locker, but he can be pretty funny, too. He drinks a lot. You don't want to see him then."

Usually, the fan would say, "Aw, no. Not the Mick."

The sports deities are with us long after they retire. Dave Anderson of *The Times* and Steve Jacobson of *Newsday* sometimes write sympathetic columns about Mantle as an aging hero, sadder and wiser, looking back at his playing days, but I cannot do it. I remember too many chilling stares, too many muttered "Fuuuck"s when I came around as a young reporter.

Mantle is a blind spot for me. The older I get, the more I appreciate the charming rogues, the hustlers, and the wise guys. I don't believe that all athletes must be role models to adults and children. In fact, it's unrealistic, totally against human nature, to expect it.

A judge in Kansas City sent four Kansas City Royals to jail on drug charges that would have brought suspended sentences to almost anybody else. The judge tossed the book at them because, he suggested, they had let down the fans of Kansas City. This is a responsibility no athlete deserves, no matter what the salary.

But I have to remember there are athletes who deserve their good image, deities I admire after years of watching them play and meeting them away from the arena.

I can't claim to be neutral about Julius Erving, who was the best man at my brother Peter's second wedding. For most fans, he is Doctor J, the man who launched the game into its rocket-ship generation, but I can never bring myself to call him anything but Julius, the name his mother gave him. At Pete's reception, Julius was clearly uncomfortable when people tried talking jive to him, expecting him to be as flamboyant in a tuxedo as he was in uniform. I think he's glad he wears glasses and has a touch of frost in his hair. Or maybe they're props.

A quiet adviser to troubled athletes, a low-key witness to his Christian faith, a willing volunteer for many charities, Julius Erving has helped bring new dignity to the National Basketball Association.

At the All-Star Game in Denver in 1985, a lot of fans and reporters thought the new slam-dunk competition was just playing up the simplistic side of basketball. Sitting on the court with his oldest son, mapping out the strategy for the next dunk, Julius gave instant legitimacy to the contest. He dignifies anything he touches.

As a writer who works in crowded press boxes under early deadlines, I would love to have the poise and consistency of Chris Evert. Whenever she is in trouble, she will take a deep breath, shrug her shoulders, and nod her head, as if to say, "Now I understand what the problem is. Now I'm in control."

Chris is also in control in her public appearances, winning the female reporters with her apparent friendliness and frankness, and charming the male reporters with just the slightest innuendo, the smallest of winks. She displays a trace of striptease queen or frontier barmaid— Mae West with a backhand.

Reporter: "Chris, how did you prepare for the big match today?"

Chris (Mona Lisa expression): "That's my secret."

According to Martina, Chris is far more earthy than she lets on, a master of the bawdy joke after a glass of wine. But it is Chris's public posture I admire most. In the tight little world of tennis, there are not many secrets. I have seen Chris shrug off a lot of things, from ptomaine poisoning to romance problems, when she got on the court.

While Chris Evert seeks simplicity on the court, Reggie Jackson makes life complicated for himself with his ego and his rhetoric, but then he almost always makes it come out all right.

I can still see Reggie trying to hit the ball to White Plains but managing only a four-hundred-foot out to center field. I can still see him stopping at first base, watching the runner tag up and move to third base after the catch, and Reggie pounding his palms together, as if he had planned it just that way.

Reggie had to be in control. There was a game when Bobby Brown, a reserve outfielder, stole second base with Reggie at bat and two outs. I don't remember whether Reggie got a hit or not. I do remember that after the game, Reggie ambled over to Brown's locker and said:

"It's all right. You were safe, so it's no problem. But if you try to steal second with me at bat, you must always be safe. I've got a chance to help the club by hitting a dinger with you on base. If you get thrown out, we don't get anything, you know what I mean? But like I say, you were safe. You must always be safe."

I also remember Brown rolling his eyes, knowing Reggie was right but also knowing Reggie had embarrassed Brown in front of a reporter. For all that manipulation, Reggie backed up his talk. The Yankees have not won anything since George Steinbrenner let him go.

Even in exile, Reggie had to be the critic. Entertaining twenty writers before a championship game in 1982, he suddenly pointed at me:

"Look at the man from *The Times*," he said. "Tweed jacket. Paisley tie. Blue jeans. Cowboy boots. But it works. It works."

Almost the opposite of Reggie is Steve Garvey, who never provokes, never confronts. When I first came back to sports, I would watch Garvey signing autographs before a game, posing for pictures, patting children on the head. Yet some players and some reporters would tilt their heads toward Garvey as if to say, "What a jerk."

I kept waiting for some sign that Garvey was a phony, but win or lose, he would stand in front of his locker, stick out his cleft chin, and answer almost any question. His answers may have been overly optimistic, but he could fill up a notepad for you, while many of his teammates scurried to the safety of the shower, glaring at Garvey as if he were doing something wrong.

The final week of the 1982 season was not the best in Steve Garvey's life: The Dodgers were about to finish second; the front office was about to turn down his contract request; and Cyndy Garvey was living in New York with another man.

One evening in Dodger Stadium, I waited until Garvey was alone at his locker, and I started asking questions. When I asked about the absence of his wife and children, he looked me in the eye and said, "I'm sorry, but I just won't talk about my private life. I hope you understand."

Almost any other deity might have cut me dead for the next decade or so. The next day I found myself trudging up the hill outside Dodger Stadium, carrying my word processor, unable to park in the press lot for lack of the right ticket. I heard a voice ask, "Want a ride?," and it was Steve Garvey, at the wheel of an ornate car—American, of course. The way I looked at it, the lift up the hill was his modest way of saying he understood I had a job to do.

Another sports deity who has always impressed me is Bill Bradley, now a senator from New Jersey. I first met him when he was a solemn sophomore at Princeton University, talking about wanting to have an impact on the world.

In 1968, I was visiting a group lobbying to keep South Africa out of the Mexico Olympics. Suddenly, the organizer asked me to wait in a side room because she had an important visitor. Through the flimsy wall, I recognized the hesitant voice of Bill Bradley, who had just finished his first, inconclusive season in pro basketball and wanted to help the cause in some way.

While he was on the road with the Knicks, Bradley used his spare time to meet people, to broaden his contacts. From everything I have seen of him since, including his reticence to talk about the old basketball days, it is clear he has not lost that appealing undergraduate earnestness.

The athlete who fascinated me most? When I woke up early on New Year's morning and went for a run on Flagler Street, I put on my treasured yellow-and-green T-shirt with BRASIL written across the front. This shirt is a souvenir from the World Cup in Spain in 1982. One of my perversities as an American sports columist is my love for *fútbol*— soccer—which I played so badly at Jamaica High School a million years ago.

As soon as I pulled on my BRASIL shirt, I became Socrates Sampaio de Souza Vierà de Oliveira, known simply as Socrates to *fútbol* fans in Brazil. Tall and slender and cocoa-colored, deep-voiced and introspective, Socrates was not merely a brilliant midfielder but also a physician, a folk singer, a political activist. I got to meet him a few times and found him committed to making things better in his country—a cross between Bill Bradley and Julius Erving, Brazilian style.

When I wear my yellow-and-green BRASIL T-shirt, I think of Socrates' long strides, the way he can move a soccer ball upfield with a flick of his foot. It helps me run better.

CHICAGO, JANUARY 5

My flight has been slowed by headwinds, and I am going to miss the kickoff of the Giants' play-off game with the Bears. We have five writers at Soldier Field, and I doubt I will even be missed, but I feel anxious about being late for the Giants' biggest game in twenty years.

The Giants were the last team I covered before becoming the Appalachian correspondent for *The Times* in 1970. I used to tell people, "I went from one depressed area to another."

Sports reporters are not supposed to root, but we cannot help having our passions and our opinions. I like the Mets because they filled the gap left by the Brooklyn Dodgers. I don't enjoy the Yankees because of

George Steinbrenner and the manager he keeps hiring. And I have mixed feeling about the Giants.

Some New Yorkers think Wellington Mara, the owner of the Giants, is a fuddy-duddy who held the Giants back for two decades with his mom-and-pop operation, but when I covered the club, I came to like Wellington, jogging around the practice field or shepherding his little blond children.

It is the Giants fans who put me off, yowling and whining when the rest of the league passed the Giants by. Giants fans of a certain age got spoiled when Huff and Tittle were winning the championships, when Rote and Gifford were the toast of P. J. Clark's. The malicious side of me enjoys it when Giants fans stage temper tantrums during a losing game.

As my plane pushes its way toward Chicago, I do have a rooting interest in this game. When I was ten, my father brought home the autobiography of Sid Luckman, the old Bears quarterback, who is Jewish, like many of my friends, and is from Brooklyn, the home of our beloved Dodgers.

Even though I don't much like pro football, I still check the Bears' score first every week. Chicago was also the first big city I ever visited, when I was nineteen, walking the Loop and Lake Shore Drive all by myself, taking the el to the White Sox game, thrilled to be in the town of Studs Lonigan and Al Capone and Carl Sandburg—and Sid Luckman.

After decades of interviewing politicians and religious leaders and athletes, I am rarely excited about talking to a celebrity, but the ten-year-old in me was secretly thrilled recently when I interviewed Luckman for a column about the Bears' renaissance.

As the plane lands at O'Hare, I realize that the last thing I want is for New York to get caught up anymore in Giants-mania. This is a madness that breaks out whenever a New York team gets close to a championship. In my life, I have seen Mets-mania and Knicks-mania and Yankees-mania, friends calling about tickets, strangers wanting to talk sports with me, but the worst is when newspapers get New York-mania.

If the Giants ever reach the Super Bowl, we will have to go over the tortured feud between Wellington and his nephew, Tim, how the team was rebuilt, what Lawrence Taylor thinks about nuclear disarmament, what subjects George Young taught in high school, all the sociology of who goes to Giants games, what they wear, what they eat at tailgate parties, and why a football is shaped the way it is. I don't want to hear any more from petulant Giants fans. Go, Bears.

My cabbie is from Ghana, so we spend most of the ride downtown talking about Kofi Awoonor, the Ghanaian poet I wrote about when he was in exile on Long Island. The Chicago skyline is terrific against the cold blue sky. No time to glance at the Chicago sports sections on my lap.

I rush into the press box five minutes into the game and see the scoreboard showing the Bears already ahead, 7–0. The press box at Soldier Field seems to stretch from end zone to end zone, with dozens of reporters mixed in with people I assume are local politicians getting out of the cold.

"Catch me up," I say, squeezing next to Dave Anderson.

These are the time-honored words of one sports reporter to another, Barney Kremenko to Harold Rosenthal, Bob Klapisch to Marty Noble. The generations change, but nobody ever refuses a catch-me-up.

"Landeta missed the ball," Dave says. "Gayle ran it in. Welcome to the Windy City."

In thirteen words, our Pulitzer Prize–winning sports columnist catches me up. We all talk in code, share the same perceptions, after years together in press boxes. While Dave fills me in on a few details, I struggle to take off my coat in the narrow space.

"What are you thinking about writing?" asks Joe Vecchione, our sports editor, a few seats away.

In the last few years, Joe and some of the other sports editors have been going to major events, partially to keep in touch with the scene, partially to coordinate their troops. It's not a bad idea. I have seen Mike Lupica and Dick Young write essentially the same column for the *Daily News* after a World Series game, because they were not speaking to each other. That would never happen at *The Times* or *Newsday* or the *Daily News* now that Vic Ziegel is the editor.

I have trouble telling Joe Vecchione what I'm writing this early in the game.

"Hasn't happened yet," I say, using one of Dave's favorite slogans.

We watch the game swirling far below us. In the second half, it becomes apparent that Richard Dent, a defensive end as lithe as a limbo dancer, is spending much of the afternoon in close proximity to Phil Simms, the Giants quarterback.

Dave Anderson slips a clipping in front of me.

"If it goes the way I think it's going, I'll probably focus on Landeta missing the punt," Dave says. "You may want to do something on the Bears defense. I saved this for you."

The clipping is from the Sunday *Chicago Sun-Times,* about Dent suggesting, through his agent, that he might skip the Super Bowl if he does not get a new contract.

"Just a thought," Dave says.

Dave Anderson is full of thoughts. He won the Pulitzer Prize in 1981 for columns like the one about George Steinbrenner firing Dick Howser for merely winning 103 games. Steinbrenner told reporters that Howser was resigning to accept an "unbelievable" real-estate deal—George's own adjective. Dave pointed out that reporters at the press conference were not touching the trays of sandwiches, that nobody had any appetite for what Steinbrenner was serving that day.

When I began filling in for Red Smith in 1980, Dave and I would talk at least once a week to get our schedules straight. I tend to do more personal and offbeat columns than Dave, and he tends to write more about the big names and big events. I know we disagree on some issues, but I have never heard the slightest inflection of disapproval from him. The world needs meat and potatoes; Dave makes it easy for me to bake my quiche.

You need to play on the same team to appreciate somebody. Dave is an All-Star who takes over the big events, Dave DeBusschere getting the big rebound, Emlen Tunnell deflecting the big pass, Tommy Henrich swatting the home run in the World Series. Old Reliable, that's what Mel Allen used to call Tommy Henrich.

Late in the game, after Richard Dent has conducted dancing class in the Giants' backfield, I tell Vecchione I will write a column about Dent and the Chicago defense. I can relate to somebody who thinks he does a helluva job but is underpaid.

"Dave showed me the clipping about Dent's contract problems," I say.

"Hey, we're all on the same team," says Old Reliable.

PORT WASHINGTON, NEW YORK, JANUARY 7

"Do you have any homework?" Marianne asks, stepping in front of the hockey game on the television.

"No, ma'am," I say.

"Not you, jerk. Your son. Him."

"All done," David says.

"It better be," I say, giving it my best Robert Young. I really don't want him going upstairs to do homework.

This is my dirty little secret, my version of the beer commercials, the clean, well-lighted place where all the good buddies hang out. Instead of beer and pretzels with the boys, this is tea and popcorn with my son.

One of the reasons I succumbed to going back to sports was that David was already a good sports companion, and I knew he would enjoy my new job. He's sixteen now, and has accompanied me on trips to Philadelphia and Boston, riding shotgun, digging out change for the tolls, reading the signs, stopping at historic sites, watching the games in the stands, waiting outside the press gate until I was done.

I try to remind David of the mindlessness of sports, I keep bringing up the "real world" out there, but I cannot conceal that I like sports as much as anything I ever covered.

Even when I was a news reporter in the seventies, baseball was an antidote for boredom. When I covered the convention of the Roman Catholic bishops in Chicago every spring, I would jump on the B train in time to grab a sausage and a coldie and join the Wrigley Field Bleacher Bums. Around the seventh inning, I would call downtown in case the bishops had voted to canonize Martin Luther.

After nearly a decade away from sports, I found I still respected athletes not only for their skills but also for dealing with constant mental pressure and physical stress, for living with the fragility of career, the public criticism. I missed the gallows humor of players, the talk of "dying" when they are cut from a team. I did not like politicians or public officials nearly as much as I liked cops and coal miners, people who live on the edge.

In our own way, journalists live on the edge, producing articles that will not read as if they were written in forty-five minutes. Once your system is used to that regular jolt, it is very hard to give it up. You become, as Jim Bouton called it when he was out of baseball, "a thrill freak."

Our family is full of people who found ways to express themselves, starting with Marianne, who lives on the edge by creating paintings from within. Laura is part poet, part high-school basketball player, and worked for newspapers until her current job with our state assembly-woman. Corinna has tested herself on long-distance bike trips and mountain hiking, worked for the *International Herald Tribune* and for Jane Kramer of *The New Yorker* in Paris, and now works for a literary agency. Both girls have won poetry contests, both have good Sarah Lawrence College educations, and now they both miss the buzz of the newspaper business.

And David? I keep reassuring Marianne that watching the games on television is training David to think like a writer, that sports are a laboratory of human behavior.

Last spring, David began talking about a young Met outfielder named Len Dykstra, with his peculiar smirks, his thick hair, his belly-whopper catches. In his youth-league days, David always played like a human cannonball. Sitting around the den, watching the Mets on television, David developed the myth of Lenny, a name and a persona straight out of Steinbeck's *Of Mice and Men. Tell me how it's gonna be when we get into the World Series, Davey.*

Whenever the opposition started a left-hander, Len did not get to start the game—but Len was too hyperactive to sit still in the dugout. David imagined manager Davey Johnson telling the rookie, "The game is going to start late, Len. Don't bother coming until eight-thirty." David imagined the Mets spinning elaborate tales to explain to Dykstra why the game was already in progress when he arrived.

The biggest moment in David's life to date was working in the local supermarket and spotting a scruffy little fellow in jeans wandering in the aisle.

"Hey, man, where's the white bread at?" Dykstra asked.

David directed him to the white bread, then followed him to the cash register, where he found the voice to congratulate Dykstra on a good rookie season. After that, David practiced Dykstra's squinty smile and added a lisp to Dykstra's reedy voice—"Thankth, man."

Having studied his hero up close, David began perfecting his Len Dykstra routine, a latter-day Edgar Bergen developing a puppet halfway between Charlie McCarthy and Mortimer Snerd. Lenny became another member of the family, like a child's imaginary pet.

"You know, Lenny's mother doesn't like him chewing tobacco," said David, who had dabbled in chewing last summer while working at a camp in Vermont.

"I can just see Len in the clubhouse, getting a call from his mother," David said, warming to his routine. "Of course, his mother calls him 'Leonard.'

" 'Mom, pleathe, not here. The guyth are lithtening. Yeth, Mom, I know it'th bad for me. I'll thtop after thith year. I thwear. All right, don't watch the game. I'm thorry, Mom. I didn't mean to yell. Aw, come on, Mom . . .' "

When David weaves these stories about Lenny, I can sense him making the leap from undisciplined teenager to imaginative writer. Marianne warns me to start developing friends for when David goes to college. I remember the terrible emptiness, the feeling of mourning, when each of the girls went away. I don't want to think about the last of our children leaving.

NEW YORK, JANUARY 9

With the wariness of a kickoff receiver squirming his way upfield, I maneuver past men urinating against buildings, addicts lurching down the sidewalk, pimps in doorways, women waiting in corridors of cheap hotels. I'm on my way to work at the world's greatest newspaper.

It is one o'clock in the afternoon, relatively safe for West Forty-third Street. At night you wish you had Wyatt Earp at your side.

I have just covered a press conference for Willie McCovey, who was elected to the Baseball Hall of Fame this morning. With his high cheekbones and silent stares, McCovey used to seem as remote as an Easter

Island statue when he played in the cold and sullen environment of the San Francisco Giants. Most players do not weather well in retirement, but McCovey seemed happier and healthier today than when he was playing.

Fortified with anecdotes and good impressions, carrying my power lunch of a half-pound of mixed nuts and fruits and a container of coffee from the Egyptian stand down the block, I rush to *The Times* to write my column.

The *Times* office is a block from its ancient headquarters in Times Square, where the neon sign flashes the news headlines. *New York Newsday* produces those headlines now. When I was a copy boy at the Associated Press in my teens, I had to walk down to *The Times* and pick up the first edition on Saturday night, right where the papers flowed from the assembly line into the delivery trucks. Now the gruff, protective men bustle around the docks loading columns I write.

I love walking toward our building, with its sense of urgent purpose. Every afternoon we must do it again, in our grim *Les Misérables* neighborhood, a blunt reminder that nobody goes into the newspaper business for the creature comforts.

A few years back, when I was working as a news reporter, *The Times* hired somebody from the Midwest. He did not like the bus trip from New Jersey every day, and he was not enthralled with the taut atmosphere in the city room, but he particularly loathed the war zone of the West Side.

One day he had an assignment over on Madison Avenue and came back with wondrous tales to tell:

"Maybe you already know this," he said. "But over on Madison Avenue there are people with suntans and nice suits and pretty dresses. Not as many neurotics. People are carrying squash racquets and sports bags from health clubs. They look sleek and relaxed and healthy."

"We know about this," we told him. "It's called the East Side."

He doesn't work for *The Times* anymore.

After passing the scrutiny of the guards on the ground floor, I take the elevator to the sports department on the fourth floor. Six years ago, I was a religion reporter on the third floor, the main floor. If the Iranians captured hostages or the Pope was coming to town, I had to produce on deadline, the tension heightened by the immensity of being *The New*

York Times. I still miss the excitement in the late afternoon, the editors rushing to their conferences, reporters rushing back from breaking stories, the air of suspense, a Flagler Street all its own.

For a long time, I had resisted identifying myself as a *Times*man, having grown up at *Newsday* and worked outside the building so much. After a few years in the newsroom, I knew what I had become—a lifer. But I was becoming tired of some of the editing, and the religion beat was being stifled by office politics, and I started coming to work muttering "second career, second career."

One day, as if by magic, the long shadow of Arthur Gelb fluttered across my desk. Arthur was then the assistant managing editor, a former theater critic with a great love for Manhattan and great energy for innovation. As a metro editor, he had so many ideas that a secure reporter had to say no to Arthur at least one out of three times, but I listened carefully to this brainstorm: The expanded Monday sports section needed a hired gun to write showcase features. Arthur "suggested" I talk with LeAnne Schreiber.

The first female sports editor in the country, LeAnne was young, she was female, she had taught at Harvard, she had written about sports for *Time* magazine, she had done a hundred other interesting things, but she had not come up through the ranks of daily sportswriting, and she was resented by many of the older people in the business.

She took me out to lunch to an Afghan restaurant, fixed her piercing eyes on me, and talked. I did not understand half the things she said, because LeAnne is one of the smartest, most complex people I have ever met.

One thing that filtered through was: "Why don't you come back to sports and write long pieces, as if they were plays or short stories? Just have fun writing."

Have fun writing? Nobody had said *that* to me in a long, long time, so I went back to sports, with extremely mixed feelings, quite aware that I might be looking for a soft spot to land.

Within six months, LeAnne made the mistake of getting out of New York for a few weeks, sleeping under the stars in Baja and realizing she did not want to be a sports editor another day. (The fiction remains that she was demoted; a friend of mine at another paper recalls his sports editor gleefully holding a piece of wire copy and shouting, "They fired the broad!" In fact, the *Times* editors were stunned that she didn't want to be sports editor anymore. They made her the assistant editor of the Book Review, which she improved for five years before heading off to the woods to write.)

The new editor was Joe Vecchione, who had worked with me when I was a reporter and he was a photo-assignment editor. Most people in the sports department have no history on the third floor, but Joe knows how the paper works, and I try to keep up my contacts, too.

Today there is no time for visiting the third floor, because I have to write my McCovey column. Other people use my desk when I am not there, so the first step is to wipe off the telephone and clear old lunch bags and newspapers from the desk. I feel like Bette Davis issuing her famous line: "What a dump."

Time to write. There is no word processor anywhere near my desk, so I plant myself at a terminal in the center of the copy desk. It is hard to get down to business surrounded by friends I have not seen in weeks, with the Mixmaster voice of Sam Goldaper, our basketball writer, explaining that he sensed Dave DeBusschere was in trouble weeks ago, but couldn't bring himself to write it.

This is an exclusive club, a home away from home, not unlike a baseball clubhouse except that we don't sit around in our underwear and chew tobacco. The old *Front Page* raffishness is long gone, the business has gotten sober, but there is still an earnest grubbiness about it, a sense of desperation, almost an addiction.

If we can just somehow get it right, just right enough, they will print it, and we will have justified ourselves for another day. My boss will like me, people will have something to read at breakfast, maybe some little thing will be changed in the world. It's all possible, midway through the afternoon.

We are newspaper junkies, as flawed as any other humans. Whoever claims newspapers are infallible, given clairvoyance by some occult power, is guilty of self-delusion. Most of my colleagues try to get everything right; there is a zeal approaching terror in those late-afternoon meetings. Still, we are always one step away from putting misinformation into print.

How close? Minutes, sometimes seconds. I will never forget how close I came to becoming the Wrong-Way Corrigan of the sports page, only to be saved by the reporter's best friend, the cop on the beat, the noble Saint Bernard of journalism, an editor.

My escape from ignobility happened on a Sunday afternoon in 1981, in the white heat of deadline. I had ridden in the open jeep of Fred Lebow, the organizer of the New York Marathon, for the entire 26 miles, 385 yards, from Staten Island to Central Park.

I watched Lebow shout through a bullhorn, warning late starters on the bridge, "Get off, you hot-doggers, I know who you are!"; bark orders at the lumbering photographers' truck; plead in Yiddish for Hasidic Jews to cheer as the runners passed through Brooklyn; and he even fired his aide in the jeep over some momentary disagreement.

When Lebow's jeep squealed into the parking lot at Tavern on the Green, I was convinced I had been on the grandest military expedition in history. After the race, I hustled downtown to the office, composing the column in my head. Once the caffeine took over, I banged out my lead:

"He was William the Conqueror catching the south wind into England. He was Charlemagne crossing the Alps with a cortege of elephants. He was George Washington crossing the Delaware in a rowboat. . . ."

I continued in that vein, with the cacophony of a newspaper office around me, and the clock moving faster and faster toward six o'clock, push-the-panic-button time. Right on deadline, I transferred the finished column into the editor's directory, then relaxed for the first time in twelve hours.

A few minutes later, Bill Brink, the assistant Sunday editor, a polite young man out of Notre Dame, strolled to my desk.

"Uh, just checking something," Bill said casually. "In your lead, uh, did you really mean, uh, Charlemagne? I was thinking you might have meant, uh, Hannibal."

No guilt, no recriminations, no "ah-ha, we gotcha" snickers. He was saving my ass, and being nice about it. Of course, I knew the difference between Charlemagne and Hannibal, but that moment, on deadline, when it really mattered, I had confused them.

I was so grateful that I got down on my knees and pressed my palms together in the Zen Buddhist salute of maximum respect. Because of Bill Brink, I was not going to be immortalized in *The New Yorker,* in the *Columbia Review of Journalism,* in *The Village Voice,* in *The Nation,* in

Winners and Sinners, forever remembered as the pompous ass who sprinkles historical references in his column, and then gets it wrong.

Today I have another chance to make a fool of myself in print. At this shared terminal, I must write fast because the copy editor starts putting his belongings in his desk drawer, near my knees.

"Take your time, no problem," he says, shuffling papers.

I debate asking him to please move a few feet away until I am finished. But then I remember Bill Brink and Charlemagne, and I hold my fire. A writer needs all the friends he can get.

NEW YORK, JANUARY 10

Keith Hernandez and I are having lunch at the Ballroom on West Twenty-eighth Street, but Hernandez does not seem very interested in their grand selection of tapas. The tensions of last season do not seem to have gone away. He seems preoccupied, withdrawn.

The Times has asked me to write a magazine article on Hernandez in the wake of his testimony last September, in the trial of an accused drug dealer in Pittsburgh, that he had used cocaine for several years while playing in St. Louis. He was pictured on television and in newspapers walking into the court in a business suit. *Sports Illustrated* ran that picture near a headline SLEAZE IN BASEBALL. In the *New York Post,* Dick Young called him a "druggie."

"God, I hate that word," Hernandez says with a shudder.

Many people would not have been surprised if Hernandez had fallen apart, but he managed to drive in twenty-four game-winning runs, the major-league record, and he helped keep the Mets in the pennant race until the final weekend.

Now the suspense seems to be working on him. Hernandez is waiting to find out if Peter Ueberroth is going to suspend him for his past use of drugs, and his divorce case is still pending in St. Louis. I am sure the main reason he agreed to meet me at all is that I have often written that Hernandez is the best everyday player the Mets ever had.

Hernandez is also one of the most compelling athletes I have ever covered, a superb defensive player, a skillful hitter. It is like getting a master's degree in baseball to stop by Hernandez's locker after he has relaxed with a beer.

I have never spent any time with Hernandez away from the ballpark; we are both trying to work out the ground rules of our interview. After an hour of small talk, he relaxes a bit. A couple of times he tells me, "Don't write this," or "This is off the record," and I draw elaborate lines and print *OFF* in the margin.

There is no denying his background in drugs. Last September he testified he had awaked one morning in November of 1980 with his nose bleeding: "I had the shakes. I wound up throwing a gram down the toilet. I stayed away from it the rest of the winter." He later went back to cocaine until early in 1983. In the trial in Pittsburgh, he called cocaine "a demon in me."

Drugs are the new dimension in sports, touching just about every team, complicating every judgment about athletes. Some addiction officials say athletes are no more prone to drugs than any other segment of the population, but the money and the fame make it that much easier for them to get it.

When I broke into sportswriting, we used to allude to Mickey Mantle showing up "under the weather" and hitting a home run. Mantle was "merely" hung over. But even then, other stimulants were around. I remember one of the best pitchers in the sixties, a model of conservative propriety, babbling a blue streak in the clubhouse just before going out to pitch. Smoke was pouring out his nose and ears, like in a medieval drawing of a dragon. A reporter who knew the pitcher made a covert motion of a man popping a pill in his mouth. Greenies. Amphetamines.

I've seen star quarterbacks rambling incoherently on the flight back after a game, as the greenies faded and the beer took over. They shoo us out of clubhouses earlier these days, and I think I know one reason why.

I am no longer an innocent about chemical abuse. In 1981 I wrote a book with Bob Welch of the Los Angeles Dodgers about his treatment for alcoholism. To understand what Bob had gone through, I spent a week at the Meadows in Arizona, going through heavy confrontational therapy with patients and their family members. I laughed and cried with people who were wrecking their lives with alcohol and drugs, sometimes with abuses of sex or food.

The experience at the Meadows made me wonder how many times I had interviewed athletes who were flying high. Before a game in Montreal, Ron Leflore once gave me a fascinating rap about dedicating his career to Jackie Robinson, and maybe it was true. But a year or so later, Leflore admitted he had sometimes come to the ballpark high on drugs. Was it the drugs talking, or Leflore's heart?

Nowadays, when a player's career plummets, I suspect drugs. When players show up late for work, become careless, talk in grandiose circles, I suspect drugs. When a friend insists, "I only have a couple of drinks with lunch," my ears perk up.

As Hernandez and I fence with each other over tapas, I find myself wondering what led this seething man to seek refuge in cocaine. He is intelligent, loves to read history books and tour Civil War battlefields, reads the papers, is the backbone of the Mets' team, and has been a model citizen since coming to the Mets in 1983.

I have never been a good hard-news reporter, able to threaten and cajole information out of people, but I like to think I am good at getting people to talk about themselves. For the feature, for the column, it is important to listen to them, to try to see things from their point of view. A journalist should always do some homework, but it is just as important to encourage people to open their hearts.

Trying to get Hernandez to relax a little, I ask about his three daughters back in St. Louis, his love of travel, his making New York his full-time home. Then I bring up the first game in Shea after his appearance in the Pittsburgh trial, how people gave him a standing ovation and Dick Young claimed the fans were "soft" on drugs because they cheered Hernandez.

"My impression was that fans were saying, 'Let's go on from here,' " Hernandez says. "People were not condoning what I did. Maybe the fact that I played well has something to do with it. If it were some fringe player, would it be different? It probably would."

A woman walks out from the kitchen, gesturing with open hands that she is not about to ask for an autograph or interrupt his lunch for long. She says, "Mr. Hernandez, I just want to thank you for a wonderful season. And next season? One place higher?"

He smiles and thanks her, but after she returns to the kitchen, he says, "I fall asleep at night wondering what people really think. To my face, they may smile and say nice things, but how do I know they don't go back and say, 'There's Keith Hernandez. What an asshole.' It will always be like that, I guess."

His dark mood unabated, Hernandez prepares to leave. I keep thinking there is something missing, something that makes him seem incomplete. As we shake hands near the front door, I realize what is absent from Keith Hernandez today—a ball game, to absorb all that energy, all that skill, all that tension.

STEWART MANOR, NEW YORK, JANUARY 12

It looks like the all-American birthday party—potato salad, gooey cake, sentimental speeches, a handsome suburban house, the matriarch sitting in the center, waving her hands to deflect the praises while grandchildren and old friends fuss over her seventy-fifth birthday.

From the poised way my mother greets her friends, you could not tell she has been fighting multiple sclerosis for a quarter of a century, exercising every day with the diligence of a champion athlete. She often tells me where the will is hidden, but in the meantime she runs a ten-room house by herself, and drives her friends to church and luncheons and college reunions.

"Face it, Mom," I tell her. "You're going to be one of those little old ladies I see in England, driving around the countryside, visiting tearooms, and knowing everybody's business into their nineties. So you'd better get used to it." She smiles when I tell her that.

The party looks so wholesome, but really we are honoring a couple of radicals here—my father, George Stephen Vecsey, who died on Thanksgiving night a year ago, and my mother, May Spencer Vecsey.

Among the guests today are some of my parents' newspaper friends from the thirties, old lefties, unionists. J. Edgar Hoover should be hiding behind the pickle tray, taking down names.

My parents met at the water cooler at the *Long Island Press,* a shoestring-budget, union-busting newspaper in Jamaica, which some-how collected a newsroom full of bright, hopeful people who would work for anybody during the Depression.

He was the sports editor. She was the society editor. He was a high-school dropout, an adopted son in a Hungarian family, probably of Rus-sian or Jewish ancestry (a mystery that makes me feel part of all three cultures). She was a graduate of the College of New Rochelle, born in England of an Irish mother and English-Australian father. My father was an agnostic, my mother is a Roman Catholic.

Given their disparate backgrounds, I always wondered how they struck up a conversation at the water cooler.

"Pop was buying," says my brother Peter, who writes a basketball column for an Australian-language tabloid in New York.

They did have something in common—the poor pay and the dreadful conditions at the paper. They also had mutual friends who believed there was a more equitable way of sharing the wealth, the kind of thing people talked about in the thirties.

The two young editors joined the new union, the Newspaper Guild, and they both went on strike along 168th Street in Jamaica. The com-pany hired goons who pushed people through plate-glass windows, the usual stuff, while people like Heywood Broun came from other papers to back up the *Press* people.

One day, somebody offered my father an extra five dollars a week to go back to work. The management man suggested that my father could use the money more than ever, since he was getting married. My father turned down the raise, and somebody else took my father's job and kept it for forty years, and lived in a fancy house up the street from us. I never heard my father say anything vicious about the man who took his job, but the name of the owners was pronounced with a sneer ever afterward.

When the strike was over, my mother went back to work until one of the owners got nervous about her wearing a maternity smock. The bulge was me. I was in the newspaper business before I was born.

My father eventually got back into the newspaper business, filling in at the *Daily News* during the war, later writing for the radio sports wire at the Associated Press. He used to have nightmares, afraid somebody would turn him in for going to meetings in the thirties, afraid it could cost him his job. When Joe McCarthy was stalking the land, one of the old *Press* reporters, a former neighbor, turned in my father's name. My parents did not speak to him for years, but my father's job was never threatened.

I grew up idolizing the people who worked for newspapers, the chattery, energetic, compulsive, underpaid, overworked, charming know-it-alls at my father's offices. My father would point out Buddy Roberts, the drawling political writer for the Associated Press, who had been a childhood friend of Thomas Wolfe, the favorite author of my youth, or my father would introduce me to Hal Boyle, the Pulitzer Prize–winning war correspondent.

In 1954, Boyle returned to Brussels and interviewed my mother's Irish-born aunt, one of the survivors of Boyle's war. During the war, the Duchene family had shielded two Scottish soldiers for fourteen months, until Nazi soldiers discovered them. In Boyle's column, I learned for the first time that my mother's cousin Florrie Duchene had died in Bergen-Belsen.

"Did you know her?" I asked my mother.

"Of course I knew her," my mother answered. "My father died when I was fifteen, and my mother and I visited Europe. Florrie was my age. We played together."

Knowing that a blood relative of mine, a Catholic, had died in the camps strengthened my bond with the Jews of Europe, the Jews of New York. Madame Duchene died soon after the column, the last of one more family ruined by the war. My mother's father had died in a car wreck in upstate New York when she was fifteen. She talked wistfully about him, about the Spencer side of the family, ship captains who had taken perilous voyages to Australia in the settlement years.

My Irish-born grandmother lived with us until she died, when I was eleven, and we had American relatives. We had diaries of those earlier sea journeys, family photographs, a street named after my grandfather in upstate New York, but no more family in Europe. My mother came from "a good family," but we could not benefit from it, no stern-faced Australian great-grandfather materializing from the oval photograph to tell me sea stories, no Irish-Belgian aunts singing Christmas carols in two languages, no cousins in England or Ireland inviting us over for the summer holidays. I miss them now. I think my mother mourned them all along.

My mother never worked after I was born. My father would go off to work in the afternoons, and I would feel envious of that bustling world of subway trains and elevators and clacking typewriters and jangling bells and shouts of "caw-pee" and news bulletins and baseball scores, long sheets of paper and glossy photographs of baseball players and soldiers and pinup girls and plane crashes. The world was out there, in a newspaper office.

While my father worked seven days a week, my mother stayed home to raise five children. As the oldest child, I got the most undivided attention at an early age, the stories of the old *Press* days, talk about books and politics, the notion of "doing the right thing," whether it was going to church every Sunday or being polite to people or sharing the wealth with the less fortunate.

Sometimes my mother laments "wasting" her life, but I never heard her talk about going back to work in those days. She probably never had time to think about it. To this day, I don't know how she managed. At one point, while my grandmother was still alive, we had eight people living in a four-bedroom house, with no dryer, no dishwasher, and sometimes no car. And my mother was always there, fixing meals, caring for us when we were sick, and talking and listening.

My mother revered Franklin Delano Roosevelt for leading us out of the Depression; I think the patrician upstate New York president was a surrogate for her lost patrician upstate New York father. I can still see her sobbing by the telephone in 1945 when my father called from the office to tell us FDR was gone.

The records we played most on the Victrola were by Marian Anderson and Paul Robeson. We despised the Daughters of the American Revolution for not allowing Marian Anderson to sing for them. We were sure Paul Robeson had his reasons for seeking a more equitable life in Russia. In 1946, my father called from the office to say the Brooklyn Dodgers had signed a Negro named Jackie Robinson. Our home had another hero.

Saint Augustine says the first seven years are quite sufficient to capture the heart and mind of a child. In my first seven years, I had two parents still fighting the battles of the Depression, still railing against injustice. Marvin Siegel, one of my favorite editors in the *Times* newsroom, once called me "a Depression writer," because he knew I was more comfortable on the street than at City Hall. I took it as a great compliment. My sports column in the eighties has its roots in the thirties.

The other children are products of later decades. Liz, who is throwing the party today, is a member of her school board, a civic activist, and a mother of five, just like our mother. Peter, when he is not savaging people in his basketball column in the *Post,* is a loving husband and father with his second family. Janet, an office manager, is the most introspective of the children. And Christopher, a professor of American Indian history at Colgate University, laughs at the same jokes I do. He should. I took him around a lot when he was little.

It's rare for all five of us to be together, but a seventy-fifth birthday party is special. My mother, who is not a sports fan in the least, has given me a wonderful excuse not to travel to the football play-off game today.

After dessert, a few of us take turns saying a couple of words about my mother. My turn:

"For years my mother has been living in terror that someday I would write a novel about my family," I say. "Mom is afraid I will reveal the worst family secrets. Remember how Thomas Wolfe described his mother saving string and watering the soup at the boardinghouse? I've got good news for you, Mom. Up to now, I've shown no gift for fiction. Our secrets are safe."

My mother looks relieved. She is never quite sure what to expect from me. I think she thinks I'm too self-assured, too opinionated; I think we're a lot alike.

I look around the room at the family and the friends, particularly the old newspaper people I have known all my life.

For a few more minutes, I talk about growing up in a house where my two biggest heroes were not even Franklin Delano Roosevelt or Jackie Robinson, but the two young newspaper editors who met at the water cooler and walked a picket line together.

NEW YORK, JANUARY 17

Riding in on the Long Island Rail Road, the man in front of me searches through *The Times* for the sports pages, which we cunningly hide in a different section every day. Eventually, he folds the paper into quarters, so the only thing showing is a column. My column.

Today's column is about producer Michael Weisman of NBC planning to have the network go blank for ninety seconds during halftime of the Super Bowl next Sunday. Football people are always talking about game plans, I said. Here is a ninety-second game plan for Sunday—time for exercise, food, bathroom, and conversation, but in four staggered sections, like campers singing "Row, Row, Row Your Boat," so as not to blow out plumbing and electricity all over North America. In the middle is a cartoon of a television set with a shade being pulled over it.

The commuter in front of me moves his eyes back and forth, but not an emotion crosses his face. I am sitting three feet from him, and I cannot tell if he loves it, hates it, or is totally neutral.

When I was a news reporter, my mail helped me to form an impression of the "typical" *Times* reader. I used to picture her as a retired librarian who lives by herself on the Upper West Side near Columbia University. Every morning she goes down to the corner newsstand and buys *The New York Times* and reads it over tea and a bran muffin at the neighborhood luncheonette. She cares a great deal about grammar and fact, gives money to *The New York Times* Neediest Fund, and is not a sports fan.

Only recently did I stop to think that, with a few minor changes, my typical *Times* reader just might be my mother.

When I moved back to sports and started writing an occasional column, I did not want to lose the retired librarian on the West Side and all the other *Times* readers who might read about the broader issues of money, drugs, race, civil liberties, medicine, law, etc., pertaining to sports. But I also did not want to insult the sports fans who wanted profiles of players, strong opinions, the passion for sports at their best.

It bothers me when *The Times*'s sports section is sometimes criticized as "dull" by some sports reporters, fans, and athletes. I have a theory that many of these critics are not *Times* readers. I have to gear my column for the million people who do buy the paper every day.

Before *The Times* made me a columnist, I had not written a regular sports column since my old *Newsday* days, when I had managed to annoy most of the coaches on Long Island by interviewing their players for my column, "All Scholastic."

Most of the coaches made me feel like a child molester when I covered their games, but a few were secure enough to let me talk to their players. I wandered into a basketball game at Seaford High School and heard the coach bawling out his own son, a fifteen-year-old freshman. The coach would not criticize anybody else, but took it all out on his son.

After the game, I asked the coach, "Rocky, do you mind if I talk to your kid?" Rocky had no problem at all with that, so I went into the locker room and asked the boy, "Say, what is it like to play for your own father?" The kid smiled and practically went into a song-and-dance routine: "Hey, let me tell you about my old man . . . " A funny little kid. It was the first column anybody ever wrote about Jim Valvano.

The circle went around. The week before Jim's North Carolina State team beat Houston for the national title in 1983, I did a column on how proud Rocky Valvano was of his son. Rocky died not long after the championship. Whenever Jim and I run into each other, we talk about the old coach who wasn't afraid to let a columnist into his locker room.

Later at *Newsday,* I occasionally filled in for the regular columnists, writing one very tough column about Warren Spahn a few days before the Mets fired him as pitcher and coach.

At *The Times,* I wrote a few soft substitute columns when Arthur Daley went on vacation. Later, as a news reporter, I wrote a column for the Long Island section, encouraged to be opinionated about life in the suburbs. Stewart Kampel, the editor, was preparing me to be a sports columnist, and he didn't even know it.

Coming back to sports was something of a jolt. Since I had left the beat nearly a decade earlier, sports had become vastly more complex, the tabloid war between the *Daily News* and the *Post* was starting to smoke, and *Newsday* was growing ever more influential. Dick Young was presenting his conservative vision of "My America," my brother Peter was vilifying the likes of Spencer Driftwood and Bob McAdon't in the *Post,* and Mike Lupica was everywhere, hip and knowledgeable, at two hundred revolutions per minute.

Relying on my own enthusiasms, I wrote columns about diet and conditioning, covered the Tour de France and the World Cup of soccer in Spain, pondered what Saint Ignatius Loyola and Thomas Jefferson would have thought about the hugely publicized basketball game between Georgetown and Virginia. One of my first efforts was a column about Corinna, my number two daughter, volunteering for a mostly male gym class at high school to prove that women could play touch football, only to realize that one miscalculated spiral pass could damage her cello-playing fingers.

At first, when I had to deal with the harder issues, like the George-Reggie-Billy craziness in Yankee Stadium or the major sports events, I stayed close to anecdotes and quotes and reporting, slipping my point of view between the lines. But gradually I began asserting my natural opinionated self.

One of my first tough columns came in February of 1981, when Jim Craig, the goaltender hero of the 1980 Olympic ice-hockey champions, refused to let the Boston Bruins demote him to the minor leagues.

I pointed out that Craig might not have enough emotion left to back up his limited skills, and I also noted that Craig wanted to be a star in his hometown, but did not want to work for it, or give up his privacy, or take criticism.

"He can't give signals he wants it both ways, not indefinitely," I wrote. "The fans in Boston will eat him up if they sense ambivalence."

As criticism, that was pretty tame and impersonal compared to what I would write today, but a family friend of ours felt that I should have been more considerate toward an Olympic hero.

"He's only twenty-three," our friend said.

I pointed out that many athletes that age were making big money, that criticism is part of the package.

"But who are you to criticize him?" our friend asked. "Maybe there are things you don't know about him."

My friend was uncomfortable with me as pontificator, pundit, judge, and jury, Mike Hammer on the sports pages. For the first time, I had to verbalize my role.

"It's a column," I said. "I try to be fair, I try to be kind, and I have to be accurate with my facts, but I'm entitled to an opinion. You know, like Rocky said, 'I gotta, I'm a fighter.' I gotta, I'm a columnist."

Some readers would call me the most sensitive, literate fellow that ever lived, at least since Red Smith, and others would say I am a knee-jerk liberal or a right-wing male chauvinist pig.

One time I came home from the local fish market and discovered they had covered the fish with my column. Since they do not know me at the market, it was pure chance, not a friendly prank. Journalists suspect our words are perishable, but there was the final, stinking proof.

Sometimes the hardest part is disinterest, like this morning on the Long Island Rail Road. Please, Mr. Commuter, do something. Put down the paper with a contented sigh and announce to your fellow commuter, "That guy can really write." Or angrily jerk the paper to the next page and mutter, "What an idiot." Something. Anything. Just react. But he merely folds the paper neatly to the next story, and keeps reading, stone-faced. I spent four hours slaving over a hot word processor for this? What does my little old lady on the Upper West Side think?

NEW YORK, JANUARY 19

In the last hours before I take off for the Super Bowl in New Orleans, we made a pilgrimage into the city today to hear Rick Danko and Rich Manuel. They were part of my favorite music group, The Band, which started as Bob Dylan's backup group and finished as a legend in Martin Scorsese's movie *The Last Waltz*.

Seen at Pete Fornatale's annual "Mixed Bag" party, nearly ten years after the last waltz, Danko was overweight and overly enthusiastic, Manuel gray and sodden, but they evoked the sounds from the albums I carry with me on all my trips. I do not know how I existed before the cassette player and earphones. They are a buffer against unwanted conversations on airplanes and in press boxes, and they let me take my best companions with me everywhere.

The Band never retires on my cassette player, never stages the Thanksgiving Night farewell party in San Francisco. They are always young, always in their prime, unlike the two aging rockers in the Lone Star Café. Will I be listening to them when I am fifty? Sixty? Seventy?

I guess we have a formative age for everything. John Kennedy will always be "my" president. The Brooklyn Dodgers will always be "my" team. And The Band and Joni Mitchell and Dylan and James Taylor and Judy Collins will always be "my" music, frozen in time from the sixties and early seventies.

Sports journalism has no mystique for me—it's my business—but a songwriter who can compose a ninety-second ballad about a lost love, like James Taylor's "Fire and Rain," or an ode like Judy Collins's "My Father" leaves me in awe.

Popular music and disk jockeys fascinated me when I was young. I'm the last of the radio generation. Television is still an innovation to me. I can remember getting up in the dark, listening to Arthur Godfrey's dawn morning show, talk about airplanes and the Blue Ridge Mountains of Virginia. With the radio, you could visualize things in your mind. You could think.

I grew up listening to William B. Williams on WNEW, raging when rednecks roughed up Nat King Cole during a southern concert. Frank Sinatra. Tony Bennett. Other stations played Fats Domino and Hank Williams. One day somebody played Billie Holiday. Who'd been hiding this stuff?

I lost touch with pop music after college—too much to do, getting married, starting a family, building a career. One day I heard William B. Williams, with that beautiful urbane voice, stage a diatribe against the Beatles. I seem to recall him breaking a record on the air. What could disturb him so much about these English kids with funny hair? I had to go out and see *A Hard Day's Night.* Christ, they were fun. My younger brother Chris entertained in folk joints around New York, playing guitar and harmonica, just like Dylan, singing against the war, and I was proud of him before I was touched by the music.

Then in 1966, while touring Europe, we bought a car with an FM radio, and had it shipped back to the States. When I flicked on the FM band, I heard all kinds of amazing things. The Beatles were becoming dark and mysterious. Dylan touched a nerve about the Vietnam War. There were groups out there you couldn't believe. Cream? Traffic? The Kinks? I went from a young fogey of twenty-seven to an aging teenager with the flick of a switch.

On the road with the Mets and Yankees, you would drive across the

Bay Bridge at night, every car pulsating with the Doors, through open windows. "Come on, baby, light my fire." One night at the old Fillmore they introduced a band to fill in for a group that didn't show. The new group was named Santana. "You've got to change your evil ways—baybee." Whip out of Dodger Stadium, down the hill, L.A. glittering below you, Beach Boys on the radio. Miss my wife and daughters. I wish they all could be California girls. H. Rap Brown muttering about burning down Madison Square Garden during a boycott of a track meet. Otis Redding on the car radio. "I can't do what ten people tell me to do." Jonathan Schwartz on WNEW-FM, announcing the birth of our third child and playing a song by the Incredible String Band. Everything was incredibly alive.

Most of the music was about dope, but it couldn't touch me. I watched a few friends work at getting high on grass at dinner parties, but I had no interest in the stuff. The music and the decade were quite enough, and being alive, and being in love and raising three children, and trying to cope with Lyndon Johnson and the war and everybody I admired in public life getting blown away, the Chicago convention, the Democratic party handing us Richard Nixon on a leaden spoon. I was in muggy Connecticut, covering the first Giants-Jets exhibition, while Woodstock was going on a hundred miles away. Football fatties frying up grease-burgers in parking lots in New Haven while everybody was going to Yasgur's farm. Never had I felt more out of place.

Cambodia happened on April 30, 1970, and Kent State on May 4. I was out in California with the Yankees. I remember hearing Thurman Munson, a Kent State athlete, telling somebody that they should have gotten more of the protesters. What kind of country was this becoming? I had a beard and hair down to my shoulders, and I tried to slip protest themes into my sports copy, playing journalistic chicken with editors twice my age, and when Cambodia and Kent State took place, all I could think of doing was to stop standing for "The Star-Spangled Banner" at the ballpark. Sat down for ten days on the road. Just couldn't get up anymore.

John Drebinger, the merry *Times*man who had covered the Yankees since Wee Willie Keeler was a pup, was now working for the Yankees. Drebby didn't think my little insurrection was very *Times*like, so he decided to keep tabs on me when the club got back to New York. I was done with my protest by then, but I heard Drebby was going to catch me in the act. Before game time, he stalked me up and down the press box. Just when the anthem was about to be played, I ducked into the tiny one-person toilet, discombobulating the old gent. It was time for me to get out of sports. By November, I was a news reporter in Appalachia, covering a riot—a football weekend Michigan–Ohio State riot—in Columbus, humming "Four Dead in Ohio" while I watched a cop, standing right next to me, take a bottle in the head for no good reason, thrown by a sneaky drunk in the dark. The kids were getting nasty. The sixties were over. The music lived on.

I have never read a perfect sports column, but I have heard perfect songs. Elton John's "Your Song." The best of Anna and Kate McGarrigle from Montreal. Nina Simone singing "Memphis in June." The Beatles doing "Here Comes the Sun." The whole side of that album. The Band doing "Ophelia," about a girl who disappeared, or "Makes No Difference," about a broken heart, or "Acadian Driftwood," Robbie Robertson's ballad about the migration from Quebec to Louisiana, and one man's return trip—"Point my compass north/I got winter in my blood." The Band was a mélange of styles and instruments, too soft to be pure rock, too hard to be pop, four Canadians and one Arkansan, strange touches of Soul and Cajun and Bluegrass, simplicity stopping just at the edge of sentimentality, human feelings, historical honesty, unique chords, never quite put that way before. The best.

When athletes had long stopped having much fascination for me—when they became mostly what I wrote about—my love of music grew deeper. Classical music took hold, Bartók and Satie took my attention away from Mozart and Bach, but I worshiped classical music from afar. Who could write such beautiful pieces? Who could play them? Rock and folk music were accessible. I could almost fantasize writing or performing it, if I had any talent.

As a news reporter, I got to meet a few musicians. I liked country music before I ever wrote the book *Coal Miner's Daughter* with Loretta Lynn, but I was a bit dismayed by how isolated her music seemed, not listening to and learning what was being done by other people. Sitting around her ranch one time, I played a tape of Judy Collins singing "Some Day Soon." Loretta listened briefly and said, "It's nice—but it ain't country."

I got to see Joan Baez, the Madonna, one time, backstage after a concert in Montreal in 1969. She was pregnant and long-haired and beautiful onstage, dedicating antiwar songs to My Husband, David, Who's in Prison While His Child Is Due. She sang for an hour, left us limp. In the reception afterward, she haughtily informed the hosts that she could not stay "unless my people can come in." Her fans were pressing their noses to the glass door of the tiny reception room. I was sorry I had seen it. I understand Judy Collins lives in the building where we go for Passover seder most years. I always hope I won't run into her in the elevator. Want to worship her from afar.

I had my glimpse of Bob Dylan in 1974, when I covered the four New York dates on his triumphant tour with The Band. I needed an early-edition article on his first date at Madison Square Garden. DYLAN RETURNS. THE KID FROM GREENWICH VILLAGE COFFEEHOUSES PLAYS THE GARDEN. As a favor to *The Times*, Bill Graham, the organizer of the tour, the famous rock impressario from San Francisco, sneaked me into a Dylan sound check in the Garden that afternoon. Even the ushers and the sweepers had to stay outside while Dylan checked the acoustics. He liked his privacy. But Graham told me to crouch down between some seats and get a few details, enough to pad out a homecoming story. Dylan sings a few bars. Dylan taps his foot. Dylan scratches himself.

That night, when the Garden was full, Dylan looked out at the crowd and spoke his first sentence of the entire damn tour—DYLAN SPEAKS! "It's an honnuh to be heah!" he said. The place went crazy, and I rewrote my homecoming story for the second edition.

Long after midnight, back in his suite, Dylan picked up the first edition of *The Times*. And went crazy. He had been seen. Observed. Witnessed. Spied upon. Deceived. Somebody had watched him making his sound check. He called David Geffen, the producer, who called Bill Graham, who sadly informed me the next day that I had screwed him. I started to remind Graham that he had allowed me to peek in on the paranoid troubador, but then I did the gentlemanly thing.

"Bill," I said, "you're absolutely right. I disguised myself as a red seat and played a trick on Dylan. My fault."

I never let it affect my love of Dylan's music. Carry it with me wherever I go. In the long, dreary hours of a football game, I will play the entire album from the tour by Dylan and The Band, my enduring heroes, gone their separate ways now.

Not all first encounters are disillusioning. We met Levon Helm when

Coal Miner's Daughter opened in Nashville. He played the role of Loretta Lynn's father, the great opening scene with Sissy Spacek riding the horse to deliver a lunch bucket to her daddy at the mine. A glorious performance by both of them. After the opening, there was a party back at the hotel, with Sissy and Loretta singing country music, side by side. Levon played his guitar and shook a tambourine and sang backup, never intruding on the ladies' show. And he was bombed, in a sweet, happy, funny way.

During a break, somebody congratulated Levon on his acting and added, "And you can sing and play the guitar, too." As bombed as he was, he realized the guest did not know he was Levon Helm from The Band. With utter southern gentility he said, "Yes, ma'am, I might take up singin' sometime."

There is talk that Levon and Garth Hudson are going to join Danko and Manuel to resurrect four-fifths of The Band on a tour later this year. In my fevered, hero-worshiping mind, if Robbie Robertson is not going to make The Band whole for one gallant, nostalgic romp, it would be a kick to stand up in front of an audience and sing Robbie's parts. Forget for the moment that my anxieties include getting up in front of crowds. Forget for the moment that I do not have any performing ability. That's what fantasy is all about.

Fantasy is what draws so many of the people I see in stadiums, trudging up ramps, dreaming of running for touchdowns. One of the great stereotypes about sports journalists, believed by most athletes and fans, is that we go into the business because we are frustrated jocks. I confess that I used to have a recurring dream of being a pinch hitter with the Brooklyn Dodgers—never the Los Angeles Dodgers—but I knew better. This dream may have had as much to do with retrieving lost youth, reviewing a lost Brooklyn I wish I had known better, or maybe it was about going to games with my father, talking about sports and the old days, living up to his dreams.

In real life, I may daydream about being Socrates when I wear my BRASIL T-shirt out on my daily run. But the last time anybody handed me a varsity uniform was as a soccer player at Jamaica High School, and I am too close to athletes, have too much respect for what they do, to harbor any strong daydreams about being them.

Athletes pretty much exist on the field or on television, heroic at the moment they make the great play, diminished even on "the tapes at eleven." Musicians are forever. The Band gets older, paunchier, grayer, more wrinkled, like the aging civilians who come back for baseball old-timers' games. But when I wait in a crowded airport lobby, The Band fills the space around my ears, floods my mind, reaches my emotions, and we stay young together. Within the headset, we are always young.

On March 4, 1986, Richard Manuel committed suicide in a hotel room in Florida, shortly after a performance on the return tour with his three old mates. He had seemed terribly gray and withdrawn and reluctant that afternoon in the Village. Maybe he just didn't want to go back out on the road again. He was forty.

COLUMBIA, MISSISSIPPI, JANUARY 21

Up before dawn, I stopped for biscuits and coffee in a truck stop, where the good old boys gazed with disdain at my beard and my sport jacket. I thought to myself, Hey, Buddy, this is my South, too. I used to work down here, but I refrained from saying it out loud.

The truck drivers probably wouldn't agree with my definition, but I consider myself part southerner, too. I lived two years in Kentucky as a news reporter in the early seventies, and spent enough time in truck stops to become a lifetime member. Don't these old boys remember me?

When I was based in Kentucky, Gene Roberts, the national editor, who had covered the civil-rights movement, used to tell me, "If I ever assign you to Mississippi, you'll have two hours—one for getting to the airport and one for getting a haircut."

When I returned to Jackson yesterday, the hotel clerks and the government workers all had longer hair than I do. There are *New York Times* vending machines on street corners, and I could see black and white women swimming in the same indoor YWCA pool. I ate home-made gumbo in a luncheonette and said it was better than anything in New York, but the lady who owns the store could not be coaxed into giving out the recipe for the hot sauce.

Why do I feel such a fascination for the South? I was raised to hate segregation, of course, but when we were kids in Queens, playing Civil War in the backyard, I never minded playing a Confederate soldier. Maybe the South appealed to me as a lost cause, just like my Brooklyn Dodgers.

Some parts of North America turn me on more than others. New England seems a bit cold for my bones, but Boston is a delight. The Midwest gets interesting in Iowa and Minnesota. In my next life, I will live in California and not worry so much about things. Seattle and Vancouver are two of the best secrets on this continent. I've never had much chance to get to know the Southwest. Cincinnati is a lovely mixture of hills, river, and urbanity. When I lived in Kentucky, my personal compass tended to point southeast. I liked it where they serve iced tea even in the wintertime.

I learned to say "you all" (not "y'all"—that would be an affectation). I think a southern buttered-grits accent sounds better than a New York chewing-gum accent, and yesterday tried to exorcise any vestigial Edith-and-Archie accent while Eastern Airlines took me circuitously to Jackson.

As soon as the Chicago Bears qualified for the Super Bowl a week ago, I claimed a column on the home state of Walter Payton. This will be the first and perhaps the only Super Bowl for the man who has rushed for the most yards in pro football.

I want to write about where Sweetness came from, where his high-pitched voice and hyper-energy were cultivated. I want to break away from the pack and find some private truth, like in the old days when I was a national reporter. This morning I have an appointment with Payton's favorite high-school coach, Charles Boston.

The sun came up as I headed south to Columbia this morning, watching the rolling hills, the pine woods, the yellow school buses, the new split-levels and the tar-paper shacks of the New South. I had the feeling of wanting to drive forever, to cruise back and forth across the South, combined with the tension of knowing there is a column to be written on deadline when I reach New Orleans later today.

This was the same creative tension I used to feel as a national reporter in the seventies. All it would take would be one phone call, maybe even on Saturday evening, with dinner in the oven and guests due in an hour, Gene Roberts or Dave Jones, the next national editor, saying, "There's been a disturbance in Baton Rouge, a few people dead. There's a plane to New Orleans at eight o'clock. . . . "

As I drove through Mississippi this morning, I remembered heading toward a coal-mine explosion in Hyden, Kentucky, offering a lift to a woman walking along the road. She got into my car silently, looking straight ahead, knowing that her husband had been working on that shift. When I let her off at the mine, she forgot her gloves and a can of cat food on the front seat. Late that night in a snowstorm, everybody knew that all thirty-eight men were dead. I could not bring myself to move the gloves or the cat food until weeks later.

Most of my sports assignments involve games scheduled months or years ahead, making me feel more like a meter-reader than a news reporter. I knock on doors, jot down some numbers, and move on. But on this day in Columbia I will be on my own, just like the old days as a national reporter, best job I ever had.

As I approached Delta country, I noticed the white sandbanks on the edge of the Pearl River, where, according to legend, Sweetness developed his powerful legs. I found the school-district office, and the secretaries offered me coffee, asking me questions about New York, so feminine, so solicitous, with warbling voices that could break your heart.

Charles Boston is a trim, middle-sized black man, with traces of white in his moustache. There is an air of upbeat caution to him that I remember from working in the South, the survival tactics of older black men. Boston was already a grown-up when the civil-rights movement arrived in his hometown. Nobody knows the trouble he's seen.

Boston was the football coach at John J. Jefferson, the "separate but equal" black high school in Columbia, when Eddie Payton and his kid brother, Walter, came along. Columbia became the first district in Mississippi to be integrated after the United State Supreme Court abolished the "all deliberate speed" doctrine. The way it worked, they made a white man the head coach at Columbia High and made Boston the assistant.

"The band never played 'Dixie' at the games," Boston recalls from practiced memory. "The class presidents from the two schools got up at an assembly and told everybody to get along. And Walter scored two touchdowns in our first game, and we won it.

"To me, that put to rest any doubts about how people would get along," Boston continues. "People saw Walter with the ball, and he wasn't a black boy, he was a Columbia Wildcat. We won eight and lost two, and that helped, too.

"People had to get used to each other's ways. At Jefferson, our way of getting prepared for a game was to make noise. At Columbia, their way was to get quiet. On the bus to our last game, Walter was bouncing around the aisle, pulling ears, patting backs, talking loud, the way he does.

"One of the coaches said, 'I'm going to put a stop to that,' and I said, 'Naw, I wouldn't do that. That's just Walter's way.' And the man understood."

I ask how often Payton comes back, and Boston gives me a vague, every-so-often answer. I ask him whether people have hard feelings because Payton does not live here anymore. Boston says people understand that Payton's work is in Chicago now.

I keep thinking there is something more Boston wants to tell me, some essential part of Walter Payton's history. But we are playing an intricate North-South, black-white ritual with each other. One of the rules is that I will not be direct with him. But there is something. Something.

Although Boston never did become the head coach at the integrated school, he became Payton's link to Columbia. When Payton broke Jim Brown's rushing record, the Bears brought Boston to Chicago to be part of the festivities. And when reporters come through Columbia, the lawyers and the businessmen and the school officials direct us to Boston. In fact, Boston tells me, *USA Today* was here the other day. He thinks the *Boston Globe* and the *Washington Post* are coming tomorrow.

Why does a reporter always assume he's the only one with a good idea? Well, at least I'll get this in the paper for tomorrow. I say goodbye to Charles Boston and head south, already composing the lead in my head:

Jazz moved up the Mississippi from New Orleans to Chicago, but Sweetness reached Chicago by way of the Pearl River.

Sweetness is Walter Payton, who by the sweetest of coincidences is about to appear in his first Super Bowl 105 miles south of here in the sinful mecca of New Orleans. But his river is the Pearl, not the Mississippi.

It was on the sandy banks of the Pearl River—once navigable clear through to Jackson, but now silted and shallow—that Payton developed the powerful legs that have churned him . . .

The next morning I found the national edition of The Times *in a vending machine outside the Hyatt and felt pretty good about my column—until I glanced at* USA Today. *Reporter Carolyn White had discovered the little secret I sensed in Charles Boston: In 1979, Payton's father, Edward, died from an aneurysm in the Columbia jail, after being picked up on suspicion of drunken driving. This explains why the Paytons rarely return to Columbia.*

Like many journalists, I sometimes snicker about USA Today's *short articles, its lack of descriptive writing, but White's article about Columbia was filled with good color and details about this small southern town, plus the one hard fact I did not have. I felt annoyed at myself for not doing more research, but I was still glad I had made a detour to Walter Payton's hometown, to my old roots as a national reporter, before getting caught in the crush of the Super Bowl.*

NEW ORLEANS, JANUARY 22

Whenever I am introduced to somebody who does not know me or my work, just the uttering of the word *sports* induces a crafty smile on the stranger's lips. He feels he knows me, probably from watching Walter Matthau or Jack Klugman in *The Odd Couple.*

"You get to meet the players? You get to go to the Super Bowl?"

"I'm afraid so," I say with a sneer, Monty Wooley playing Sheridan Whiteside in The Man Who Came to Dinner.

The Super Bowl has become the most desirable sports event in America, with corporate vice-presidents competing for a seat on the company jet, wealthy people milling around the lobby looking for scalpers, and several thousand journalists jamming into news conferences. We are living out the American fantasy, right along with Las Vegas and Disneyland, but for me there is the tedious feeling of slogging through a convention.

The Super Bowl is the best organized sports championship I have ever seen—and why shouldn't it be? The league has several years to prepare for a week of rigid scheduling. The identity of the two teams matters not at all. The league produces both teams, on schedule, for two days of interviews; it produces coaches, and it even produces Commissioner Pete Rozelle. Everything's available, and nothing's available. Wherever we go, there are hospitality rooms with coffee, Danish, fresh fruit, and lavish hot breakfasts, too. All of this for one game, on Sunday afternoon, when the ball will be in play for approximately twelve minutes.

For some reason, I have never liked "American football," as I snidely call it to differentiate it from the real football, or soccer. I have never been touched by the sudden bursts of motion, the pileups, the long intervals between plays. By the time they start the next play, I can never remember who has the ball, who's in the lineup, what down it is, what the score is. I just don't get it.

I don't think I've ever written a good column about a football game, never really gotten any dramatic feel for one player making a difference. Football always seems to be an apologetic business of coaches whining, "We won't know until we see the films," or players mumbling, "I'm just trying to do my job." They always seem afraid of being cut from the team, or saying something inflammatory that will wind up on another team's bulletin board. They're so big, but they're so small.

Paul Zimmerman, my old pal from *Sports Illustrated* who knows the game better than any journalist, often talks fondly about the old Packers or the old Raiders or other teams that were fun to be around. I've missed it, and I'll never catch up.

This morning I had a minor panic attack when I realized I had nothing to write. Maybe I made a mistake by writing three early columns about the Super Bowl—Sweetness Payton's hometown for Wednesday, and two last week, about the ninety-second game plan for halftime, and one confessing to being a closet Chicago Bears fan ever since I read Sid Luckman's autobiography when I was a boy.

Caught in the Super Bowl swarm, at the sportswriters' convention, I am reminded that the main reason I don't like football is that nothing happens for six days at a time. The big questions of the week are whether Jim McMahon, the punk-rock quarterback of the Bears, is troubled by a bruised buttock, and whether the New England Patriots' receiver, Irving Fryar, is recovered from the mysterious knife wound on his hand, suffered in a spat with his wife.

With Dave Anderson looking at the big picture, my role is to illuminate some little corner of the Super Bowl. I can't goof on it in every column. That becomes a cliché in itself.

For my Friday column, I decide to write about two college teammates who will be playing on opposite sides of the line—Steve Moore, a guard with New England, and Richard Dent, the defensive end with the Bears, both from Tennessee State University. They will be assigned to other opponents, but I am curious how they feel about playing a few feet from each other.

Forsaking the press bus, I walk a few blocks to the Patriots' hotel. Right on schedule, the Patriots lumber into the room, carrying playbooks, looking for their names on placards on the thirty-odd tables.

I have met Moore, a bright and decent man who weighs nearly three hundred pounds and is nicknamed "House." Offensive linemen are often my favorite interviews, because they tend to be social beings, because they really know what is happening on the field, and because they do not often have big crowds of reporters around them.

"Steve, George Vecsey, *New York Times,* we met up in Foxboro last year," I say, shaking his huge hand.

"Oh, yeah, yeah," he says, perhaps remembering a column I did on him going back for his degree through Richard Lapchick's center for athletes at Northeastern University.

Four or five other journalists and I stare at Moore's huge thighs and arms as he recalls how he and Dent lived across the hall from each other in Boyd Hall on the Nashville campus. He tells how their coach would match them against each other in practice, just to feel the earth shake.

"You know how it is," Moore says. "Tempers will flare, but you'd leave it on the practice field."

When the Patriots' session is over, I walk a few blocks to the Bears' hotel. In a dark conference hall, Richard Dent has a big crowd around him. He has decided to play in the Super Bowl after all, despite his contract problems. I hang around the crowded table until I can interject a question about his old teammate.

"Steve is such a good player, such a strong man, that you'd go out to practice and say, 'Whew, do I have to line up against this man again?' "

Dent says the two friends had dinner last night. I am somewhat surprised to find that the guardians of pro football do not have a rule against fraternization during this holy week. Both Moore and Dent insisted they never talked about the game. The only gamesmanship came when Moore asked Dent what he was doing with his eighteen thousand dollars—the losers' share, you understand.

When the interview session is over, I have a column in my notebook and an afternoon to kill. I walk along Rampart Street, enjoying the bright sunshine. I eat by myself in Mother's Po' Boys, a popular sandwich shop. I keep saying we shouldn't send so many reporters to the Super Bowl, but I personally find it hard to turn down New Orleans in January.

NEW ORLEANS, JANUARY 23

Sticking an electric coil into a cup, I boil water for my Twining's English Breakfast tea. Electronic gadgets have reinforced my hermit's instincts. I can snack in my room, write my columns in my room, and file my copy by telephone.

I file my column for Friday, and then go out looking for a Sunday column. Jim McMahon has been keeping us all busy, first by mooning at a helicopter, to show that his sore buttocks muscle was healing quite nicely, thank you. Yesterday's Big Mac news was the rumor that McMahon had called the women of New Orleans "sluts," but that turned out to be the invention of a radio broadcaster, who has been suspended by his station.

Today's flash is that the Japanese acupuncturist Hiroshi Shiriashi is in town to treat McMahon and Willie Gault, the Bears' receiver. Not every Super Bowl has a Japanese acupuncturist in the cast, so I walk over to the Bears' hotel and ask Gault about it. A world-level sprinter, Gault says he first tried it before a track meet in Japan.

"Hiroshi uses thinner needles than most people," Gault says. "You don't even feel it when he's working on meaty muscles, and when he's around the knee, where there's more bone, you feel a tingle."

I try to arrange an interview with Shiriashi, but Gault says the acupuncturist is keeping a low profile. I come back to my room and call the Bears' team doctor, who is not thrilled with the acupuncturist's presence but cannot keep the players from seeing him.

Judy Greenfield in *The Times*'s invaluable research department calls back with some background, including the reminder that James Reston, the *Times* columnist, had acupuncture following an anesthetized appendectomy during his China visit in 1972. Now I'm ready to write about the ancient process of acupuncture, using the modern convenience of a word processor.

My constant companion on every trip is a four-pound Radio Shack Model 200 word processor, one and a half inches thick, six by eight inches, usually carried in a shoulder bag, with the strap resting on my right shoulder. With my headset, a few cassettes, a notebook, a wallet, a newspaper or book, and an extra set of batteries, my shoulder bag weighs over ten pounds.

When my career as a traveling reporter is over, I suspect I will be as readily identifiable as old pitchers like Carl Hubbell and Warren Spahn, whose throwing arms hang further down than their other arms, with palms facing outward, from decades of screwballs and curves and fastballs.

Is there workmen's compensation for a shoulder permanently ruined from carrying a writing machine through a million airports? Tennis elbow? What about sportswriter shoulder?

When I first started traveling with the Mets and the Yankees in 1962, I walked around with an Olivetti portable typewriter in my hand. This was when Western Union was still in the business of transmitting copy at press rates. Every sports event would have a familiar Western Union operator who would take the typewritten copy, jumbled with scribbled inserts, coffee stains, arrows, and deletions (and a few drops of blood from the writer's veins, according to Red Smith), and retype it into the electronic system. By mysterious relays, it was sent to our offices.

In New York, our copy was supervised by Howard Smith, a gracious old man with a slightly hunched back who served as an unofficial warden, chaplain, and arbiter of the press rooms.

One time I wrote a rather nasty article about a biased Yankee writer —let's call him Homer, after the comic-book pigeon, not the blind poet. Homer, who doubled as official scorer, something most papers don't allow anymore, had given Mickey Mantle an utterly gift single on a bobble by the shortstop. Howard filed my copy but took me aside to say, "George, I didn't think that was big-league, to criticize Homer that way." You would accept the criticism from Howard as long as he filed the copy.

On the road, we would sometimes write in our hotel rooms, charming the civilians on our floor with the clackety-clack of our portables at all hours of the day and night. Working for *Newsday*, with its old deadlines of four and five in the morning, I would often finish my story at one o'clock. Then I would stride confidently into the refreshing cool night air, through the deserted streets, to the beckoning yellow sign and glowing lights of the ubiquitous all-night Western Union office.

Sometimes I had to wait on line while a poor soul tried to wire home for money or solve a domestic crisis with a telegram. With no misgivings, I would slide my sheets of paper across the counter, mutter "press rates," and take off into the night, searching for an all-night coffee shop.

At three o'clock, I would return to my room, hoping there were no messages from the office. Then I would sleep the righteous sleep of the reporter who is done for the night, protected by a carbon copy at my bedside. In all those years, I don't think my copy was lost more than once or twice.

Sometimes we had to type on the trays of airplanes, even if the other passengers did not much care for the clacking noise of our machines. I will never forget writing on a Met charter flight in the mid-sixties, describing a home run given up by Galen Cisco, a pitcher who had played linebacker for Ohio State.

". . . but then Cisco hung a curveball, and it was mashed into the upper deck . . ." I gaily typed.

Suddenly I heard a growl from the seat behind me, and I saw a very large and very angry man reading the yellow Western Union paper sticking out of my machine.

"That wasn't a curveball, it was a slider!" Cisco growled. "And it was a good pitch, too!"

When I left sports, I discovered there were no press rooms or Western Union offices at your local coal-mine disaster. So I got in the habit of dictating stories into the recording room at *The Times,* where they would be transcribed from cassettes.

One day in 1976, we came to work and found our typewriters gone. Flat-out gone. The thankless task of teaching us to operate word processors went to Howard Angione, a former reporter.

In my usual mature fashion, I acted out, treated Angione poorly, threw raging temper tantrums when the system went down without warning and swallowed whole chunks of my articles. Angione had the patience of a saint with me, adopting me as his Everyman. His theory was: If Vecsey can learn the computer, anybody can.

As a result of my childish frustration and technical incompetence, I always managed to take the newest equipment on the road. Howard had me using a Teleram, a large, square machine that ran on electricity. Somebody would spill coffee into a machine in a crowded press box and short it out, or unplug the wrong extension cord and lose half a dozen stories in a crazed World Series press room.

In 1982, Howard broke me in on the Radio Shack, a little beauty that operates with electric power but also has a backup of four batteries, which saves every last word in case of power failure. Howard recently handed me the newest Model 200, with a raised screen that holds sixteen lines of copy, double the old size, and contains twelve thousand words, more than twice the old capacity. I can write on planes or in airport lounges, I can write during a game in antiquated arenas like Boston Garden, where there is no electricity on press row.

At Wimbledon, where European writers smoke lethal cigarettes in the press room, I can sit in the deserted stands after a match and tap out my story on battery power. (Nobody has ever explained to me why, when smoking is being banned in airplanes and restaurants and public buildings, press facilities are the last bastions of unconscionable smoking. Are we so disreputable that our health falls outside the law?)

When word processors were first used, I was sure they would hurt my writing, would keep me from making the magic last-minute arrows and deletions with a pen or pencil, but the opposite is true. With the press of a few buttons, an entire story or a few paragraphs can be moved, or duplicated, or turned inside out—no more angry jerking of an offending sheet from a typewriter, no more balled-up paper on the floor. (However, I suspect editing at newspapers has suffered because copy editors have become typesetters, more concerned with mechanics than with the flow of a story.)

For better or worse, technology has reinforced my lone-wolf tendencies. I can still write a story on deadline with all hell breaking loose in a press box, but the word processor has liberated me to write easier in my hotel room. And breathe better, too.

NEW ORLEANS, JANUARY 24

"I'm afraid I have some bad news," Lawrie Mifflin says on the phone from the New York office.

In my years on the road, I have grown accustomed to hearing bad news while in distant hotel rooms. I measure the tone in our deputy sports editor's voice and decide she is not talking about a family member.

"What is it?"

"Flo Hyman just died. She fell over during a match in Japan. They're assuming it was a heart attack."

I can immediately picture Flo Hyman, six feet five inches tall, her thick shock of hair, her full, bittersweet smile, smashing a volleyball over a net. She was my favorite athlete at the 1984 Olympics, the Old Lady on one of the strangest teams this nation ever fielded.

That team was put together by Arie Selinger, a driven Polish-Israeli-American coach who would have been equally at home storming a hijacked jet on the tarmac at Entebbe. Instead, he accumulated a dozen female athletes, sequestered them near a marine base on the California coast, and drove them in quest of an Olympic gold medal.

The first time I met Flo Hyman in 1983, she described how Selinger had prodded her to throw her long body on the hard volleyball floor, an absolute requirement for world-level players. She could evoke the pain with an arch of her eyelashes or a curve of her mouth. She had Lily Tomlin eyes.

"I know how much you liked her," Lawrie says. "I just wanted you to know."

Lawrie and I were part of the *Times*'s 1984 Olympic team, rooming down the hall from each other with our respective spouses. Lawrie is a field-hockey player from the first class of women at Yale; I think she is pleased that I find so many interesting female athletes to write about. How could you not write about Flo Hyman, the Old Lady?

Because of Jimmy Carter's ill-advised boycott of the 1980 Olympics to protest the Soviet invasion of Afghanistan, Flo Hyman and her teammates had to wait four more years, a full generation for athletes.

Their mission and their haunted emigré coach made the best ongoing story at the 1984 Olympics, and I drove down to Long Beach for every match. I was there the night this proud athlete lost the gold-medal match to the lithe young women from China. Flo Hyman, who was self-conscious about her height, never stood taller than that night, as she urged her teammates to be proud of their silver medals.

Now she had died, pursuing her sport in a small city in Japan.

We are always shocked by death in sports. One of the attractions of sports, it seems, is a rebuttal of death, an affirmation of living forever in the presence of athletes who are always young, always healthy, always confident. The death of an athlete is often taken as a personal affront by fans and by sports reporters. This news of mortality, coming after two mundane Super Bowl columns, leaves me numb.

"We'll handle the obituary," Lawrie says. "I know you won't be able to write anything about Flo until after the Super Bowl, but I just wanted you to know."

The league is throwing its annual Super Bowl party tonight, but I have already given my ticket to one of our reporters for his wife. Other friends have reservations all over New Orleans, but I need to be alone.

The hotel coffee shop is too jammed with football people; I slip out through the lobby, jammed with fans holding up TICKETS WANTED signs. I am sure my colleagues would make jokes if they saw where I am headed on a Friday night in New Orleans—a small Wendy's restaurant tucked into the huge medical center across Rampart Street. I noticed it on a run a few days ago. I'm always on the lookout for Thai restaurants and Mexican restaurants, and I never go near other fast-food chains, but the fresh salad bars and baked potatoes and even an occasional hamburger at Wendy's are a constant to a reporter racing around Middle America.

This Wendy's is a replica of all the others, except that it is tucked into a medical center. Weary-looking nurses and interns and orderlies eat reflectively, talking quietly, many of them in their hospital uniforms. The institutional tone fits my mood ever since I heard about Flo Hyman. The people in this Wendy's are connected to life and death, to the pain of living in the real world. I am around people, but I am also alone. I read the papers and sit around the Wendy's for a long, long time.

Weeks later, doctors disclosed that Flo Hyman had died from a ruptured aortic aneurysm, associated with the Marfan syndrome, a disorder of the aorta. Because some of the symptoms can be detected, many other people were helped by the publicity over Flo's death. That would be a legacy even greater than the gold medal the Old Lady never won.

NEW ORLEANS, JANUARY 25

There are two great parties at the Super Bowl every year—the one thrown by the National Football League and the one thrown by Dick and Trish Schaap.

I'm glad I saved my appetite for the Schaap party.

The Schaaps teamed up with two friends, Hamilton and Midge Richardson, to rent K-Paul, the popular Cajun restaurant. Dick did a story last year when Paul Prudhomme moved his operation to New York for a few weeks and Dick fell in love with the food and ate there twice a day for three weeks, which is a lot of pepper and pecan pie. The Schaaps became so friendly with Prudhomme that he closed his place to the public tonight and personally cooked blackened redfish for over fifty guests.

This intimate little party included two senators, Gary Hart of Colorado and Christopher Dodd of Connecticut, Representative Lindy Boggs of Louisiana, John Roberts, a former member of the Trudeau cabinet in Canada, Jimmy Buffett, the singer, Ed Bradley and Bryant Gumbel from television, Bob Pettit, the former basketball star from Baton Rouge, three former Green Bay Packer stars, Willie Davis, Marv Fleming, and Jerry Kramer, and Nick Lowery, the placekicker for the Kansas City Chiefs.

Somebody whispered to me, "This must be a big event. Gary Hart is here with his wife."

I am always amazed at Dick's ability to remain friendly with the people he has interviewed in his long career as television correspondent and writer for the *New York Herald Tribune.* We go back to when he wrote a nice piece for *Newsweek* about our Kiddie Corps at *Newsday* in the early sixties; he has covered Robert F. Kennedy and he has covered Vince Lombardi and he has written dozens of books. You never know who will show up at his parties; Billy Crystal is a regular, and Martina Navratilova has dropped in at the Wimbledon party.

Jerry Kramer is the constant at all Schaap parties. Shake hands with him and you feel the lumps from all the broken bones a lineman receives, plus the metallic hardness of his championship rings. Dick and Jerry collaborated on *Instant Replay,* about Kramer's days as a guard with the first Super Bowl champions. Kramer is a businessman with investments in energy; we sometimes discuss the many charms of strip-mining. Tonight Kramer proudly told how he was recently crossing the street in New York and a cabbie leaned out the window and yelled, "Nice block" —for some heavy hit he laid on a Dallas Cowboy two decades earlier.

The best sight of the night was Trish Schaap, with her honey-blond hair and lovely Scottish accent, working in the kitchen alongside Paul Prudhomme, who is about three times her size. Prudhomme had his first string of waitresses on duty, putting Mardi Gras beads around our necks and forcing pecan pie on us.

Everybody was enthused about meeting each other. I told Ham Richardson that I used to watch him play the U.S. Nationals at Forest Hills. Ed Bradley congratulated Jimmy Buffett on a good show last night. Kit Dodd, who is a real sports fan, wanted to know how the Yankees and Mets are going to do this year. We all apologized to John Roberts for some idiots in Yankee Stadium booing "O Canada" during the Blue Jay series last September.

During the party, I wound up with a roommate for the night. Dick once did a feature on Nick Lowery working for a member of the House of Representatives between seasons for the Chiefs. When Lowery arrived at the party tonight, straight from the airport, he found out the Schaaps did not have room for him at their borrowed house. The best way I could thank the Schaaps for a great party was to offer Lowery the extra bed in my hotel room, and give him my extra key before he went out on the town. Sometime long after I went to sleep, I heard him wander in.

NEW ORLEANS, JANUARY 26

My new roomie is still asleep as I get out for my Super Bowl run. I cross the gangway from the Hyatt, and do my stretching in the chilly sunlight alongside the Dome, where vendors are already setting up tables with shirts, caps, and banners with Bears and Patriots colors. Sunday morning peaceful in the South.

After six revolutions of the Dome, three miles, I put on my sweat clothes and stretch again in the cool air. Fans are already inspecting the souvenirs. This place is going to be a zoo in another hour or two.

When I come back to my room, Lowery is just waking up.

"You've been out already?" he asks.

"Got to run off the pecan pie," I say.

I shower and change. Now I'm on company time. The game will not begin until five o'clock here, which means I must write an early column before kickoff—the curse of *New York Times* sports columnists.

Since most major events begin after our first-edition deadline, it is difficult writing a column, knowing that events probably will make that column seem irrelevant before it ever reaches print.

Some papers let their sports columnist miss the first edition, or else their deadlines are late enough for them to work an event before writing. I am always jealous when I see Jim Murray from Los Angeles or Barry Lorge from San Diego working slowly after a game.

Last April I had to write an early column about the championship game of college basketball, Georgetown against Villanova. I felt justified writing about the four-year bond between John Thompson and Patrick Ewing, sort of a "Now they are for the ages" column. I never said Georgetown would win, but I did say they were "heavy favorites last night." Of course, Villanova upset Georgetown, and I rewrote my column for the next edition, but people who saw the national edition had to think I was out of touch, writing about Thompson and Ewing rather than the upset.

The deadline problem is a little easier at the Super Bowl, because the paper holds the first edition open for the lead story and for Dave Anderson to insert the score in his column. That allows me to write about the mood of the day, what New Orleans was like on Super Bowl Sunday.

My idea for today came from Gerry Eskenazi, one of our best reporters, who told me about a charter train from Chicago, carrying Bears fans. As soon as Gerry told me about the train from Chicago, I thought about the beautiful feature Roy Reed did around 1971, when he was *The Times*'s writer-in-residence in New Orleans. I have long lost the article, but I remember the haunting description of Roy's ride on the City of New Orleans passenger train from Chicago to New Orleans.

About the same time Steve Goodman wrote a song about the train:

> *"Riding on the City of New Orleans*
> *Illinois Central, Monday morning rail.*
> *Fifteen cars, fifteen restless riders,*
> *Three conductors, twenty-five sacks of mail . . . "*

I have no idea whether the *Times* story influenced the song, or the song inspired the article, but the two masterpieces blend in my memory as two halves of a perfect whole. I would personally kill to be able to write as gracefully as Roy Reed, now teaching writing back home in Arkansas, or to write a song as perfect as the one by Steve Goodman, who died of leukemia a few years back.

I hum Goodman's song as I walk a few blocks to the train station, thinking about the train slashing through Jackson, Mississippi, Monday night, thinking about the link between New Orleans and Chicago, jazz going up the river, Chicago Bears fans coming down the river.

And here they come, wearing blue-and-orange hats, shirts, pennants, scarves, jackets, buttons, long-suffering fans celebrating the Bears' first Super Bowl. Jack and Judy Fitzpatrick from Northbrook, Illinois, looking remarkably chipper for people who have just spent eighteen hours jouncing on the Illinois Central roadbed, recall the bitter cold of the Bears' last championship game, in Wrigley Field in 1963—"Eleven degrees," Fitzgerald says, with a shudder. No, he won't mind the climate-controlled sterility of the Superdome, not at all.

Other fans rush past us, a blur of navy blue and orange, looking to snap up more souvenirs, take a taste of Bourbon Street. I am energized by the sight of Bears fans, like a throwback in time, before all the nouveau teams from the American Football League. This is the team of Sid Luckman and Bulldog Turner that I saw play when I was ten years old. These people are happy, excited about coming all this distance to watch a football game.

After five years of doing a column, I know when I'm ready to write. I rush back to the hotel, find a nice thank-you note from Lowery, plug in my computer, and write about the train and jazz and Steve Goodman and long-suffering people; create an ambiguous second paragraph where I can insert the result on deadline.

The column begins: "The train arrived backward, which was not necessarily an omen, you understand. . . ."

Now it's midafternoon. I look out the window and see the crowd assembling outside the Dome, and I know it's time to go to work. For the next six hours, I will be engulfed by noise and crowds, trying to make sense of a big event. I remember the blend of tension and curiosity and sadness that I used to feel when I knew I was going to cover a street demonstration that could turn violent, or a coal-mine disaster that had already killed dozens of miners.

That was life-and-death, with so many details unknown. This is fun-and-games, with the National Football League handing you a mimeographed description of every play in the game. There is no comparison, but I will have to reach back for some of the same mental toughness, inner peace, physical strength, to keep my poise for the next six hours. People will say, "You get to go to games," but I call this work.

I assemble my machine in my black shoulder bag, stuff a few thick press guides inside, and I dress in neat slacks, a jacket and tie. Until a few years ago, I was partial to jeans and sweaters, but then I decided I was living up to the public image of the sloppy, casual, freeloading "sportswriter." Maybe it's middle age catching up to me, but I want to look like a serious adult journalist even in the madhouse of a football dressing room. When I walk up to a coach or player who does not know me and I introduce myself as being from *The New York Times,* I want him to think of me as a representative of the adult world "out there."

Before we leave the hotel for the Superdome, we have a Team *Times* staff meeting in our rented office. We have sent down a full dozen— Pete Alfano, Dave Anderson, Ira Berkow, Gerry Eskenazi, Mike Janofsky, Frank Litsky, Malcolm Moran, and me, two photographers, Vic DeLucia and Barton Silverman, one photo editor, Steve Fine, and our assistant sports editor, Arthur Pincus. A former clerk from City College who worked his way up as a copy editor, Arthur has never been a writer, but he understands the psyches of reporters as well as any editor I've ever met.

Most of us fidget as Arthur talks, all of us involved in our own stories, our own logistics, our own little worlds. Journalists are essentially lone wolves, producing what we do by prowling for ourselves, surviving on our wits, but *The Times,* more than any paper I know, expects us to coordinate our efforts. We're all impatient now. I don't guess it's too different from a locker room, where players clatter their feet on the floor, fidget with their equipment, make quick trips to the bathroom. They say the Boston Celtics knew Bill Russell was ready to play when he rushed off to the bathroom and threw up. Nobody throws up here, but we all talk a lot. Nervous energy.

Somebody decides to take a group photograph of Team *Times,* including all the wives, but we also want to make sure our photographers are included.

"Set it up and show me what to press," I tell Barton, not mentioning that my protruding thumb has ruined a number of once-in-a-lifetime photographs in Europe. Thumb goes to Falaise. Thumb goes to Nuremberg. Thumb behaves himself on Barton's camera, I think.

As our meeting breaks up, I decide to add a little football flavor.

"Let's kick ass!" I shout.

My colleagues stare at me. A few of the wives smile tolerantly.

The next stop is lunch, in a private dining room under the eaves of the Superdome—trays of shrimp and shellfish and pasta, the normal high standards of the National Football League.

I fill my plate and sit next to Karla Hudecek, Malcolm Moran's wife, an enthusiastic young reporter in Bridgeport as well as a Russian major who has studied in Leningrad. I usually tease her about her affinity for the Indy 500 and for Bobby Knight's Indiana basketball team, but this time we talk about my impending trip to the Soviet Union for the Goodwill Games in July.

"Three weeks in Russia," Karla says with a sigh, no doubt thinking about all the stories she could dig out for Malcolm, with her familiarity with the language and the country.

A few minutes before game time, I take my seat in the press box above the fifty-yard line, with all the regulars, the old war-horses, together again.

The Bears break the game open, and I find myself enjoying it, as if George McAfee and Johnny Lujack were still wearing those blue-and-orange uniforms. After I update my column about the Bears fans enjoying their first Super Bowl, Arthur Pincus asks if I can write a sidebar about Walter Payton, who has not scored a touchdown in his first and maybe his only Super Bowl. Refrigerator Perry and a million other Bears have scored in the 46–10 romp, but the Bears have not made any concerted effort to get Sweetness into the end zone.

Somebody in the office wonders why a Payton story is necessary since Payton has not done much today. Pincus rolls his eyes and says, "That's the point." Man bites dog, and all that.

The press box is beginning to vibrate, with hundreds of writers filing on deadline, the adrenaline kicking in, all the talent and the skills and the experience being called into play. We may look like a scruffy mob, with our beards and our bellies, our jeans and our piles of paper, but most of us once were the brightest scribblers in our grade schools. Over the years, we have acquired a few tricks for informing and entertaining the readers.

Late in the game, the ragtag army follows a wavy red line down the ramp toward the dressing rooms. We watch the end of the game on huge television monitors, and then we wait as both locker rooms are closed for a few minutes. Then the league officials bring players and coaches to the interview area, to stand on lecterns and speak to huge knots of reporters.

After fifteen minutes, Walter Payton still has not shown up. I am a little nervous about the second-edition deadline, but Joe Browne, the capable public-relations man for the league, assures me Payton will be coming along soon. Instead of waiting, I rush into the Bears' locker room to see what Payton's teammates think about Payton not scoring. Steve Fuller, the reserve quarterback, still wearing a drenched T-shirt and game pants, says he tried calling a special play so Payton could score a touchdown, but that Payton "didn't like it a bit."

Fuller adds, "He's the heart and soul of this organization. I don't think scoring a touchdown would have made any difference."

Jay Hilgenberg, the Bears' center, tells me he didn't realize Payton had not scored until we told him.

"He doesn't need a Super Bowl touchdown to be the greatest," Hilgenberg says.

It sounds like the company line to me. I think they should have kept handing the ball to Sweetness until he got into the end zone. But what does Sweetness think? My next deadline is nine-thirty New Orleans time, and by nine o'clock, he is still taking the longest shower in history. He finally dresses and walks to the interview room. Nearly a full week after visiting Payton's hometown, I finally get to see him in person: high-pitched voice, nervous energy, looking smaller than his listed size of five-ten, two hundred and two pounds, curly black hair still wet from the shower.

He looks tired, and his voice is edgy and defensive, but he tells us everything is fine. No, he did not think he should have scored.

"I had my chances," he says over and over again.

Besides, he says, the Patriots' defenses were designed to stop him.

"When they're keying on you, you can't mind. I don't mind being the rabbit."

I don't believe him. I think Sweetness is upset, just barely controlling his emotions, too polite to share his hurt with reporters who are prodding him to open up. It's a funny duality. I want him to say something controversial, but I respect him more for not complaining.

After ten minutes, Payton starts to vibrate like a tuning fork. I have heard he is hyperactive, that he has trouble staying in one place for long, which makes him a great running back but not a great interview. Then, zip, he's gone. Now it is time for me to make like Walter Payton and run to deadline. I rush up the ramp, hoping I never get old or out of shape, and I pound out a fast five hundred words on what Sweetness said.

This is a sidebar, and I cannot editorialize the way I would in my column, but I lay out the quotes to suggest there was more than what Payton was willing to say. My final paragraph includes a Payton quote that he was quite happy to be with a winner, and I conclude: "Most of those around Payton would have to take his word for it."

I push the buttons, and the story flies to New York. Then I pack up and get out of the press box as quickly as Payton bolted from the interview room. Many of my friends may hold a glamorous image of sports reporters fraternizing with Jimbo and Sweetness during Super Bowl week, but our contacts have been formal and peripheral. Now that the game is over, we go our separate ways.

The league holds yet another sumptuous buffet for the media after the game. I spot Roz Eskenazi and Arlene Litsky holding a large table in the back, and I tip the waiter ten dollars to bring silverware and napkins and wine for the arriving troops. People are talking about how good the Bears were, and the halftime show, and what it was like in the stands, but the room is noisy, and my mind is shot.

When our other reporters arrive, one by one, carrying their bags and their computers, weary soldiers home from the wars, I excuse myself and bolt back to my hotel room. I immediately pack and take a shower and jump into bed, along with my headset and a cassette by The Band, with songs about Canada and the South, small towns and railroad trains. Before long, the Super Bowl is pushed from my mind as if it never happened.

NEW ORLEANS, JANUARY 27

Today is called a "travel day" on my schedule. I hope that's prophetic. For a convention city, New Orleans does not have a lot of flights. The travel desk at *The Times* could not come up with a Monday flight months ago, and I do not love the idea of an extra day on the road.

I wake up in darkness, and take a cab out to the airport. Lines everywhere. I try TWA first, but realize my case is hopeless when I see Jim Kensil, the general manager of the Jets, arguing for a seat on the plane—and he's got a ticket for it! Why do airlines overbook for events like the Super Bowl, when they can assume everybody who went in with a ticket is going to want to go out?

Everybody has travel horror stories, but our travel horror stories are aggravated by always going to the hot town for the hot event. The bastards overbooked at the NBA All-Star Game in Indianapolis last year. I'm convinced the only way I got my seat back on the last USAir flight was when I started screaming I was going to write a column in *The New York Times* about the misery of an extra night in Indianapolis. They didn't want me in their town nohow. I somehow don't think New Orleans will care.

I trudge with my luggage over to Eastern, and ask for anything heading east. That means Atlanta, where deceased southerners change planes on their way to heaven or hell. The man says he is sold out all day, but he will check my baggage to LaGuardia and put me on standby. My weight reduced, I run out to the gate, carrying my portable computer on my right shoulder.

The first flight leaves for Atlanta, but only one or two lucky souls are saved from the standby list. The man tells us to come back in an hour.

I find a national *New York Times* at the stand and forage for a quiet corner of the breakfast room. When I am finished, I call home.

"Don't know if I'm going to get home today. What's new?"

"What's new?" Marianne says. "Oh, not much. Just David changing schools, that's all."

In his junior year, David has totally stopped trying to adjust to the disciplined little private school. He says it's time for him to move on to the public school, and he's probably right.

"I've been up at the high school all morning helping him register," Marianne says. "I'm exhausted."

She often says she'd like to trade places with me—let me run the house for the next quarter-century while she travels. She's been around enough to know that travel is more tedious than dangerous—but she insists it beats talking to school officials and waiting for repairmen to keep their appointments. I don't offer to trade.

The flying's not bad. In fact, I love flying, particularly to California. The office can't find you. Salesmen can't call you during dinner and try to sell you credit cards or municipal bonds or chimney service. The world is almost always tidy and serene at thirty-five thousand feet. And sunny. Marianne thinks the airlines could make a fortune in the wintertime by offering brief flights above the cloud cover—a glimpse of sunlight to cure midwinter depression.

In twenty-five years on the road, I've had very few bad flights. There was one flight when we flew over the tower in Pittsburgh for a visual inspection of our undercarriage. One flight into Atlanta in tornado weather, when the pilot slapped us down on the runway like a short-order cook making pancakes. A couple of shaky flights in the early days of the 727 jets, when pilots had to blast on the power to reach the runway. A popped door on takeoff from LaGuardia, a loss of cabin pressure, a routine landing. A couple of aborted landings where we went around again. A few brutal final approaches in electric storms. The usual.

The biggest scare I ever had was on a late flight home from Chicago, when we realized we were circling over Lake Michigan. After a while, the pilot announced there were indications the landing gear was stuck. He said he was trying to lock them manually, but that he could not be sure. We were using up fuel, and then we were going back to O'Hare. Just for safety's sake, you understand, the attendants would show us the correct crash positions.

On a clear evening, bright stars, twinkling lights of the city, we made a long, low approach. We could see trucks with their red lights moving toward the runway. The passengers were extremely quiet, anticipating anything—sparks, fire, spinning, grinding, our lives turning upside down. We braced ourselves, and the plane bounced once on its wheels, bounced again, and made a perfect stop. They told us we would all be put on the next flight to LaGuardia, with drink chits all around.

When I called home to say I would be late, I was stunned to hear Marianne sobbing on the other end.

"They told me your plane was making an emergency landing," she said.

Because airlines are not always great about giving information on delayed flights, Marianne has become proficient in asking to speak to the supervisor. In this case, they gave her real information.

"I didn't know you loved me," I said.

"I thought you were going to crash," she said, still crying—my tough little wife who is always calm when she has any control over emergencies.

"I'm too mean. They can't get me," I said.

The airlines will get me by overbooking, not by crashing. I head out to the Eastern wing, to watch two more flights head toward Atlanta. It is already one o'clock. All the standby people are getting tired of each other.

I run into a colleague, Dan Foster from the *Greenville News* in South Carolina, a genial regular at the big events. Dan has his ticket home, via Atlanta, and he commiserates with me.

"Hey, the Eastern manager here used to be based in Greenville," Dan says. "I'm going to tell him there's a columnist from *The New York Times* who needs to get back today."

Dan has more faith in the power of *The Times* than I do. His friend courteously examines my ticket and says he'll try to do something, but that he cannot jump me ahead of other people. That satisfies my sense of justice, but won't get me home.

A few minutes later, Dan walks over and says, "My friend says there's a flight leaving for Houston in five minutes. He says just get on it, then turn around in Houston and fly to Atlanta. Plenty of space."

I rush to the gate, wave my ticket. They have no time to rewrite it, but they wave me into the walkway. The door is closing, but the agent opens it, and I sink down next to Sam Skinner, a colleague from the Bay Area.

"You going west?" he asks, surprised.

"Going east, Sam."

"Oh."

Dan Foster's friend was right. I get off at Houston, flash my ticket and my air-travel card, pay a few more dollars, and get a seat to Atlanta. When we land in Atlanta, I race for the subway, race up some stairs, race down the hall, carrying my computer on my aching right shoulder, the O. J. Simpson of the press box. I make the next LaGuardia flight with five minutes to spare. Three seats to myself.

At LaGuardia, my luggage has already arrived on an earlier flight. I lug it to the Avis terminal and rent a car to get home, because I don't want to deal with cabbies after my exciting day in the wonderful world of travel. At nine o'clock, I walk in the front door.

"How'd you get here?" Marianne asks.

"Friend of mine from South Carolina," I say.

FEBRUARY

NEW YORK, FEBRUARY 5

The deputy sports editor and I are meeting to plan our coverage of the World Cup of soccer in June. But first the deputy sports editor displays the latest photographs of Daniel, a beautiful boy of two.

"Great smile," I say.

The deputy sports editor knows I'm a softy for baby pictures. I know the deputy sports editor is a softy for pictures of Michel Platini, the graceful star of the French national soccer team.

Lawrie Mifflin has been looking forward to covering the World Cup of soccer since she came over to *The Times* and later was promoted to deputy sports editor. But now she is not going.

"Lawrie," I say, in mock admonition, pointing at her waist.

"Don't say it," she says, with a mock groan.

Whenever I get together with Lawrie and her husband, Arthur Kimmel, we talk about parenting, not sports. They had planned to have a second child, but not quite this soon, around the finals of the World Cup.

Lawrie is an All-Star in the first generation of female sports reporters. She has written for the *New York Daily News,* for Howard Cosell, and now for *The Times.* She still plays field hockey, as she did at Yale, when she is not busy having children.

In the office, she is a huge asset, because she knows what it is like to be a reporter, and because she has a strong knowledge of hockey, soccer, gymnastics, the Olympic movement, and women's sports.

In my first tour of duty in sports, there were almost no women covering sports. The only women we saw were in bars or hotels. The conversations in the press box were pretty graphic; the air was full of cigar smoke. Bob Lipsyte, the young writer who expanded the parameters of the sports column at *The Times* in the sixties, would occasionally venture out to women's games, but most sports sections covered only the most important women's golf or tennis tournaments.

As a news reporter, I was impressed by female ecologists, female lawyers, female soldiers, female coal miners, female journalists. After never working with women before, my head was turned a few times, but when you stand watch in the snow at a coal-mine disaster with male and female reporters all bundled up in the same thick coats, it tends to minimize the differences.

When I came back to sports, women were already in place at most papers, but having a hard time doing their job. The National Football League would not force every team to open its doors. While the male reporters were crowding around a player, getting the first, most honest reaction after a game, a female journalist had to stand outside and request that a player be brought out to her. By the time the player steps outside, of course, he is bored, tired, and anxious to get on the bus.

One of the lowest moments in Bowie Kuhn's career as baseball commissioner was when he actively fought the suit by *Sports Illustrated* seeking equal access for Melissa Ludtke, one of their writers. I found Kuhn to be a humorous man who loved and understood the game, but he had an establishment lawyer's blindness to the injustice being done to an entire gender.

At first, the resistance to women as sports journalists appeared to be the Weenie Issue, as Geoffrey Stokes called it in *The Village Voice*. Athletes are used to walking around the clubhouse naked, giving interviews or playing cards or eating a sandwich while wearing absolutely nothing. More than once, I have interviewed athletes who were preoccupied with scratching, stroking, and inspecting a rather personal part of their bodies. I'm sure an anthropologist could tell me what that was all about.

Having played a lot of ball in my time, I'm used to being naked in all-male lockers, and I've been in a hot tub or two in mixed company, and have never been overly modest around my family, but if I were a player, I think I would wear a robe or a towel in mixed company. How hard can it be for players making four hundred thousand a year to buy a five-dollar robe?

But I think the issue goes beyond modesty. Many athletes have had so much "success" with women that they tend to perceive women in very functional terms. The majority of them have never worked or socialized with women on any sort of equal basis, and are not prepared to be questioned by female reporters.

With lack of support, and you could even say lack of respect, coming from the commissioner, it is no wonder some women were treated with contempt by some baseball players. Some of the more observant Christian players like Dale Murphy and Bob Knepper still do not cooperate with women in their locker rooms. I never was sure if it was because they had dirty minds or because they regarded women as inferior, or both.

And then there was Dave Kingman, a man avoided by most of his own teammates even when he was hitting forty home runs a season. This strange bird, known as Texas Tower among his peers because he reminded them of a mass murderer, used to make vile remarks to female reporters who visited the many clubhouses to which he was shunted. He once sent a shoe box, gift-wrapped with a pink ribbon, to Susan Fornoff of the *Sacramento Bee.* The box contained a dead rat.

One of the ugliest legacies of Kuhn's policy came during the 1984 National League championships, when Claire Smith of the *Hartford Courant* entered the San Diego Padres' dressing room. A few of the players made vicious remarks and dispatched a club official to eject her, while the league official wrung his hands and whined, "What can we do?"

Fortunately, Steve Garvey of the Padres heard about the problem and went outside and gave Claire as long an interview as she needed— just another example of why Garvey has been one of the class acts in baseball. Later, Goose Gossage, an old friend of Claire's from the Yankees, assured her, "No problem, you're in there tomorrow."

Peter Ueberroth, in his first days as commissioner, put pressure on the Padres to open their doors during the World Series, which they did, reluctantly. The Padres then lost in five games. No offense to Garvey and Gossage, but—good.

Lawrie Mifflin has had a few problems with athletes who did not want to talk to female reporters. The worst came from Tiger Williams, the most penalized player in the history of the National Hockey League, who is just as offensive off the ice. One night Lawrie and the rest of the writers trooped in to the Vancouver Canucks' locker room to interview Mario Marois, a former Ranger who had tossed a puck at the Ranger coach, Craig Patrick, in the heat of the game.

While Marois was talking openly with Lawrie and the others, Lawrie heard Tiger Williams screaming, "Get her out of here! What is that fucking bitch doing in here?"

She knew Williams had recently come over from Harold Ballard's Toronto Maple Leafs, the most backward organization in hockey, with a ban on women in the locker room. She did not think that Tiger, as bumptious as he is, would take matters into his own hands on his new club.

But he did. She suddenly felt his powerful hands, which had earned him weeks' worth of penalties, grabbing her by the arm and shoulder and giving her the bum's rush out of the Canucks' locker.

"I was stunned," Lawrie has told me. "I couldn't believe this was happening to me. I knew I had to do something right away, because I couldn't let him do this to me. I had to get my story."

She sought out Harry Neale, the coach, and persuaded him to intervene. He smoothed the way for her to get back in to interview Marois, but he could not stop Williams from screaming at the young player, "You don't have to talk to that bitch!"

Lawrie later got her sports editor, Buddy Martin, to write a letter of protest to John Ziegler, the president of the league, but Ziegler was as passive about women's rights as he is about violence on the ice. She never received an apology from Williams, and as far as she knows, he was never reprimanded.

Most hockey players seem relatively polite and comfortable with the many female reporters these days. Other women say professional basketball players are also generally tolerant. You could not find two more divergent sports than hockey and basketball—one sport predominantly white, rural, Canadian, the other sport predominantly black, urban, American.

Perhaps because hockey players do not have the veneer of higher education that football players have, as a broad group, they are more natural, more relaxed, about women in the clubhouse.

Perhaps basketball players, with their great individual skills and creativity, are able to think for themselves, and not be herded into any mass response against women. My hunch is that basketball players recognize the back of the bus when they see it.

One of the main reasons women are not treated better by teams and leagues is that they are not totally accepted by the sportswriting associations and individual colleagues. Some of the older male reporters may be courteous and helpful on a personal basis, but they really don't believe women should be covering sports.

It was curious that Dick Young, who became bitterly conservative writing for a Rupert Murdoch paper, came right out and said women have a right to earn a living in the locker room, while Red Smith, who became more liberal in his *New York Times* years, felt it would be better for women not to work the clubhouse. How do you figure that?

I've heard colleagues say women should not write about sports because they did not trade bubble-gum cards when they were little, because they did not wait their turn for "winners" at the local basketball court—assuming this to be the case.

Of course, some of the female reporters are athletes. Christine Brennan, one of the best reporters at *The Washington Post*, impressed a Redskins' coach by tossing a perfect fifteen-yard spiral pass. Jackie MacMullan, stylish writer for the *Boston Globe,* is a willowy ex-forward for the University of New Hampshire. A lot of the men on the beat never were handed a varsity uniform, anywhere, but that's not the point. Writers, whether novelists or songwriters or sports journalists, male or female, learn to inquire and empathize and imagine and report and create. That's the transcending, transforming act of being a writer.

It is also possible that some athletes and male reporters are opposed to female reporters because their wives are not comfortable with the idea of women in the locker rooms—and press boxes, and long road trips. But in the six years I've been back in sports, I have never been aware of a female sports journalist having a "reputation" among her male colleagues or with the athletes, although a few long relationships between reporters did begin "on the beat."

The work we do tends to make us equals—tired, hungry, grouchy equals, with planes to catch and deadlines to meet. Not much romance there. Women tend to order room service more than men, because they are just not comfortable going out by themselves, or they are not welcome with the boys all the time.

"I know I cramp their style," says one of my best female friends on another paper. "I go out for dinner once in a while, but then I head back to my room."

The gap between men and women may be changing rapidly. As the older males move out of the business, the younger men are used to being around women from college dormitories, coed softball teams and even Little League, shared apartments, and more equal working backgrounds. The sixties did leave some permanent changes.

Now that women are bringing their diverse talents to sports, I'm waiting for the next step—the first outrageous female sports journalist. This may be totally to their credit, but the women have not yet shown that overt need to impress and dominate that I would categorize as a male trait. It may be offensive and macho, but it produces dialogue and controversy.

You could not find more zealous, competitive journalists than Jane Leavy of the *Washington Post* or Helene Elliott of *Newsday* or Jane Gross of *The Times,* but women do not show the same show-off, gunslinger egos that the men have among their pals—Mike Lupica, Tony Kornheiser, Steve Jacobson, and me in the same western saloon, this town ain't big enough for all of us.

As part of my duality about life, about success, about sports, about roles, sometimes I enjoy raising my voice and sticking out my chest with all the bad little boys of the press box. But I'm also glad there are sports reporters named Pam and Lesley and Robin in my second tour of duty. No matter what feminists may say and believe about ultimate equality, I'm grateful for the difference I feel when I talk with some of these younger colleagues.

Peter Richmond of the *Miami Herald,* one of the best young people in the new generation, once said, "You know, I recently noticed that most of my best friends are women." I knew exactly what he meant. Being around women, being around some female journalists, brings out a less competitive, more comfortable side of me than I ever felt in the old cigar-smoke days.

Women can obviously write pointed and knowledgeable columns, as proved by Charlotte Curtis, Flora Lewis, and Anna Quindlen at *The Times,* Judy Luce Mann at the *Washington Post,* Ellen Goodman in the *Boston Globe.* There is not a funnier, more devastating political satirist in the country than Molly Ivins of Dallas, who can cover a gubernatorial race in Texas and make the reader pray that nobody wins.

If there is one thing missing in the first wave of female sports journalists, it is the overview, the critical vision, the irreverent voice, the mocking tones, teasing the heroes, prodding the officials, pointing out great truths with exaggeration or scorn or fury.

We need sombody like Molly Ivins in the press box, the first truly smart-ass female sports columnist, as quick as Jim Murray or Leigh Montville to tease the idols of sports. Maybe the problem is that male sports editors have not seen the wittiness, the inspired crabbiness, in their female reporters, or do not want to encourage it. A smart-ass male columnist is a curmudgeon. A smart-ass female columnist is a bitch. Antics with semantics, as Sydney Harris used to write.

Maybe women have been working to prove they know their beat and can write well and quickly. Maybe women still have an element of socialization, of not disrupting, of getting along with others. Maybe it is a male trait to be ornery. LeAnne Schreiber used to say about a male colleague, "Oh, he just has a strong case of testosteronitis." Don't we all.

As an editor and former reporter, Lawrie Mifflin is particularly good about phrasing suggestions with "Do you think?" or "Maybe you already know this." This is not to say male colleagues cannot be reasonable and compassionate. Joe Vecchione, our sports editor, is strong-willed when he has to be, but he is also one of the best administrators I've ever met in dealing with problems.

Lawrie was a little hesitant about breaking the news to Joe that she and Arthur were going to have their second child a bit sooner than they had anticipated. As a family man and a friend, Joe told her it was terrific, to take as much time off as she needed—and not even to think about working in Mexico while she was pregnant.

Now we are sitting in the *Times* cafeteria, Lawrie three months pregnant and starting to show it. She's getting grief from the estimable Paul Gardner, the soccer expert and friend who will not forgive her for missing the World Cup.

We place our World Cup schedules on the cafeteria table.

"I guess you'll be based in Mexico City and travel around," Lawrie says.

"One of us should be based in Guadalajara and covering Brazil," I say, lowering my eyes to Lawrie's midsection. Guilt. Guilt. Guilt.

"Don't start," Lawrie says.

"The next one's going to be beautiful, too," I tell the deputy sports editor.

DALLAS, FEBRUARY 7

Back in the corner of the Webb Soul Market are two billiard tables with large green lightshades overhead.

"Spud can play that game, too," says David Webb, Jr.

This is the home of Spud Webb, all five feet seven inches of him, a rookie in the National Basketball Association. Tomorrow the league is holding its annual slam-dunk competition, and the little man from the Atlanta Hawks is going to be the hometown favorite. He's my Sunday column, no matter who wins the slam-dunk.

Janice Smith, Spud's sister, is wearing a button that says I'M A SPUD NUT. These are good, hard-working people who run the family market for sixteen to eighteen hours a day, all year round. Their big day is New Year's, with the Cotton Bowl just down the street.

Walking into the market, with its six-packs of beer and disposable diapers, pig's feet and dresses, messages tacked up on bulletin boards, neighbors keeping warm indoors, I felt immediately at home, back out in "the country"—on the road again, as Willie Nelson would put it.

"I remember when he was in high school and they wouldn't put him on the varsity because the coach was always doubting his size," says older brother David. "But in his senior year, Coach put him in, and nobody's stopped him yet."

This afternoon reminds me of the nice day in Mississippi a few weeks ago, on my Walter Payton tour. Reminds me of the old Kentucky days. I chat with Spud's family for as long as I can, then I pick up some orange juice and crackers for my hotel room. Time to head downtown.

DALLAS, FEBRUARY 8

Sleek blond hair, shimmering pants suit, exotic cheekbones, Martina spots me near the court. I forgot she was going to be a judge in the slam-dunk contest. I walk over and give her a kiss, reminded once again how pretty and unassuming she is without a tennis racquet in her hand.

"Jana's here," she says, pointing toward the stands.

Jana Navratilova is Martina's half-sister. When I was doing research for Martina's book, I spent eleven days in Czechoslovakia, visiting her family. Jana, a dental student in Pilsen, hit it off with my daughter Corinna, giggling and talking the entire day. When we left the family home that Sunday, I told Jana, "I am not telling you what to do with your life, but if you ever feel you need to make a change, you have a place with us."

Seeing Martina makes me realize how much I gained from the three collaborative autobiographies I have written—with Loretta Lynn (*Coal Miner's Daughter*), Bob Welch of the Los Angeles Dodgers (*Five O'Clock Comes Early*) and Martina Navratilova (*Martina*). In all three projects, I was allowed into places, trusted, given insights, that would never be available to me as a journalist.

I love the immediacy of journalism, trying to get it right on deadline, trying to build the associations, store the information, but I am not sure it would be enough. The part of me that is a writer, the part of me that loves detail and dialogue and description, the layering of theme, is not satisfied with 950 words, four times a week.

The books started with a few modest children's books, then *Joy in Mudville,* about the Mets going from ragged losers to world champions in 1969. Four years later, I wrote *One Sunset a Week,* about a radical coal-mining family in an isolated corner of Appalachia. The book was well reviewed and nominated for several awards; it forever gave me an identity outside sports, allowed me to feel I had touched and described America.

After a while, it became normal to be working on a book in my spare time. Blessed in being able to write quickly, I enjoy working in the early morning, before the phones start ringing or I have to go out. My books are my hobby, my private life, my self-expression. When I'd go too long without a book, I'd start having a midlife crisis; work became a great cover-up for thinking and feeling too deeply about anything else.

After the Martina book, *The Times* decided that reporters should not do collaborations with people they cover, a decision I totally endorse. I'm just glad I had my experiences before we all thought it through.

I first met Loretta as a news correspondent in Kentucky. I had been a country-music buff since spending summers in a small town in upstate New York, listening to Kitty Wells and Hank Williams on the radio. Loretta was a throwback to them, pure country, none of this hundred-and-one-violins uptown sound that Nashville got itself into.

In 1971, Loretta ran a benefit for the families of thirty-eight miners killed in the first coal-mine disaster I covered, in Hyden, Kentucky— poor souls carried out boots-first in the snow right around New Year's. I got to know some of the widows, and I saw how they resented a Kentucky girl like Loretta becoming rich and famous.

The morning after Loretta became the first woman voted Entertainer of the Year in country music, I interviewed her in her motel room. Charlotte Curtis made it the feature article in the Family Style section, and a year later, Loretta's manager asked me to write her autobiography.

For the next six months, I would catch up with Loretta on the road in her touring bus or at the ranch in Tennessee or back home in Butcher Holler, Kentucky. She would bring me up onstage and introduce me. I was part of the act, like the lead singer who eyed the girls or the bass player who made the bad jokes, or Mooney, her husband, out counting the house.

"This is *Jo-erge*. He's mah *wrahter*."

I was her *wrahter*. If she and Mooney had a fight over money or drinking or his girlfriends, she would tell me about it. At first, I was afraid Mooney might shoot me for prying around in his life—there were always pistols lying around on tables and shotguns propped up in corners or bedrooms—but he assured me, "Hell, if it's true, write it," and he never backed off it.

I got to like Mooney a lot, a proud, chunky man who would have been better off running a service station than trying to make sense out of show business. He has a few flaws, but in the movie he got played by Tommy Lee Jones, a big, handsome football player from Harvard. What a guy, Mooney.

Loretta became like a cousin of mine. I came to feel protective of her, sorry she did not enjoy her fame or her money. She was often fatigued and depressed, camped in dark motel rooms while I was itching to get outside and hike in the countryside.

After six months of interviews, she told me, "Jo-erge, you know me better than any other man." I would read my manuscript to her, splicing in some Appalachian history and country-music background and interviews with friends and family. Loretta does not read well, but she would make changes orally and tell me entire new chunks of stories, and I came to appreciate the creative side to her.

"I may be dumb—but I ain't stupid," she would say.

When Bernard Geis published the book, all of us were shocked that it sold nearly 150,000 copies in hardcover. Readers were surprised to discover that Loretta's life is anything but glamorous, with the long bus rides, her illnesses, fights with Mooney, children divorcing, relatives squabbling, bickering with her manager. Loretta's life seemed to me the ultimate country-music song. Hollywood movie? I wasn't sure.

When Bernard Schwartz, the producer, and Michael Apted, the director, and Tom Rickman, the screenwriter, put together a movie, I never saw a script, never visited the set, never was consulted, and frankly was afraid Hollywood might turn Loretta's story into a caricature, the Beverly Hillbillies of Nashville.

When they invited me to a screening in New York, I brought along a disguise, like Floyd Patterson bringing a mask to the Sonny Liston fight, ready to slip anonymously into the swarms on Sixth Avenue and deny any connection with the movie. But as soon as I saw Sissy Spacek riding a horse, bringing lunch to her daddy, Levon Helm, working at the coal mine, the mood was so engrossing, so faithful, that I knew I would always be proud of *Coal Miner's Daughter*.

In 1982, I wrote Bob Welch's book about his battle with alcoholism, which has inspired dozens of people to seek treatment for chemical abuse, according to letters we receive. Two years later, Martina's agent said she felt my closeness with Loretta was a sign Martina could be comfortable with me.

I had been around Martina at the U.S. Open and had been impressed by her ability in English, her complexity, her pride. I was excited about the chance to write about life in the Soviet bloc, and also about sexual values in America. That Martina was a championship athlete who had been pushed to new heights by her friend Nancy Lieberman, the basketball player, was only the third inducement.

We had never met until we were put together at dinner on a rainy night during Wimbledon in 1982. Martina was gracious and complimentary, but she hung back whenever the book was discussed.

"Just out of curiosity, how much time are you going to need?" asked Peter Johnson, her agent.

"Fifty hours of personal interviews, spread out over the next year," I said.

A groan escaped Martina's lips. She seemed to slip down further into her chair. But Nancy, always direct, turned to her and said, "Look, Tini, if you want to do this, you've got to do it right."

Martina remained wary when I said we would obviously have to write about her "life-style," as I cautiously put it. She did not want to hurt anybody, but my answer was that since she had been involved with Rita Mae Brown, the writer, who is openly proud about being gay, we could let that relationship stand for any others that might have taken place.

Martina agreed. It was clear she is complex and intelligent, ambivalent about mixing her public and her private lives, part killer shark, part timid fawn. I found it an appealing combination, even during some sharp financial negotiations, provoked, I suspect, by Nancy. (When they split up a year later, I realized how much I had come to like the redheaded schoolyard basketball player from Queens, sharp elbows, sharp manners, and all.)

Whenever I showed up over the next two years, in Los Angeles, Dallas, the Poconos, New York, Wimbledon, Virginia Beach, Palm Springs, Martina bustled around the kitchen with those powerful forearms, making coffee and supper, opening beers, a good hostess. Then she would settle in for a few hours' work, often telling me to turn off the tape recorder, trusting me with intimate details "that can never be printed" but that she felt I should know.

We have several gay male friends who are quite close to us, but I had never spent much time with a gay female before. Martina helped me see how important it was to her to have a strong emotional-support system, that sex was only one aspect of the relationships. She had very good things to say about almost all her friends, even when the friendship had ended badly. She allowed herself to be open with me; I began seeing her as a friend, beyond labels.

When she reached for the box of tissues and wept over the story of the death of her grandmother, I saw the vulnerable child in Martina. One moment she could plead for fans to show more tolerance toward her, the next moment she could shrug off old friendships with a coldness that was impenetrable.

Just like Loretta, Martina had great recall of her childhood, perhaps an indication of unresolved feelings about growing up, about fame. She could remember names of teachers in her village, the numbers of trams she used to take in Prague, the face of a locker-room attendant at the only indoor court in Czechoslovakia ("a little old scuttlebug," Martina called her, so comfortable with English, her fourth language.)

Martina could not take me on a walking tour of her childhood, because she had not been granted a visa to visit Czechoslovakia, even after she had become an American citizen.

In late October of 1983, I visited Martina's family in Revnice, a pretty town between a river and a mountain, on the commuter line to Prague. Martina's mother cooked a Sunday dinner for us, and Martina's step-father gave us a caustic vision of life under "our good friends" from the East. They admitted they had suffered somewhat at work and school from Martina's defection, and later from revelations about her sexual orientation, but they would not let it defeat them. Good people. Strong people.

The saddest moment for me was visiting the pleasant little red-clay tennis club where her parents had introduced Martina to her sport. In the clubhouse, there were tennis posters of Bjorn Borg, Jimmy Connors, and Czechoslovakia's sweetheart, Chris Evert—but not a trace of the little girl who had grown up a few blocks away.

After eleven days in a country suffering from terminal depression at being cut off from the West, I understood better why Martina had asked for political asylum. This bright, athletic girl knew she was different, knew she had to leave her homeland to be herself, as an athlete and as a woman. I knew that Martina's story—like Loretta's story, like Bob's story—was a ready-made novel, plopped in my lap, and I was grateful for the chance to write it.

Martina's book became a best-seller, but just as important, left me with friendships that do not go away. As the slam-dunk contest begins, I go upstairs to find Jana and Judy Nelson, Martina's best friend, mother of two sons, a former beauty queen with reddish hair. Always smiling,

Judy gives me a big kiss, and I settle down to catch up on the news with Jana.

Smaller than her half-sister, once a promising tennis player, Jana seems frail and foreign in her return to Dallas. She and her parents once tried living here for one tense year, but the parents were used to working, having lives of their own. Most of the pampered children in the swank Dallas private school had assumed that because Jana was from Czechoslovakia, she had to be a Communist.

Sitting in the stands today, Jana seems pale. I cannot tell if this is the light Czech skin color, or the paucity of fresh fruits and vegetables in her country, or a touch of suffering from the distance between her and her famous sister.

She tells me officials at the dental school gave her a hard time when Martina's book had some critical things to say about Czechs who aligned themselves with the Russians. The government will no longer allow all three members of the family out of the country at the same time.

"I know I've told you this before," I say, "but if you ever feel the need to come to New York, you must stay with us."

She nods, too much on her mind. She is trying to find her place in the world, caught between the possibilities in the West, and her love for her parents, rooted to their home in Revnice. If she leaves, they will have no children left.

Down on the court, Spud Webb, the hometown favorite, wins the slam-dunk contest. At least the Webb family is together today.

Rushing downstairs to update my column, I kiss Jana and Judy goodbye.

"Please remember me to your parents," I say to Jana. "I think of them often."

DALLAS, FEBRUARY 9

Great weekend for little men. Spud Webb on Saturday, Isiah Thomas today. I keep waiting for the big boys of the National Basketball Association to wipe that sweet smile off Isiah's face, but let's face it, ain't never gonna happen.

Isiah, named for the prophet, spelled his own way, isn't even close to six-feet-one, the way the program says. He scored thirty points and made ten assists in the All-Star Game today, and of course we voted him the Most Valuable Player.

This weekend is an annual pilgrimage for me, to remind myself what a superb game pro basketball can be. I don't do enough with it back home. The Knicks are lackluster, the Nets are worse, hardly worth struggling over two bridges to New Jersey at rush hour, and sometimes it's mid-January when I taunt Sam Goldaper—who covers pro ball for *The Times*—with the question: "Sam, when does the NBA season start?"

Shame on me, teasing Sam, ignoring pro basketball. Then I go to the midseason jubliee for a refresher course. Slam-dunk and three-point contest and old-timers on Saturday, the big boys on Sunday.

The league became big business when David Stern started putting together the television deals, and now he's the commissioner, maybe one of the best any sport ever had. This weekend is the finest All-Star celebration of any sport, with parties, dinners, games, and the dignified elegance of the players.

This is the only sport in which the All-Stars create new levels of brilliance. With 6:55 left in today's game, K. C. Jones put Larry Bird, tall blond guy from Indiana State, in the backcourt with Isiah, short black guy from Indiana. They just tore it up.

With the West still leading by six, Bird was near halfcourt with the ball, and he threw a sidearm bounce pass to Thomas, coming down the left side. The little man took a few dribbles, then whipped a cross-court pass to Sidney Moncrief to a basket. East won by seven. Can't tease Sam about pro hoops—at least till next year.

NEW YORK, FEBRUARY 10

The papers say Alexis Arguello won his fight in Reno last night. A reporter is supposed to be neutral, so let's say I'm glad he survived.

Since I'm the only sports columnist loose in the land who has called for the abolition of boxing, it may sound incongruous for me to be worrying about one particular boxer. But as a writer, I've always had the strongest feelings for people living on the edge, like Alexis Arguello, trying to make a comeback at thirty-three.

Most of my friends, who share my repulsion for boxing, do not believe me when I say that boxers are about the nicest group of athletes. Boxers' violent work in the ring and their isolation in training tends to make them open and decent, realistic and fatalistic.

I have liked Arguello since I spent a few days in 1981 working on a long profile about him. There was something vulnerable about him, a man who could not go back to Nicaragua, a champion with sad eyes.

After that, I followed his career at a distance as he was battered into retirement by Aaron Pryor, went down to Latin America to work against the Sandinistas, who had confiscated his home. I read how he had lost his money, tangled with cocaine, how he once held a pistol to his head and contemplated suicide.

Last December I read that he was making a comeback. I visited him at a gym in Miami, just before sunset, his eyes a little more haunted, same shy smile, a new wife waiting for him outside. I asked him what in the world he was doing making a comeback.

"Everybody said I was broke," he answered. "But if being broke means only having a few pennies, I'm not broke. I have a couple of good investments. I just want to win the fourth title, to give boxing fans another good performance from Alexis Arguello."

For the fans. Performers often talk about the fans. Loretta Lynn rides around in the back of her customized bus, playing the state fairs, "for the fans." What performers mean, I think, is that they keep going for the glow from the lights, the rush from walking onstage, the image of themselves in their fans' eyes. For themselves, in other words.

When I got to the word processor, I reasoned that Sugar Ray Leonard was foolish to risk his repaired retina just for the thrill of winning another championship, but that Arguello does not have Leonard's security. As long as this sordid business exists, I could not bring myself to advise Arguello to stay away from it.

Today's papers say Arguello lost the first three rounds against Billy Costello before scoring a left-right combination for a knockout. It sounds as if Alexis delivered a knockout from memory. He may not be so lucky next time in a business that does not leave room for error. Ask Duk Koo Kim's orphan about that.

My distaste for boxing stems from the first match I saw. I had somehow avoided the sport until I was twenty-five, when *Sport* magazine asked me to do an article on Carlos Ortiz, a tough guy from the Bronx. I spent some time at an old farm in rural New Jersey, enjoying the routine of the camp, the running, the eating, the ring work, the talking; even the sparring seemed benign, with the headgear and the large gloves. I enjoyed talking with Ortiz, talking about Puerto Rico and the Bronx and the army.

Then came the fight—a Friday night at the old Madison Square Garden, with half of San Juan, Santurce, Mayaguez, Caguas, Ponce, Arecibo, and the South Bronx packing the upper deck, cheering for Ortiz against Flash Elorde from the Philippines.

I had a press credential in the first row, where the sweat and the blood of the preliminary fighters spattered me. I found myself flinching at the blows, ducking my head when one man backed another into a corner and flailed away at him. The primeval spectacle seemed a bit too much like the nature movies on television, the lion cornering the antelope.

Then it was time for the main event. The wily, complex man I had been interviewing stalked Elorde, pounded him, harassed him, jabbed at him, physically weakened him, minute by minute, inch by inch. Trapped, Elorde lowered his head, tried to hide behind his gloves, but the code of boxing said he had to stand and take it, and the referee had to wait long enough to satisfy the fans, who had paid their money to see one man beat up another man.

Finally Elorde went down, hit the deck right above me, his eyes gone blank, his body twitching. I felt physically sickened to see a man twitching a few feet from me. At that point, I had not yet seen a man die, and I thought this was about to be the first time. But the ring technicians worked over Elorde, revived him, sent him off to the dressing room a few minutes later. As I recall, he received a nice round of applause for absorbing so much punishment to entertain the fans on a Friday night.

With no moral qualms yet, I covered boxing in many forms—heard Joe Frazier exclaim, "Free at last!" when he finally won the title, got my pocket picked of thirty-five pounds while squeezing into Joe Bugner's dressing room at Earl's Court in London, tracked down a Quebec boxer named Gaetan Hart who had put Cleveland Denny into a fatal coma in 1980, and I covered the last fights of Joe Frazier and Muhammad Ali late in 1981.

The Frazier fight was in Chicago, where the nonentity named Jumbo Cummings spattered Frazier's blood all over my typewriter. I wrote about the rust-colored spots to make the point that Frazier's comeback had become a bloody fiasco.

Why do I love boxers? The morning after his ineffectual draw with Cummings, Frazier was as spunky as ever.

"Champ, this is my daughter who's visiting from college," I said.

"Where do you go?" asked Smokin' Joe.

"Well, uh," Laura said. She was enrolled at Sarah Lawrence College but was spending her junior year at the University of Iowa. She couldn't decide which school to claim.

"Huh," Frazier grunted. "You go to college, but you don't know the name."

We all roared with laughter, including Laura. That was vintage Smokin' Joe. You kill the body and the head will die. Then, gallantly, sensing he might have made the young woman uncomfortable, he redirected his salvo.

"Her mamma must be pretty," Frazier said, staring at me.

Ali's last fight was against Trevor Berbick in the Bahamas shortly before Christmas. I had admired Ali since the sixties, when he stood up against the Vietnam War. I had bumped into Ali on street corners in New York and Chicago, seen him rally young blacks and whites against the war, made them laugh, made them think.

After the George Foreman fight in Zaire, I covered Ali's triumphant return to Louisville, where he introduced a tiny African pilot: "This nigger flew our jet from Zaire to New York. A nigger. Flying a great big jet."

In the Bahamas in 1981, I got up before dawn to take a run with him, but the superb athlete had become so lardy, so befuddled, that I was moving faster than he was. After one mile, the great champion Muhammad Ali summoned the limousine hovering behind him.

"Let's go back," he said. He spent most of the day performing clumsy card tricks in his hotel room.

But why do I love boxers? That same week, I escorted Marianne into Ali's dressing room after a workout. The old champion was lying on his back on a training table, wearing a robe, looking like an African chieftain about to expire. His voice was low and husky.

I edged up to him and said, "Champ, I'd like you to meet my wife."

We lowered our heads as if to catch his last words.

"Can't you do better than him?" he whispered to my wife.

People told me later it was his standard line with reporters' wives. He lost to Berbick, and the next morning he retired. His slurred speech and loss of energy is indictment enough of boxing.

Up to then, I had tried to be a good reporter, balancing facts and quotes with a few observations of my own, not taking a stand on the essence of boxing, but when Red Smith died early in 1982, I was suddenly *The Times*'s columnist, licensed to give my opinion.

Marianne had always been telling me boxing should be banned, but I was not comfortable telling mostly black and Hispanic men how not to make a living. I knew I did not like most of the promoters I met, was suspicious of some of the managers and the television matchmakers, and I sometimes thought I detected a whiff of condescension in some of the most celebrated boxing writing. It sounded a little easy, encouraging desperate people to bleed so we could write about human grace under pressure.

In November of 1982, I had to take a stand. On a Friday night in Miami, Arguello took a fearful pounding from Aaron Pryor, twelve straight punches to the head. I caught the news clips of that one, Arguello twitching the same way Flash Elorde had done in the first boxing match I had ever seen.

The next afternoon in Las Vegas, a Korean boxer named Duk Koo Kim was pounded into a coma by the popular American Ray (Boom Boom) Mancini. As the news grew worse, I reviewed the news clips of fans standing in the sunlight, cheering the American as he pummeled the Asian visitor. Kim fought back bravely, but Mancini kept battering him, doing what a boxer is trained to do.

The faces in the crowd looked pleased. This is what they had come to see—our guy beating their guy, both fighters bravely taking their punishment like men. I was watching a mob exhorting two human beings to destroy each other for money, not much different from a crowd gathering where a man was dangling from a sixth-story fire escape and chanting, "Jump! Jump! You'll be on the six o'clock news."

With Kim in a coma on Sunday, I knew I would have to write a column about boxing. I could not blame Mancini, a nice man licensed to partici- pate in a legal business. My problem was with the faces in the crowd, the promoters who made money from it, the government officials who sanctioned it, and the writers like me who kept pecking away at their word machines without asking the deepest questions.

So I wrote a column comparing boxing to the cultivated beast in Jean Cocteau's movie *La Belle et La Bête.* One night Beauty looks out the window and sees the Beast, with his elegant silk shirts and his elegant French, gnawing at a dying stag on the front lawn. When Beauty berates the Beast, he says something like, "What did you expect from me? You know I'm a beast."

What did we expect from boxing? It was all about two humans being paid to damage each other. It was time to ban the Beast, I wrote. Some sports columnists had a good time with that. I was called a wimp, a liberal, a bleeding heart, and was told that if I didn't like sports, I shouldn't cover them. Of course, I hadn't liked coal-mine explosions, either, but I used to cover them anyway.

One of the strongest hairy-chested rampages came from John Schu- lian in the *Chicago Sun-Times:* "For if you want to change the order of things in boxing, you must alter human nature. You must wash the bloodlust from the paying customers' souls and tame the fighters' hun- ger for combat." I never thought you could change human nature; I did think you could try to control it.

Two weeks after Kim died, a heavyweight named Randall (Tex) Cobb became a human punching bag for Larry Holmes to batter for fifteen gruesomely boring rounds. That was the night Howard Cosell broke with his network, saying the match should have been stopped, later refusing to work any more professional matches.

There are a lot of Cosell-bashers in the world, but I am not one of them. At his best, Howard has been a positive force, talking about race and politics and money when no other celebrity sportscaster would touch the issues. Some people saw Howard's stance as hypocritical, others saw it as a sign of self-destruction, but I saw it as a personal awakening, a statement that he had had enough of a business he had helped make popular. Obviously, I don't think journalists should abstain from covering boxing; Dave Anderson and many others cover it honorably and perceptively.

I enjoy meeting boxers, particularly José Torres, the chairman of the New York State Boxing Commission. The first time we met, he listened to me talk, and then he said, "You are sincere. You really do not like boxing."

Of course, Torres disagreed with my abolitionist stance against a business that had given him a life as champion and writer. Until we got to know each other, he was prepared to consider me an elitist who did not understand that boxing is one of the few avenues out of poverty.

My own view is that so few boxers benefit from their business that there is no justification for the damage. Many of the greatest fighters, including Joe Louis and Ali, could not escape the cruel tangle of poor financial management and physical and emotional damage.

I once found myself telling Floyd Patterson that cities should build computer centers and martial-arts centers instead of boxing centers. One of the gentlest people you could meet, Patterson was perplexed at my message. Without boxing, he might still be hiding in the subway tunnels, as he did as a delinquent child, or he might be in prison. But for every Floyd Patterson, there are dozens of men who learned the discipline of boxing but came away with less than when they started.

It is disappointing to me that more black and Hispanic leaders have not expressed disdain for boxing. Instead, I see Jesse Jackson and Bill Cosby having a great old time at the fights. Boxers are asked to receive violence and commit violence to satisfy the fans. How far is that from the slave block? Yes, they are free to choose, but the temptations of boxing amount to exploitation for most boxers.

From time to time, supporters of boxing come up with the statement that many other sports are more dangerous—the old Hang-gliding Theory. The danger of boxing is not only in the few ring deaths per year, but in the long-range brain damage as well.

I am hardly against violent sports. I don't enjoy the ruined knees of

American football, and don't condone the damage from steroids and amphetamines that football encourages, but at least football rules are constantly being adjusted to cut down on danger. I have played enough soccer and basketball to appreciate a marginally legal elbow—at least when it was wielded by me. I hate to see baseball players injured, but I understand why pitchers throw inside, and why runners slide hard into second base. I have little interest in auto racing, but I doubt the drivers want to crash into each other.

Then there is the old Riverboat Barge Theory, advanced by some of the greatest names in sportswriting, that if we tried to ban boxing, it would be held on the sly rather than in enlightened places like Las Vegas and Atlantic City. I find that argument cynical and even corrupt.

Society has the responsibility to stop people from doing certain destructive things. We are getting tougher about drunken driving. We have chosen to ban cocaine because it is harmful. We expect drivers to stop at red lights. Cock fighting, dog fighting, prostitution, drug traffic, smoking in public, slavery—whatever we think is destructive to the public, or to individuals. We could ban boxing, too. Our choice.

NEW YORK, FEBRUARY 11

There are three reasons why I've done a couple of columns on the dog show in recent years: It falls in the abyss between the pro basketball All-Star Game and the Big East tournament. It is indoors at Madison Square Garden, at the end of my train line. And while I'm not interested in dogs, I've talked to a few cute owners in my time.

Today I strolled the grounds for a few hours, talking to trainers, groomers, handlers, preparing a chatty midwinter column. But I felt uncomfortable, thinking something more newsworthy might be going on.

Around noon I called the office and found that Micheal Ray Richardson of the New Jersey Nets is being tested for drugs again. I am growing weary of drug stories, but I know this is what we must cover, along with the fun and the games. I made my apologies to the dog-show people and walked through the garment district, toward *The Times.*

As I dodged the pushcarts packed with plastic-covered pink and yellow spring clothes, a promise that spring will surely come, I thought about all the times I had gone to the Garden when Micheal Ray was young and a Knick.

His was a wild, uninhibited talent, full of herky-jerky motions and emotional sprees and eccentric shots like the "finger roll," a lay-up off his fingertips. He is also the only man I know who spells his name Micheal. Maybe he made a pact with Isiah Thomas.

Sometimes Micheal Ray made perfect sense in his street grammar, as when he surveyed the Knicks' season a few years back and proclaimed, "The ship be sinking." (Nowadays, whenever the Knicks go bad, one reporter will turn to another and say, "The ship be sinking." To an outsider, this might sound like racial stereotyping, but how could any writer with an ear for language miss Micheal Ray's speech patterns? You would never hear a white reporter making fun of Bill Cartwright or Bernard King's speech, because they are articulate and grammatical. You should hear Peter Alfano do Ivan Lendl, or Junior Feinstein do Lefty Driesell. We may not be poets, but sometimes we are mimics.)

At other times, Micheal Ray seemed disjointed, barely understanding what his coaches or the older players were trying to teach him.

He seemed like one of those victims of big-time sports—emotional problems, broken home, exploited by scouts and coaches, no visible signs of education, not very bright, scary future. Micheal Ray could score twenty-five points in a game, put on a fur coat, and walk out into the night with a beautiful woman on his arm, but you could still feel sorry for him.

Now his ship is listing badly. He has been treated four separate times for drugs, but he missed a practice and failed to consult a team doctor on Monday, leaving the Nets no alternative but to suspend him. If he tests positive, under league rules he must be banned for life.

I do not agree with the National Basketball Association policy that any player caught with drugs must be banned for two years. My experience at the Meadows on the Bob Welch book taught me that denial is the essence of addiction, that you cannot expect most drug users to come forward. In my opinion, anybody caught the first time deserves rehabilitation and one more chance, but Micheal Ray's case goes way beyond even my tolerance.

When I got to the office, I placed a call to the Net's general manager, Lewis Schaffel, a bright man whose wife, Barbara Kolonay, is a psychologist. Maybe he could tell me something hopeful about Micheal Ray.

"He cannot do the simplest things," Schaffel said. "He cannot follow the rules anymore. It's the saddest thing in the world. This is sadness."

Not even Micheal Ray's boss was asking for leniency. After talking to Schaffel, it was not hard for me to write the last paragraph:

"The latest disappearing act shows that Micheal Ray Richardson is in the wrong business, that for his own good he should leave basketball behind forever and get about the business of saving his life."

I was making a judgment that a man should be thrown out of his sport for life. The old days of sports reporters writing about the merry banter around the batting cage seemed a million years ago.

RYE, NEW YORK, FEBRUARY 24

I've always had a soft spot for the talented scamps of sports, the outlaws, the breakers of rules who kept the games from belonging too much to the authoritarians and the bureaucrats.

Today I have a luncheon appointment with one of those charming rogues, Pierre Larouche of the New York Rangers, one of the most deft offensive players in hockey. I've met Larouche—long hair, squeaky voice, appealing Quebec accent, sly and funny and charming to a visiting columnist. A wildman, at least when he was younger. Impossible to coach. Traded three times. Lucky Pierre.

Nobody said the people at Gulf and Western know how to run a team, but what they did with Lucky Pierre was ridiculous. With the Rangers struggling to make the play-offs, they sent their only pure scorer to their Hershey farm team for four months.

The general manager, a third-generation hockey executive named Craig Patrick—called Vague Craig by anybody who has tried to have a conversation with him—and the coach, a grim automaton named Ted

Sator, kept insisting they wanted Larouche back as soon as he learned toughness or humility or maturity, whatever it is they instill in Hershey, Pennsylvania.

It was hard to believe they wanted Larouche back, considering they gave away his uniform number before his tumbrel even reached the Lincoln Tunnel.

Somehow, Larouche did not let the exile break him. He scored so well in Hershey, and the Rangers slumped so badly, that they had to bring him back. He has now scored seven goals in his first nine games, and it is definitely time to giggle a bit about the return of Lucky Pierre.

It is winter break at the high school. I called Larouche and asked if it was all right to bring my sixteen-year-old to lunch. No problem. David and I drive up to the Rangers' training rink at Rye Playland, along the shore of Long Island Sound, barren and melancholy on a late winter day. Larouche is dressed and waiting in the clubhouse, his long hair still damp from the shower.

"We'll go to a restaurant near my house," Larouche says, with traces of Canadian French in his English.

He looks at my son, nearly his size, half man, half teenager, and makes a judgment.

"David, you want to ride with me?"

I know we are going to have a nice lunch.

I follow Pierre's car. He is driving with one hand, tapping on the dashboard with the other, obviously to the beat of rock music, and he and David are chatting away like old friends. David does not warm up to strangers easily, does not suffer fools at all gladly, and I can see his head bobbing as he and Pierre trade life stories.

One of David's problems in school is that he tends to do things his own way, regardless of the rules. I have a feeling Lucky Pierre is not going to be a very good role model for David.

"A little wine?" Larouche asks at lunch, and proceeds to have "*une p'tite.*" Even off the record, he is genuinely cautious about criticizing the prim Ranger management, because he does not want to stir anything up.

I remind Larouche that Herb Brooks, the former coach of the Rangers, once said that asking Pierre to fight for the puck in the corner was "like asking Picasso to paint a garage."

That seems to strike a responsive chord in his artistic soul. He takes another sip of the red and concedes that he has never worked hard in training camp.

"You go around some guy," he says, waving his supple hands derisively, "you put it in the net, and you know he could have really let you have it. He's your teammate, he doesn't want to hurt you, and you don't want to make him look bad. Games are different, it's a war out there, but in practice, why go around your teammate?"

Homework. Lucky Pierre does not like doing homework. David is staring at him with open admiration.

Between bites of lunch, Lucky Pierre continues to talk with his hands, describing his love for the pure game, the jittering back and forth across the ice, the slapped shots, the impromptu passes. He describes for us how he was a "pond skater" back home in Amos, Quebec, three hundred and fifty miles due north of Montreal, where "We'd play all day, even after dark, when you could tell where the puck was by the sound, the slap of a stick on the ice, eighty kids chasing it."

His voice grows soft and reverent as he describes the beauty of a game played in the dark, under the stars. He still wants to play that game, even though Gulf and Western is paying him a few hundred thousand dollars a year to follow Ted Sator's instructions.

"Some people are just different," Larouche says.

Wonderful. Just what I want my son to hear. David can write as easily as a baby otter can slide, but he resists direction from outside forces. Just like his two older sisters, just like his mother, just like me. As a young reporter, I was a pretty agreeable chap—until I was asked to spend a winter on the *Newsday* copy desk.

You want me to edit articles about harness racing, stock cars, bowling? You want me to make paragraph marks or rewrite them completely? There is no in between, you know. Why not let me go out and write, and instruct other people just to make paragraph marks on my copy?

The Rangers want Larouche to spend some time on the copy desk, too. They want him to chase the puck, to crash his body into defenders, to "muck in the corners," as the hockey people say. Larouche thinks he is most valuable writing the feature story.

"I don't care what kind of defenders they have," Larouche says. "If you can skate and move without the puck, you can score—if you have talent."

David and I do everything but give him high-fives. You tell it, Lucky Pierre. We have another *"p'tite"* and then we order coffee. This could be the sequel to the movie *My Dinner with André. Our Lunch with Pierre.*

We part outside the restaurant. By now, I am dropping appropriate French phrases into the conversation. We do everything but kiss on both cheeks. Pierre says good-bye to David.

"You coming to the game tomorrow?" Larouche asks him. "Maybe you'll bring me luck."

On the way home in the car, I clear my throat.

"Ahem, son," I ahem. "You do know, of course, that Pierre's work habits are not the best."

"Right."

"I mean, he was kind of a wildman when he was younger. Didn't take care of himself."

"Probably."

"That is to say, there are good reasons why he's been traded three times already."

"I'm sure there are."

"You did hear Pierre say he's trying to work with the team."

"Of course, Dad."

Glad that I have put things in perspective for the young man, I drive home, thinking about a moderate, neutral, objective, fair, responsible column about the Rangers and Lucky Pierre.

It begins: "First they took his job, then they took his number . . ." and it goes on from there.

NEW YORK, FEBRUARY 26

Joe Goldstein, the king of the sports publicists, came up with a new approach to me last week.

"How would you like to do a column on the most beautiful female athlete I have ever seen?" he asked.

In these sensitive days, we males are supposed to appreciate women for their achievements, not for their attractiveness. We are not supposed to reserve one dark and swinish corner of our souls to categorize attractive female athletes.

"More attractive than Pam and Paula McGee?" I asked. "More attractive than Peggy Fleming? More attractive than Chris Evert?"

"Have I ever lied to you?" Joe asked.

For the record, Joey has never lied to me. He is part historian, part hustler, the leading sports publicist in New York, and also a friend, calling up with unusual column ideas—all of them, coincidentally, his clients.

In the old days, Joey was considered the unofficial sports editor of *The Times,* until LeAnne Schreiber and Joe Vecchione took back the turf, but Goldstein does represent some of the major track meets, including the nationals Friday night, sponsored by Mobil Oil.

"Are you interested?" Joey asked. "The most beautiful female athlete I have ever seen?"

"Who, Joey?"

"Tamara Bykova, a high jumper from the Soviet Union—and not only that, she's a journalist herself," Joe said. "She was voted the outstanding female athlete at the nationals two years ago. The Garden loved her. She's coming to our luncheon Wednesday, and I can arrange for you to sit next to her."

As Joe very well knows, this is a slow few weeks in sports. There is usually room for a column on the big indoor track meets—and Joey plays "Matchmaker, Matchmaker" between athletes and scribes. Besides meeting a beautiful woman, I can justify writing a column on a Soviet athlete as part of my preparation for the Goodwill Games in Moscow in July. Yes, I told Joe, I think I can attend that luncheon, indeed.

The luncheon is in the Library of the Helmsley Palace on Madison Avenue. The waiting room is crowded with Czechoslovak and Romanian athletes, their eyes bulging at the cacophony of American reporters, photographers, and press agents. Joey guides me to a couch, where Tamara Bykova is waiting.

In a better world, I would see her business suit and frilly blouse and almond eyes and curly hair and think of her only as the world indoor record holder in the high jump. To my everlasting discredit, I think mostly that she is the most beautiful female athlete I have ever seen. Joey's reputation for integrity is intact.

"I am sorry. I do not speak English very well," she says.

"Sounds good to me," I say.

We try to talk, but the room is too noisy. Don Hogan Charles, our photographer, is giving her orders on how to pose. Bulgarian shot-putters and East German sprinters amble back and forth in sweat suits. Tamara looks frightened, like Bambi's mother at the start of the great fire.

"Where is Lyudmila?" she asks.

Lyudmila, the interpreter with the Soviet team, is busy translating for Sergei Bubka, the champion pole-vaulter. Without Lyudmila, Tamara seems to be developing the world's worst headache.

We sit together for an elegant luncheon, and in halting English she tells me she is a journalism student in Rostov-on-Don, in the southern part of the Soviet Union. In fact, she says, she has a Greek grand-mother.

After Lyudmila drops by to translate, I learn that Tamara writes features about other athletes for the newspaper in Rostov. I also learn that Tamara, as one of the outstanding Soviet athletes, has visited Italy more than twenty times. Her almond eyes glow when she talks about the beaches and the cities and the food of Italy.

"Pizza," she says. "Tell me," she says, "where can I find good pizza in New York?"

"I think I might be able to work that out," I say. "My wife and I would like to take you and Lyudmila out for pizza tonight. There is a neighborhood called Greenwich Village, where many Italian people live."

I know Marianne will understand this important business appoint-ment. When I was a news reporter, I was known to bring home antipoverty officials, civil-rights activists, anti-strip-mine protestors, Appalachian folk singers, civil-liberties lawyers, former nuns—all in the interest of sound journalistic research.

"We will have to see," Tamara says.

The manager of the Russian team hovers behind her chair, saying something like "Last question" in Russian.

From some convoluted corner of my memory, I blurt out the words, *"Pyat, pazhaloostah."* Five, please. I can't remember how to say "minutes," but it works. The man says, *"Da,"* and walks away. My spare moments studying the Russian phrase book have paid off. For the first time in my life, I have said something intelligible in Russian, and gotten what I wanted.

Tamara and I make tentative arrangements for pizza this evening. I am to call Lyudmila's room around five o'clock. I even remember to arrange for Marianne to come into the city.

But when I call Lyudmila at five o'clock, she says, "I am sorry, but it is not possible." Her crisp Russian-British accent tells me there is nothing more to discuss.

I will write my column, and gaze at Tamara's long legs during Friday's high-jump competition, but never will we share pizza in Greenwich Village. I think of all we might have talked about, the Goodwill Games, athletic training in the Soviet Union, our mutual interests in journalism, the first stirrings of *glasnost* under Mikhail Gorbachev, but now it will never happen. My heart is broken.

Exactly a year later, I wandered over to the very same track luncheon, thinking about the beautiful athlete I had interviewed a year before. Joe Goldstein told me Bykova was not listed on the Soviets' roster for the indoor meet, that she was probably phasing into retirement.

But when I walked into the luncheon, she was sitting by herself, her hair long and straight this year. I hesitated for a moment, and then walked over to her table.

"I don't know if you remember me," I said, "but we met here a year ago."

Tamara fixed a warm smile at me and said, "Of course I remember. Last year I could not go for pizza with you. But this year I could." There was no Lyudmila in sight.

That night Marianne and I took her to dinner—at an Italian restaurant, per certo—*and we also gave her a tour of* The Times. *The next day Marianne took Tamara to the Metropolitan Museum of Art. It was interesting to watch the two of them chat like old sorority sisters despite the language gap. Now I believe in* glasnost.

NEW YORK, FEBRUARY 28

The drug beat goes on. There have been reports the New England Patriots were riddled with drug problems on their way to the Super Bowl last month. Eleven baseball players, including Keith Hernandez, were fined and given community-service penalties for previous drug usage.

Peter Ueberroth's requirement of fifty to two hundred hours of community service could be an eye-opener to some of them. I'd like to see Bulldog Fred, one of the counselors at the Meadows, get his teeth in the shins of an athlete who thought he could breeze through a celebrity-style lecture.

Also this week, Micheal Ray Richardson was banned for life from the National Basketball Association—"a tragic day," said David Stern, the commissioner.

After the press conference regarding Richardson, one of my colleagues asked the league's doctor-counselor, "But if somebody just used drugs recreationally, you know, on weekends, that person wouldn't be an addict, right?"

"Actually," the doctor said softly, "that person might have a problem."

MARCH

NEW YORK, MARCH 9

Looie Carnesecca has an Australian accent that he dusts off every March. Ever hear a diminutive Italian New Yorker speak Australian through a classic hook nose? "Oy wuz in Froymantle dooring duh woor." It's a beauty.

He does his Aussie imitation every time the committee sends St. John's to distant ports for the opening round of the national basketball tournament. He says nothing could be further than sending a young sailor from the Lower East Side to Fremantle during World War II.

Last night Looie's team clawed back to beat Syracuse, 70–69, in the finals of the Big East tournament. As a reward for winning, Looie's team is going to play its first-round game in Long Beach, California. As a consolation for losing, Syracuse is going to play its first-round game in Syracuse, New York. The Carrier Dome, with its 30,000 seats, is already selected as a site for the first two rounds, and the committee wants to sell tickets.

We try to prod Looie into knocking the system, but Looie's too smart for that, and college basketball is too big-time for that. The Big East Conference is only seven years old, but its tournament in the Garden every March is one of the highlights of the New York sports season. Last spring three Big East teams got to the Final Four in Kentucky. That put a lot of meatballs in the St. John's hero sandwich.

I keep trying to moralize about the growth of the Big East Conference. Chris Mullin and Duane Washington never struck me as having spent much time in a classroom. Georgetown's program seems idealistic, but the players seem to cock their fists too quickly. Did Villanova make any compromises for its national title last April? But I confess, I look forward to the games, the intensity, the earnest, mostly black basketball players, the fervent, mostly white student bodies, the priests, and the mascots.

You walk in the locker room, and they're nice young men. I walked into Syracuse's locker the other night and met Wendell Alexis, a quiet forward from Queens with a 2.7 classroom average. Met Rony Seikaly, a wealthy Lebanese center who grew up in the affluent Psychico Hills of Athens. Perfect gentleman. Met Joel Katz, classic last man on the bench, from the unlikely hometown of San Juan, Puerto Rico, where his father runs a hotel. Katz taps the table as he runs past me in warm-up drills. "Hello, Mr. Vecsey." I've got kids their ages. I have a theory that if you keep covering sports and don't look in a mirror, you'll never grow old.

And Looie. I know I should be tougher on Looie, on the low graduation rate of his players, on some of his strategy, but I'm totally co-opted by the little man who dances in front of his bench. I remember him umpiring college baseball games in the spring, a little man dwarfed by his own chest protector, a high-school coach hustling for a few bucks on the side, waiting for his break.

When my middle brother, Pete, was on the freshman team at Molloy High in Queens, he came home and told us, "The varsity coach chases us around with a broom." Years later, during dinner at some Italian restaurant, I turned to Looie and said, "Looie, you used to chase my brother with a broom."

Big eyes. Straight from confession. Head cocked to one side. Hands in front of chest, palms out.

"I would nevuh chase a kid wit' a broom. I would hold da broom in front of da basket ta make dem shoot at a higher angle. Chase a kid? Nevuh."

Now Looie's going to Fremantle again. He won't complain. Nevuh.

PORT WASHINGTON, MARCH 12

"This is Mario Cuomo," the voice on my answering machine said. "Sorry I missed you, but I'll try again tomorrow afternoon."

I've been trying to get in touch with the governor of New York for a column about sports role models. The first time I met him was outside the St. John's basketball locker at the Garden a few years ago. He bumped into Frank McGuire, the hallowed former basketball coach, and they greeted each other with respect. Hey, Coach. Hey, Governor. Somebody told me later that McGuire, as varsity baseball coach, once made a casual remark that he would convert Cuomo from a center fielder to a catcher.

The threatened conversion was not the reason Cuomo took a modest bonus to play minor-league ball with the Pittsburgh Pirates, but Cuomo has never forgotten it, my source told me.

I've been hearing about Mario and Matilda Cuomo for more than a decade. Marianne's Aunt Bettina lived in their neighborhood and was helping Matilda around the house while Mario sought public office.

"I don't agree with Mario on everything," said Bettina, who is somewhat to the right of Jerry Falwell, "but they are the nicest people."

From what I read in the papers, I used to tell Bettina that her friend Mario was too intellectual, too private, too solid a family man to run for office. He should work behind the scenes, solve community problems, write books, maybe be appointed a judge.

During one of Mario's campaigns, Matilda Cuomo visited our house for a few hours, a bright and gracious woman. She could be First Lady any time. Still, I was amazed when Cuomo was elected governor.

A few days after Cuomo's speech to the Democratic Convention in San Francisco in 1984, Marianne and I were sitting in a café in Santa Barbara, on our way to the Olympics. We eavesdropped as two Reaganite real-estate executives discussed the election.

"The president will beat Mondale," one man said to the other. "But I am very impressed with this Mario Cuomo. We don't have anybody who can beat him in 1988."

I probably should tell Cuomo that, but I promised his aide that I would zero in on my topic. The state has a program called Athletes Against Drunk Driving, using John Woodring of the Jets and Ron Darling of the Mets as spokesmen. I wanted to ask the governor, who calls himself "a broken-down old ballplayer," why athletes make good role models.

Right on schedule, the governor calls back today. We make small talk about his alma mater's chances in the NCAA tournament this weekend, and then his fine legal mind clicks into our selected mode.

"The role model is the best teacher," he says, his South Jamaica accent sounding familiar in my Hollis ear. "You start with the song 'Mrs. Robinson.' 'Where have you gone, Joe DiMaggio?' We're looking for heroes. I'm saying, the best thing is to send a Woodring, a Darling, into the schools to say, 'Look, I'm an athlete, I don't drive when I drink, I don't take drugs.'

"Laws are good, of course we have laws," the governor continues, referring to the state's new twenty-one-and-over drinking law. "But if a person doesn't understand what will hurt him, laws don't do anything. You need role models talking about social conduct."

I ask the governor who his role models were when he was growing up.

"A guy named Joe Austin who ran the CYO program at St. Monica's," Cuomo says. "He was my coach."

"Joe Austin?" I repeat. "Wiry little Irishman? White hair? Ran half a dozen basketball games every Sunday—won every one of 'em? Hey, I've been there. They'd run you right off the court."

The governor chuckles contentedly at the other end of the phone, as if he had just run me into a wall in a narrow parish gym in South Jamaica.

"Yeah, well, home-court advantage," he says.

I ask the governor what ever became of Joe Austin.

"He's still my coach," Cuomo says. "I brought him up to Albany for my inauguration. Told him I couldn't do it without him. When it was time for me to make my speech, I could see Joe Austin, clapping his hands together the way he used to on the bench, to say, 'Let's go, let's go.' "

All during the election campaign of 1988, I kept waiting for both political parties to approach Cuomo and say, "Look, Governor, we've both made ghastly mistakes. Could you help us out?" Never happened. Guess the joke is on them. Or us.

PORT WASHINGTON, NEW YORK, MARCH 13

In bed, lights out, classical music on the radio, eleven-thirty at night. The telephone rings. My first thought is fear about our two girls, grown up, out on their own, but still our girls. I pick up the phone.

"Hello, Pete?"

"No Pete here."

"Peter? Pete Vecsey?"

"This is George Vecsey. His brother."

"Oh, my gosh, I must have made a mistake. I'm really sorry. This is Howard Howard, you know, the agent. I'm out here in California, and I need to get in touch with Pete. Heh-heh, I guess I've lost Pete's number. You wouldn't happen to have it, would you?"

My brother-the-basketball-columnist has an unlisted number. I don't. Sometimes I remember his number and sometimes I don't. At eleven-thirty at night, I do not remember it. Sorry, Howard.

My brother accuses just about everybody in basketball of chicanery and incompetence, but he hears a lot of accurate gossip in late-night calls from people like Howard Howard.

Pete is truly one of a kind, the Rona Barrett of sports, somebody once called him. Only Pete could invent nicknames like Cloudy Werblin for Sonny Werblin, the former impresario of the Jets and Knickerbockers, or Spencer Driftwood for the well-traveled Spencer Haywood. Pete is tough.

Having a brother working in the same town has its good points and bad. I find I get very good service from clerks and porters at the airport when they see my last name on my suitcase. They all love my notes column, "Hoop du Jour," in the *Post*. Once I tried to leave a message at the city desk at *The Times*, and the male clerk said. "Vecsey? You write the basketball column in the *Post?*" No, I said, I merely work for *The Times*.

Pete is the biggest attraction the *Post* has: He sells the paper, and Murdoch recognizes it every payday. It bothers me that we are not paid as well as some sports columnists around the country, but at *The Times*, with all its specialists and its editors, the sports columnist is one of a cast of thousands.

A lot of my friends ask me, "How can two brothers be so different?" People probably ask the same thing of Pete. Dick Schaap once wrote that Pete and I are as different as Nate Thurmond and Strom Thurmond.

"Who is Strom Thurmond?" Pete asked.

"Who is Nate Thurmond?" I asked.

We were both kidding, I think.

The way I explain it, Pete and I handle the New York sports scene like two cops in a station house. Pete works them over for a while in the back room. Then I come in and offer them a cigarette and a cup of coffee and I say, "You really ought to talk, or I'm going to have to let that animal back in."

Sooner or later, they all talk, either to Pete or to me.

We are very different people. I am forty-six, four years older than Pete. I was never more than a schoolyard athlete, but Pete was the sixth man on a very good Archbishop Molloy High School team, and he also played a bit of freshman ball at Hofstra before the first-semester grades started coming in. I have a degree in English; Pete worked on a ship and joined the Airborne. I write books in my spare time; Pete was the player-coach of a team in the Rucker League in Harlem. My best man was an actor; Pete's best man was Julius Erving. We vacation in Europe; Pete and his wife vacation on Shelter Island. Different folks.

We see each other at Christmas, or at the press table at Madison Square Garden. I don't think Rupert will mind if I tell the world that Peter is always explaining the game to me, always introducing me to basketball people.

For a long time, Pete had a running feud with the ultra-cool Joe Barry Carroll of the Golden State Warriors. Carroll was offended just because Pete called him Joe Barry Apathy. No sense of humor.

After a few years of feuding, they resumed nodding to each other. One day Carroll came over to Pete at a party and said, "Hey, I read where you came out for the abolition of boxing."

"You read?" Pete asked with a sneer.

"I'm telling you," the patient Carroll said. "I bought Howard Cosell's book and you're in it."

"That's two upsets," Pete said. "You read. And you bought a book. But look, Joe Barry, that wasn't me. That was my brother who works for *The New York Times.*"

Long silence. Then: "You mean there are two of you motherfuckers?"

A few months later, we were at a game, and Pete pulled Carroll over and said, "Hey, Joe Barry, this is my brother."

Carroll shook my hand politely and said, "There really are two of you motherfuckers."

Every few minutes during the game, I would catch Joe Barry staring over at us, shaking his head. I'm no lip-reader, but I knew what he was saying.

Pete's style is not mine, but I respect the work he does. That he has not been beaten up by twelve tall men in an alley indicates the players realize he has the goods on all of them. Some of my colleagues who question Pete's sources don't realize how hard he works. Pete is always on the phone with an agent or a general manager, players, and coaches. There are executives in the league who check with Pete before concluding a deal. Pete just might know something about a player's knees, or his nose.

Pete's style is a few hard paragraphs and on to trashing somebody else. He has contempt for some sports journalists who don't "tell the truth" in black and white. Pete may not think that the varied topics I cover have much relevance to the fans on the street, the *Post* basketball buffs he serves so well, but it is hard to explain the broader vision at *The Times*.

I would like to have seen what a more catholic sports editor, somebody like Vic Ziegel, might have done to stretch Pete's horizons, to expand his confidence. The best editor Pete ever had was our father.

When Pop died on Thanksgiving Night of 1984, Pete sat down and wrote a flowing, gentle memoir of how Pop used to spend hours advising him about his writing. Pete's column was so good, I never even tried to write one.

The column ran on the morning of the funeral.

"That's the first time I've ever seen Uncle Pete write a whole column on somebody and not rip him," said my son, David.

Wait till Joe Barry runs into David.

SYRACUSE, NEW YORK, MARCH 16

Some sports reporters stay up all hours of the night absorbing ESPN and *USA Today*, every sleeper, every outsider, every junior-college transfer, every three-point artist. I don't know what I do with my time, but I arrived here Friday blissfully unaware of Cleveland State. Didn't know they existed.

Bobby Knight knew about Cleveland State, but then again, that's his business. Knight is the thoroughly repulsive coach of the University of Indiana, chronic sneer on his face, big belly sticking out of his red sweater, part bully, part genius. He's won the national title twice, coached the U.S. Olympic team in 1984, made a jackass of himself during the Pan-American Games in Puerto Rico in 1979, made anti–Puerto Rican comments at public meetings, a beauty. Of course he had heard of Cleveland State.

When Kevin Mackey, self-professed "fat little streetcorner kid from St. Polycarp's parish," waddled over to Knight before Friday's game, Knight was prepared. Mackey is the coach of Cleveland State, a master recruiter who found twelve black kids nobody else wanted, plus two white walk-on players.

"Hey, take it easy on me, big guy," Mackey said in his Boston, corner-of-his-mouth accent.

What did Knight tell Mackey?

"Hey, he's no fool," Mackey recounted later. "I'll paraphrase his answer for you. He said, 'I'm not gonna give you any breaks out there.' "

I would never root against an entire university just because its head coach is a swaggering lout. That would be unprofessional. But I nearly dislocated my neck performing body English on a couple of shots rolling around the rim as Cleveland State beat Indiana, 83–79.

As everybody knows, journalists don't root for people, we root for stories, and Cleveland State is a story, with its freshman guard named Mouse McFadden, who did not play high-school ball in New York. Mackey entertained us for an hour after the game, portraying his team as outsiders, city boys, reclamation projects.

"In the eastern ghetto, the kids who used to be boxers are now basketball players," Mackey said. "The midwestern player takes shots from the perimeter, but the eastern kid has some attack in him. There's a difference in a kid from the projects."

We saw through Mackey's underdog speech, noticing that the Cleveland State players were thoughtful, polite, curious. There were also some faculty representatives who clearly had an interest in the players. Kevin Mackey aside, this was not exactly the Wild Bunch.

There were four games on Friday in the opening round of the regional tournament. Yesterday morning, all four winning teams sent representatives to a press conference. David Robinson of the Naval Academy, all seven feet of him, all hundred and fifty IQ points, his face a kaleidoscope of thoughts, showed up in his midshipman's uniform, spit shine, polished brass, white shirt.

While Robinson answered questions, the entire Cleveland State team slipped into the back of the room. They were neatly dressed in slacks and sweaters, no chains, no black leather jackets, fourteen polite young men a long way from Cleveland.

And they gaped at David Robinson. I mean gaped. Open-mouthed, where-did-they-find-this-brother? gapes. It probably wasn't the introverted smile, it probably wasn't the five-syllable words, it may have been as basic as the pressed white shirt and the elongated navy-blue uniform and the shiny black shoes. He could have been representing the Martian Naval Academy and not seemed any more extraterrestial to the Cleveland State players. I don't remember a word David Robinson said, just the looks on the Cleveland State players.

Today, both Cleveland State and Navy won their second-round games. They both play in the regional tournament in New Jersey next weekend. I leave town with enough notes for separate columns on Navy and Cleveland State during the week. No Bobby Knight to think about, plenty of Mouse McFadden. Some days it just works out.

The following year, Bobby Knight won the NCAA title for a third time, which did not surprise me at all, and was the subject of a best-selling book, which surprised me immensely.

There used to be an old publishing axiom that "sports books don't sell," that people who buy hardcover books and people who follow sports live in two different worlds. The success of the John Madden books, the Ron Luciano books, Martina's autobiography, and a dozen other sports books obviously demolished that theory, but I was not prepared for the success of the Knight book.

I had always seen Knight as a regional phenomenon who was allowed by the state of Indiana to throw chairs, bully officials, rough up his players physically and emotionally, because he (a) won championships and (b) ran a "clean" program, mostly (a).

Knight did not seem anything like Patton or Chuck Yeager or Lee Iacocca, other individualists who fascinate Americans. I was flatly amazed that men and women (women!—this is a man who uses phallic words to express his contempt for women) would walk into bookstores on Fifth Avenue or Michigan Avenue or Wilshire Boulevard and buy a book about a gristle-bellied, cigar-smoking, misogynist basketball coach. It either proves that John Feinstein is one hell of a writer, or I don't know jack about the American mind. Or both.

ST. PETERSBURG, FLORIDA, MARCH 23

I am reading a novel called *The Sportswriter* by Richard Ford, which makes me remember why I prefer to be called "sports reporter."

Sportswriter? The way the word is usually used, when introduced to strangers, it takes on the condescending sound of a rumpled, childish soul who goes to games for free, uses terms like "these tired old orbs have seen," eats free meals, rattles off statistics, bitches about the high salaries of the athletes, and stumbles through the week ill dressed, ill conditioned, and hung over. Oscar Madison in *The Odd Couple* is a sportswriter.

My image of the prototypical "sportswriter" has always been Krazy Kress, in Mark Harris's classic novel *The Southpaw*. Krazy Kress makes up quotes, shills for management, and usually manages to make a buck.

"In his column he is always promoting 30,0000 things on the side, and if you keep a close watch you will see where whatever comes along Krazy is somewhere where the cash flies," writes Henry Wiggen, the Southpaw. "If it is some kind of a benefit dinner who is handling the tickets? Krazy. If it is a collection being took up for some sick kid in the hospital who is all of a sudden the chief collector? Krazy. Is it a new suit of clothes you wish to buy? Or a car? Who will get it for you cheap? Krazy.

". . . I was a full year catching wise to all this, but I done so at last," Wiggen adds.

I have always been afraid of becoming Krazy Kress. After a few days at the Super Bowl, in the stultifying clutches of the National Football League, I have to glance in the mirror to make sure I have not started wearing plaid pants, checked jackets, striped shirts, and polka-dot ties.

Or, as Garth Iorg, a former ballplayer, said in 1985, when he agreed to cover the baseball play-offs for the *Toronto Star:* "I guess this means I have to put on thirty pounds, smoke smelly cigars, and wear clothes that don't match."

There have been a few Krazy Kresses, colleagues who tumbled head-first out of team buses, groveled to management, or made up stories from the top of their heads. I'll never forget poor Johnny Keane inheriting the disintegrating New York Yankees in the spring of 1965. Early in camp, one of the older reporters shuffled apologetically up to Keane one sunny morning and mumbled something about "doing something that might cause you some problems." The "something" was a concocted story about a feud between a few of the older Yankees and Keane, the result of a midnight collision between too much whiskey and a first-edition deadline.

The rigid demands of modern, computerized sports journalism—the tight deadlines, the travel requirements, the demand for greater knowledge of law and economics and medicine—have weeded out most of the real stumblers and bumblers and connivers.

My vision of sports journalism was high because I started at *Newsday* back in the late fifties. We felt ourselves part of the Red Guard of sports journalism, formulating what we thought were new approaches—asking questions, relying on quotes, writing long profiles that focused more on the psychological than the technical.

We were a combination of playful and dead serious, consciously proud of our craft, and having very little in common with the lone-wolf magazine "sportswriter" in Richard Ford's novel.

Ford is a serious novelist who has created an uncommitted modern man, buffeted by divorce and the death of a child. My first reaction was that it made sense for Ford to use the emptiness of one "sportswriter" to make his point about the anomie of contemporary life. Ford made his protagonist a sportswriter the way Arthur Miller made Willy Loman a salesman, making his living out of a suitcase, "a smile and a shoeshine."

But the more I thought about it, the more concerned I was that a "sportswriter" should be the convenient symbol for detachedness. Is that what people think of us? Is that what we are? I suspect Ford did not make his man a foreign correspondent or a cityside reporter because they work with life-and-death subjects, whereas "sportswriters" deal enough in the superficiality of games and press conferences to qualify as contemporary, rootless people.

In Ford's novel, there is one episode in which the sportswriter is exposed to the drug-supported anguish of a broken athlete. But much of the time Ford's sportswriter seems to dash off to games carrying only his press guide and his notebook and his airline schedule, unencumbered by conferences with editors, research into the files, the ringing of the telephone, or the jangling of professional conscience.

How true is that? There certainly are times when I go off to the arena without the slightest thought about what I will write or what the main issues are today. This is the old "God will provide" theory of Red Smith, still quoted by some of his admirers today. Something will happen.

But beyond that studied nonchalance of Red's, many "sportswriters" take a complicated vision and agenda with us to work every day. We read the papers, we monitor the radio and television, we make and receive phone calls, and most important, we are the products of everything we have learned up to that point.

Most sports columnists may not be actively working on a theme or a story, but when something happens, when somebody says something, we link it with what we already know and feel, not unlike a doctor remembering a seminar on chicken pox when he was in medical school, or a patient he saw three years ago.

In New York, with its tabloid frenzy, no sports columnist can stay too far away from the issues, from getting involved. As a writer, Richard

Ford should have known that even a magazine writer, who regularly produces copy once a week, cannot be too detached.

Having come along at *Newsday,* I have never been able to get far from social consciousness. After eighteen years at *The New York Times,* I still think of the old *Newsday* sports staff as "we," the way older veterans regard their old army days as the most vital time in their youth. *Newsday* is linked in my mind to the heady first few hours of the sixties, to my graduation from college, to my marriage, to the election of John F. Kennedy, to the shining promise of a new era. We had our own charismatic leader, a sports editor named Jack Mann, whose tenure lasted even less time than Camelot.

When I first encountered *Newsday* late in 1956, it was already a fat, respectable suburban tabloid, just beginning to cover events away from Long Island. I was a seventeen-year-old college freshman, hired by the "local" sports editor, Bob Zellner, to take high-school games over the telephone a couple of nights a week.

In the same office, there was a "national" staff whose editor was Jack Mann, who had served with the marines at the end of the Pacific campaign. Like Ernie Pyle and Bill Mauldin, Jack maintained a foxhole perspective of sports, seeking out the testy old grunts, the pinch hitters and the bullpen pitchers, who understood how the game really worked.

His "national" colleague was Stan Isaacs out of Brooklyn College, part social activist, part anarchist, who wrote a column called "Out of Left Field," which it surely was. Stanley once spent an entire evening with the sheep on the grassy slope behind the outfield in the old Kansas City ballpark, and *Newsday* ran a wire-service photograph with the caption: "Stanley, Is That Ewe?" His next column would be about how whites viewed blacks in baseball, years ahead of almost all columnists.

When I came back from my first assignment, a riotous club basketball game, Mann and Isaacs fussed over my article, encouraged me to be impertinent. In February of 1960, I was hired full time by Zellner, but a few weeks later Mann was running the whole department.

Sometimes Mann or Isaacs took me to Yankee games, introducing me to players and writers. Late one spring night, I watched Jack drawing squares on a huge cardboard sheet, carefully etching in the daily assignments. He could not help but notice me peeking over his shoulder, and he finally turned his head and asked with drill-sergeant irony, "You think you're ready for this?"

Inked on the assignment sheet was: CHISOX @ YANKS.

"Hell, yes," I said. I was twenty years old.

Mann recruited Steve Jacobson to cover baseball, Bob Sales to cover basketball and work the desk, Dick Sorkin to cover hockey. He took advantage of the varied skills of Ed Comerford, Bill Searby, Tony Sisti, and Dick Clemente from the old local staff, and he hired Bob Waters, a former boxer and marine, to work the desk and cover boxing.

The first thing we established was that we were honest. We didn't write program pieces for the Garden. We paid for our trips with the teams. We did not take gifts at Christmastime, or any other time. We did not work as official scorers in baseball, since that could make us part of the story. We could take a free meal in the press room if there was nothing else to eat in the joint—but we tipped copiously. Sometimes we bought breakfast for road secretaries, rather than the time-honored "sportswriter" way of hanging outside the hotel coffee shop, waiting for Bruce Henry of the Yankees to show up. We were big-time.

Fighting inexperience and bad habits, Mann issued a series of style pages, his Yellow Pages, a version of *The New York Times*'s august "Winners and Sinners" if issued by Mao Tse-tung instead of Ted Bernstein.

Nobody was "affable" anymore. Show it. No more comparing high-school rivalries to the Sharks and the Jets of *West Side Story*. Too many chances for ethnic or racial mischief.

Some of us still keep our Yellow Pages tucked in a drawer. Jack's message of April 25, 1960, said:

"Soul-wise, these times are trying. Trying enough, that is, without words like schedule-wise, money-wise or anything-wise. They're out."

And he strung together words we could no longer use, like "fray, tilt, donnybrook, stanza, heat, canto, chapter, merman, natatore, cindermen, hurler, twirler, netmen, hardwood, circuit clout, twin killing, kegler, and so on, and on." This would have eliminated half the vocabulary for some sportswriters of the time.

Jack's last paragraph was: "Maybe it isn't possible to put out a sports section without this kind of drivel. Certainly it hasn't ever been done. But let's try it, anyway."

Maybe we were a bit xenophobic. Old *Herald Tribune* people talk about Stanley Woodward as the best sports editor who ever lived. From my perspective, Jack Mann was the best teacher and editor a twenty-year-old could have had. He would sharpen a pencil and, with some dramatic arrows and cross-outs and a pithy insertion here and there, could pare a thousand-word feature and ask, "Is that what you had in mind?" Often enough, it was.

In the late fifties, television was on its way to purchasing the control of sports. (In those days, television merely told teams when to take a time-out for a commercial. Nowadays, television tells baseball what time to hold the World Series, and it tells the Olympics what events to hold at what time.) But if television did one good thing, it exposed athletes, politicians, and entertainers to the public eye. Reporters could not create an "affable" Willie Mays or a "kindly" Frank Sinatra or a "humane" Joe McCarthy; all you had to do was see them on the tube for thirty seconds and you knew better.

Mann was insistent that we explore the myths and legends of sports. Was Joe DiMaggio the perfect warrior, so often fawned upon by city columnists, or was there also something empty and aloof at the core? Seek him out, ask him some questions. Was Mickey Mantle a courageous hero, or was he also a gruff rustic who cursed at fans and reporters and sometimes showed up for work hung over? Hang by his locker and find out.

We thought we were pretty hot stuff when Dick Schaap of *Newsweek* wrote a rave piece about the *Newsday* "Kiddie Corps," but we were not alone. Mann and Isaacs had kindred souls in Larry Merchant and Stan Hochman of the *Philadelphia Daily News* and Leonard Shecter at the *New York Post.* Our office was always piled high with recent copies of Merchant's section, the way revolutionaries and philosophers in England, France, and the Colonies must have exchanged pamphlets during the second half of the eighteenth century.

Eventually, the true believers were blended among the entire younger generation of sports reporters. The acerbic Jimmy Cannon spotted young Phil Pepe, then of the *World Telegram and Sun*, who happens to have prominent front teeth.

"He chatters like a chipmunk," Jimmy snapped.

Before long, we were all Chipmunks, anybody under forty, anybody who did not wear three-piece suits. Dick Young and Jimmy Cannon were too old to be Chipmunks, although many Chipmunks admired them. The professorial Leonard Koppett (once accused by Jimmy Cannon of carrying decimal points in his attaché case) insisted he was no Chipmunk but belonged to a rival group, the Badgers.

Chipmunks were constantly digging up quotes the way their rodent cousins seek acorns. The definitive question of the entire Chipmunk movement was posed by Stan Isaacs in the Yankee locker room. It came after Ralph Terry excused himself from the group interview to make a call to his wife, who had recently given birth to their first child. When Terry returned, he mentioned that his wife was busy nursing.

"Breast or bottle?" Isaacs blurted out.

Over the years, those three words have become the symbol of Chipmunkery, even as we become middle-aged and do not scurry and chatter quite so much. The Jack Mann era at *Newsday* ended abruptly when Jack got involved in some intramural feuds at the paper, and was fired in July of 1962. Jack covers racing at the *Baltimore Evening Sun* these days, having worked just about everywhere else in between. But once upon a time he created a sports section that is still one of the best in the country.

There are still some Krazy Kresses around—some of them my age, or younger—but except for an occasional tabloid frenzy, most of us are under the surveillance of corporate officials concerned about criticism and inaccuracy. I can understand Richard Ford's literary device in making his man a "sportswriter." The character just doesn't remind me of my favorite people in the business.

ST. PETERSBURG, FLORIDA, MARCH 24

When practice ends, we follow the players into the clubhouse, a few steps into a time warp. In the cool darkness, I expect to see Charlie Neal and Frank Thomas and Rod Kanehl bantering as they were on my first day of spring training. Instead, there are youngsters named McDowell and Mitchell and Dykstra, but the talk is the same. Your wife does this, your girlfriend does that. And the clubhouse attendants still put celery sticks and soup out for lunch.

Why isn't it 1963? Why am I no longer twenty-three years old? Why isn't Casey Stengel rasping, "Listen, you asshole, I'm trying to tell you something"? I always changed the word to "ironhead" to get the feeling into the paper.

Spring training has marked the spiritual beginning of my work year since 1963, fulfilling the childhood dream from the radio on snowy March days, hearing the good news that baseball had survived, that pitchers were getting ready to go nine.

During college, gray winters, long term papers, I used to say to myself, "Just hang in there until baseball season." Daily box scores would be better than chicken soup, something to think about every day. Even when I was a news reporter, I found excuses every March to visit this pretty little lakeside camp. I couldn't give up baseball.

In earlier spring clubhouses, I have seen old players agonize when they were cut from the worst team in the major leagues, and I have seen young players insist they would be back soon. This year there is very little suspense about who will make the squad. The Mets are loaded.

Last September the Mets staged two epic series with the Cardinals, one in New York, one in St. Louis, falling just short on the final weekend. This year, Davey Johnson thinks the Mets should not only win but dominate. His confidence spreads to the players.

I have been coming here since the second lunatic spring of Casey Stengel, but these players have the strange notion this is their clubhouse, not the writers'. Since most athletes read the tabloids rather than *The Times*, to most of these players I am another writer with a beard but no name.

A few players make eye contact, Ron Darling with a nod, Gary Carter with a smile. Carter came to the Mets in 1985 with the Steve Garvey Syndrome, mistrusted by his Montreal teammates because he was constantly charming to fans and polite to reporters. I kept waiting for one sign of phoniness, and haven't found it yet. In his first year, I wrote that if Carter kept hugging people every time they made a good play, he was going to break somebody's ribs. He looked at me a little strangely for a while.

Keith Hernandez greets me with a sideways "Hey, George." *The Times* never did publish its planned sports magazine, after I had gone through agonies with waves of editors, but I recycled the interview with Hernandez in the sports section. He let me know he was not happy with one or two things, but we're both big boys.

A few other Mets make eye contact—Rafael Santana, the Dominican shortstop who is constantly underrated as a player and as a personality (some of the announcers seem unsure whether he speaks English, which he does); Ray Knight, an absolute sweetheart, trying to make a comeback; and Terry Leach, an older pitcher with true Alabama grit, destined to return to the minors. Most of the players go about their business. Then I spot Robby.

I don't know what other players and reporters think about a coach and a columnist giving each other a hug, but Bill Robinson and I go back to his first spring with the Yankees in 1967.

"How's the family?" we ask, in unison.

Robby was one of those rare players who could make you lose your objectivity. Mike Burke, who was running the Yankees, told Robby he could be a black Mickey Mantle, he could own the town. Robby was so sweet, so earnest, so discouraged when it didn't work out. Every few months I would write another "Bill Robinson is making his move" article, wishful thinking for all of us.

Eventually, Robby rebuilt his career with the Phillies, and in 1979 he was a regular for the World Champion Pirates. Mike Burke sent Robby a laminated photograph of Robby scoring the winning run in the Series. When Mike retired to Ireland a few years later, Vic Ziegel and I arranged for Bill and Mary Robinson to be the surprise at a little farewell dinner in the Village, a way of remembering Mike Burke's dreams for Robby and the Yankees. That's how far back Robby and I go.

"Good winter?" I ask.

"Great. I operated my hitting school again. Worked on the house."

While Robby and I catch up on family news, Dwight Gooden walks past Robby's locker. The young pitcher with the forty-one victories in his first two seasons pretends to glare at Robby. Robby dismisses Gooden with a contemptuous wave. They both break out laughing.

"Great kid," Robby says, after Gooden pads away.

"I don't really know him."

"He's shy," Bill agrees.

Does anybody know Dwight Gooden? He arrived from the lower

minor leagues in 1984, so poised and athletic that he seemed almost alien. I came to call him "The Brother from Another Planet," in honor of the classic John Sayles film about a black extraterrestrial plopped down in the middle of Harlem. In fact, has anybody seen Gooden and actor Joe Morton at the same time? The Brother was a black Billy Budd, an innocent at large in hurting, scheming, brawling Harlem. With no power of speech, the Brother sometimes seemed lost in this raucous corner of a foreign planet.

Gooden's planet is the pitching mound, but he seems to lose his powers when he steps into the clubhouse. The Mets have kept him isolated by not allowing anybody to interview him except in stilted mass press conferences, where Gooden relies on the most innocuous clichés.

Since the end of last season, Gooden has been involved in several questionable events. In January, he did not let the Mets know he had sprained his ankle, and he told enough versions to give himself a Pinocchio nose. A few weeks ago, Gooden missed a spring exhibition and told a story about a car accident that was less than accurate. The Mets are hoping he is not developing bad habits. He is only twenty-one.

Like a lot of the Mets, Gooden lives in Port Washington. Last year David used to serve hamburgers to Gooden at the local Burger King. A friend of ours delivered pizza to Gooden's apartment, and she reported he did not give her a tip.

Aside from not being a tipper, what kind of person is Dwight Gooden? I've tried talking to him a couple of times and got a quick "Gotta go." He always seems furtive, like a man wearing permanent dark glasses.

I get in my rented car and drive across town to Al Lang Field, where the Mets will play the Dodgers. Even with a few modern high rises and the art museum and the marina, St. Pete is still a languid southern town, funky boarding houses and greasy coffee shops, and I love it for that.

My nostalgia is shattered at the stadium when somebody drops the news that in two years the Mets are moving across the state to some place named Port St. Lucie. The reason I hear is that Nelson Doubleday and Fred Wilpon, the owners, are pretty damn tired of having to fly clear across the state from their mansions near Palm Beach to watch their hirelings perform.

It is true that the Mets do not have a perfect spring-training camp, having to shuttle to three different bases here, but there is something homey and familiar about St. Pete, just as there was about Brooklyn before Walter O'Malley moved the Dodgers to Los Angeles.

I stand behind the batting cage and take a good look at St. Pete—the small planes landing behind left field, the sailboats on the bay, the fading rooming houses behind right field, the singing vendor who sounds like William Warfield with a popcorn tray. In a year or two, this delightful scene is going to be a memory, like the rasping voice of Casey Stengel, now scattered in the moist breeze, saying, "Now wait a minute, you asshole."

ST. PETERSBURG, FLORIDA, MARCH 24

The game is still going on, but I'm keeping an eye on a Dodger pitcher running laps in the outfield. When he is done, he jogs toward the visiting clubhouse.

"Welchie!" I shout.

He reaches past the guard and opens the metal gate, and we hug each other, the way people do at the rehabilitation center where Bob Welch went to fight alcoholism. I followed a year later to spend five days in a treatment session, to work on his book. As far as I know, Bob hasn't had a drink in six years.

"Come on in," he says.

"There's a game going on," I say.

"It's almost over," he says. "Fuck it, it's spring training."

As a reporter, I don't like other journalists getting favored treatment; I also don't like being chased from places where I don't belong. But Bob half shoves me through the clubhouse door.

"Come on, man," he says. "I got to get out of these clothes."

Since Bob and I worked on his book, I have become friendly with Al Campanis, the Dodgers' courtly general manager, and Tom Lasorda, the garrulous manager. I have tried not to take advantage of their hospitality, but as Bob says, fuck it, it's spring training.

Bob is tall and hyperactive, with a wild look in his light blue eyes. A few reporters tell me they can never forget how unpleasant he was when he was drunk. I've never seen him that way, but I see the look in his eyes. Sober, he's a sweetie.

As Bob goes off to change into a dry shirt, the thought strikes me, I am in the Dodger clubhouse. It was my boyhood dream, catching a glimpse of Jackie Robinson and Gil Hodges trudging through the tunnel to the clubhouse in their creamy white uniforms with the blue trim.

Bob has been with the Dodgers since 1978, when he struck out Reggie Jackson for the dramatic last out in a World Series game. Because of *The Times*'s new rule that reporters cannot collaborate on books with people we cover, I don't write about Bob when he pitches. But I follow his games, rooting for his continual recovery rather than his earned-run average.

"The last time I saw you was after Clark's home run," I say.

"Pissed me off," Bob says. "I was psyched to pitch the seventh game."

That was in Los Angeles last October, after the Cardinals won the pennant on a home run by Jack Clark off Tom Niedenfuer. Following my instincts that losing clubhouses are more interesting than winning clubhouses, I went to find out why Lasorda had chosen to pitch to Clark with first base open.

I was standing with the other reporters in the gloomy clubhouse when Welch sidled up to me and whispered, "Some of the guys are getting hammered, but I choose not to."

Bob reinforces his sobriety by verbalizing his decision not to drink, day by day. He has been doing it that way since 1980, when he spent a month at the Meadows, in Wickenburg, Arizona. *The Times* heard about the young Dodger who was openly talking about his treatment, and we thought it would be a good profile. I caught up with him, and he told me how he had been chugging wine in his hotel room before going out to the ballpark, suffering blackouts at the age of twenty-three. Through John Newton, an alcoholism counselor at Union Oil, the Dodgers had persuaded Bob that his career was in jeopardy if he did not seek treatment.

At the Meadows, they told him he was going to die young. His family and his girlfriend, Mary Ellen Wilson, and Rick and Robin Sutcliffe from the Dodgers, had come to the Meadows to help confront Bob with the reality of his drinking. In his first tenuous weeks out of treatment, Bob was going to Alcoholics Anonymous meetings nearly every day. I wrote a long feature about a young pitcher who was saving his life, day by day, and I rooted for him the way reporters often quietly root for somebody nice.

Late that season, Bob's old agent called and said he had heard about my collaboration with Loretta Lynn. He thought there was a good story in Bob Welch, too.

"Welchie's a good kid," the agent said. "You'll like him when you meet him."

I said I had already done a two-thousand-word profile on Bob in *The New York Times*. The agent said he would have to look it up.

We got together late in the season, in San Francisco. Bob took me on a walking tour of some of his most famous drunks. This was where his roommate had found him sprawled in a bar. This was where he had lurched onto the team bus at four in the afternoon.

Bob's stories of drinking since he was in junior high school, getting drunk before playing in a high-school basketball game, hitting the bars and the liquor stores at night, sounded like foreign territory to me. But Bob was so straight, so vulnerable, that I found myself liking him. This was not going to be a book about sports, not a book about the Dodgers, not a book about a celebrity, but a book about a young man in danger of losing his life.

After a few weeks of research, I realized I had to visit the clinic where Bob had been treated. The officials agreed to let me visit, but they had a house rule for visiting writers: You had to sit in the circle and partici-pate with patients and their family members. The Meadows treats ad-diction as a family disorder, on the theory that patients turn to alcohol or drugs to try to numb the feelings of sadness or anger that have gone unresolved in many families.

No problem, I thought. I would be a nice fellow, sit at the edge of the family-therapy week, and observe. Bob had warned me they would prod any visitor to reveal something about himself. Bob told me how the Dodgers had asked—made—Tom Lasorda attend one of Bob's ses-sions. Tom showed up signing autographs and playing his self-created role of Manager with Blue Dodger Blood in His Veins.

That act got Tom as far as the first group session, where he introduced himself as "Tom Lasorda, the happiest man in the world." Immediately, Fred Downing, the head counselor, snapped, "Tom, you don't look too happy to me," which is true. Lasorda can be hilarious, the Rodney Dangerfield of managers, but his eyes don't laugh. At the Meadows, they have no qualms in voicing their perceptions of other people. Tom did not stay long at family week.

I anticipated no problems that way. At the first family meeting, I introduced myself as a writer who was doing a book about the Meadows. I did not mention Bob, because I did not want to trade in on his celebrity status.

"I don't have any alcohol or drug problem," I added, "but I hope I can be part of the group and help somebody."

Immediately, a man who was visiting his wife at the center said, "George, I hope you're not going to just hang back and observe us intellectually. From your words, it sounds like you might do that."

Coming from a family where feelings are not easily shared, I was not used to such a blunt critique. I felt as if I had been punched in the stomach. This was the role I had chosen in life—the observer, the writer, gathering up my clues and my impressions and sharing them in print. As soon as the man said that to me, I began to suffer one of the anxiety attacks I had been having periodically since I was a child, watching the door, wondering if my legs would be strong enough to carry me that far.

My claustrophobia vanished at lunchtime as I interviewed Bob's counselor, Lynn Brennan. Now I was back to being myself again: in control, with a mission, interested in other people. With Bob's permission, Lynn opened up all his records, all the notes she had taken on him. I was living in Bob's life. I was safe. But that afternoon, back in family session, an agonized family was bringing up ways the patient had hurt them. People from other families were voicing their reactions.

"George, what do you think?" Fred Downing asked.

"I agree with what the last lady said," I answered.

"Don't you have any feelings of your own?" he snapped. "Do you think you're better than other people?"

Fred's caustic remark jarred me. Of course I had reactions to other people. One elderly Hispanic couple reminded me of my parents. Some of their children could have been the children in my family. The divisions within a family, the distances between people, the things left unsaid, were not so different from what went on in my original family, or the family I had created as an adult.

Watching people cry as they brought up the jealousies and resentments made me think about things that had hurt me as a child. There was nobody from my family here to talk about me, no pattern of alcohol or drug abuse, but I could remember the selfish little boy, angry because his mother was having other children. It wasn't hard to dredge up the feelings that had perhaps turned me inward, made me caustic and flippant and distant on one level, loving and concerned on another level. Somebody in college once expressed amazement to find I was the oldest of five children. He had always assumed I was an only child. I did not think it was a compliment.

At night, I would bring these dislodged feelings back to the motel. Marianne, who was not taking part in the sessions, would sit up for hours listening to me, sobbing by now, talk about how I had put up walls between myself and other family members, how I had not paid attention to her feelings. I began to think of things I wanted to tell Marianne, my children, my parents, my brothers and sisters.

The next day I would go back to the Meadows, shift my gears after the sessions, become the concerned writer again, talking with Lynn Brennan about Bob Welch. One day Lynn said that Bob had used beer to blot out fear that people liked him only because he was a star athlete. "A piece of meat," somebody had called him, meaning he had value only as long as his arm was healthy.

The more I thought about it, the more I felt a connection with Bob Welch. I remembered the fat little boy, the class clown who could write, laughing and showing off and acting out in a bid for attention. I realized how much of my adult self-image was caught up in being a writer, having a skill, having a name, being able to perform in public, giving off one image and perhaps hiding the other corners of my personality.

We were both performers for famous companies—the Los Angeles Dodgers for Bob, *The New York Times* for me. I recalled how only a year earlier I had been tempted to walk out of the tense, stifling *Times* city room, to seek more independence, more creativity, more self-respect. But I had held back, knowing I would be giving up a major source of my identity.

Who would like me if I didn't work for *The Times?* Would all those people call for favors, would people defer, would they still be interested in me if I did not have a byline in *The Times?* Did Bob ever wonder about what his life would be like without the Dodgers, without baseball? Would his friends and family think he had let them down? Would he be just another hard drinker in a factory town?

Lynn Brennan told me how group members had prodded Bob about what he really felt behind the athletic swaggering, the cool pose. Why did he become belligerent and destructive with a beer or two in him? What demons were really inside?

Facing my own insecurities, the cut-and-dried ways I had come to deal with emotions, I began to realize I had my own demons, which sometimes prodded me in closed rooms, in quiet moments, setting off anxiety attacks. I recognized that my own way of hiding from my feelings was to work, to keep busy. A day off with no writing, with no phone calls, with no appointments, would leave me feeling loose, uprooted. No wonder I would describe working for a demanding newspaper as an addiction.

One day in a session, I talked a little about myself, and felt better for it, but I could also see that everybody else in that room was dealing with life-threatening addictions—overdoses, binges, car wrecks, stolen money, compulsive affairs, broken families. My problems were garden variety, but I no longer felt like an outsider.

On the last day of family week, Bob flew down to the Meadows and gave me a walking tour—his room, where he had cried, where he had written letters to Mary Ellen, the first time he had faced his fears, the first time he had admitted he is an alcoholic.

"Pretty rough?" Bob asked me.

"Wasn't bad for me," I said. "But they can get pretty close to you."

"Man, they got on my case something awful," Bob said, shaking his head. "If they thought I was holding back, they'd say, 'Man, you're going to die if you don't open up.' They all said I was angry, holding back. I said, 'Fuck, I'm not angry.' " And he laughed.

From that day, we became even closer. We'd both been through the Meadows. We had learned when other people were bullshitting us. We had learned when we were bullshitting ourselves. After that, when we worked on the book, I could say to him, "Come on, there's more to it than that," and we would both laugh.

Bob really did want to beat the thing, day by day. He wanted to be a star. I came to think of the song Robbie Robertson wrote about Bob Dylan, called "Stage Fright": "But when he gets to the end, he wants to start all over again."

The book came out, got some nice reviews, sold a few copies. I know three people in my business who have looked into their own lives as a result of reading the book. I've participated in a few confrontations, helped a few friends check in for treatment.

Having seen people walk out of the Meadows with a new attitude, having seen Bob not touch a beer for six years, I am a strong believer in rehabilitation. My boyhood idol, Dick Young, thinks I'm "soft on druggies" and writes about a month at a rehabilitation center as a paid vacation. But I spent five days at a center, and I can attest to the knot in your stomach, the tension in the room, and the love and the hope that can save lives.

In 1984, Bob and Mary Ellen were married in a candlelight service in the Boston University chapel. I have never seen a happier, more beautiful couple. They spent part of their honeymoon in our guest room, visiting New York. Bob is one of those rare baseball players who loves New York, who takes the subway to Shea Stadium, who roams from Greenwich Village to Central Park.

Bob has learned to live a disciplined life, discovering his sober personality. He remembers names, keeps appointments, studies his investments, makes speeches about addiction, plans to open a treatment center when his baseball career is over. But mostly he takes care of the body that allows him to be a baseball player.

"I've been throwing all winter," he says with great zest. "I feel awesome, ready for a great season."

I hear the familiar clatter of spikes and bats, and the Dodgers troop into the tiny clubhouse. Tom Lasorda wanders by and gives me a big handshake, his eyes distant and suspicious. He has never been comfortable with Bob's frankness about alcoholism. The room is getting crowded, and I have work to do.

Bob puts his arm around me and says, "Say hello to Marianne and David."

"I'll see you and Mary Ellen in New York," I say.

* * *

In 1987, my associations with the Dodgers began to unravel. Al Campanis, whose long and honorable career shows no trace of racism, made a disjointed appearance on television and blurted some foolish comments about blacks not having the "necessities" to be baseball officials, and was forced to resign. Bob had a terrific 1987 season but was traded to Oakland as the Dodgers rebuilt their starting lineup. He and Mary rented a house near the Golden Gate Bridge in San Francisco, and he won seventeen games with his new team. Day by day.

PORT WASHINGTON, MARCH 29

The big news in television is that Al Michaels is being moved over to pump some life into *Monday Night Football*, which has gone stale ever since Howard Cosell and Don Meredith lost the feel for it years ago. Howard should be glad that a professional announcer who never played the game is getting such a big assignment, but he and Michaels will probably not celebrate together—or even nod to each other in the hallway.

It is sad to see Howard cutting off ties with his network and the best young people in his own business. It's almost like a professional death wish. He should be allowing himself to be treated the way I gather CBS is treating Walter Cronkite—kindly Uncle Walter who still has a thing or two to teach us—but Howard is choosing to distance himself from everything, the good and the bad.

Howard has worked up his feud with "the print media" over the years, bitterly attacking Red Smith in his later years for taking a trip to South Africa (also because Red twitted Cosell so perfectly). But I get along with Howard and give him credit for being a positive force in television sports. He has raised issues nobody else would raise, even if he did it in the grating, egotistical persona he created. He has even been willing to criticize his own business, constantly taunting what he calls the "jockocracy," all the former athletes now working as broadcasters.

This has been a bad week for the jockocracy. Frank Gifford, who still comes across like a star athlete wearing a tuxedo at an awards banquet, is being moved from play-by-play to color commentator. O. J. Simpson, who probably got bad advice by some network adviser to play the role of the braggart, is being moved out to college football. And Joe Namath, who lost his Broadway Joe glamour the day he stopped being a quarterback, has been dropped.

I'm not gloating at the career turns of a few former athletes, but it is nice to see Michaels reaching the top of his profession. I first noticed him broadcasting the Cincinnati Reds on a network that reached every holler in Appalachia. His crisp, intelligent calls—with echoes of Vin Scully, and why not?—helped keep me in touch with baseball while I rode the ridges. Michaels and Marv Albert and Bob Costas are the deservedly highly paid, highly prominent television versions of dozens of lower-paid, less visible print reporters like me, who grew up knowing exactly what they wanted to do, who studied and practiced and prepared any way they could.

I have great respect for the skills of radio and television broadcasters, but I still make a distinction between journalism and broadcasting. To me, journalism is news and opinion, words and articles carefully selected and edited and printed—in a journal. Broadcasting is much more immediate, images and descriptions, heard and seen—and vanished in the air. Born in 1939, I'm the last of the radio era. We did not have television in my home until I was twelve, so I learned to read newspapers and listen to the radio and amuse myself before the flickering images arrived.

To this day, I watch almost nothing on regular television except sports events and an occasional movie. No *Miami Vice.* No Dan Rather. No Vanna White. No Warner Wolf. No Carson. No Letterman—although my son keeps me posted on him. (The arts on cable television are a blessing of my middle age.) I get my spot news from the radio, and doubt that I watch the evening news three times a year. There's always something more important happening—dinner with my family, working at the ballpark, out for the evening, exercise, classical music on the radio, reading, whatever. Just don't have the patience to sit still for a few brief impressions and the intonations of the larger-than-life celebrity broadcasters. My theory is, if something really serious happens, we'll hear the warbling of the air-raid alarms. Otherwise, the news will still be there on the doorstep tomorrow morning, written by reporters, packaged by editors.

I tend to fret about the regular coverage that newspaper sports sections give to the occasional bon mot of a broadcaster and the technical wizardry in the control booth. We publicize them, while they get information from us. But there is no denying that television has purchased control of sports, so I guess it's necessary for newspapers to cover that impact.

From occasional glimpses, I know that friends and former newspaper stars like Dick Schaap, Larry Merchant, and Bob Lipsyte are doing good work on television. But mostly I'm concerned with live events on television, things I need to see to do my own job. I used to gleefully support Howard's theory that almost all former jocks were out of their element in the word business, but it's hard to ignore a former coach like John Madden, who loves to talk to Everyman, or a former catcher like Joe Garagiola, who made baseball lovable for generations of network viewers, or a former shortstop like Tony Kubek, who loves his game and has no problem criticizing anybody in it.

Tim McCarver's emergence with the Mets and ABC has been a big surprise to me. When he played in St. Louis, he seemed like an amiable foil for bright older players like Bill White, Ken Boyer, and Bob Gibson. But McCarver has been listening and learning and reading for the past twenty years. He loves words and he loves ideas and he loves his game.

Shortly after taking off his Islanders' jersey with the captain's "C" on it, Ed Westfall moved into the booth with Jiggs McDonald and immediately became a broadcaster and a critic, not just a celebrity-athlete. When Billy Smith would flail his stick at opponents, Westfall would say, "Jiggs, there's no place in hockey for *that.*"

Both McCarver and Westfall have taken lessons, have practiced their new trade when the red light was not on. McCarver is no longer a secret, because of his work with WOR-TV and ABC, but Westfall is mostly a regional treasure for those of us fortunate enough to be plugged into the SportsChannel system.

For tomorrow's column about "The Athlete in the Booth," I interviewed Westfall, who said, "Sometimes I feel awkward knowing that people like Al Michaels and Jiggs McDonald have spent all their time in school and in their career preparing to be announcers. But that's the way it is." By being so good, Westfall and McCarver have made it impossible for print journalists to chortle about the jockocracy.

APRIL

THE BRONX, APRIL 8

Turning north on the Major Deegan, just past the Triboro, I catch a glimpse of Yankee Stadium, blue and gray majesty, nestled alongside the Harlem River.

I have seen Yankee Stadium a million times in my life, but to see it on Opening Day is thrilling, like the drizzly April day ten years ago when I escorted my children across the Seine to the Louvre. This is it. April in Paris. April in the Bronx. The real thing, the big ballpark. Opening Day.

The Yankees were never my ball club. When the Brooklyn Dodgers went away, I had to make do with rooting for the Kansas City A's and the Washington Senators when they came to town. I once saw Ryne Duren walk Herb Plews, Ossie Alvarez, and Neil Chrisley, with the bases loaded, for the Senators' winning run. From 1958 through 1961, that was baseball in New York for a lot of people.

When I started covering the Yankees a little bit in 1960, they were like a crusty men's club, about to win five pennants in a row. I came to like the Yankees more in the late sixties, partially because Michael Burke and Lee MacPhail, two of the finest people I ever met in sports, were running them, partially because the players were from my generation, partially because they were a mediocre ball club, pleasant and humble.

When I came back from my decade away from sports, George Steinbrenner was running them, so it was back to square one.

For the moment, it does not matter who owns them, or what tensions I will encounter inside. Just a glance at the great cathedral of the Bronx makes me feel like a pilgrim. We have gotten through the winter. We have survived.

Every year we write the same thing, whether it is Roger Angell or Tom Boswell, Mike Lupica or Peter Gammons, and it is always the truth. There is no sports event like Opening Day of baseball, the sense of beating back the forces of darkness and the National Football League.

From now into October, there will be games every day, athletes with faces and personalities, the Cubs in the afternoon and the ultimate security of going to bed knowing that at that very moment they are playing in California. Tomorrow there will be enough box scores and probable pitchers to read right through lunch. This is real life, starting today.

While pulling down the ramp from the Deegan, I decide to write about the Yankees being part of New York, that there should always be an Opening Day in the Bronx. Yet my hometown is threatened once again because New Jersey is lusting to build a baseball stadium alongside its sports complex in the swamplands. They've already got the Jets, the Giants, and Nets, and the Devils, without even bothering to put in mass transportation.

Because I live on Long Island, the hoarding of teams by New Jersey has been the single most depressing thing about my return to sports. I became a sports journalist for better or for worse—but not the Jersey Turnpike.

Now the swamp-dwellers want a baseball team—and guess which one. Steinbrenner has been putting pressure on New York to build him better parking facilities and put a railroad stop alongside Yankee Stadium, a reasonable request, assuming good faith on his part. But when Steinbrenner talks about New York not keeping its "promises" to him, he sounds suspiciously like Walter O'Malley just before he took my Dodgers to Never-Never Land.

O'Malley was at least from Brooklyn. Steinbrenner is from Cleveland and Tampa, for heaven's sake; he would have no qualms at all. The Secaucus Yankees. The Tampa Yankees. Whatever.

A Bronx assemblyman, John C. Dearie, has been passing out pamphlets to fans, urging the city to provide better rail and parking facilities at the Stadium, to give Steinbrenner no excuse to move the Yankees to New Jersey. That will be a good hook for my column about the threatened Jerseyfication of the Yankees.

Like Howard Cosell, I have serious reservations about cities using tax money to build stadiums, to lure franchises, but the Yankees are vital to the Bronx and important to New York, not just because of the income they generate but because of their presence. I don't care that the football teams play in New Jersey, except that they are an inconvenience to me, but the Yankees help hold New York together.

George. It's bad enough to have "Georgie Porgie, pudding and pie" in the nursery rhyme, along with George Bush, Mr. Male Menopause, shrieking at Geraldine Ferraro in 1984. Why couldn't Steinbrenner be named something else?

Ever since he carpetbagged into town, that lovely name of English kings and Magyar violinists has been used with the mocking inflection one would normally reserve for the village eccentric, the cranky old man down the block who talks to himself and keeps your baseball when it goes over his hedge. *George* is at the game today. *George* is holding a press conference. Did you hear what *George* just did? Why couldn't he be named Tom, or Dick, or Harry? Damn, we've even got the same birthday, July 4.

The first time I heard about George M. Steinbrenner III, Red Smith was referring to "George III," the king who let the Colonies get away. Then Bill Nack in *Newday* began referring to "Hair Steinbrenner," a play on Steinbrenner's Teutonic grimness and his fetish for GI-Joe haircuts for his players.

The first time I met Steinbrenner was in 1976, when I was assigned to write a cityside feature about the rich and famous who had been invited to watch the World Series game from Steinbrenner's private box. John V. Lindsay here, Joe DiMaggio there, Gay Talese over there.

On the eve of his first game as a World Series host, Steinbrenner was quite charming for most of the interview, but for some reason or other, he suddenly summoned his stadium manager.

"Goddammit, get me Kelly," Steinbrenner shrieked. All work—indeed, all breathing—ceased in the office until Kelly was located, somewhere in the big ballpark, supervising a thousand details. Steinbrenner then proceeded to threaten the man with being fired if the problem was not solved immediately. I had heard that Steinbrenner bullied his employees, but I could not believe he had done it in front of a stranger, a reporter. Every time I see Kelly trudging around the Stadium, I feel sorry for him.

When I came back to sports, I decided to give everybody the benefit of the doubt while I formed my own impressions. That fall, I was assigned to write a long piece about Steinbrenner after he had eased Dick Howser out of his managing job. I tried to observe Steinbrenner at the Howser press conference, but was kept outside the doors because it was an invitation-only press conference. I had never heard of such a thing in sports, but Steinbrenner frequently chooses which journalists to admit.

When I finally reached him on the telephone, Steinbrenner said, "Gee, take it easy on me, will you? My wife is pretty sick right now, and a bad article could really hurt her." I probably held back an adjective or two in my subsequent story, just to be kind. A few months later, reading Dick Schaap's book on Steinbrenner, I learned that the Boss often uses a sick relative to ask for sympathy.

After I became a columnist, Billy Martin verbally abused a pretty young researcher from *The New York Times* who had been given a press pass to the Yankee clubhouse. I wrote that the real problem was not Martin himself but the owner's pathological need to bring Martin back. Steinbrenner has admitted to me that he knows "Billy has a problem," but he cannot stay away from the man. So who's got the problem?

I concluded by saying that one of Steinbrenner's main problems is that he is not a New Yorker. He loves the glamour, the gawking on the streets, the rush from rubbing elbows with business tycoons and cardinals and entertainers, but he does not have the leavening sense of humor, the sentimental street smarts, of a New Yorker. He was really a visitor from Cleveland who now lived in Tampa, I wrote, and he should sell the Yankees and get out of town. A nice, reasoned column.

The next day, a group of reporters surrounded Steinbrenner in the corridor of the Stadium. He said he was giving Martin the benefit of the doubt in the case of the female researcher. Steinbrenner then noticed me standing there, and he smiled and he said, "One of the finest journalists in this town wants me to get out of town, and I have always respected him greatly, and I know he has the right to his opinion because of freedom of the press, but I just want you to know I'm not going anywhere."

Son of a bitch, I thought to myself, the man can take a punch. Here was George—the Boss, George III, Hair Steinbrenner—standing up like John Peter Zenger and defending the First Amendment.

I still criticize Steinbrenner whenever he needs it, like last September, when he took the heart out of the Yankees by belittling them in the middle of a pennant race. I cannot conceive of a man having so little respect for, so little understanding of, the talented athletes he acquires, and I have to wonder whether Steinbrenner has some deep-seated need to punish himself. The way I understand it, he was never able to satisfy his father when he was young, so nobody is able to satisfy him now.

But I confess, I've grown accustomed to George. I refer to his name with the same winking patronization as everybody else. I like writing about his temper tantrums, his feuds with his players, his energy, and his endless sense of being right. We can talk easily on the telephone, we gab in the dugout during spring training as if we were pals. I guess I need him as much as he needs me, as much as Frick needed Frack, as much as Punch needed Judy.

I still suspect his loyalty to New York could change in a flash. He stays in a hotel when he visits New York, and he runs the Yankees from his shipping office in Tampa, or from pay phones in airports. Because of his compulsion to control, he never has a real general manager, somebody to take charge, somebody accountable. Everybody quivers, waiting for George to call in.

A certain show-business figure used to be nicknamed Dimes, because he did all his work from pay phones. In today's age of inflation, the Yankees are directed by another man on the run, Quarters Steinbrenner.

I park the car and walk toward the stone facade of Yankee Stadium, where dozens of fans are already gathered by the entrance, waiting for the visiting team. The guard spots my word processor and waves me in before I even shout my number from the Baseball Writers' Association of America—"three-six-nine, writer." Jack Mann, my mentor, used to say that anybody could crash a sports event by carrying a portable typewriter. Security is tougher at the big events these days, but a blunt sense of belonging will get you a long way.

I walk down the steps to the clubhouse level, the inner sanctum, wearing my trench coat and carrying my writing machine—doing the same thing I did twenty-six years ago, covering Opening Day at the Stadium. But the coal miners and the nuns, the politicians and the cops, the people I covered as a "real" reporter—they helped sharpen my perceptions as a sports columnist. I take them wherever I go.

The clubhouse is jammed with more visitors than players. Opening Day brings out anybody with credentials—writers, television crews, radio reporters inserting their microphones into other people's conversations, plus the usual mix of agents, publicists, equipment salesmen, family, friends, and hangers-on. Lou Piniella's father and uncle have just flown up from Tampa to attend his first game as Yankee manager, between Billy Martin terms, one always assumes.

The Yankee players try to function in this Opening Day crush, the younger players peering sideways at the mob, the older players ignoring us as best as they can. We are all part of it, Opening Day, the media crush, New York, New York.

Perhaps because of the Steinbrenner-Martin tensions over the years, my connections with the Yankee players are not very good. I used to get the feeling the established white players kept tabs on which reporters enjoyed talking to Reggie, or maybe I'm paranoid, but I never got very close to the Graig Nettles–Ron Guidry–Piniella axis.

Except for Rich Gossage, the recent Yankees I enjoyed most have been Reggie, Don Baylor, Rudy May, Billy Sample, Bob Watson, Bobby Brown, and Willie Randolph, all of them black. Some reporters find Randolph testy and self-centered, but I've always found him warily friendly, a survivor in this snakepit, a New Yorker with a softening touch of Holly Hill, South Carolina. Plus, I like the pictures of his babies in his locker, the baby shoes dangling from a hanger, the way he rushes home to his family after a game.

"Hey, man, how's it going?" Randolph asks. I'm not sure he knows my name or my paper, but the contact is always there.

"You think Bernard's ever going to play again?" he asks, referring to the injured knee of Bernard King of the Knicks. Willie and I see each other at the Garden several times a winter.

Willie was just named co-captain, along with Ron Guidry. Without making it sound too bitter, he says softly, "They could have done it two years ago." Gotcha, Willie. I steer him toward talking about the old days, Reggie and Thurman, Billy and Looie, all the desperadoes, and he says, "I've seen everything—on and off the field. I've seen things you wouldn't believe."

I'd believe them, all right, but Willie is not about to share them. Just enough to give me the mood. I've got enough for an off-day column on Co-Captain Willie. You always try to keep one in your notebook.

The clubhouse is closed to reporters forty-five minutes before game time, and we all swarm to the press room for old home week. The beat reporters have just spent six weeks covering the Yankees in Florida, which means they all need vacations—and it's only Opening Day.

The Yankees beat might be the toughest one in sports. Late last season, Billy Martin got into a fight with Ed Whitson at the hotel in Baltimore and started banging on Whitson's door, screaming, "I know you're in there, come out and fight some more!" Some of the reporters had rooms in the same wing, and they peeked their heads out the doors and broadcast blow-by-blow, oath-by-oath descriptions to their offices for the next edition. Most baseball writers can file a story and go out to eat, but Yankee writers lead the league in room service. You never know.

Today, every paper has sent a sidebar writer or a columnist, maybe both, and we all congregate in the work room, leaving the dining room to the Opening Day visitors. The beat writers are more at home in the press rooms at Shea and Yankee Stadium than at their papers. It is a standard joke when Murray Chass visits *The Times* to introduce him to the staff.

In the press room, no holds are barred and secrets are few, just like at the police shack or the city-hall press office. Everybody bitches about something—duplicitous news releases, lack of parking passes, the Yankees' perennial lack of a general manager with authority, editors who mangle copy.

We take the elevator to the press box, an apparent afterthought by the architects, steep and cramped, three rows of seats where there is room for only two, all the comfort of a submarine. At rickety Shea Stadium, *The Times* has four seats, and you can wander around and schmooze, the way reporters like to do. Here, our two seats are crammed into the furthest corner, up against a screened television booth. I feel like a hamster.

I visit Bob Sheppard, the cultured and gracious teacher whose august public-address announcements have added dignity to Yankee Stadium since I was a boy. Hearing Bob's voice in the Bronx makes me feel I am in Westminster Abbey. I watch seven innings from our corner of the hamster cage, but when the Yankees go ahead, I take the elevator downstairs to watch the last two innings on television.

"Georgie Boy," says Louie Napoli, the venerable bartender, once a decent club boxer from Brooklyn. Louie and I have worked it out that he was working the press room at Ebbets Field when my father took me to my first game back in 1946. Either he or the late Bill Boylan was the gruff man pushing a soda to me across the bar on that day when I realized you could live your whole life going to ball games.

When I came around to Yankee Stadium in the late fifties, Louie was there. He's worked for the Mets since they started, but this year Louie is being replaced by a new crew at Shea.

"Whaddaya gonna do?" Louie asks. "They didn't give no reasons."

Most of the reporters watch the press-room television as Dave Righetti nails down the victory with two innings of relief.

When the game is over, we rush down the corridor, knowing we will be stopped for five minutes outside the clubhouse, until all the players have arrived from the bullpen. As they clump up the runway, the players turn their heads to the right, perpetually surprised to see a shuffling, milling mass of reporters and television crews. Then the guard bellows, "Show your passes," and we squeeze past him, one at a time. Some of us go, "Moooo."

It is after four o'clock. I have less than two hours to file a column on my theme of not letting New Jersey snag the Yankees.

Somebody told me Righetti is the only Yankee who actually lives in the city. I don't know him very well, except as a nice kid from northern California. He sits at the table in the center of the clubhouse and meets the press after his save. I ask him about the New Jersey rumor.

"I don't think we need to go anywhere. We can draw fans and be successful right here," says Righetti, a bit more strongly than I might have expected.

I ask Righetti about living in the city. He declines to identify his neighborhood, saying, "People know I'm around, but they keep it pretty quiet."

Most of the radio reporters look impatient to change the subject, but I try to keep Righetti on the same theme by saying, "Most of the guys live in New Jersey. . . ."

"I'm sure the Meadowlands would be a nice place to play ball, and New Jersey is definitely family-oriented," Righetti says. "If I had a wife and kids, I'd want to live there."

Most players answer only the question, but Righetti is actually chatting conversationally.

"I looked at Brooklyn and Queens, but it was too much of a hassle to get to the Stadium," he continues. "I drive my own Bronco in the city —I wouldn't want to try to get a cab—and I don't mind the hustle and the bustle. When you get home, you don't just want to take a nap. You want to look around. That's what New York does for me. It gets me up."

At nearly five o'clock in the afternoon, one hour before deadline, the Yankees' star relief pitcher, a kid from San Jose, is willing to talk a bit about how much he loves New York. While Righetti is answering another question, I tap his shoulder and say, "Thanks." In the dark tunnel between clubhouse and press room, the headline comes to me: RIGHETTI SAVES TOLLS, TOO.

UNIONDALE, NEW YORK, APRIL 12

Plaid shirts and polyester, the crowd streams in for the Islanders' playoff game with Washington. This is the home of the best team and finest athletes I ever covered, but it is still a dull suburban arena, with none of the electricity, none of the urban mystique, of Yankee Stadium or Boston Garden or the Forum in Montreal.

From 1980 through 1983, the Islanders willed themselves to four straight Stanley Cups, but playing hockey in the Long Island suburbs was like pitching horseshoes in Kamloops, as far as most New Yorkers were concerned. The Islanders did not penetrate the newspapers, the television, the public consciousness, the way the city teams did. The Islanders could have walked en masse down Broadway and been taken for just another bunch of white guys on vacation.

But I saw them at their best, able to come up with the big goal, the big defensive move, rarely acting spoiled in the locker room afterward. I tried not to show it, in person or in print, but I admired the Islanders more than any team I ever covered.

Having grown up on legends of the Boys of Summer, I always believed the Brooklyn Dodgers were the best team of players and people. Robbie and Campy. Pee Wee and Gil. Skoonj and the Duke. They were the heroes of my childhood, but they were largely dispersed by the time I came along as a reporter.

From my early days in sports, I felt the St. Louis Cardinals, with Bill White, Bob Gibson, Tim McCarver, Curt Flood, and Lou Brock, were the best bunch of players I ever met. The Baltimore Orioles of Frank Robinson and Brooks Robinson were a close second, with their kangaroo court, fining teammates for obscure offenses, loose and human. The old Yankees of the early sixties were a bit too crusty, the Amazing Mets of 1969 a bit too callow, and the other dynasties, the Green Bay Packers and the Boston Celtics, were just teams I covered from time to time.

When I came back to sports in 1980, I came to relish Saturday nights in the winter, driving to the Coliseum in the darkness, listening to Garrison Keillor on American Public Radio, and then arriving at the circular outpost on the tundra, watching the Boys of Winter pull out another one. I would never let my head twitch or my neck flinch when the puck careened crazily in the vital seconds, but the reporter in me knew that the Islanders would find a way to pull it out.

When the Islanders were in trouble, blustery Billy Smith would make a save, arrogant Denis Potvin would rush the puck up the ice and fire it into a corner, cold-eyed Bryan Trottier would elbow somebody in the small of the back and dig out the puck from a tangle of ankles, strapping Clark Gillies would level somebody ("Don't hurt Gillies!" my wife would shout, hockey and the handsome Gillies being two of her few sporting enthusiasms), and the pale, sensitive marksman, Mike Bossy, would flick the winning goal past the goalie's shoulder. The dressing room would smell of liniment and tape, crisp, wintry smells. The coach, Al Arbour, would give his intentionally bland critique, a hint of a smile behind his thick glasses. And the players would change into their fur coats, in a rush for dinner with their wives, but always with time to explain the game. There were some excellent people in that clubhouse —Bob Nystrom, Bob Bourne, Bossy and the Swedes, Anders Kallur and Stefan Persson, and others—a higher ratio than any team I ever covered.

It's all over. The Islanders have been dethroned for two years now, most of the old hands traded or infirm, but I am out looking for an Islanders column, for old times' sake.

Edging my way through the crowd, I spot a security agent, wearing a blue uniform and cap, his back to me, guarding the gate against crashers. I sneak up behind the guard and slip my arm around his waist, rubbing my cheek against his steel-wool sideburns.

"You're doing a good job," I whisper.

Jimmy Hill cocks his head sideways and says, "Georgie!" We exchange the Soul thumb-to-thumb handshake that was big back in the sixties.

Jimmy ran the laundry and did the tailoring for the athletic department of Hofstra College, a few hundred yards from this arena. His laundry, warmed by dryers, smelling of soap, rocking with music, was the hub of my college life from 1956 to 1960. His radio was always turned to WINS, before it became an all-news station. Jimmy was Chuck Berry and Lloyd Price, Jackie Wilson and Sam Cooke, he was Fats Domino and Little Richard to me.

He was not supposed to lend out the new gray T-shirts and the fresh white socks and the cushy white towels and resilient new jocks to anyone but varsity athletes, but for four years he kept me supplied with fresh clothing. He altered my clothes for moderate prices, he watched my valuables, he warned me who the sneak thieves of the locker room were, he shared gossip, and he lent me money when I was short.

In his spare time, Jimmy managed a rock 'n' roll band, waiting for the big break that was sure to come. I arranged for his band to play at a school dance, cool black dudes entertaining the white-bread students, and for a few years Jimmy's band was a fixture around Hofstra.

"If I can ever do anything for you . . ." Jimmy said.

I took him up on it when my car died and I was assigned to cover a woman's golf tournament for *Newsday*. They loved me at the exclusive Creek Club, interviewing socialite golfers, probably in a Hofstra T-shirt, then va-rooming out of the parking lot full of Cadillacs and Lincolns in Jimmy's yellow 1953 Mercury. Jimmy also lent me his car so I could take my co-editor of the yearbook out for a drink. I ended up marrying her.

Nowadays, Jimmy and I keep in touch in the smoky corridor of the Nassau Coliseum, where he moonlights as a security guard. His hair is gray and his teeth need work, and he lost a son in an automobile crash, and he doesn't talk about getting set up in the tailoring business or getting the big break for his band the way he used to. But he is as cheerful as ever.

"I wouldn't be married to Marianne if you hadn't lent me your car that night," I tell Jimmy. "Wouldn't have my job, either."

Which is true. I almost gag when I hear people boast how they made it "on my own." Nobody does it alone.

I think of all the people who gave me a push: Nathan Chalfin, an old Russian immigrant who gave me my first job as a newspaper deliverer, who lovingly called me a "jackass" and made me place the paper safely out of the rain; Irma Rhodes, my English teacher at Jamaica High School, who discovered me, a truculent dropout from the honors program, in the "general" classes and made me read my essays out loud in class; Dick Gordon, the Fox, the sports publicist who hired me at Hofstra; everybody who encouraged me at *Newsday;* all the people who protected me at *The Times;* and Jimmy Hill, whose laundry was my den, my hideaway, my refuge, for four years of college.

Jimmy's eyes keep darting toward the gate for crashers. I check my watch and discover it is almost game time. We've gone over the past, the good old days in the laundry. Now we've got to get to work.

FLUSHING, APRIL 14

Waiting around the press room at Shea Stadium for the home opener to begin, Frank Cashen walks up to me and says, "You know, I was just thinking about your father, how much he loved being here."

The general manager of the Mets is the only sports executive who ever lent me a Lawrence Durrell book about Cyprus, or any book, for that matter. We've had some lunches and some beers, and I like him a lot—he was a sports journalist until he went straight—but he usually hides his feelings behind a breezy facade.

"I'm not just saying that," Cashen adds, speaking softly so no other writers can hear this side of him. "Your dad was a great guy. He got such a kick out of being at the ballpark. He really loved Opening Day."

I thank Cashen for his nice words, and he waves his hands, having used up half a season of sentiment.

He leaves me with memories of Pop. These are Pop's colleagues, Pop's cronies, all around me, gabbing away the hour before the game. I'm glad to see Dick Young and Jack Lang, the Don Quixote and Sancho Panza of the Mets' press corps, who still provide me with an older generation.

Lang is a chunky man in his early sixties, with boyish nervous energy. He has been the secretary-treasurer of the Baseball Writers' Association of America for many years, deciding who gets writers' cards, chartering the writers' flights at World Series time until the airlines' mileage plans put his charter out of business.

"Captain Jack," I call him.

"Doctor," he greets me.

We go back to late nights in Milwaukee and St. Louis, watching Casey Stengel filibustering for hours on end, drinking anything put in his hand, calling everybody "Doctor." Now we are all "Doctor" to each other, like a fraternity handshake.

When Captain Jack was working for the *Long Island Press* in the Mets' first season, the club was reluctant to keep negative statistics. If you wanted to know the number of vagabonds given a tryout at third base, you shouted over to Jack to take out his little black notebook: "Hey, Jack, I need some neggies."

When I see Dick Young in the press box, I can remember my father coming home from his wartime job at the *Daily News*, telling my mother, "They're putting Dick Young on the Dodgers." My father knew that when all the reporters came back from service, his job at the *News* would be in jeopardy, but my father admired the brash man nearly ten years his junior.

Dick became a great baseball reporter, the first New York writer to haunt the clubhouse, to report what the players and the managers and the owners were saying. His pithy leads drew readers out of their homes on soft summer nights, down to the local candy store for the first edition of the *Daily News*.

"Geez, did you read Dick Young?" people would ask. "Listen to this:

'The tree that grew in Brooklyn is an apple tree.' " In Dick Young's language, that meant the Dodgers were choking in the clutch, feeling the apple in their throats.

My father got another job, at the Associated Press, but he continued to moonlight at the *Daily News*. Sometimes he would take me there, past the giant globe in the lobby, to visit the sports department, introduce me around. And when I was seventeen, my father got me a job as a copy boy in the *Daily News* sports department.

One of the few compensations, besides the forty dollars a week, was spotting Young on his irregular visits to the office, in bright-checked jackets, a cigar jutting from the side of his mouth, his voice as cutting as a crow's. I would think up questions about Reese's ankle or Robinson's knee, and he treated me like a mensch rather than the subhuman species known as copy boy.

When I first started coming around as a young reporter for *Newsday*, Dick would introduce me to the biggest names in the business, sometimes adding, "You've got a nice old man."

Long moved over from the *Daily News* to the *Post*, Dick writes about "My America" these days, spreading his and Rupert Murdoch's cynically reactionary philosophy that organized labor is corrupt, that drug addicts are evil, that there can be no change in people's hearts, no shadings, no subtleties.

We are rival columnists and sometimes we attack each other's positions, but whenever we meet, we pat each other on the back and call each other "Doctor." If the young reporters want to think of Dick as the last angry dinosaur, I see him as a faded giant, a friend, a reminder that my father was in this press room only two seasons ago.

I can still see my father in his final season of 1984, long retired but still calling in Met stories for the AP, emaciated and weak, his clothes too big on him, his nose and his glasses and his white moustache dominating the wrinkled shell of his face, the way people look when they are dying.

I think of the hot night in his last summer, the game long over, papers all over the country jangling for the box score, Pop unable to locate a crucial putout or base hit. The more he searched, the later it got, the more jumbled the score sheet became. I didn't want to shatter Pop's dignity as he worked, small and lost in the dark midnight, so I waited quietly until he found the missing statistic and recited the box score over the phone. Then I drove him home.

Pop loved to work. He was happiest with his glasses on his forehead, his shirtsleeves rolled up, arranging words and figures. One time he was driving us back from a vacation in upstate New York, seven of us jammed into an old jalopy, and we saw the lights of the city from the Taconic Parkway and he muttered, "Back to the hellhole," but I did not believe him. He was never very comfortable away from a newsstand and the subway and the ball game on the radio.

He had started to work when he was fifteen, when his adoptive father slipped out the back door. He always had a job, right through the Depression, first with an insurance company and then as a reporter at the *Long Island Press*. I often wondered what kind of writer Pop might have been if the scab had not slinked into Pop's chair while Pop was on the picket line. It was hard to tell from a few clippings about the amateur sports on Long Island in the late thirties. Pop always told the story on himself, how he had advised a young shortstop from Brooklyn to become a jockey or something else befitting a small man. Little fellow named Rizzuto.

Part of my image of Pop was from his physical condition, balding, glasses, wisps of gray hair on his forehead by his midthirties, short and stocky, a truss bulging across a massive hernia that he would not have fixed for many years. Pop did not run or swim, although he did teach me to hold a bat and shoot a two-handed set shot.

Fathers were older then; they did not run around in sneakers and sweat suits the way they do today. Once I was surprised to discover a pair of baseball spikes in his closet, and he told me he had been a pretty fair baseball player in his earlier days. I guess I thought he had been born old.

Not many years ago, my mother uncovered a photograph of my father in his midtwenties, with a full head of hair and a proud, defiant, handsome face, with a slightly wistful look in his eyes, like Kirk Douglas playing the businessman who can never quite forget the poverty of his childhood. I was stunned to see that my father had been more rugged-looking, more handsome, than I would ever be. But that was in his early days, before the union business, before he became a deskman, before the troubles.

After the Guild strike, Pop struggled to make money. I remember driving around the open spaces of eastern Queens with him while he delivered mail. During the blackouts, lights out, shades drawn, he was gone on a publicity job with Pepsi-Cola, taking a long train trip across the country, stopping in towns that would always have a magical sound when he said them—Reno, Frisco, Sacramento, L.A. When I started traveling to California, I would tell him, "Pop, nobody out there calls it 'Frisco.' They hate that word." But he persisted in calling it Frisco, like in one of those old movies he loved. He could tell you who played every role in every movie ever made. Sometimes when I am working on my column, I think to myself, Damn, Pop would know that, wishing I could call him to pick his brains. My mother says she finds herself thinking the same thing.

For as long as I can remember, there was enough money for food and clothing and sometimes a modest cabin near a lake, but there was also a vague mystery, a sadness, a tension, about money in our household. I attributed it to my parents raising five children on a newspaperman's salary.

When I was little, Pop worked the overnight shift, coming home at dawn carrying the *News,* the *Tribune,* a couple of afternoon papers, dropping a few penny chocolates he had bought in the subway vending machines. Then he would wander off to sleep, having enchanted me with the world out there of newspapers and subways and candy machines.

When I was a teenager, Pop worked the evening shift, but sometimes he would come home at dawn and stumble up the stairs to sleep on an extra bed in the attic, in my room. I could hear him emptying his pockets, taking off his clothes, falling onto the other bed. As I dressed for school, he would open his eyes and push a couple of quarters at me, lunch money for a hungry adolescent, muttering, "I'm sorry there isn't more."

Sometimes he would moan in his sleep, waking me with his cries of "No, no, no."

When my father first got copy-boy jobs for me, I could tell he was respected for his professionalism, liked for his sense of humor, and treated gingerly for his sharp tongue. Sometimes I would see him talking with people I instinctively did not like, seedy men with furtive eyes who huddled together in secret conversations, who met in the back rooms and played cards on lunch hours, who hunched over the sports wire looking for scores and race results.

Sometimes when he came home at night, my father's pockets were filled with score sheets from hundreds of gin-rummy hands. Once, in the Associated Press, he pointed out a grubby-looking man and whispered to me, "Don't ever play cards with him," which seemed like a strange thing to say, because I had no plans to play cards with that man, or anybody.

In those days I never mentioned these signs of gambling to my father, or brought it up to my mother. People did not talk about those kinds of things.

When I was seventeen, the phone calls began.

"Tell your father Joe called," the voice would say.

I could smell the man over the phone, could smell his hair oil and his cigars and his ugliness.

The next time the man called, I asked him, "Is there a message?"

"Your father has business with us," the man said.

The third time, the man sounded annoyed that my father was not there.

"Where is he?" the man asked.

"None of your business," I told him. "And if you ever call again, I'll kick your ass."

I told my father I had threatened to kick the man's ass. My father said that would not be a very good idea.

By that time, I was working my way through college, pretty much full of myself. If my father wanted to keep doing business with the bad people, that was his business. That's how I looked at it. But the men continued to call until the family secret finally came out. My father had run up thousands of dollars of debts to loan sharks, had lost thousands of other dollars over the years. My father and mother took out legal loans wherever they could arrange them in order to pay off the brusque men on the other end of the telephone. And my father began to attend meetings of Gamblers Anonymous.

I was angry and did not want to know about Gamblers Anonymous, their meetings and their family support system and their successes. My mother asked me to go to a meeting with my father, but my position was simple: "He got himself into it; he can get himself out." Other members of the family did give him support, did go to meetings with him, did encourage him, day by day. I was too busy with my bitterness, my own life.

One day when I was twenty-five, already a baseball writer, already ahead of him in my way of looking at things, my father dropped over to my house one afternoon while my wife was at work.

He took off his glasses and sat back on the sofa and started telling me about his life. He said he was sure his troubles went back to his early years in the orphanage, being dressed up and put on display for prospective parents, finally being adopted by the Hungarian couple, the Vecseys, then later seeing his adoptive father disappear.

He felt better about himself now, he said, and he wanted me to know that. There were no tears, no emotions, that was not my father's way, but I saw him lying on the sofa, a happier man, a relieved man. Those meetings at Gamblers Anonymous had given him a purpose, a pride, I had never seen before.

In 1981, while going through the Meadows for my research on Bob Welch's book, I realized how badly I had failed my father when he needed me. I saw how important it is for family members to support a person battling addiction.

As soon as I got home from that trip, I rushed over to see my father, and told him I loved him and respected him greatly for gaining control of his life. He waved off my apology, said it wasn't necessary, that he knew how I felt. He was never comfortable with emotions, with talking about himself. He once told me, "I know if I get started, I won't be able to stop."

I have often wondered how much gambling affected my father's view of journalism. Did the fears and sadnesses that led him to bet extravagantly on horses and athletes and gin rummy make him see sports with a gambler's impatience, the desire for results, rather than with a writer's interest in technique or strategy or personality?

My problem with gambling continues to this day. I cannot help feeling that people who gamble, who play poker late at night, who frequent elegant casinos, who bet on horses, who stop off at the candy store and buy their daily lottery tickets, are lacking some inner peace, some self-confidence, some satisfaction with the rest of their lives. I see people on line at the track, and they seem to be a vision straight from Hieron-ymus Bosch. I cannot believe that television executives who call them-selves journalists hire people like Jimmy the Greek, who talk about odds rather than news developments. I find it grubby that newspapers run columns that focus on gambling odds rather than the events themselves.

When I cover racing, I am bemused at seeing racing writers betting on races they cover, some of them sweating and shouting as the horses approach the finish line, some of them cursing jockeys and trainers for costing them money. I understand that much of racing is about bet-ting, but I'm not comfortable seeing journalists handling thick wads of money on company time. I don't think drama critics are allowed to in-vest in the plays they cover, and there are increasingly tight regula-tions for journalists who cover the stock market. What's different about racing?

Thanks to Gamblers Anonymous and my father's courage, he was unshackled from the gambler's view of the world. In his late sixties and early seventies, after his official retirement, my father began filing sto-ries from the ballpark. He was free to be a writer, to find the right word, the right detail, the right quote, from something that had just happened in front of him. He also had to deal with athletes as real human beings, not as myths and abstract figures whose names clattered across the wire in somebody's else's stories.

The observant Frank Cashen could see the smile on my father's face as he stood around the batting cage before a game, thrilled to be out of the office after nearly forty years, trying to discover in some belated way what he might have been.

Pop had his share of successes as an Associated Press stringer, but nothing to match the taming of Dave Kingman, a brooding loner who hit 442 home runs but had far fewer friends and admirers.

One day I went to Shea and saw my father chatting comfortably with Kingman at the batting cage. Not only that, but when it was Kingman's turn to hit, he told my father, "Excuse me, I'll be right back." He belted four or five pitches toward Flushing Bay, and then resumed the inter-view. The rest of us kept our distance—and gaped.

"Pop, how did you do that?" I asked him later.

"Maybe he felt sorry for me because I'm an old man," Pop said. "Who cares? I got a story."

After a few good years around the ballpark, my father became ill. In

November of 1984, knowing there would not be another baseball season, we threw a seventy-fifth birthday party at our house, surrounded by family and friends and colleagues. Millie Morabito told how Pop used to fling telephones into wastepaper baskets, and Charlie Morey told how Pop used to kick chairs. Withered and slight, Pop flexed his arms to let us know he was proud of every telephone he ever threw, every wise guy he ever set straight.

That party took his last bit of strength. He went home to bed and never came downstairs again. On Thanksgiving Night, a few of his granddaughters dropped by to say hello. Pop looked up at their solicitous faces and he snapped, "What is this, a death watch?" My daughter Corinna thought he was a howl, even in his final hours.

After the girls had left, he settled down for a nap. Just before closing his eyes, he asked me, "Leave the papers by the bed, would you?" Not a bad last line for an old newspaperman.

The baseball seasons go on without Pop. Today, the Mets kick away their home opener to the Cardinals, 6–2, not a very promising beginning for Dwight Gooden. I tend to think Pop would have thrown a telephone, or at least kicked a chair.

Dick Young died late in the 1987 season, and Jack Lang retired from the Daily News *after that season. The* Post, *unloaded by Rupert Murdoch, and the* News *stagger onward, in a death grip that only one of them seems likely to survive.*

In January of 1988, CBS sacked Jimmy the Greek for making dumb comments on how black athletes were so superior that the only jobs left for whites were in management.

PORT WASHINGTON, APRIL 28

"Why are you smiling?" Marianne wants to know.

She has caught me smiling at my own idea, a character flaw of a sports columnist who works at home.

I have been up early, chopping wood behind the house, thinking about what I am going to write today. Last night the Rangers stunned everybody by winning the series against Washington, as Lucky Pierre scored two goals. Larouche has been talking about the *"petit miracle,"* but last night when I rushed into the locker room afterward, he winked at me and said, *"Ça n'est pas petit."* It made a good headline in the late editions: NOT 'PETIT' ANYMORE.

Madison Square Garden has been as vibrant as any arena I have ever seen, with rabid fans caught up in the sheer surprise of the Rangers' victories. The press box is directly behind one of the goals, about ten rows up. Sometimes a wayward shot comes screaming over the glass partition, making it foolhardy to take your eyes off the game.

All around us are the same fans, game after game—Sid-the-Lawyer-from-Queens; Herbie Mann, the jazz flutist, in his season box; the cretin who shouts at enemy goalies, "Hey, get a Porsche," a vicious reference to the high-speed death of Pelle Lindbergh last fall; and Rob Ingraham, the sports businessman who sometimes brings his childhood pal Patti Lupone to the game. Patti likes to press her mobile features against the glass and make faces at some of her friends on the ice.

What makes the Garden so vital? It is not just witless fan noise, but the selective, verbal soul of the big city—the creative and hard-driving people in the expensive seats, the hardy, cynical survivors who chant their vulgar slogans up in the blue seats. (I once sat in the upper press box and asked a few fans in front of me stop smoking. It's against the law, I said. They flashed police and fireman badges at me and told me to shut the fuck up. My town.)

But I have written enough about the excitement in the Garden, enough about miracles and upsets. I want to write something new and different about this preposterous event. And nothing is more preposterous than the return of Lucky Pierre.

While I was chopping wood, I kept thinking about how he did not let his will get broken when Craig Patrick and Ted Sator banished him to Hershey, Pennsylvania. *Sports Illustrated* cajoled Pierre into wearing a full tuxedo and posing alongside a wooden fence with a cow grazing in the background—Lucky Pierre in Chocolate Town.

Then my mind asked the question: How did Lucky Pierre spend his nights of exile in Hershey? I conjured up the image of the temperamental scorer practicing in his seedy hotel room, flicking puck after puck against his mattress propped in the corner, muttering Gallic imprecations to himself.

I could see him sitting around the humble little motel office regaling the desk clerk with tales of the old days, a Napoleon dedicated to another campaign. I kept chopping wood until I had it all worked out in my mind. Then I sat down at the machine and Marianne caught me giggling.

Coming from the Chipmunk Ashcan Realism School of Sports Journalism, I have found it hard to develop a light touch as a sports columnist. In the sixties, there were so many serious issues that it seemed almost immoral to be flippant or funny. Then ten years watching coal miners die, covering Nixon's America—not a lot of laughs there.

When I started writing the sports column, I realized I had never enjoyed the chatty, smile-over-breakfast, good-old-boy style of sports columnists. My first mission was to talk about the subjects I thought were important—race, drugs, women's sports, labor issues, recreational sports, cheating at the colleges. One of the greatest talents in sports journalism has confided to friends that he finds my work "preachy" at times, and I guess he's right.

Recently, I have tried to keep the preachiness to a minimum. Two columnists I feel close to are Ellen Goodman in the *Boston Globe* and Colman McCarthy in the *Washington Post*. Nobody covers trials and hearings better than the dean, Murray Kempton. The ultimate goal would be to approach Russell Baker, who wrote the single best column I ever read. Back in the seventies, when Craig Claiborne gushed in *The Times* about a two-thousand-dollar boondoggle meal he had taken in France, Baker responded with a column about beans and ketchup and hot dogs and mayonnaise, dinner at Chez Baker. Ever since then, I have not been able to take French cuisine quite so seriously.

Trying to develop my own voice, I began to write about a mythical college called Sunbelt State, a stand-in for all the abuses of college sports—timid college presidents, devious coaches, crooked boosters, dishonest recruiters, ignorant players.

From a formula like Sunbelt State, I began to trust myself to find new voices when I wanted to comment on something. We all have voices and visions buzzing in our ears, but I am convinced that our educational system, with its tests and its SAT scores, discourages us from recognizing them.

My wife still has not gotten over a grade-school principal saying, "Mrs. Vecsey, the other art teacher's students all make the same thing at Halloween. Why do your students all make different things?" Nobody had ever told him it was all right to be creative.

I've been struggling to hear those voices. Last year the Yankees were giving a day to Phil Rizzuto, retiring his number, partially to console him over not making the Hall of Fame. I found myself wondering how Phil himself would describe the event:

"Anyway, they've having this day for the little guy from New Jersey on account of. . . . Wait a minute, thank you, Frank Messer, but it's not his birthday. His birthday isn't until September twenty-fifth. Nineteen eighteen. That makes him, don't tell me, he'll be, well, it's pretty close to seventy, I bet."

After sketching Rizzuto's convoluted speech patterns, I went to the ceremony on Sunday to capture the details, which would include Rizzuto being knocked over by a real live "holy cow." Friends and colleagues liked the column, which reinforced my confidence in trying to be funny.

Today's column on Lucky Pierre is written from the point of view of the room clerk at the mythical Candy Kisses Motel back in Hershey, with the clerk describing how Larouche spent his exile, on a diet of chocolate.

"He carried his hockey stick with him everywhere," the desk clerk recalls. "We thought it was a little weird, but after a while we realized, a doctor always carries a stethoscope in the jacket pocket, a writer always carries a pad and pen, so an *artiste* like Mr. Larouche should carry his stick with him."

At the end, the interrogator suggests that Larouche's exile room be turned into a shrine, the way the Russians did with Lenin's old room number 107 at the National Hotel in Moscow.

"Gulf and Western has already reserved that room for a year. They say they've got some executives they're sending down for the Pierre Larouche treatment," the desk clerk says, my way of twitting the Rangers for keeping Pierre down on the farm.

The editors at the paper have commissioned Gary Zamchick, an artist, to draw a cartoon of a player flicking pucks at a mattress. I guess it's understandable why I have a soft spot for the bad little children of sports. To be a sports columnist, you have to rediscover the bad little child within yourself.

MAY

MONTREAL, MAY 9

You can only do something for the first time once. After that, whatever else it is, it is not the first time. Your first kiss. The first time you drive a car all by yourself, pull away from the curb, in charge of your own life. The first time in Paris, crossing the Seine, knowing they didn't exaggerate, all of them who wrote and sang about Paris. Painting your new living room late at night, the radio on, hearing Victoria de los Angeles sing *Songs from the Auvergne.* Being twenty-five and discovering cassoulet in a little French bistro off Ninth Avenue. Waiting in town for two hours for the first edition of *The Times* with your first byline.

Two years ago, it was a little like that for me in Montreal.

I've been coming to Montreal since 1969, for the Expos' first game in Jarry Park, where the paint was still drying at game time. I came back that summer for a Mets' weekend, while astronauts were walking on the moon. And that September I heard New York Giants fans chanting *"Bon soir,* Allie," at their beleaguered coach, Allie Sherman, as the Giants lost an exhibition game.

But somehow I never visited the Forum until the spring of 1984. It was always there, waiting for me. A gentleman named Camil DesRoches, nearly seventy, with a fine Gallic mustache, who has worked as a publicist in the Forum for nearly half a century, escorted me on my first tour. DesRoches showed me where Howie Morenz had lain in state after his death from an injury in 1937. Then DesRoches escorted me to the Canadiens' clubhouse, where the World War I poem by Dr. John McCrae, "In Flanders Fields," is inscribed in English on one wall, in French on the other.

Then DesRoches took me for lunch in the Forum restaurant, *vin rouge, mais oui.* I did not tell him he reminded me of my father.

"I always say that hockey is like a religion here in Quebec," he told me. "We are perhaps ninety percent Catholic, but we are all hockey fans."

From the moment I stepped into the Forum, it was in the highest level of my universe—like getting off the elevated on a steamy July noon, climbing to the bleachers in Wrigley Field; crossing Causeway Street on a dank winter evening for a Celtics game in Boston Garden; watching Johnny Unitas lumber onto the field in homey Memorial Stadium, until somebody named Robert Irsay moved the Colts out of Baltimore; sitting in the tenth row of a delightful little candy box of a soccer stadium in Barcelona; watching the Tour de France whiz through the countryside.

To be in the Forum is to feel the unity of a people, to appreciate the color and manners and history of one province, one team, one sport.

The two escalators in the lobby are crossed, like two hockey sticks artistically arranged. The three tiers of stands are colored red, white, and blue, a perfect Gallic tricolor.

I would never say the Yankees should always be in the World Series. I believe it would be good for somebody other than the Celtics and the Lakers to win the basketball championship. Even though I never met an Australian I didn't like, it is good that the Aussies no longer win the Davis Cup all the time. I never was comfortable with the conceit of the Dallas Cowboys as America's Team. Who started that?

However, I honestly feel the Montreal Canadiens should always be seeded into the Stanley Cup finals. Let the Oilers and the Islanders and the Flyers, whoever, fight it out for the other finalist spot, and send them to the Forum for a crack at *Les Habitants*.

In actuality, the Canadiens have not won the Stanley Cup since 1979, but they are on their way to the finals. Pierre Larouche was the first to know it. The minute he walked into the Forum for the eastern finals, he knew exactly what the Rangers were up against—"The Rocket and the Flower, more than five skaters against you."

Pierre wasn't exactly packing it in; he just knew in his *Quebecois* heart that it wouldn't just be his old teammate Bob Gainey clamping on to him, it would be *les anciens*, Maurice Richard and Guy Lafleur, whisking around on the ice.

Tonight the Rangers are down, three games to one. The cretins in the Garden booed "O Canada" on Wednesday night, making Montreal fans eager for revenge tonight. It is a gorgeous early spring in Montreal, and I wouldn't have missed this for the world.

When the American anthem is played, the fans boo lustily, drowning out the organ. My friend Camil DesRoches, who loves New York second only to Montreal, walks through the press box, looking ashen.

"I have never seen anything like this in my forty-eight years," he says.

The Canadiens demolish the Rangers, 3–1, a just payback for loutish New Yorkers who do not know the difference between supporting their home team and insulting a good neighbor to the north. When the game is over, Pierre Larouche, who has not scored in five games, skates last on the reception line, hugging and congratulating the Canadiens.

Afterward, I visit the Ranger locker room. Craig Patrick turns his head and stares at the wall rather than notice me. After my Larouche columns, I can't say I blame him. Ted Sator, who looks like David Letterman without the twinkle in his eye, strides through the locker room.

"Good season, Coach," I say, but he keeps walking. Can't say I blame him, either. The Candy Kisses Motel column had to be embarrassing to the Ranger officials, perhaps even jeopardizing their jobs. It's what we do.

With fans honking horns on Rue Ste.-Catherine, Mike Farber of the *Gazette* and Eddie Swift of *Sports Illustrated* and I repair to a bistro on Peel Street, French and English swirling around us. Journalists never win the Stanley Cup, but we get to go to the Forum in early spring. Close.

PORT WASHINGTON, MAY 10

"Hey, Pop," my oldest daughter begins. "Know anybody on the Albany papers?"

Laura has been working as the press aide for May Newburger, one of the best legislators in New York State, but May has decided not to run again. Bad for us in May's district, and particularly bad for Laura, who has friends in Albany and wants to stay.

"Got to get back on the beat, Pop."

The family sickness, rearing its ugly head again. My father and my mother. Peter and I. And now my three children, all leaning toward journalism. Laura has worked in public relations, in government, she is a poet, and she could certainly teach. She has also worked as a janitor and as an editor of a low-budget chain of weeklies—more or less the same job, actually.

She never felt better than when she was a part-time clerk, or what they call a "casual," at the *New York Post,* the brutal hours, the raffish company, the gallows humor, the sudden crises, the blend of boredom and reality, all appealed to Laura the same way they appealed to me and most of the family.

"I miss the business," Laura says.

"Call Clemente," I say.

Clemente. When Laura was little, I used to take her to the *Newsday* sports department while I picked up my check or dropped off a story. I would plop her at my desk, give her a pencil and copy paper—in the old days we used pencils and copy paper—and tell her to create something.

While I was busy, a man with the handsome Latin looks of a Ricky Ricardo would walk over to my desk and inspect the newcomer.

"You little brat!" he would snarl. "But you write better than your old man!"

That was Dick Clemente, one of the survivors of the early years, who had grown from covering bowling and stock-car races into covering the football Giants. Clemente was not a great writer, but he worked like a pack mule, and had the ferocious loyalty of a junkyard dog.

He had tried to bully me when I was a seventeen-year-old taking high-school games over the phone. I laughed at him and said I would plant him on the copy spike. We became friends. His favorite expression, which he used on the average of once a minute, was "You know what I always say—fuck 'em!" I went through four years of college imitating Clemente.

In addition to frightening little children, Clemente liked to poke his head into the style department and tell lovely Penny, lovely Nadine, lovely Aurelie, how beautiful they all were. George Usher and I knew that if we talked like that, we would get our faces slapped.

While the rest of the world was home, washing the dishes, watching *Gunsmoke* on the tube, putting the 2.5 suburban babies to sleep, we worked in an isolated office, made all the sadder once the style reporters had gone home. We sent out to the diner for greasy cheeseburgers and salty french fries, and we waited for baseball games to end in California.

When the going got slow around midnight, Clemente would rise from his desk and snap his elastic belt for effect.

"Ready for a game?" he would ask. "Ready for a game of glue-pot roulette?"

This was in the old days, before computers, when newspapers used massive amounts of paper. The excess paper was stuffed in large cardboard barrels placed strategically around the office. We also used massive amounts of glue, which were stored in glass jars about the size of a pickle jar.

The code said I could not refuse the challenge to play glue-pot roulette. Clemente would tamp down the paper in the cardboard barrel, making sure there was a soft base. Then he would grip a glue pot in his right hand and take three steps back from the barrel. With a nice, soft toss, Bill Sharman on the foul line, he would toss the glue pot neatly into the center of the barrel.

"Your turn," he would say, snapping his elastic belt.

Inevitably, I would feel a weakening in my knees, a shortness of breath, I would start giggling at Clemente's ferocious intensity, and I would choke up. My shot would hit the outside of the basket and crash to the floor, breaking into shards of glass and globs of glue. Loser cleaned up, you understand.

Loser cleaned up quickly, too, before a giant maintenance man named Duke Wellington made his rounds. Duke was our pal, who came around to see if Willie Mays had gotten any hits that night, but Duke was not so much our pal that he would tolerate glue and glass on his floor. It was nights like these that taught me to love the high calling of journalism.

Many years later, Clemente made an odyssey to Albany, where he works on the sports desk. Once you have looked into a man's eyes in glue-pot roulette, you are always *amigos*.

"Call Clemente," I tell Laura.

A few hours later, she calls me back.

"Clemente gave me the name of a guy on the *Times-Union*. I've got an appointment tomorrow. I've got a feeling I'm back on the beat."

"How's Clemente?"

"He said I'm still a little brat."

NEW YORK, MAY 12

Sitting in court this morning, listening to prospective jurors explain why they did not have months of their lives to give to the United States Football League, I tried to justify for spring football. Employment for football players? Fair enough. Something else on television? Let 'em watch soap operas. Mileage on my frequent-flyer plans? Selfish.

Then I realized that the best reason for the new league was making a national celebrity out of Donald Trump. Up until then, Donald had merely been a brash young builder, putting up glitzy buildings and trying to muscle elderly people out of rent-controlled apartments. Once Donald purchased the New Jersey Generals, he had access to the back page of the *Post* and the *News*.

I'd much rather have publicity-conscious club owners like Donald—or even George Steinbrenner—than conglomerates like Gulf and Western, which throttle the fun and individuality of sports by making decisions based on accountants you never met and executives you never saw because they were in Europe or on the other coast. Where have you gone, Horace Stoneham?

Donald, who grew up in the same part of Queens that I did, is a true rogue New Yorker. Just watch him slouch around with his long hair and his elegant topcoat; he's not a preppie or a yuppie. He walks like a kid from Queens, head forward, shoulders hunched, ready for anything that comes along—dogshit on the sidewalk, street gangs, pigeons, truant officers, a city block for sale, somebody to evict. Whatever.

The best thing about Donald is his beautiful wife, Ivana, a bright and determined woman of Czech heritage, definitely a civilizing influence on Donald.

What a glorious time it was when Donald burst upon the sports scene. It did not matter in the slightest that Doug Flutie was not a prospect as a professional quarterback. What mattered was that Flutie was an appealing little guy, fresh from his Heisman Trophy season with Boston College.

Donald signed him for a huge amount of money, and held the ceremony in the atrium of his own Trump Tower, attended by every television crew on the island of Manhattan. There was no room for reporters, so Dick Young had to stage a screaming fit before they sat him right up on the dais, practically on Donald's lap. They tried to sedate Walt Michaels, the coach of the Generals, with an elephant stun gun, but the poor devil broke into the press conference, brandishing the Generals' playbook and screaming, "You gotta know the plays!" like a demented street preacher. Improvisational theater, right in the atrium.

Now, the league has gone to court, claiming the leaders of the National Football League conspired to keep lucrative television contracts away from it. Why wouldn't they?

Today I went to the first day of the trial and interviewed the earnest USFL attorneys about why the league should survive. I tried not to laugh. Lord knows we don't need more football, but I have a feeling we haven't heard the last of this Donald Trump.

PORT WASHINGTON, MAY 15

Ira Berkow's biography of Red Smith arrived in the mail last week. I circled the book for a few days before finally opening it, to learn more about the man regarded as the greatest sports columnist of his time.

It has been four years since Red died and I was named to write the column. When people sometimes praise a column of mine by saying, "Red Smith would have been proud of that one," I know they could not say anything nicer. In truth, I grew up regarding him as yet another fine New York columnist, and I spent my churlish early days in sports thinking of him as a pleasant older man I did not know very well.

When I came back into sports in 1980, I took note that some of the best people who had emerged while I was gone—John Schulian, Tom Callahan, Ira Berkow, Jane Leavy, Mike Lupica—clearly worshiped Red, saw him as something of a mythic figure. Something was going on.

Because journalism is a young person's business, like war and athletics, it is not often that journalists get a chance to grow in their later years. When reporters think they have reached the stage of life where they have something to say, they often run out of energy and patience for following orders, particularly dumb ones, from editors. I know I did.

Columnists have a better chance at growing older gracefully, because they are allowed to use their experience and their point of view. As Ira's book makes clear, Red Smith is one of the rare journalists who matured at an age when other columnists might calcify into stylists. Red's renaissance in his sixties was something I had overlooked, or minimized.

One thing that struck me from Ira's book was that Red was not a New Yorker, that much of his character was formed in Green Bay and South Bend and St. Louis and Philadelphia, working long hours for low pay. The book, entitled *Red*, made me understand Red's attachment to Toots Shor's, the bright lights, the celebrities at the head table. He'd come a long way from St. Louis, and now he got to drink with Joe DiMaggio.

The perception of Red as not a New Yorker reminded me of my own taste in sports columnists when I was a schoolyard kid in Queens. Our teachers were always holding up Arthur Daley's columns in *The Times* as an example of sportswriting, but I was never excited by his fond columns about Frankie Frisch and other legends. Red Smith in the *Tribune* often seemed to be writing about fishing and horse racing rather than coming up with quotes from the locker room.

In junior high school, we would stop for an egg cream on Queens Boulevard and thrill to Jimmy Cannon's latest streetcorner analysis. ("You're Leo Durocher, and you've been dealt a straight flush . . ." sounds like something Jimmy would have written.) Dick Young used clubhouse lingo like "ribbies" and nicknames like "Skoonj." Milton Gross rode home in a car with Don Newcombe after another bitter World Series failure. Real stuff.

The new face in the early sixties was Bob Lipsyte, hanging around city playgrounds and suburban tennis courts, listening to racial and labor complaints from jockeys and boxers, dragging *The Times* sports section forward fifty years nearly by himself.

Lipsyte began sharing *The Times* column with Arthur Daley, a lovely man who had batted out six columns a week for decades. Having enough trouble filling four columns a week, I would find it hard to criticize how Red and Arthur filled six a week—but the rules were different for columnists in the forties and fifties:

Baseball was the absolute king, and a columnist could go to spring training for six weeks and file breezy, anecdotal columns every day, without being expected to rush off to the Final Four in Albuquerque, a hot Stanley Cup final in Edmonton, or the pro basketball finals between Boston and Los Angeles. The issues were lighter, and expectations from sports editors and higher-ups were minimal. You could call them the good old days, or you could call them ancient history. Need a column? DiMag. Sunny Jim Fitzsimmons. Ben Hogan. Stan the Man. The Babe.

Writing six a week must have been brutal, but it was made slightly easier in the era of day baseball, when a columnist could sit in the dugout and chat with managers like Danny Murtaugh, Al Lopez, and Casey Stengel. Managers talked comfortably back then, giving the regular reporters a rundown on who was healthy, who was playing well, a synopsis of interesting games and weird plays in recent weeks. However, that familiarity has all been demolished by the tabloid wars and the radio people sticking out their microphones and interrupting every conversation. You go to the ballpark early now and half the managers are hitting fungoes or collecting baseballs behind a screen near second base rather than chatting on the bench. Nobody chats anymore.

When my *Newsday* mentors started breaking me in during the late fifties, a familiar face in the old dugout huddles was Red Smith, eyes twinkling behind his thick glasses, not asking searching questions or demanding special treatment. He just sat there, tossing off a line now and then, one of the pack, and then he toddled back to his typewriter and zipped off a lovely tone poem on the life and times of Casey Stengel, or whoever. He seemed so casual, and his column seemed so light that, as a young lout, I just assumed it was easy.

By the time I came around, Red had his own point of view, and did not feel he needed the daily exposure to the excuses, the tantrums, and the celebrations of the postgame locker room. Given the Chipmunks' preoccupation with quotes, there were times when I thought Red was missing the story, like in 1964, when he and Arthur Daley wrote about the Yankees going down gallantly to the Cardinals in the World Series, while we foot soldiers knew that most of the Yankees were pouting in the trainer's room.

When the sixties began to heat up, I became impatient with both Red and Arthur for persisting in calling Muhammad Ali by what he called his "slave name" of Cassius Clay when people like Lipsyte, Howard Cosell, Bud Collins, and the Chipmunk gang honored his Muslim name. To continue to refer to "Clay" seemed a reactionary statement against the civil-rights and antiwar movements.

Once I got on the circuit as a reporter, my path seemed to cross Jimmy Cannon's more than Red Smith's. Red was a social man, in the center of the World Series party, while Jimmy was not drinking by then, and tended to sit in hotel lobbies, catching your eye as you went out for a walk. Jimmy would talk about Hemingway and Lardner and Runyon, the gangsters he had known, the assignments he had away from sports. Sometimes you might not get your walk at all.

As Ira's book makes poignantly clear to me, Red also had lonely days after his wife, Catherine, died in February of 1967 and the *Herald Tribune*'s successor folded in May of that year. After he moved to *The Times* in 1971, Red began to slash away at the political climate, the new breed of club owners, like the man he called George III. His new energy came partially from the young children of his second wife, Phyllis.

By the late seventies, Red Smith seemed almost like a different columnist—or maybe for some of us it was the old fable about the son thinking the father was growing wiser as the father grew older.

In April of 1976, Red was awarded the Pulitzer Prize. I don't know that he ever knew this, but the editors had asked me to write the letter of recommendation. I praised a man who got wiser as he got older, and I quoted Bob Dylan about "The times, they are a-changing."

(I remember the day the prizes were awarded, but not for anything concerning Red. As a cityside reporter, I was assigned to interview our own Sydney Schanberg, who had won the Pulitzer for his work from

Cambodia. To get him talking, I said something innocuous like, "You must have many strong memories . . . " and Schanberg dissolved into helpless tears. It was only then that I understood the depth of Sydney's pain about the disappearance of his colleague Dith Pran during the holocaust in Cambodia. Dith Pran managed to survive, and later joined *The Times* as a photographer and became a focus of the film *The Killing Fields.*)

When I moved back to sports in 1980, working as the so-called third columnist, I wrote for Saturdays and when Red and Dave went on holiday. It was easy to coordinate with Dave, but Red was a bit more vague. I would ring him up in Connecticut, and he would say, "Oh, I'll knock out a few things this week. . . . Do whatever you feel like. . . . God will provide." He had always been gracious to me, but it must have been threatening, a vision of mortality, to see somebody thirty years younger filling up the space.

In 1981, Tom Callahan, the sports editor at *Time*, who loved Red as much as anybody did, told me, "You know, you really ought to get to know Red. He's not going to be around much longer." It made me stop and realize I had never taken a meal with him, never spent an hour at the bar with him. We just had different friends, different tastes. He was Toots Shor's; others were the Lion's Head; still others were Runyon's; I'm a cappuccino bar on Columbus Avenue.

When Red died on January 15, 1982, my wife asked me if she had ever met him. I said I did not think so. Since *The Times* does not run photographs of its columnists, she had no image of the man behind the byline. But when *The Times* carried his obituary and his photograph on the front page, Marianne exclaimed, "Oh, I know him. Oh, what a nice man!"

"How did you meet him?"

"Remember the Colonial Inn in St. Petersburg?" she said. "While you guys were at the games, this very nice couple used to sit out by the pool. He would talk with all the wives for a while, and then he would go off to a table by himself and write. I never knew his name."

"What made you decide he was nice?" I asked.

"You know how most people are not interested in what wives do? Well, he asked what I did, and he talked for a while about my being a teacher and an artist. He was a gracious man."

At the funeral in St. Patrick's Cathedral, many other people told stories about the graciousness of Red Smith. I was, quite honestly, stunned at the attention Red received, because it seemed in such contrast to his own modest pose as just another "working stiff." At some point, he had been transformed from a craftsman of a sports columnist into something of a national laureate. Sitting in St. Patrick's, I thought for the first time ever about the immensity of replacing Red Smith.

The Times waited a polite ten days or so after the funeral, and then Abe Rosenthal, the executive director, called me into his office.

"It's your job," he said, extending his hand. "You earned it months ago. We were working you into the lineup. Red Smith was a great columnist. We expect you to be one. Don't even think about replacing Red."

After Abe's advice, it was easy for me to keep the emotional distance necessary to develop my own voice. Only now does Ira's book make me realize the passionate concerns behind the graceful prose, the anger when Arthur Daley was the first sports columnist to win a Pulitzer Prize, the desire to be recognized as the best in his business.

There has been some rumbling at other papers since 1981, when Dave Anderson became the third sports columnist, all from *The Times*, to win the Pulitzer. The very talented Frank Deford, who is not eligible for a journalism Pulitzer because he works for *Sports Illustrated*, has campaigned for a separate category for sports Pulitzers, and for Jim Murray to receive one. I feel strongly that a sports Pulitzer would, in the very short run, tend to reward the regulars, the old war-horses. Pulitzers ought to be given for special efforts, the big story, the exceptional series.

In my Young Turk era, I used to be suspicious of Murray because he was not a clubhouse quote-monger. I used to be bothered by his one-liners. But I began to appreciate Jim a lot more when I was a news reporter in Louisville and he would pop into town for the Derby and would tackle the pretentiousness of the Derby with his opening sentence: "Well, here I am at Appalachia Downs. . . ."

Fighting off serious eye difficulties and family problems, Jim has stayed closer to the big events than anyone might have imagined. I saw him struggle through antiquated Tiger Stadium to get the feel of the Tigers' clubhouse in 1984. But the real time to appreciate Jim is the off-season, a week in Los Angeles (hey, make it Palm Springs) in early February, after the Super Bowl, before spring training.

Slip some coins into the newspaper box, read Jim Murray at breakfast, maybe a column about an offbeat golfer, maybe a midwinter visit with Leo Durocher, maybe a slashing comedy script about a pompous sports commissioner or a larcenous club owner or a bumptious athlete. It is then that you realize how well Murray has served his audience, with its show-biz familiarity with the one-liners of Jack Benny and Johnny Carson.

But then there are sports journalists in a few dozen other cities who don't exactly curdle your coffee or burn your toast.

Sometimes when baseball managers are asked to name the ideal manager, they answer by listing the best qualities from many managers— the patience of Gil Hodges, the self-confidence of Earl Weaver, the knowledge of Gene Mauch. If you were creating the ideal sports jouralist, you might include:

The singular style of Jim Murray.

The experience of Dave Anderson.

The personality of Bud Collins.

The interviewing tenacity of Steve Jacobson.

The versatility of Stan Hochman.

The fierce integrity of Jack Mann.

The gentle integrity of Dave Kindred.

The youthful energy of Christine Brennan or Peter Richmond.

The reporting ability of Murray Chass or Jane Gross.

The sense of humor of Tony Kornheiser or Leigh Montville.

The international vision of Phil Hersh or Randy Harvey.

The storytelling flair of Ira Berkow.

The social conscience of Stan Isaacs or Derrick Jackson.

The writing talent of John Ed Bradley.

The sheer gall of Dick Young or Peter Vecsey.

The California poise of Scott Ostler or Diane Shah.

The deceptive southern humility of Hubert Mizell.

The opinions of Mike Lupica.

The contacts of Milton Richman.

But there is always the human need to proclaim somebody as number one. Who was our best president? Was Babe Ruth our greatest baseball player? The greatest American novelist? Does it matter?

In boxing, they have a category called "pound for pound," which eliminates the weight difference and throws all boxers into one category, based on power and speed, instinct and knowledge, durability and personality. When they talk about "pound for pound," Sugar Ray Robinson is often acknowledged as the greatest boxer of his time. After reading Ira's book, that sounds like a good way to remember Red Smith, too.

MEXICO CITY, MAY 28

As the plane dips, I see the new scars from last year's earthquake, buildings gutted and twisted. The city extends five more miles of cinderblock shacks since the last time I was here, five years ago. Poor Mexico. When I first came here in 1968, you could see the volcanoes from the center of the city, before the smog came to stay.

My job has brought me four times to Mexico City. The first was with the Yankees for exhibition games in 1968. The second was to cover the first trip of Pope John Paul II in 1979. The third was to cover the strike of baseball players in 1980. And now this trip, to cover the finest moment in sports in all the world.

Forget the World Series or the Stanley Cup, which are only for Canada and the United States. Forget the Super Bowl, which is an American sport, just beginning to be exported. Forget Wimbledon. Even the Olympics are too diverse, too individual, to have the impact of the sports event I am going to cover.

For the next month, in cities all around Mexico, teams from twenty-four nations will be playing in the World Cup of soccer. In Spanish it is called *El Mundial.*

There is no grander moment in all of sports than when two national teams stride onto the grass field and trade banners. At this moment, these players are not hired hands, not professionals, not state-supported amateurs, but eleven representatives of their nation—*La Selección,* as they say in Spanish.

When the two teams stand at attention for their national anthems and then briefly pose for the traditional pregame team photographs, six standing, five crouching, I always get a chill, no matter how many times I see it. People will be following this game in Africa, Asia, Europe, Latin America, even in those backward places north of the border, the United States and Canada.

I come by my enthusiasm honestly, having played soccer two years at Jamaica High on a team that had a couple of Frenchmen, a couple of Italians, and assorted Puerto Ricans, Greeks, Colombians, Swedes, and Germans. We were the most disorganized team imaginable, a tower of Babel in short pants, but I came to love the fall afternoons, the sun slanting in my eyes, watching deft forwards from Grover Cleveland High School run circles around me.

Most American sports reporters scorn soccer, ridicule its low scores, its subtle thrusts, its lack of contact, but they have never collided with a wiry halfback with knees and elbows like metal shields, both of you trying to control a hard, round ball with your insteps, running full tilt.

Those two autumns of playing inept fullback made me love soccer the rest of my life. As a journalist, I have sought out *fútbol*, covering the Mundial in Spain in 1982, writing more columns on the fading North American Soccer League than I probably should have, and going to soccer games on vacations in foreign countries. I am a soccer junkie.

Marianne will never forget her first few hours in Czechoslovakia, while I was working on the Martina book. Exhausted from an all-night flight from New York via Frankfurt, she arrived in Prague at noon, to be met by me and Corinna, our second daughter, who had taken the train from Paris. Corinna and I had already scouted out the big doings in Prague that day.

"Let's get the bags to the hotel," we told Marianne. "There's a European Cup match between Sparta of Prague and Lodz from Poland at four o'clock."

We bought standing-room tickets among the pale youth of Prague, buying beers and sausages, cheering the Sparta victory, both women noting that soccer players have the best physiques of any athletes, without the emphasis on bulk as in American football or height as in basketball. Or, as Corinna put it, "Look at those guys in shorts."

I'm a journalist, not a blind fan, and I know about the dangers of mob violence, the ultranationalism, the shady deals concocted by the equip-

ment manufacturers, the stadium builders, the men who run world soccer. But this assignment is partially a labor of love. Soccer in Mexico.

We get off the plane in a humid crush, and I find the driver from the
Times bureau, José Trinidad Lopez, a polite young man with a withered
right hand. He lugs my suitcases into the car, and drives the stick-shift
car expertly despite his hand. José does not speak English, but he is a
born communicator, speaking every Spanish word slowly, making sure
I understand before he goes to the next sentence.

It is beginning all over again, the love of learning, the infatuation with
language, the thrill of being in another country, trying to survive from
hour to hour, to get things right, the old fantasy of being a correspondent, a real journalist. I am in Mexico, covering the Mundial. Can't think
of anything else I would rather do.

MEXICO CITY, MAY 29

I've got a room on the twenty-sixth floor facing Chapultepec Park. I've
got laminated credentials for the Mundial. I've got our rented office in
the press center, complete with computer and printer and telephones.
For the next five weeks this will be my base. Now I need a column.

I have read that an exhibit, the Ball Game, will open this weekend at
the Museum of Anthropology, to coincide with the opening of the Mundial. I walk from the hotel to the museum, taking in the low-cost mini-
buses, the giant buses, the honking horns, the mixture of smells,
gasoline from the cars on the Reforma, animal smells from the zoo in
Chapultepec Park. The giant fountain in the center of the museum plaza
creates a misty timelessness, with giant galleries recreating the world
of the Aztec, the Maya, the Zapotec. I want to embrace strangers with
their brown mestizo faces and say, "I am home. I came back."

Journalists learn to have many homes, to feel proprietary about many
cities, many countries. Since my three weeks covering the Pope's trip,
Mexico has been another of my homes, like Paris, like London, like
Wales, like Madrid, like Rome, like the Tampa Bay area of Florida, like

Louisville, like Los Angeles. If you sleep in a place a certain number of nights, it becomes your home. If you read the papers and order breakfast and joke with the people in their language, it becomes your home.

Mexico may be one of my homes, but the polite young publicist tells me she is sorry that nobody is allowed in the exhibit until this evening. I pull out all the stops for her. *The New York Times.* A worldwide circulation. Deep respect for the tradition of Mexico. Deadline in a few hours. Just want a peek at the exhibit.

If I were in New York, I would ask to see her superior, huff and puff and use the name of *The New York Times* in every sentence, as we are taught to do in basic training. But part of my pride in existing in Spanish countries is to maintain the facade, the point of honor between two individuals. And I know my Spanish is not equal to the next level of charm and manipulation. I do all right in Spanish until the conversation gets to normal speed and complexity, and then I am gone.

The publicist offers me a brochure with photographs from the exhibition and says, "Perhaps this will help," and she directs me to a few displays with sports themes in the permanent section of the museum. I think they are silly to refuse me a ten-minute escorted peek, but I will not make an issue of it.

Then I stop in the open-air museum cafeteria and order *molletes*, chili and cheese on French toast, and listen to half a dozen Brazilian men, wearing the green-and-gold national shirts, chat up a waitress in their throaty Portuguese-accented Spanish. She tells them about her memories of the Brazil team that won the Mundial here in 1970. Brazilians are the heart and soul of world soccer, the players exhibiting a samba-style game, the fans in constant euphoria. My hero, Socrates, has postponed his medical career to represent his nation in yet another Mundial.

I stay and listen to the Brazilians as long as I can, but my deadline is approaching. I go back to the hotel and spend an hour reading the brochure about Mexican ball games, before Cortés, before Columbus. I have a love affair with Mexican history, feeling that no nation in the world has the same rich blend of fact and legend.

Whenever I read about Mexico, I wonder what would have happened if Montezuma had told his soldiers to garrote Cortés in the night. Of course, Montezuma was guided by the prophecy that the god Quetzalcoatl, with his reddish beard, would return with the eastern sun one day, but aside from the reddish beard, there was no trace of deity in the vandal from Spain, or his soldiers or most of his priests.

One self-protective thrust in the dark of the night and the Aztecs and the Mayas and the Toltecs might rule Mexico today, instead of merely being symbols for subway stations. But would Mexico have streets named after Galileo and Oscar Wilde? Would Mexico be host to the Mundial?

According to this brochure, the tribes used a hard rubber ball, slightly smaller than today's soccer ball. Some tribes used only their hips and shoulders, others used their feet, still others used their knees, but hands were rarely used. The object was to propel a ball through a narrow ring, suspended above the reach of the players. Sometimes they played for hours and even days before somebody scored.

In the early days, it was considered a great honor for the winning captain to be sacrificed, but when athletes became professional, the losers were sacrificed instead. There will be plenty of calls for the heads of losers in the next month. No nation takes well to a loss. The Italian team was spat upon when it returned from a loss in Mexico in 1970. Fans throw themselves into rivers or shoot the television set when their team loses. This is the World Cup, the center of the universe.

I begin my column by describing the poor people, squatting in the shrubs in front of my hotel, eating tortilla in the same posture as statues at the museum. Men dressed as Aztec warriors sell chewing gum in the middle of traffic jams. Poor *campesinos* huddle in front of elegant boutiques. Past and present. Indians and Europeans. Montezuma and Cortés. The red-bearded stranger carries a word processor.

MEXICO CITY, MAY 31

Tere Parra suggests we leave early for the opening game to avoid the dreadful traffic jams predicted for today and the next month. Tere is the office manager of the *Times* bureau, the daughter of a Mexican surgeon and an American woman. With her reddish hair and light skin, she looks more German or Swedish than mestizo.

She and José drive by the hotel at nine o'clock. We stop at an open-air market for a fruit-flavored milkshake with an egg in it—"perfect if you've been up late partying," Tere says in English. We sip the smooth, sweet concoction from milk cartons as José expertly zips onto the Periférico, the superhighway that circles the central city, a rival to the Long Island Expressway as the world's longest parking lot.

On this steamy Saturday morning, hundreds of officers in uniform are waving traffic onward. Children stand by the side of the road and wave Mexican flags and chant "May-hee-co! May-hee-co!"

We park close to the giant chafing dish of a stadium and walk through vendors hawking Mundial T-shirts and caps. Then we reach the barricades. For more than a year, there have been rumors that terrorists from Libya, from Lebanon, from Nicaragua, from Cuba, from Mexico itself, will try to disrupt the Mundial. With President Miguel de la Madrid Hurtado due here today for the opening ceremonies, hundreds of nervous-looking little brown soldiers and police officers wave automatic weapons half their size. There is no doubt in my mind that any demonstration, perhaps even sudden excitement or loud words, will be met by a murderous hail of bullets.

To get into Aztec Stadium, we have to pass through checkpoints, like subway turnstiles with X-ray machines. We are among the first customers on Opening Day, so we are getting the full treatment from squads of officious soldiers, hands patting my chest, my waist, my calves, my buttocks, my crotch.

A small brown soldier peers inside my shoulder bag. He asks to inspect my word processor. No problem, *amigo*, whatever you want. He inspects my bottled mineral water. No problem. He inspects my package of snacks. No problem. Then he notices my Swiss army knife for opening the bottled water and cutting some cheese and crackers. The knife must go, he says. I am embarrassed at the trouble I am causing José, who with his impassive face, walks back through the checkpoints to drop the knife in his car, knowing he must be poked and prodded all over again on his way back.

We climb to the press box, crowded with reporters of a dozen languages. The committee has engaged hundreds of handsome male and female volunteers in pastel uniforms to assist the press. Some of them are skilled in operating the computers, some are translators, most of them stand around and look attractive. The committee has leaned heavily to light-skinned Mexicans, partially because they may speak English or German or French at home, but also because blond is beautiful in the Mexican mind. You do not see pure Indian features doing the six o'clock news or the commercials.

We arrange for our telephone, giving square blue *New York Times* pins to every worker who helps us. Pins are the grease of international sports events and conventions. People collect them, trade them, sell them, and display them on caps and jackets. The pins bring smiles and *"muchas gracias"* and a bit of extra service.

The press box is out in the muggy sunlight. I am sitting next to a correspondent from the Chinese news agency wearing his correct beige Mao suit. In perfect Spanish, he asks how I like my Radio Shack computer, so I give a demonstration to my old *amigo* from Peking.

Because of our Sunday-paper deadline, and not trusting the telephone and electric systems once the crush begins, I write an early column an hour before the ceremonies.

Remembering the killer earthquake of last September 19, I write a lead: "Mexico literally rose from the rubble yesterday. . . . " I am relieved when the New York office says it has received the transmission.

When the ceremony begins, a chorus of impolite whistles fills the stadium as President de la Madrid is introduced. He continues his speech, right through the whistles.

"This is a terrible insult," Tere Parra whispers.

"Just like New York," I announce, making a joke for the Americans near me. "We do the same thing when Mayor Koch shows up for a baseball game."

Tere realizes I have missed the point.

"We never do this to our president," she says. "I think it's news."

In a nation with one political party that acts as surrogate parent for the obedient children-citizens, this public display is a surprise. Mexicans who had the money and the pull to come up with the twenty-dollar ticket for the opening game—Mexicans for whom the system works at least slightly—are using the anonymity of a huge crowd to razz their president.

Are people upset with inflation, the terrible state of the peso, corruption, lack of political power? When I call the office with my color inserts, I make sure to mention the rude reception given the Mexican president.

The two teams march on the field and exchange their banners, the anthems are played, the team photographs taken, the ritual of soccer. The game, as often happens, becomes an anticlimax. On a muggy day, on a field softened by the rainy season, Italy scores a goal early and goes into its traditional defensive posture, the *catenaccio*, the bolt. In 1982, that defensive mode was good enough to win the World Cup, but today Bulgaria scores, in the eighty-sixth minute, to stun the Italians with a 1–1 tie. Mexican fans happily chant, "May-hee-co," proud to be at the center of the world.

JUNE

TOLUCA, MEXICO, JUNE 1

Because of the war with Iran, the Iraq national team has been forced to qualify for the World Cup by playing totally on the road for the past two years. Sue Mott of the London *Times* and I drove out to the Iraqi base to interview the road warriors.

Iraq is staying in a motel at the edge of town, a Mexican version of a Holiday Inn. There is a concrete guardhouse at the entrance, with a few Mexican soldiers with machine guns. They ask to examine the trunk and engine of my car, and I am glad to comply.

We wait in the bar and drink fruit juice and watch the opening game between France and Canada. When it is over, we are joined by a handsome, rangy man carrying gifts: travel guide to Iraq, key chains, pennants, posters of Baghdad. The man is Raad Hammoudi, the goalkeeper for Iraq, a worldly man who owns a clothing factory and plays goalie in his spare time.

"We are amateurs," he says, talking about the permanent road schedule. "It is not like professional sports. The fans are nice to us."

We ask him how he feels playing in a sports tournament while men his age are dying in the war with Iran.

"When we come to the World Cup, people ask us, 'How can you play when you have a war?' " Hammoudi admits. "We say, 'The war is on the border, it is far from Baghdad, and we are sportsmen, so we must play football. We go to hospitals and meet with the soldiers.' "

The idea of a war seems very distant from this sterile, comfortable motel. We thank Hammoudi for his presents, and I give him a handful of *New York Times* pins. He says he plans to take a master's degree in Greenwich, England, and he invites us to look him up. We wish him well in the tournament, and then we drive past the concrete guardhouse and back into the evening thunderstorm in the valley of Mexico.

MONTERREY, JUNE 3

My legs were shot by the time I arrived in Monterrey yesterday. I am guessing it was the fruit juice back in Toluca, but how do you know? I'm here six days and I'm sick already.

My reason for flying at dawn to Monterrey is a column about the most notorious soccer fans in the world, the English. Scorned for their murderous riot in Brussels, known for tearing up trains all over Europe, the English fans were warned to behave at the Mundial. I interview a World Cup official, Enrique Gómez Junco, who guessed that hints about long jail sentences for drunken behavior, and the high cost of travel to Mexico, may cut down on the rowdies.

At first, the English players and officials were unpopular here because they had expressed unhappiness at playing in hot, dry Monterrey. But Gómez Junco said the English team has won over the population by playing a "friendly" game against fourteen-year-olds when they arrived.

After sleeping twelve hours last night, I take a cab out to the stadium for today's 1–0 victory by Portugal over England. Dozens of white-skinned English fans are lurching around the stadium, wearing skimpy shorts with a Union Jack printed of them, their bodies burned crisp from the sun.

"*Animales?*" asks Delia Zárate, a giggling teenager. "*Ah, no. Los Ingleses son guapos.*"

The English fans who can speak coherently say they are being treated nicely, even invited to people's homes. Mexican graciousness seems to be solving the problem.

MEXICO CITY, JUNE 4

Marianne was waiting in the hotel when I returned from Monterrey last night. She has brought me reinforcements—cranberry juice, peanut butter, Pepto-Bismol, herself, all welcome. Like a true reporter, I leave her on her first day in Mexico, but she knows the city and can do just fine. I have lunch with Bill Stockton, *The Times*'s Mexico City bureau chief.

Times correspondents are like diplomats and Jesuits—always a bureau somewhere, with phone and cable contacts to New York, and gossip, and the latest papers airmailed in. I barely knew Bill back in the home office, but *Times* people invariably drop their barriers when they meet in distant bureaus.

He takes me to a charming restaurant a few blocks from the hotel, El Invernadero, the Greenhouse, where they serve an excellent grille, Argentine style, on braziers at the table. We talk about *The Times*, as all correspondents do, particularly the sense of separation and disjointedness. When I was based in Louisville, I always wondered what they really thought of my work, always tried to read a meaning into random telephone comments. To be a correspondent is to be paranoid. It goes with the territory.

Bill has just returned from the States, where he attended the high-school graduation of his only child. We discover our sons have a lot in common—independent, seekers, not one of the crowd. After a three-hour Mexican lunch, I feel I know Bill—and his son—much better.

PUEBLA, MEXICO, JUNE 5

Our hotel is straight out of Fellini, with Italian soccer journalists crowding the lobby, arguing, gesturing, flirting, singing, smoking, hours before the big game against Argentina.

My trip here in 1979 was one of the most controversial assignments

I have had. This was the Pope's first trip out of the Vatican since his election, and everyone was watching to see what signals he sent out.

When the Pope got off the plane and gave a speech warning priests and nuns to get back into uniform and stop dabbling in "politics," I had to report not only what he said but also what his words meant. This managed to work against the objectives of both sides at the bishops' conference in Puebla. I was scolded in public by the bishop of Panama, a Notre Dame man who should have known better than to scapegoat the free North American press. I also managed to be scolded privately by some of the best liberal journalists in the region, who didn't want the Pope to be identified as a conservative just yet.

After the Pope went back to the Vatican, I spent two weeks in this old regional capital, working back and forth between the two camps of liberal and conservative bishops and theologians, who literally had separate strategy headquarters. It was like covering a war, without the barbed wire and the bazookas.

Now I'm back in Puebla, half expecting to see my playmates, the religion reporters, from seven years earlier. Having covered the Vatican, I am prepared for the lack of information and the lack of access in that other traveling carnival, the world of *fútbol.*

My introduction to the World Cup came in Barcelona in 1982, when I covered the Italians' big upset over Argentina. The next day, curious how the Italian players were taking their sudden success, I hooked up with Enrico Jacomini, an American-born reporter in the Rome bureau of Associated Press.

The Italian team was staying at a motel in the suburbs, with armed guards on the rooftops. The players were lounging around the pool in skimpy bathing suits, but none of them would talk to the press. They were on a slowdown strike because they wanted more money for playing in the World Cup. Also, they were upset because some Italian journalists had written that two of the players were rooming together—"like man and wife," I think the phrase was. No sense of humor.

That day in Barcelona, I discovered the truth about world soccer, and the state of world sportswriting. After a quarter of a century of covering North American sports, I had taken for granted the interviews after every game, the access to the clubhouse, the travel on the same planes, the respect and even friendships that spring up along with the inevitable distrust and dislikes.

Compared to our home sports, world football (soccer) was mysterious, duplicitous, a secret society. In world football, the clubhouses are off-limits, and the players rarely come out for interviews, which leads to rumors and suppositions, and spite and distaste, and further alienation. I could see that around the pool in Barcelona in 1982.

After a bit of brokering with team officials, Dino Zoff, the forty-year-old goalkeeper, agreed to talk to the press. Because my Italian is limited to maybe a hundred words, Zoff gave me a separate interview on our middle linguistic ground of Spanish. I learned that he had never heard of contemporaries like Pete Rose and Carl Yastrzemski, elderly baseball players who were also having terrific seasons at the age of forty, and he had no idea of the strenuous conditioning methods they used. Zoff's idea of conditioning for the World Cup was to cut down a little on wine and cigarettes. Of course, he played excellently.

Zoff was quite gracious with me, particularly given the language problems, but it seemed pretty clear that he and most other European athletes are not used to long, thought-provoking interviews. I saw how the press was given almost no information, and had no clout in asking for clarification. The attitude of FIFA, the world-football body, seemed to be, "You get a seat at the game. You write whatever you damn please. What else could you want?"

A Brazilian who ran a soccer team in the United States told me that athletes in Europe and South America assume writers are either paid off by the clubs or not paid off and therefore take it out on the players. Either way, the athletes see the sporting press as nothing more than mercenaries.

"When I get a new player from Europe or South America," my friend told me, "the first thing I do is tell him I am not paying anybody off. I also tell him that if Hubert Mizell or Larry Guest or most of the press asks for an interview, he will listen and try to be fair."

European sports journalists are more like critics, analyzing the play on the field and guessing at the motives of the participants. At Wimbledon, it is almost exclusively the Yanks who crowd into the tiny interview room for the seven questions we are allowed with each athlete. Sometimes the English club officials try to rescue the players by saying, "I don't think that's a suitable question," only to be waved off by old pros like Martina and Chrissie and Jimbo, who are used to being psychoanalyzed by American sports reporters.

It has crossed my mind that American openness kept the United States from being the host of this World Cup, which Colombia was supposed to hold until it backed out because of financial problems. When American soccer interests tried to make a bid for the 1986 World Cup, the world-football body snubbed them, even—or maybe particularly—when the good Dr. Kissinger got into the act.

I could just see the world soccer officials thinking to themselves, Oh, sure, Kissinger. His President Nixon couldn't even hold his office once the press found a few missing tapes in Watergate. We want to stage the World Cup in countries where nobody will ask too many questions. You think we want American businessmen and reporters nosing around in our business?

So here we are in Mexico.

The Fellini swarm heads out to the soccer stadium to watch this year's Argentina-Italy game. Italy gets a break in the seventh minute when the referee charges an Argentine player with using his hands within the penalty area. From the press box, high in the upper deck, it is impossible to tell what happened. Italy scores on the penalty kick to take a 1–0 lead.

Then Diego Maradona goes to work. This squat, muscular little chunk of rock was vilified in Barcelona in 1982 (one Spanish paper called him "Mini Doña"—a pun on his name, meaning "Little Lady"), but now he looks ready to take over the World Cup. His massive thighs churning like pistons, Maradona pressures Italy again and again until the thirty-third minute, when he powers a left-footed goal. Italy goes into its defensive crouch and escapes with a 1–1 tie, to derisive whistles from Mexicans and Argentines.

After the game, the usual circus of a pentalingual press conference. We are herded into a small room under the stands. Enzo Bearzot, the Italian coach, puffs on his pipe and defends his team's defensive posture. They way I hear it, Bearzot is saying, "We did what we had to do."

Next comes Carlos Bilardo, the Argentine coach, who is said to be a medical doctor. Somebody asks him about the penalty called against his defender, and he says, "I never comment on the officiating." I love hearing clichés in other languages; they sound so much more interesting than when Tom Landry and Don Shula say them in English.

What did the players think about the penalty kick? What did they think about the tie? Will the rain hurt the rhubarb? We'll never know. In world soccer, the doors don't open.

The 1994 World Cup has been awarded to the United States, more for its commercial possibilities than its soccer skills. I am curious to see whether soccer officials will make players more available in a country where report-ers are used to interviewing athletes. If they don't, I predict major press frenzy.

MEXICO CITY, JUNE 6

A friend invites us to a party in the Polanco district, where a distin-guished architect is showing a film he made of an archaeological dig. Because we just arrived back from Puebla, we are an hour late, but our hosts reassure us: "You are not late at all. You are right on time for Mexico."

Mexicans tend to mock their driving habits and their sense of time. A young friend of ours roared through a couple of stop signs the other night, laughing it off by saying, "I drive just like a Mexican, don't I?"

Our hosts tonight are all European-looking, barely a trace of Indian or mestizo in the coloring or the cheekbones. There are language profes-sors, poets, business people, lawyers, and we could just as easily be in Madrid as in Mexico City. But I note how proud they are of the history of Mexico, and pre-Columbian culture. They do not act as if the original Mexicans were "them" but rather "us."

These people used to visit their favorite cities in the States several times a year, but the falling peso has taken away their access to world culture and goods that used to be part of their life.

Once they sense they can trust us, in a three-language conversation, one woman chatting to Marianne in French, they tell us in hushed voices that the country is falling apart. The government is corrupt. The peso is wiping out their pensions and their savings.

"I do not see why there is not some kind of revolution," says a man in a gray business suit. "If one broke out on the sidewalk tomorrow, I would understand."

Marianne and I walk back to the hotel along streets named for poets and artists. The rain has temporarily sweetened the midnight air, like spring flowers, making us more aware how ghastly the air is most of the day. Poor, poor Mexico.

The narrow, disputed victory by the Party in 1988 came as no surprise to me. The derisive whistles in Aztec Stadium and the talk in my friends' homes had told me the people were growing impatient.

MEXICO CITY, JUNE 7

The biggest star of the host nation is Hugo Sánchez, who was paid five hundred thousand dollars to play for Real Madrid in Spain this season. Sánchez has come home to play for Mexico during the Mundial, lured by the extra money from commercials that show him booting the winning goal and praising the delights of chocolate milk. Whenever you turn on the television, there is Hugo, smiling at the camera with little boys calling him *"Campeón."*

Just as in the commercials, in the final minute of a tie match with Paraguay, Sánchez is jostled in the penalty area, and he takes a dramatic swoon on the grassy pitch. The English referee goes for it, and gives him a penalty kick from twelve yards out. Sánchez takes an itty-bitty step and lets go a relatively soft kick to the far left side of the goal, but the Paraguayan goalie, Roberto Fernández, has been anticipating it; he deflects it out of danger, and the game is over. You can hear the air going out of the lungs of the Mexican fans. This was no commercial. This was real life.

MEXICO CITY, JUNE 8

We drive through a section of downtown where buildings are empty since the earthquake last September. This neighborhood feels haunted, too empty for a city of crowds.

We have been hearing earthquake stories since we arrived. One friend was driving along the Periférico when she saw buildings swaying. She drove to her office, where she was a personnel manager, and she spent the next few days helping her employees hunt for their relatives.

A reporter I know was lying in bed when she felt the room swaying. She grabbed her camera and film and rushed out of the apartment, and never went back.

I was in an earthquake in this city in 1979, lying in bed in the Alameda Hotel, thinking I was being sick to my stomach. But when the plaster started falling on my head, I realized it wasn't something I ate. I looked out the window and could see electric lines snapping off in Alameda Park, sparks flashing in the darkness. The building shuddered a few more times. I could hear people screaming as they ran down the stairs of the hotel, but quite clearly we had survived. We all stood around on the sidewalks until the management told us we could go back upstairs.

The next day a cabbie told me there was nothing to worry about when the building sways back and forth. But, he added, undulating his hand up and down, "When it goes like this, then it's bad."

Every new tremor brings new cracks, new odd listing to the buildings of Mexico. But this quake last September emptied whole sections, killed entire families. Whenever I come to Mexico, I always remember this city is built on a lake. The center is not holding in Mexico.

PUEBLA, MEXICO, JUNE 10

Casey Stengel used to say that every day you see something in baseball that you never saw before. Casey was right about today.

Marianne joins me for another jaunt through the mountains, this time for a soccer victory by Italy over South Korea. Then we hang around so I can pick up a column on Willie Mays Aikens, one of the four Kansas City Royals who served jail sentences for drug possession because a judge felt they had let down the fans, a judicial double standard if ever I heard one.

Now, Aikens is trying to resurrect his career in the Mexican League, which has dropped in quality in recent years. After a tremendous thunderstorm delays the game, we sit shivering in the stands while workers try to dry off the field. They pour kerosene on the base paths and toss a match, sending thick waves of acrid smoke billowing into the stands. I have never seen a kerosene fire on the base paths before—but they manage to get the game started.

I am supposed to interview Aikens after the game. He belts a huge home run up on the hill in right field, but the game goes into extra innings, and after the thirteenth inning, we give up. Shivering and damp, I follow the big trucks back through the mountains, and we arrive home in Mexico City at two in the morning—just your usual twenty-hour day covering the World Cup.

MEXICO CITY, JUNE 10

Our driver, José, has been able to sit in the press section for each of Mexico's games. Even though some Mexican journalists do not restrain themselves, José understood that it is bad form to cheer in the press box. When Mexico beats Iraq today to finish first in its division, José turns to me and gives a shy thumbs-up signal.

When this tournament began, Mexicans were proud just to be the hosts. Now the team has played well enough to advance with fifteen other teams into the single-elimination round.

As we leave Aztec Stadium, all of Mexico City seems to be lined up along the Periférico, cheering this momentous event. Traffic is so bad that José tries a side road, zipping along for a few minutes—until a police officer pulls us over. The officer inspects José's license and snaps unfriendly remarks at José.

The way I see it, there are two alternatives—a bribe or a threat. Money or fear. Mexican officers accept fines on the spot to supplement their low income. A Mexican friend visiting New York once tried to slip a twenty-dollar bill to a Long Island officer when she was caught speeding. The officer told her, "Ma'am, please put that back in your pocketbook and I'll forget I saw it." Her daughter was horrified, but Mamita said, "In Mexico, that's how it works."

Drivers are not always innocent in Mexico, either. I heard of a legitimate police sweep in the Zona Rosa to investigate car registrations. Apparently, dozens of motorists, driving hot cars brought over the border, just abandoned the vehicles in the streets.

What to do about this officer? I suspect that sometime in the past two weeks he has been told not to shake down the locals in the presence of foreigners. Bad for image. I lean across José and wave my Mundial press badge, and I surprise the officer by rattling an excuse in functional Spanish.

"*Disculpe,*" I say. "Excuse me. This was my fault. I told my driver to go fast because I am late to work. I am a journalist. *The New York Times.* I am writing a story about the kindness of Mexico during the Mundial. Please excuse us, and we will not speed anymore."

The officer grumbles, realizing he is not going to make any money from José, and he waves us on.

"I was thinking of offering him five thousand pesos," I say, meaning around seven dollars at the current rate.

"I don't believe in bribes," José says. "I don't want to encourage corruption. If I get a ticket, I pay it in court."

This morning I discovered that José has to take two buses to my hotel to drive my car to Aztec Stadium. I managed to pull out of him that he lives right off the Periférico. When we approach his neighborhood, I take the wheel and tell him to go home and spend an extra two hours with his family. No sense both of us sitting in this traffic.

QUERETARO, MEXICO, JUNE 13

We spent the night in this highland city, in a hotel filled with West German and Danish soccer reporters, pale-skinned men with beards and bellies, wearing shorts and open shirts. The motel reeked of beer and cigarettes.

This afternoon, after covering Denmark's 2–0 victory over West Germany, I called the office to confirm that my copy had arrived. Lawrie Mifflin got on the phone. Her voice was somber.

"I hate to have to tell you this," she said.

I remembered her giving me the news about Flo Hyman in New Orleans. Oh, my God, who is it?

"Bill Stockton's son died last night," Lawrie said. "He got sick suddenly on a train in New Jersey, and he died later. They think it was his heart, but they're not sure. Bill is heading back to the States to do what he can. Kind of makes a soccer game seem silly, doesn't it?"

We talked for a while, but neither of us had much to say. She had been told it was one of those inexplicable things, the sudden disruption of a young man's heart. No past history. No symptoms. Last week the boy was graduated from high school. Today he is gone.

I hung up the phone and waited for Marianne to meet me at the stadium for the long ride back to Mexico City. I thought about the long lunch Bill and I had nine days ago. Like all correspondents, he had seemed under a lot of pressure, but he had seemed even more preoccupied with his son—where he was going to college, where he was going to live. Kevin was Bill's only child.

While waiting for Marianne, I said a prayer for Bill and for Kevin. After sixteen days on the road, I could not help but think how much I miss our three children. When they were younger, all living at home, I used to ache to get home to see them, to play with them, to teach them. I surely was an inconsistent parent, but I had so much time at home when they were little that I know my children better than most fathers do. When each of the girls went off to college, I went through a modified period of mourning. This is the real thing.

The death of a child, any child, leaves me numb. I have never gotten my strength back from a few episodes of sickness in my first few days here. I've been fighting it off, day by day. Now, the death of Bill Stockton's boy brings on a great wave of weakness and sadness. When Marianne picks me up outside the stadium, I get in the passenger's side and slump down in the seat.

"You drive," I say, and then I tell her about Bill and Kevin.

MEXICO CITY, JUNE 17

As an old Mexican hand, I am always annoyed by Americans who come home telling stories about Montezuma's revenge. Is that all they can remember from the country? But how did they like the Museum of Anthropology? Did they ride the subway? Jimmy Carter even made a Montezuma's revenge joke in front of Mexican leaders, which canceled out his advantage of being an American leader who could actually speak Spanish.

Having a policy of not fussing about getting sick in Mexico, I find myself in the embarrassing position of being sick. This is not the classic *turistas*. The long hours and the daily travel, the high altitude and the heavy smog, plus the change in diet, have zapped me. Whoever designed the Chapultepec Hotel included windows that do not open, and the so-called air-conditioning circulates the same stale air, over and over again. Late at night, after the rains, you cannot open a window and breathe the reasonably fresh air outside. At home, I eat a diet of mostly pasta, vegetables, and fruit, but here I have been eating more meat and eggs and spices than usual.

Plus, I have been working too hard. *The Times* originally planned to have four people covering the World Cup, but Lawrie Mifflin is pregnant, Bill Stockton is out, and Alex Yannis was not assigned. My dawn flights to Monterrey, my midnight drives back from Puebla, have beaten me down, with two weeks to go.

Fortunately, Alex came down on his own, since there was a credential in his name. He has been covering soccer a long time, and wants to keep up on his contacts and watch this Mundial. Ever since I set up shop here, Brazilians and Englishmen and Italians and, of course, Greeks kept popping their heads into our *Times* office, asking, "Where is Alex?" Now that Alex is here, the soccer world is happy again.

Today we drove together out to Olympic Stadium, where France eliminated the defending champion, Italy. I found myself losing my temper at every small problem—the guards who give me the wrong directions, the long walk up the concrete stairways, the crush in the press area, the open seating in the hot sun, the long walk to the rest room, the telephone service, the lack of lineups and information, and lack of food and drink. Where is Pete Rozelle, now that we really need him?

After the hour on the Periférico, I was supposed to meet Tom Callahan for dinner, but I could not face the idea of dressing and sitting in a restaurant. Marianne ordered room service, and I am going to sleep at nine o'clock.

MEXICO CITY, JUNE 18

I pack a lunch and some fruit juice to try to keep up my strength, but the hot sun in Aztec Stadium wears me out. England beats Paraguay, and I am too weak to walk downstairs for the interviews with the coaches. I file a game story and get back to the hotel. I break another dinner date with Callahan—he's probably getting a complex—and I fall asleep.

An hour later, Alex knocks at the door. He peers down at me and blurts out, "Man, you look terrible."

"Yeah, I'm pretty shot, Alex," I say.

"You're supposed to go to Russia right after this," he says. "You'd better get some rest or you'll never get there. I'll help out if they want me to. Your health is more important than anything. I was sick last year, and I know. Go home if you want. It's not worth it."

It was not a good idea for me to cover the World Cup and the Goodwill Games, by myself, back to back.

"I'll take tomorrow off," I promised him. "I'm going to volunteer your services."

MEXICO CITY, JUNE 19

I get up early and wander next door to our office in the press building. The air-conditioning is on full blast, and I am shivering. I call Joe Vecchione in New York and tell him I am sick.

"Take a few days off," Joe says. "Stay in bed. We can cover it a different way."

Joe is always good about personal problems like this. But while we talk, I find myself uncomfortable with going back to my room and sleeping. I'm tired of the stale air, tired of room service, tired of World Cup press boxes, tired of the lack of services.

"Uh, Joe, the thing of it is, I'm supposed to go to Moscow on July third," I say. "I'm not going to make it at this rate. I'm not breathing well. My system is upset."

"You ought to see a doctor," Joe says. "They must have somebody at the press center."

I would see a doctor if I thought it was an emergency, but I don't want any doctor giving me medicine and telling me to rest up in my hotel room. I have never left in the middle of an assignment in all the years I have been working, but I realize I want to leave this one.

"Joe, I'm not going to get better down here," I say. "I've hit the wall."

There is a pause on the other end. Then Joe speaks: "I want you to come home," he says. "That's my decision. We probably overworked you. You need to get well."

While writing my last column from down here, I start to question my motives. Am I doing this because I am tired of the daily crush? Am I mad at being overworked? Or am I really sick? I realize how happy I am for Alex that he is about to get activated. I'm not totally proud to realize how happy I am to be leaving.

Because I am so healthy, I never used to wonder how it felt to have wobbly legs and an upset stomach with the crowd yelling and a deadline approaching. I just assumed I would always be strong, always be young.

Was Mexico a taste of my last years as a journalist? Was it a strong hint of mortality?

I remember people watching Red Smith struggle in his final months. Steve Jacobson saw Red struggling to carry his heavy Teleram computer after an all-night flight during the 1981 World Series.

"I can't carry your typewriter," Steve said, using the ballplayers' cliché, "but I can carry your typewriter."

Red was dying of cancer, but with the fierce tropism of a journalist, he was still struggling to write bright copy on deadline and then fly across the country. I thought about my father, during the 1984 season, struggling to tabulate a box score late at night. Is this what it's like to be old and tired?

At night, while Marianne is packing, I get a call from Dave Anderson from one of the ballparks.

"Hey, babe, what's wrong?" he asks. Rumors travel fast in our business.

"Nothing serious," I say. "Just run down. I'll never get to Russia if I don't go home and rest."

Dave says he'll spread the word that it's nothing serious. I am touched by his call, that he cared enough to reach me. I thank him and finish packing.

PORT WASHINGTON, NEW YORK, JUNE 20

Marianne said I looked better as soon as they turned on the plane engines. I love Mexico too much to blame her for my condition. I'll be back.

Corinna met us at the airport and drove us home to lush, comfortable Long Island on the verge of summer. The house and the deck, the trees and the grass, never seemed better—even with David busy throwing pizza boxes in the garbage. There is company coming and there is company going, but the air is fresh and the food tastes familiar. I settle down in the den and watch the Mets on television. I am embarrassed by how good I feel.

PORT WASHINGTON, JUNE 27

The office waited me out. They let me have the illusion of canceling my trip to Moscow while I consulted my doctor.

Gary Wadler is the internist for the United States Open, sometimes known as Doctor to the Stars. I met him when Martina lost to Pam Shriver at the 1982 Open and revealed she was suffering from an illness called toxoplasmosis. I was not yet working on her book, and her loss and illness were the obvious column for that day.

Some of the sportwriters made jokes about the so-called cat virus, but I looked up the doctor who was treating her, and he pulled out the laboratory results and gave me a short course on toxoplasmosis. After my column appeared, we discovered that we lived near each other, so I had new friends, Nancy and Gary, and a new doctor, too.

Gary and I often sit around his pool and joke about what we would do if we suspected we had a major disease. I always maintain that I would ignore it, pretend it was going away, rather than consult a doctor and begin serious treatment.

"There is something to be said for denial," I often say. "I'm not going to doctors. They only confirm it, make it worse."

Since I did not believe I was seriously ill, I went to Gary for a checkup after I got back from Mexico. He and his phalanx of charming nurses could not find anything wrong with me—no parasites, no infections, no heart or lung problems, no temperature.

"You're tired," he said. "You hit the wall. Your body said you needed a rest. So rest."

"What about Russia?" I asked him.

"Medically, no problem," he said. "Just get a lot of rest. You don't feel like going to Russia, you don't go."

I called Lawrie Mifflin and told her to cancel me out of the Russia trip. She was having problems getting anybody to replace me on short notice.

"It's really you or nobody," she said.

"I'm whipped," I said.

"Think about it."

As soon as I made the decision not to go, I began to wonder: Was I being a hypochondriac to feel so weak in Mexico? Did I have an anxiety attack, or was I really run down? Will the same thing happen again in Moscow? Breathing the thick sea-level air, taking naps on my deck, eating Marianne's cooking, watching Met games on the tube, I began to feel better.

This morning Lawrie called.

"Given any thought to Russia?" she asked.

I thought about Pushkin, I thought about Chekhov, I thought about Tchaikovsky, I thought about Tamara Bykova. I thought about my possible Russian genes, I thought about Stalin and the fears of bombers in the night when I was young, I thought about the country I want to visit more than any other place in the world. I thought about being sick on the road again.

"Let's do it," I said.

"Good thing we didn't cancel your flights," said Fern Turkowitz, the office manager, on one extension.

"Atta boy," said Gloria Bell, the secretary, on another extension.

"Just go as long as you can," Joe Vecchione said on yet another extension. "We wore you down. I'm sorry. Give us some good copy from Moscow. Have a good time. Have some caviar on me."

As soon as I hung up the phone, Marianne opened the pantry and showed me her cache of supplies—small tins of chicken and tuna fish, containers of cranberry-juice concentrate, Bonne Maman marmalade, Poupon mustard, crackers, cereals, tea and coffee, plus packets of pantyhose, bags of ballpoint pens, even a couple of cartons of cigarettes, gifts for Moscow.

"I stocked up, just in case," she said.

Did everybody know something I didn't?

PORT WASHINGTON, JUNE 29

Death is in the sports pages again today. While I am preparing to write a column about the World Cup final on television, the papers are full of the latest drug death—Don Rogers, a defensive back with the Cleveland Browns, who died on Friday, apparently of a drug overdose, a few hours before he was to have been married.

Rogers's death came right after Len Bias, the basketball star from the University of Maryland, died on the morning of June 19, apparently from cocaine. Bias had just been drafted in the first round by the Boston Celtics, and is probably the most prominent athlete to die from drugs in this generation.

I remember being at the Meadows and watching other addicts pressuring a young man with a drug problem. They surrounded him and said, "Hey, man, you're going to die. You're going to kill yourself with that stuff. Stop, before it's too late." Even then, they couldn't reach everybody. People would nod, and go back home, and start all over again.

Do our words mean anything? I wrote a story a few years back about the freebasing of cocaine by basketball players, leaving a trail of death and disability. Did that story scare anybody? More than a dozen baseball players were mentioned in the Pittsburgh trial last year. Micheal Ray Richardson was suspended for life for drugs. Did anybody ever have an idea that Len Bias might be involved? Or did people make the judgment —as some friends of mine make—"Oh, it's just a recreational thing, you know, weekends, at a party."

I never met Len Bias. I saw him play two games a year ago, and have no impression of him as a person. Taking the week off, feeling removed from writing, my first impulse is to say, "Stupid kid." He is somebody's son—good people's son, from what I read. At some point you get tired of writing about people taking drugs.

It's not that I'm in sports just to write about the heroes and the games. I have always cared more about the personalities than the results, always felt sports were a laboratory of human behavior, a living theater. But I guess I'm getting tired of the theater giving us this kind of tragedy, not the Greek tragedy of a noble figure defying authority, but the American tragedy of a gifted athlete flirting with death. Stupid kids.

From this distance, the biggest legacy of Len Bias is not the baskets he scored at Maryland, or what he might have done for the Celtics, but the symbol of death at an early age.

Only a few months ago, I talked with Don Rogers after a play-off game in New Jersey in which he had nearly intercepted a pass, only to have it pop into the hands of one of the Jets for a touchdown. After the game Rogers had been polite as he told reporters, "I consider it an early Christmas present. Not too many of those are going to happen."

What staggers me is that Rogers apparently took cocaine in the wake of all the terrible publicity about Len Bias. The deaths of Len Bias and Don Rogers make me realize that not enough people are being frightened, not enough people are hearing the warning signals.

PORT WASHINGTON, JUNE 30

We are leaving New York Thursday night and arriving in Moscow Friday afternoon, and I want to file a Sunday column before I leave, just in case our flight is delayed, or I have jet-lag problems, or have trouble transmitting from Moscow.

To set the scene for this strange sporting event, I want Americans to understand how the Goodwill Games were created by those two superpowers, the Russians and Ted Turner.

Until recently, I had considered Turner to be the worst of the new breed of sports owners, less interested in the tradition and the techniques of the sport than in making a name for themselves, in having a new toy.

More people heard about Donald Trump because he owned the New Jersey Generals than for all the gilded penthouses he had built for the rich. Who ever heard of George Steinbrenner before he took over the New York Yankees and started ordering his players to cut their hair? But lately I have come to think that Trump is more fun than most of the ballplayers, and we even need Steinbrenner making a fool of himself.

Turner seemed the dark angel of the new breed, part Jay Gatsby, part Rhett Butler, part Stanley Kowalski, part Archie Bunker, an unreliable playboy, Captain Outrageous, getting drunk after winning the America's Cup, lurching around at public functions, installing himself as manager-for-the-day of his Atlanta Braves until the Old Commish, Bowie Kuhn, put an end to that.

I have bumped into him a few times because of his ownership of the basketball and baseball teams in Atlanta. When I was writing about the use of freebase cocaine among pro basketball players, I felt the need to talk to some of the Hawks at a team party. When Turner arrived, he found me interviewing a few players near the front door. He fixed his evil-eye look at me, and I thought he was going to have me killed, but he only made sure I did not infiltrate the party.

When I heard he was organizing a sports event with the Soviets, my first instinct was, This madman is going to start World War III. I had always assumed Turner fit right in with the Red-baiters and the rednecks, the television preachers with the filthy eyes, the politicians who thrive on spiting the Commies.

These Goodwill Games are obviously designed for Turner's own TBS network. During the 1984 Olympics, Turner was watching television in Atlanta, and he walked into the office of his top assistant, Robert Wussler, and blurted, "Gol-durn, why can't we do something like that, but better, with the Russians?"

Wussler, who has long contacts with the Soviets going back to his days at CBS, yessed his eccentric boss, hoping Turner would forget half an hour later, which, I understand, is often the case. This time Turner did not forget. Wussler made a few phone calls, and then a few trips to Moscow. Now, we're going over there, athletes, journalists, and a modest army of TBS people, including the Mouth of the South.

My first response was to fear for our planet, but Marianne has seen Turner on all the talk shows, promoting the Goodwill Games.

"I'm telling you, he comes off very well," Marianne said. "He sounds concerned about the future of the world. There is something very committed and caring about him, like a little boy who has just figured out a great truth."

"Marianne, the guy is wacko. He's a playboy, a boozer, a loose cannon, a dabbler, an exhibitionist, a bully, a nut."

"I was impressed with him," Marianne said. "Besides, he's cute."

After twenty-five years together, I have learned to value her opinion, particularly about men. She has good instincts for bad little boys with some redeeming quality.

The other day I requested a telephone interview with the boss. This morning I heard the bizarre voice of Ted Turner—Daffy Duck on speed.

"The way I see it," he quacked, "you've got to keep up your contacts in the world. As a boy, my image of the Soviet Union was all those tanks running through Red Square, but let's face it, they only have that parade once a year. I don't believe they want to blow up the world."

To my amazement, I found myself scribbling notes as Captain Outrageous talked about world peace.

"I'm just hoping we can have improved relations between the two countries, for your children and mine," he added. "For the birds and the flowers and that kind of stuff, instead of blowing us all to smithereens."

Teasing him slightly, I noted that the Russians had burned Moscow rather than turn it over to Napoleon. Now they are letting Ted Turner in.

"Hitler never got there, either," Turner said, picking up the theme. "The Russians wouldn't let him get to Moscow. The first time I flew here, I came on Lufthansa. Ninety percent of the passengers were West Germans coming here on vacation, spending money like tourists. I wanted to grab them and ask, 'Hey, isn't this better than forty years before, soldiers lying frozen in the snow?' "

I understand Turner has a commercial reason for pumping over $10 million into these games. He wants unique programs during the summer doldrums, he wants an international contact, if things are really going to open up between the two countries. He has absolutely no qualms about possibly confusing the Olympic relationships between the Soviet Union and the West. Nobody ever said Turner was a team player, but I felt his energy pouring into me.

When I got off the phone, I told Marianne, "I was just talking to your buddy."

She said, "He's sincere, isn't he?"

JULY

MOSCOW, JULY 4

The first leg of the trip felt like the fourteen other trips we have taken to Europe: the blend of languages in the darkened plane, the sun dawning over the Atlantic, arriving at Frankfurt, ordering coffee from Turkish waiters in a West German airport. Familiar Europe.

Perhaps it comes from living in New York, between the ocean and America, perhaps it is from the European relatives I missed, perhaps it is from the trips to nearly all of Europe, but Europe has become partially a second home. We have traveled all over the United States on company time, but for our vacations we always gravitate to Wales or Spain, Greece or Norway, feeling jealous of people who can point to a specific village and say, "This is where I am from."

However, when the flight to Moscow was announced, this was not just another vacation, not just another sports event, but also a journey to a missing link in my life, the pull from the East.

When I was young, I assumed my father's ancestry was Hungarian because of the strong accent of my grandmother and the sweet Tokay wine she served. But when I was seventeen, when freedom fighters threw rocks at the tanks in Budapest in 1956, my parents explained my father's ambivalence toward his Hungarian name. He had been placed in an orphanage by his real parents, and there was reason to believe he had Russian and Jewish roots.

(They forgot to tell my second brother, Peter, until after he had dropped out of college in his first semester, worked on a ship, joined the Airborne, and gone to work as a copy boy at the *Daily News* in his early twenties. "I might be part Jewish?" he asked. "Why didn't anybody tell me? I could have made something of myself.")

Years after Grandma Vecsey died, I finally visited Budapest, and was lectured by our tour guide for having anglicized my family name. It should be "VAY-chay," not "VES-see." The guide showed me Vecsey Street, where there is a memorial to a famous general named Vecsey, massacred in the uprising of 1870, and she told me of famous violinists and writers and politicians with my name.

Further east than I had ever been before, I felt connected to the rolling Danube, the brooding hills, my own name on a historic square. When I saw huge signs for Béla Bartók Boulevard, I could hear the stirring folk dances Bartók mixed with his haunting twentieth-century music.

A few years later, on our trip to Czechoslovakia to work on Martina's book, my daughter Corinna said Prague was the first place she had ever visited where she looked like other people. Most people in Czechoslovakia resented the Russians, which I could understand, but I felt the pull of the land of deep winters and white nights.

When I was growing up in the forties, my parents had long since become disenchanted with Stalin, with communism. After it was clear the Russians also had the atom bomb, I would lie in bed in my attic room, listening to the throb of airplanes on their way to LaGuardia or Idlewild airports, working myself into believing they could be Russian bombers, on their way to destroy New York. But even in those dark nights after World War II, I never lost my fascination with Russia.

For the past few months, I have been carrying a Russian phrase book, learning the Cyrillic alphabet, listening to language records at home, reading history books about Russia. Through this strange alliance between Ted Turner and Gorbachev's *glasnost,* I will be going to a land that may have given me some of my moods, some of my skills, some of my strengths and weaknesses—in very basic terms, some of my blood.

The Pan Am plane swooped into the Moscow airport at a steep angle, the Russians obviously not believing in long, scenic approaches. The countryside looked lush and green in early summer, factories and towns, rivers and highways, but few cars on the roads.

On the ground, we knew we were in the Soviet Union when we saw the plump, elderly cleaning women with wrinkled faces, chatting in Russian. They reminded me of Nina Khrushchev, who has always been the quintessential Russian woman to me.

We were directed to passport control, where a young, sturdy soldier in khaki uniform studied my face, then my passport picture, then my face again. His face was haughty, cold. We stared at each other, right out of Ronald Reagan's greatest unmade movie, *The Evil Empire and Me*. I have heard that Russians respond well to a show of force, so I squinted my right eye and wrinkled my forehead and glared back at the soldier. His eyes glared even more coldly, and I felt good about that. He really does respect me, after all, I thought.

After five minutes of developing an intimate friendship, he finally motioned me to the the baggage-claim area, where we were met by members of the *Times* bureau, Ivan, the driver, and Irene, the translator. They whisked us through the formalities, and escorted us to the *Times* car.

After white birch forests had given way to giant housing developments, Ivan slowed down at a huge monument alongside the highway, and Irene told us this was where Russian patriots had stopped Hitler's army just short of Moscow.

Most traffic was heading out from the city, normal for a Friday night in the summer. Irene told us the authorities want the city to be comfortable for foreigners during the games, so they have forbidden their own citizens from entering except by special credentials.

Irene gave us a running tour through central Moscow, quiet on Friday evening with the sunlight still slanting through the broad boulevards. We reached our giant hotel, the Moskva, at the edge of the Kremlin, with the fantastic onion domes of St. Basil's just a few hundred yards away, on the other side of Red Square. Irene breezed us through registration, making sure they had given us a good room, and then she headed off for a weekend in the country.

At the Goodwill Games booth, a young Russian woman handed back my credentials and said in English, "Happy birthday."

She knows it is Independence Day, I thought.

Then I remembered my birthday, July 4, is inscribed in my passport. I have just turned forty-seven, and we are in Moscow.

MOSCOW, JULY 5

With an eight-hour lead on New York time, deadlines should not be a problem during the Goodwill Games. Having filed my Ted Turner columnn before I left New York, I will insert color descriptions of tonight's opening ceremonies.

After studying the Cyrillic alphabet in recent weeks, I can decipher the maps of the subway system. People study my features, my clothes, and make the judgment that I am from the West. One man in a bulky gray suit asks, "Lenin Stadium?" and points to the stop on the map. The subways are clean, no sign of graffiti, and a clock notes the intervals between trains—ninety seconds, three minutes at most. Just like New York.

As I ride in the subway, the adrenaline, the curiosity I felt as a young reporter on Flagler Street, sensing the Bay of Pigs intrigue, starts flowing again. For the next three weeks I am not going to be an old warhorse plodding off to the Super Bowl or the World Series.

The Times wants this event covered as a pageant, as yet another window onto the Soviet Union. They could have sent an expert on Olympic sports to cover the games with a tape measure and a stopwatch, but instead they sent me to write about the people and the spectacle. For the next three weeks, I can indulge the old dream of being a foreign correspondent.

The games themselves don't mean much. There was not enough money to bring in the best European athletes, and some Americans did not make the trip. This is not the Olympics, which is fine with me.

Lenin Stadium is part of a huge complex at a bend in the Moscow River. Except for the closeness to mass transit, the thick groves of trees, the classical music on the loudspeakers, the polite, well-dressed spectators relaxing in comfortable benches outside the stadium, the flags of all nations hanging from the stadium, this is just like Giants Stadium in New Jersey.

Everything in Moscow is on double scale, or so it seems to me, buzzed with jet lag. The roads are all eight lanes wide. The stadium steps are steep. The flags are gigantic. A land of giants, I think to myself.

Because of the Chernobyl disaster in the spring, I had made up my mind to avoid dairy products. Joe Gergen from *Newsday* spots an ice-cream vendor.

"Russian ice cream is supposed to be terrific," Joe says.

"Chernobyl," I say.

"Vanilla or chocolate?"

"Vanilla." The ice cream is terrific.

The sky is still light as the ceremonies begin at nine-thirty. We crane our heads to watch Gorbachev deliver his opening remarks, translated into English on the huge message board. Spectators display colored cardboard squares—just like halftime at the Super Bowl—forming a giant dove and a call for peace. The theme for the games seems to be: Sport Is Peace.

Then comes a giant extravaganza of clowns and acrobats, jugglers and beautiful women, trained bears and horses, far more impressive than the Hollywood schlock of the Olympic ceremonies in 1984. I had heard that the Russians *do* circuses. Now I believe it.

When the ceremonies are over, I call for a ride to our bureau. I have heard tales of hundred-dollar telephone bills for filing stories back to the States, and I prefer to use the *Times* wire.

Kim, a young American, drives up in his Mercedes. He was a Russian studies major in college, and he somehow wound up in Moscow as a low-paid assistant in the bureau. He drives to the apartment complex where many foreign journalists are housed, and a soldier steps out of his cubicle to inspect us. Kim growls at him in Russian, and the man steps aside. There seems to be a certain amount of ritual tension, but Kim knows how far to push it.

We take an elevator to the bureau, where I meet Serge Schmemann, our bureau chief. Serge's father was a famous theologian in the Russian Orthodox Church in America. For Serge, this tour of duty is a return to his deepest roots.

In the first hour of darkness at midnight, we sit in the bureau and talk about the Mets, about *The Times,* about the Soviets, all those great institutions. While I insert color details in my column about Ted Turner, the telex starts to clatter with a message from New York:

"Sports asks Vecsey column upcoming soon?"

At one o'clock in the morning in Moscow, it is five in the evening in

New York. I have managed to fritter away enough time that I am now filing on deadline. No journalist would want it any other way. You file early, they start expecting it.

MOSCOW, JULY 6

When I covered religion for *The Times,* I used to hear stories about the undercurrent of religious revival in the Soviet Union, the "midnight church" with millions of believers streaming to illegal services deep in the countryside. I tended to regard those claims as wishful thinking, but I am curious what a church service is like a few blocks from the Kremlin.

Serge Schmemann has told me about a Russion Orthodox church with an outstanding choir. We leave our hotel around ten o'clock and walk past Lenin's Tomb, where hundreds of European and Asian faces are lined up to visit the secular cathedral of socialism. We walk past the domes of St. Basil's, cross the bridge over the Moscow River, where a young soldier reading *Pravda* is guarding the route of the Goodwill marathon this afternoon. We file down a narrowing street, silent on this warm Sunday morning. One gets the feeling that everybody has gone to the birch forests.

We spot the Church of the Consolation of All Who Sorrow, with several soldiers standing guard, an intimidating sight. We feel them staring at us, perhaps taking pictures, as we open the door of the church. We are surprised to find over 250 people inside, standing and swaying and praying while the deep-voiced choir chants the Russian hymns. The church is dark and cool and heavy with incense, a strong contrast to the sunny, barren feeling in the streets. I stand close to the wall, and a strong old lady in a black dress nudges me aside so she can worship directly in front of her favorite icon.

I had expected churchgoers to be only elderly babushkas, grandmothers in black dresses like the old lady with the elbows, but I am somewhat surprised to see teenagers, infants, young couples, the whole spectrum, some in faded suits, some in new blue jeans.

For years I have been uncomfortable in Western-style churches, with their passive, seated congregations, but I find myself drawn by the hypnotic throb of the choir, the energy of the shifting crowd, bustling from icon to icon, shifting toward the altar, worshiping on their feet.

This service reminds me of the highly charged Hasidic synagogue in Brooklyn that I used to visit as a religion reporter. In that crowded synagogue, I felt close to the redheaded men with beards and thick glasses, releasing their physical and spiritual energy in song and prayer and swaying motion. But I am a Christian, and this Russian Orthodox church in central Moscow, with its sense of sacrifice and its hope of rebirth, also reminds me of the working-class Roman Catholic church in Queens that my family attended.

As the service continues, I become aware of three young men entering the church rather ostentatiously, wearing black leather jackets. They stroll down one aisle and back another, looking from side to side, hunching their shoulders somewhat menacingly, somewhat insolently. I have heard stories of how the government infiltrates religious services or creative gatherings or protest groups, intimidating people with young toughs in civilian clothing. Or is this the paranoia of a visitor who has been in Moscow less than forty-eight hours?

Nobody else seems to pay them any mind. Or else the people have trained themselves to not invite provocation. I find myself reacting as a member of the congregation. What is the Christian response to these men? Should we—*we?*—smile and greet them meekly? If there is a disturbance, should we—*we?*—resist? What if they do something violent? I find myself tensing, feeling protective of these Soviet Christians, who take a chance just by going to church.

The moment passes. The men leave as abruptly as they entered. I am transfixed by the smell of the incense, the candles, the Sunday perfume, the closeness of several hundred people on a warm morning. I pray for them. I think I will write about the church as much as the marathon, which begins in a little while. I will call my column "Sunday Along the River."

MOSCOW, JULY 7

Jackie Joyner-Kersee has just set a world record in the heptathlon, seven events over two days. The officials bring her into the press room for a bilingual interview. In her soft, black southern tones, she gives thanks "to God, for letting me do this." I wonder if the translator conveys this part of her talk into Russian.

After she leaves, I try to collect her times and distances, both in meters and in feet. The Goodwill Games organizers have been very helpful back at the press center. In fact, I am impressed that Turner and Wussler have managed to hire intelligent and decent people like Ken Bastian, Ken O'Donnell, Alex Swann, and Piper Parry. Unfortunately, none of them is here at the moment.

The Russians running the event at Lenin Stadium have not provided much statistical information. It is not what they do best. I ask for help from a dozen teenage boys who have volunteered as aides during the Goodwill Games. Most of them have lived in the Riverdale section of the Bronx, where the Soviets house many of their people assigned to the consulate and the United Nations. These boys grow their hair fashionably long, and wear blue jeans and Western sneakers.

They have come back with their families to be integrated into the fast track of Soviet life, the best schools, best jobs, best housing, best shopping. They are loyal Soviet preppies, not too likely to say anything controversial, but their friendliness tells me a great deal about their lasting impressions of the United States.

They have brought small gifts, pins and tiny rubber bears and lacquered wooden spoons, symbols of Russian culture, to be traded for my *New York Times* pins. They talk comfortably about New York, about "the Garden" and "Yankee Stadium" and "Billy Joel concerts." They remind me of my own son, David, with their casual confidence.

They congregate around me, a visitor from their second home, and say they will try to get Joyner-Kersee's statistics for me. But they cannot find anyone in charge, either. I am getting impatient, a typical journalist with a short tolerance for ineptitude.

"Look, fellows, I know this is not your fault," I say, "but you know how rude New Yorkers can be."

The Moscow preppies smile tentatively.

I shout at the top of my lungs: "Is there anybody here from TBS? In five minutes, I am going to write that the Goodwill Games could not supply statistics. I'm sure you do not want that."

A few Western reporters give me the thumbs-up sign, but the Soviet-bloc reporters look aghast at this outburst. After generations of people have been massacred for being the wrong ethnic group or being caught on the wrong side of a political upheaval, people have become emotional survivors, careful not to show too much of themselves in public. When American athletes take victory laps at the track meet, waving their arms to stoke up the crowd, the Soviets don't know how to respond.

Journalists do not exactly badger officials in the Soviet Union, but I know somewhere there will be a TBS official fearful of the Goodwill Games being described as a Mickey Mouse operation in *The New York Times*.

The preppies of Moscow have been around. They've been to the Garden and Shea Stadium, they've been to Record World and Burger King. They know how it works in New York. I give them a wink that says, "A touch of New York for you lads." They smile back. Half an hour later, the Turner people get their act together, all seven events in meters and feet, whatever we need. New York journalist manners win again.

MOSCOW, JULY 8

When I noticed that several rhythmic gymnasts and their coach, Alla Svirsky, were born in the Soviet Union, I immediately saw the headline: THE AMERICAN FROM MOSCOW.

Maybe I've seen the Baryshnikov movie *White Nights* once too often, but I was afraid she might be cautious about giving interviews here. However, she is an American citizen now, and does not feel any danger, so she agreed to meet me at the American athletes' hotel.

The Rossiya Hotel is a full city block in width, typically gigantic,

Russian-style, with separate entrances on all four sides. At the for-eigners' entrance, Americans congregate in the hot sun, the women basketball players sporting sunglasses and headsets, as if they were heading to the beach at Santa Monica.

Svirsky and I finally find each other, and we sit on the railing outside the hotel. She is around my age, with golden hair, a lush accent, and an erect, commanding presence. I wonder why she seems so familiar to me, and then I realize she reminds me of Mrs. Gollobin, the director of the choir and chorus back at Jamaica High School, the most charismatic teacher I ever saw. When Mrs. Gollobin clapped her hands and stuck out her chin, we would swallow conversations in midsentence. I suspect that if Svirsky clapped her hands, I would toss a colored hoop in the air and try to catch it with my big toe, no questions asked.

Svirsky was born in Odessa, moved to Moscow, studied ballet at the Bolshoi School, just a few blocks away from where we are sitting. She became a champion gymnast and was named a Master of Sport, the highest honor a Soviet athlete can achieve. She became a coach and was set for life, but her husband wanted to leave their homeland, because he was a builder who was not able to build.

"You're Jewish?" I ask.

"Yes, but that isn't why we left. It was a matter of freedom, gen-erally."

She says she did not want to leave the Soviet Union, but that out of loyalty she followed her husband to the San Fernando Valley. She tells me how she grew so accustomed to the luxuries of America that she had a second child, something she never would have considered without disposable diapers and baby food.

Svirsky laughs about the agent posted outside her hotel room, and how she enjoys opening the door and saying in Russian, "Why you walk here? You need something?" She has not contacted her relatives in Odessa because she thinks it would be "uncomfortable" for them. She says she is reminded of all the tribulations of daily life in the Soviet Union:

"When you look at people, they don't smile," she says. "They overdo their function of being serious. It's hard for me. I already forgot this, but it comes back to me."

I understand her point of view, but I cannot help telling her that I have seen Russians holding hands, playing with babies, laughing, much more secure and happy than people I had seen in Czechoslovakia, for example. The American vision of the robotlike Russian citizen just does not hold true.

"Russian people have a very good heart, they would give you their last piece of bread," she says.

I thank Alla Svirsky for her time, and she returns to the hotel for a visit with a few old friends. I walk back toward my hotel, eager to get to my machine. This is my kind of column, not an earthshaking scoop, no hard news, just the story of a former Soviet champion who has come back for a few days, the jumble of values, the tangle of emotions.

When I get back to the room, I start to write about the American coach from Moscow: "The love of music and motion began with lessons at the Bolshoi School in the heart of this city. . . . "

MOSCOW, JULY 9

Today at the press center, one of the interpreters asked if I would mind being interviewed by Radio Moscow. I have been cautious about talking to strangers ever since my trip to Mexico in 1979. Americans would show up in press rooms sporting credentials but making obtuse comments that no journalist would make.

There was a lot of serious intrigue going on that month: The Sandinistas were sensing victory in Nicaragua, and Archbishop Romero admitted to some of us that he might be a target for assassination in El Salvador. I became convinced that some of those cloddish strangers were really CIA agents.

In Moscow, what is the line between a journalist and a government agent? Reporters hear stories about overly friendly Russians who may be collecting information, or trying to entrap you for some political gain. A *Times* reporter has to remember that some people overseas believe *The Times* is practically an arm of the government. While I have no secrets, and certainly do not mind giving my opinions about America and the Soviet Union, I don't want people thinking I represent my government, particularly this one.

The interpreter introduced me to a woman in her midthirties, round-faced, dark-haired, attractive, gentle. I am sophisticated enough to know that anybody working as an interviewer for Radio Moscow is considered politically safe by the government, so I waited to hear her first few questions.

Speaking through the interpreter, the woman asked how I liked Moscow, how I thought the Goodwill Games were going, was this my first trip to the Soviet Union, the usual easy lead-in questions. Then she asked me if I thought the games would lead to better relations between countries.

"That is a difficult question," I said, "because both countries have problems. Both sides want to protect their interests, both sides have nuclear weapons, we have Three Mile Island, you have Chernobyl, we had Vietnam, you have Afghanistan. . . . "

The interpreter did not seem to be translating exactly, because I did not hear "Chernobyl" or "Afghanistan." But the interviewer nodded, and I knew she got my point.

"What is your impression of how Russians feel about peace?" the woman asked.

"I have no idea what your government really wants," I said, "but as a first-time visitor to Moscow, I do notice a great deal of signs about sports and peace. I don't know if that means anything, or if they are just slogans."

Then I added, "I do know this: The Russian people have suffered greatly from wars on their own soil, and the Americans have not. I have great respect for the Russian people for living through war in their country, and my guess is that Russian people do not want more war."

As the interpreter translated my words, tears started to stream from the radio woman's deep brown eyes. She held her microphone in one hand and used her free hand to wipe the tears from her eyes. Then she spoke several sentences in a soft voice, not her poised, professional tone.

"She says her father was injured in the war," the interpreter said. "She says her father always told her that he never wanted to see Russia in another war. She says she is glad to know that an American journalist understands this about the Russian people."

We continued the interview, looking into each other's eyes, and then I gave her one of my *New York Times* pins, and we shook hands and said goodbye. For the rest of the day, when I thought about her soft brown eyes, I felt I had accidentally glimpsed one corner of the soul of a nation.

MOSCOW, JULY 10

Victor, one of the translators in the *Times* bureau, is both an athlete and a sports fan. He and Irene, hired through a Soviet government agency, are assigned by *The Times* to pore through Soviet journals for nuggets of news about harvest and health care and social issues. In a country that has often hidden vital information, their research is invaluable to *The Times.*

One fringe benefit for Victor is accompanying me and Serge Schmemann to the gold-medal game of women's basketball today. Because the two nations have taken turns boycotting the past two Summer Olympics, this is the biggest meeting between the women's teams in many years.

An hour before the game, Cheryl Miller from the University of Southern California arrives, wearing green-tinted sunglasses and a Walkman wrapped around her ears, strutting to her own beat, as usual. She waves and points her index finger at embassy employees and other Americans in one corner of the small arena.

Before the game starts, the Americans try to get a wave going, rising from their seats and waving their arms. Some Brazilians get the picture and leap to their feet, but Soviet civilians did not survive Stalin's purges without learning to avoid attention. They remain in their seats, obediently, until it is appropriate to cheer.

In the warm-ups, our gaze goes to the seven-foot-one veteran, Yulana Semanova. Six years earlier, during a tour of the States, Semanova outplayed a slender young center named Anne Donovan. Now the grand old lady of the American team, Donovan has never forgotten the drubbing.

Age has reduced Semanova to a lumbering, tired giant. Midway through the game, she tries a flatfooted hook shot, but Donovan smacks the ball as it leaves Semanova's hand, making a loud *splat* that echoes all over the arena. As the blocked shot soars away from the basket, Donovan raises both fists in the air, exorcising her personal demon. The Americans win, 83–60, and Cheryl Miller drapes herself in an American flag and stages a victory lap around the arena.

Poker-faced and proper, Victor helps me by interviewing Olga Burjakina, the Soviet captain, after the awards ceremony. Burjakina tells Victor, "This was a healthy experience for us, and the world championships are just ahead and we will get ahead again."

After Victor passes along the quotes, Serge and I reassure him that the Russian women will get their act together for the world tournament in the fall, but Victor is not fooled by our gesture at sportsmanship. He says of the American women, "You are very good."

MOSCOW, JULY 11

Four reporters are trying to hail a cab in the rain outside Red Square, which is about as easy as hailing a cab in the rain in Times Square. In this bastion of the classless society, cabbies are a blend of J. P. Morgan and Jesse James, as played in the movie by John Belushi.

Just like in New York, Moscow cabbies want some assurance that it will be worth their while to stop. On a rainy day, people hold up two or three fingers, the universal signal they will pay two or three times the going rate. We can hear Lenin sputtering in anger in his tomb, a few meters away. Doesn't anybody believe in socialism anymore?

We are going to be late for our mass interview with Ted Turner out at the Soviet television center. John (Junior) Feinstein of the *Washington Post* spots an empty cab across the street, so he sprints across the broad boulevard to commandeer it. However, Junior is spotted by a traffic officer, who blows a whistle and races toward Junior.

Feinstein ought to be used to the authoritarian mind, since he has just spent the winter in the company of Bobby Knight. Ignoring the traffic cop, Feinstein gets into the cab to claim possession, Yankee fashion, but that trick does not go over well here. The cop blows his whistle and orders Junior out of the cab, with abrupt hand gestures. The cop then orders the cabbie to move on, forfeiting his space in front of the hotel, as punishment for encouraging this hooliganism.

We see Junior making hand gestures back at the officer before starting to race back across the street. But the cop forces him to walk to the corner and use the underpass. When Junior emerges from the tunnel, he is still sputtering at being forced to walk the line by a traffic officer.

Dave Kindred of Atlanta has located a cab by holding up five fingers. ("There're four of us on expense accounts," Dave reasons.) We speed off in the rain.

Tom Callahan turns around and looks at Junior, fuming in the backseat.

"Tell you what, John," Callahan says. "Let's say there's a war between your country and that cop's country. Who do you think is going to win?"

MOSCOW, JULY 12

Another visiting Yank has caught the attention of the authorities. Joe Gergen from *Newsday* wrote his first column about arriving in Moscow, only to find his luggage had been lost en route. He described finding himself on the same lost-luggage line as Paul Hornung, the old Golden Boy from Notre Dame, who is working here for TBS.

"I had the distinct impression we were locked in a bizarre Miller Lite beer commercial," Gergen wrote.

It was a typically wry Gergen variation on the old trash-the-locals theme, perfected by Jim Murray wherever he goes. However, a journalist from *Sovietsky Sport* wrote a rebuttal, which was translated by Tass, the Soviet news agency, under the wonderful headline PAJAMAS FOR MISTER GERGEN. It began:

Although this kind of service has not been envisaged for the Goodwill Games, we developed a philanthropic urge the other day to offer Mr. Joseph Gergen a pair of pajamas and a shaving kit.

The matter is that the U.S. journalist, who has flown to Moscow to cover the world multi-sport festival, reported that all his sleeping outfit consisted of a pocket flashlight and that there was a beard growing on his exhausted face. The man said the sorry circumstances had not befallen him through his own fault. . . .

After reading the article, we went to the press centres and stadium stands to look for an unshaven newsman in crampled [sic] clothes. There, we came across bearded, moustached and clean-shaven men but nobody looking anything like Gergen as we visualized him after seeing his *Newsday* article.

At the main press centre, though, we were shown a middle-aged, well-shaved gentleman with a tended moustache, who was busy typing at a video display. He looked not bad at all.

"Oh, my suitcase? It has been found, everything's OK," the man told us.

The *Sovietsky Sport* article went on to tease Gergen for not mentioning that his luggage had actually been lost by Lufthansa, not Aeroflot, and had been forwarded to Moscow a few days later, unharmed. The writer suggested Gergen was more interested in grumping about technicalities than writing about the competition.

Gergen's column had been a pleasant little scene-setter, with no malice apparent. I'm not surprised at Gergen being funny; I read him all the time. Why should I be surprised at somebody from *Sovietsky Sport* having a literate touch? This is, after all, the nation of Pushkin and Chekhov and Tolstoy.

MOSCOW, JULY 13

In a week's time, we have worked out a routine for living in the heart of Moscow. In the morning we pass up breakfast in the hotel in favor of breakfast in our room, with a view of St. Basil's straight out the window. I go upstairs for a huge pot of hot water from the cafeteria, and we make instant Colombian coffee and British tea, with French jam and day-old Russian bread and American concentrated juice. We have a refrigerator and a full set of dishes in our suite, normally used by Soviet officials visiting the Kremlin.

When we go out for the morning, we leave our key with the concierge near the elevator. I had heard horror stories about grumpy Russian concierges, but most of these women are conscientious, almost friendly. Because this hotel rarely has Western visitors, the concierges speak almost no English, but we get by with gestures and the few more words of Russian I pick up every day.

We take the elevator downstairs and plan our day at the service desk in the lobby. On our first day, the intrepid Bruce Schoenfeld from Cincinnati introduced us to Tanya, a buxom, dark-haired young woman who would look at home on West End Avenue in Manhattan. Tanya speaks English perfectly, and has a Western sense of getting things done.

Other Intourist guides do not dare to prod the system, but Tanya bawls out a balky post-office agent and explains things for us. Why was the metro station closed yesterday at rush hour, causing great inconvenience to thousands of commuters? Madame Gorbachev was giving a tour of the metro to Madame Mitterand, and the police blocked off the entire subway line. Tanya knows it all.

At another desk, we buy tickets for cultural events. The woman there is stylish and slender, no Nina Khrushchev. She speaks little English, but we speak French in arranging for tickets to the ballet, concerts, circuses.

Marianne is now the queen of the circuses, having seen the one in Gorky Park a couple of times. The circus was glamorous and professional, she says, on the level of our top Broadway or Las Vegas revues.

"The women are beautiful, sensuous," she says. "You don't know what you are missing."

The other night she took a subway and a bus out to the suburbs for another circus. The Intourist guide had written her destination in Cyrillic, and the women on the bus collaborated to make sure Marianne got off at the right stop. Everywhere she goes, people are friendly and attentive, no trace of hostility toward Americans.

Marianne is a resourceful Muscovite, getting on shopping lines when she sees them, even though nobody knows what is in supply that day. She found handsome books in English and Russian—Robert Frost's poems, Maxim Gorky, Lenin. She has found the bread stores and the vegetable stores, the alternative market where people sell their home-grown produce for profit. We have tried not to wear ostentatious clothes, but Russian pedestrians notice her basic English raincoat and her modest Italian shoes.

"Americanski," they say, rubbing their fingers together in the European gesture for wealth.

Today is Sunday, gray and raining. First we stroll through Gorky Park, the site of Martin Cruz Smith's thriller, but instead of bodies lying in the grass, there are young couples, families with young children, older single women, enjoying the freedom of a Sunday in midsummer. There are no panhandlers, no bag ladies, nobody whispering, "Joints, joints." Or if they are, I'm missing it. Things often seem more innocent with the language barrier.

Marushka my lovely tour guide takes me to a gazebo in the center of Gorky Park, where short-order cooks make sizzling crepes and pour apple butter over them. We buy containers of coffee and share a table with a father and a girl of around ten. I get the feeling he is a separated father seeing his daughter on Sunday afternoon, with the same tentative, hopeful manner that fathers and daughters have with each other in Central Park.

Our snack over, we stroll through the misty pink stone pathways of Gorky Park, past tree houses and little lagoons and jungle gyms. I leave Marushka my lovely tour gide at the metro stop. I am going to a water polo match. She is going to another circus. I think she's got the better deal.

MOSCOW, JULY 14

We have never stayed in a hotel with better security. Just to get inside the front door of the Moskva Hotel, we have to present our guest pass to several gruff men in clumpy suits. Then we have to walk past another series of guards, who smoke cigarettes and watch the single television set in the lobby, featuring Soviet westerns and war movies. The plots all seem the same—the hero is going back to his idyllic boyhood town to track down a capitalist smuggler or an ideological enemy of the people, with enough horses, blond heroines, and grateful old citizens to stock any three Randolph Scott epics.

When we get off the elevator, there are also security agents on our floor, who spend most of their time sleeping on couches near the concierge desk. Like alligators dozing at the edge of a swamp, they raise one surly eyelid when we walk past, letting us know they could spring into action at any moment.

After a few days, we noticed that one of the guards was monitoring our negotiations with the concierges. When the going got murky, the guard would broker a few key words in Russian and English. After a while, he began saying hello. I immediately became suspicious after hearing Alla Svirsky tell about the agent assigned to stand outside her door, and after being warned by old Soviet hands to assume that anything we do or say in our hotel room will be heard. That does tend to inhibit your love life, but maybe that's their ultimate goal in the Cold War. You tend to get paranoid.

"Be careful of anybody who seems friendly," I told Marianne.

But every time she would walk past the concierge desk, Tony would say hello, and after a few more days they became old pals. He says he is a former soldier, now a graduate student majoring in English and science. He is in his middle twenties, married, with a child, and comes from Kazakhstan, a long way from Moscow. Tony wants to practice his English with Marianne, so they sit in the lobby near the concierge desk and chat a couple of times a day. He is handsome and gentle, an all-American-boy type, from the days when we had all-American-boy types.

"Be careful of political conversations," I told Marianne, so today they were talking about Afghanistan and Vietnam and Watergate and Chernobyl.

When Marianne said she does not trust our government because we have been lied to so many times, Tony seemed indignant. He thought we were not very patriotic, and said he believed his government.

Marianne told him how radioactive clouds were drifting across Europe, carrying the spawn from the nuclear accident at Chernobyl, forcing people in Poland to not drink milk, forcing people in Wales to not slaughter their spring lambs. Under the new *glasnost* policy of Gorbachev, people in the Soviet Union have heard about Chernobyl. There is even a Chernobyl relief-fund box next to the exchange window in the lobby. Tony knows there was an accident at Chernobyl, but he seems rather ignorant about the long-term dangers of radiation.

"It's worse than you think," Marianne told him. "Check it out."

Today, Tony told Marianne he had spent his day off at the college library, where he has access to the London *Times*, the *International Herald Tribune*, and English-language papers from India.

"You were right," he told her, although he did not criticize his government.

Tomorrow she's going to bring up the dissidents and religion. If Tony's bosses debrief him, they'll get an earful.

MOSCOW, JULY 15

Bruce Schoenfeld has flipped. The nights of the hundred-dollar phone bills have destroyed his mind. He sits in the back of the bus, his headset on, undulating to the beat of a Western rocker, mumbling something about a corned-beef sandwich and going out on a date.

It's called the Three-Week Wall. Many Westerners posted in Russia are urged to take one long weekend a month in Helsinki or Frankfurt, just to keep their perspective. Bruce would just as soon it be the States.

A group of reporters are taking a bus to the Central Institute of Physical Education, where Soviet coaches are trained. We have built up in our fevered minds that this is where Soviet scientists create bionic athletes. Last week Sergei Bubka set a world record at the Goodwill Games, only to have an American pole-vaulter whine, "The guy is souped up"—meaning body-building steroids. The American did not refer to America's own history of athletes using dangerous steroids, but seemed to assume the Russians have discovered bigger, better, less detectable drugs.

We all want to see the labs where they do the experiments on Bubka, where they take him apart and put him back together again. But the guide's talk is about as revealing as a tour of Universal Studios. We realize we are being treated like tourists, not journalists.

Later, we are being led down a long corridor to another room of tumblers and gymnasts. On every wall is a photograph or a painting or a statue of V. I. Lenin. Schoenfeld loosens his headset.

"When we get to the next lecture, I'm going to ask, 'Say, as an American, I'm kind of curious about something. The Lenin Library. The Lenin Museum. The Lenin metro station. The Lenin Hills. Who was this Lenin, anyhow?"

His head starts bobbing again.

MOSCOW, JULY 16

In Mr. Gorbachev's new mood of *glasnost*, the daily avalanche of Soviet journals occasionally reveal a nugget of information that there might be one or two alcoholics and one or two homosexuals in the Soviet Union. It is usually the fault of the United States or China or Afghan rebels, depending.

Marushka my lovely tour guide was browsing in an art store when a man started talking to her. His name is Dmitri and he works in art restoration, and he was bemoaning the lack of art books and art materials available to Russian artists. Marianne said we would give him a few extra pencils and brushes if he met us near the hotel, and we invited him for coffee.

Dmitri led us to a restaurant on the second floor of a shopping center, the kind of place no tourist would ever find, and he talked the woman at the door into admitting three more people. We were excited because we were getting behind the facade, getting a glimpse of the real Moscow. It was a warm summer evening, full of promise.

The room was smoky and noisy, filled with people in leather jackets drinking beer. We asked Dmitri to order coffees all around, but he ordered two bottles of champagne and proceeded to drink the first bottle as if it were water.

Wanting to pump some information out of Dmitri to justify twenty dollars for entertainment on my expense account, I said, "I would trade both President Reagan and Vice-President Bush for your Mr. Gorbachev. What do you think of Mr. Gorbachev, Dmitri?"

Dmitri's face puckered up as if somebody had slipped him kvass instead of champagne.

"Nobody likes him!" Dmitri roared. "He has shortened the hours at the liquor stores!"

He took a swig straight from the bottle of champagne, in case Mr. Gorbachev should suddenly materialize and take the bottle away from him. We kept trying to talk about his work restoring icons, but Dmitri was concentrating on the champagne. We tossed some rubles on the table and left him alone with the second bottle.

Tonight we were taking a tour of the Rublev Monastery, where our tour guide was an impassioned young man with long hair. He talked in Russian about the spiritual values that led Rublev to paint the icons, and he pointed excitedly at the halo, at the angels, at the Madonna, his eyes burning brightly.

The translator, a proper middle-aged woman in a well-tailored suit, gave us the bare facts of the icons, the name, rank, and serial number. The young man became agitated and pointed at the bright lights framing the heads of every saint.

"He is saying these were things people used to believe," the guide said, "but of course these are not the beliefs of today."

The young guide realized something was not being translated.

"No, no," he said, switching to heavily accented English. "Not just art. Holy pictures. In church, you understand?"

The translator abruptly looked at her watch and said it was time for the concert, so we left the passionate young man in the museum. We walked to the old, desanctified church, where we heard a magnificent mixed chorus perform pop tunes and old Slavonic hymns. The translator stood at the front of the church and said the religious songs all had historical significance—from the deep past.

When the concert ended, we walked to the nearest metro stop. Waiting at the platform was our tour guide from the icon museum. Marianne and I started to thank him for trying to give us a full explanation of the icons, but we noticed another man, standing close to him. His companion said something that made the guide blush, and they moved far down the platform. When the train arrived, they boarded a different car, still standing close together.

MOSCOW, JULY 17

Normally, I do not write much about boxing, but I don't mind amateur boxing, with its short bouts, its heavy headgear, and its point system that rewards skill and aggression. Several American boxers have been complaining about the judging, and I decided to check it out.

The American coach is Roosevelt Sanders, a former marine, middle-aged, middle-class, the kind of man black civil servants from New York would call a "bootstrapper." He reminds us what this competition means to the young black boxers who harbor dreams, no matter how ludicrous, of being the next Ali, the next Sugar Ray Leonard.

"You take the volleyball team, they've got an education, they've got high-tech jobs, they've got security," Sanders says. "But our boxers are young men just out of high school. We're trying to help 'em reach their goal."

When the evening program begins, we are reminded that the Soviet boxers are battle-scarred veterans of hundreds of rounds in world competition and thousands of hours in the gym. Their names are not Russian; they come from the hard corners of this giant republic, from Georgia and Armenia and Kazakhstan rather than the urban streets of Moscow.

Boxing is a major sport to the Soviets. On Tuesday, a Soviet referee disqualified Harvey Richards for a low blow to a Danish boxer, but Richards appealed, claiming he should merely have been penalized a point. Today, we discover the Danish boxer has mysteriously, and perhaps graciously, gone home. After a long meeting, the officials allow Richards to move on to the next match.

In the third and final round tonight, Richards is knocked down by Andrei Karavev, and is counted out by the official. He gets up quickly and trudges to the dressing room.

We ask him how he waited out the protest. He says, "I took a walk to Lenin's Tomb in the morning, tried going shopping, but there wasn't that much to buy. I played cards with the guys. I tried not to think about the fight, but it's hard not knowing what's going to happen."

After chatting with some of the other young boxers, I am reminded that some of the best American sports journalists prefer boxing to any other sport because boxers do not have the layers of pretension you find in the team sports. They are good people.

A few minutes with these young black athletes make me think about America, remind me of my Aretha Franklin tapes and walking through Times Square and having brothers on the corner hail me, "Hey, Abe," my friends and colleagues, Reggie Jackson flailing his bat in the on-deck circle, Richard Pryor movies and Toni Morrison novels, black faces in the subway in my hometown. A few minutes with these brothers make me homesick.

MOSCOW, JULY 18

In the past two weeks, we have had the eerie sensation of seeing familiar faces all over Moscow, making me even more convinced that my father must have had Russian ancestry. A guard in the Pushkin Museum, dozing in a corner, was a lookalike for my father in his final years.

In the Lenin Museum, we saw a photograph of Lenin and his grandson, looking eerily like a family photograph of my father showing me how to hold a baseball bat when I was seven years old. Marianne had me divert the guard's attention in another room while she snapped a photograph of the Lenin picture.

Outside on the street, we saw a young woman who could have been our second daughter, Corinna, walking with her grandmother—same features, same coloring. Marianne casually took two snapshots of the young woman while pretending to photograph the building.

Marianne says she saw my brother Chris and his wife, Carol Ann Lorenz—together!—pushing a baby carriage, near Red Square. We have seen absolute ringers for Angela Kozuch McGuinness, who has been like an aunt to me, and my friend Al Campanis, the Greek-Italian general manager of the Los Angeles Dodgers. We realize, in walking the streets and riding the metro, that if we were not wearing Western clothes, we could blend in with the Slavic, northern faces of Moscow. I am writing my final column from here, calling it "The Faces of Goodwill." I think it is the best I have done in my two weeks here.

The most memorable figure of the two weeks was not an athlete, but the eccentric Western capitalist who funded these games. A few weeks ago, I would have sworn Ted Turner was merely a crude adventurer, making international mischief, but there is something persistently appealing about his bumbling around Moscow, squawking and honking about "my Commie buddies" and "my pinko friends."

We are becoming like political reporters who anticipate every speech the candidate has in his repertoire. Every time Turner launches into the one about saving the flora and fauna of the world from nuclear destruction, Junior Feinstein shouts out the punch line, "And what about the elephants?"

Turner is weird, but he has managed to pull the Russians and Americans together for a sports event, come up with 129 hours of programming for his network, all for the loss of merely $10 or $15 million. He says his mother worries about his deficit spending, but he ain't worried, Mamma, no way.

The Russians seem mystified by him. He is like a figure from their literary past, the slightly dangerous holy fool, stumbling around the countryside, preaching hell and damnation but fascinating the populace at the same time, part Rasputin, part Tolstoy. The paradox of the trip is that we spot dozens of Muscovites who are lookalikes for people back home, but Captain Outrageous turns out to be more Russian than the Russians.

MOSCOW, JULY 19

The last competition of the Goodwill Games is the male volleyball championship out at the Luzhniki sports center, late on Saturday night, America against the Soviet Union. Half a dozen American journalists, the survivors, have enough energy left to cover the match.

The Russians make a gallant comeback to win the match in five sets, well past midnight. Afterward, the last six American reporters scurry around to interview the American players.

Misha looks worried. He is a conscientious Soviet information officer who has made many friends in the American press corps by bustling around with information sheets and leading us to press conferences. He is the Moscow version of Bob Fishel, Joe Goldstein, Jay Horwitz, Katha Quinn, some of the best sports publicists in New York, a perfect example of the old "there are good people everywhere" theory.

"The last bus is leaving right now," Misha says, trying to hustle us out.

When we finish our interviews, it is twelve-thirty, the metro is closed down, there are no taxicabs, and there is no bus in the darkened parking lot. And there are twenty Americans and Soviets standing around.

Misha materializes from the darkness. He did not get on the last bus, as we might have expected him to do.

"Stay here," he says, rushing inside to make a phone call. In fifteen minutes, an extra bus roars around the corner. We all pile on. As the bus heads downtown toward the press center, somebody shouts, "Let's hear it for Misha," and everybody cheers.

The press center is nearly deserted in the final hours of the Goodwill Games. The survivors file our stories and say good-bye to the Russian telephone operators, hardy women who have been so patient with us, making sure we had good connections back to the States.

As the last stories go whizzing over the telephone lines, one of the operators produces half a dozen large dried fish, wrapped in heavy paper. Mike McGloin, a Yale University language student who has become a most helpful troubleshooter for the Turner people, shows us how to pluck the dry, pungent meat with our fingers. Then Mike takes up a collection and goes down to the bar for some bottles of Czech beer.

We sit around the press room and share the beer and the dried fish with the telephone operators. There is not much dialogue. The women seem to speak only telephone English, while we speak not enough Russian to get to know them. But after two weeks, there is the camaraderie of friends who have sized each other up as professionals. We all smile a lot and toast each other, and trade souvenir pins. I am not normally a late person, but I am not going to be sharing dried fish and Czech beer with friendly Russian telephone operators too soon again. It is not until three o'clock that I find a gypsy cab back to the hotel.

MOSCOW, JULY 20

Because I must attend the closing ceremonies tonight, Marianne has signed up for an all-day trip to Suzdal, an old monastery town. On this delightful Sunday afternoon, I decide to file my last column from the *Times* bureau, very much aware this could be the last time in my life I will ever walk the streets of Moscow.

I cross near the Bolshoi Theater, closed for the summer, past shops I have been too busy to visit, past a park with thick trees and tables and bright umbrellas, into a quiet neighborhood, somebody tinkering with a car, a few people sitting on stoops, most windows closed, people gone to the beloved countryside. This could be any other European city in the middle of the summer. How comfortable I have become here.

With James Taylor crooning in my headset, it takes a while for me to realize I am being followed by two long-haired young men. They catch up at a streetcorner, and after making sure no police officer is watching, they gesture to me. I take off the headset. They want to buy my Walkman. Good price. Sorry. What about my jeans? I only have this pair. They point toward the little weasel or whatever logo is on my sport shirt. I really don't want to sell the shirt off my back. Besides, I don't want to get into trouble. No trouble, we are businessmen. The two businessmen give me the thumbs-up sign, and we part friends.

I reach the bureau, and nod at the ever-present soldier in the wooden sentry box. The building is empty, quiet, with many of the foreign press away for the weekend. I do not wait for the elevator, but walk up the stairs, smelling and listening to this building for the last time.

I have visited Serge Schmemann's apartment, as well as the apartment of Phil Taubman and his wife, Felicity Barringer, the two other reporters in the bureau. The apartments are large and sunny with high ceilings, and stocked with goods from the United States, Great Britain, and Finland.

The bureau is open. By now, I know how to use the machines, how to code my stories to transmit them to New York, the telephones. I start to write my last column.

Serge wanders in sleepily and puts on a videotape of the volleyball finals last night.

"Don't tell me who won," he says, with a yawn.

He seems tranquil for a reporter being transferred after five years in the homeland of his father.

"Well, we never did get together for a meal," he says.

"We'll do it in New York," I say.

Serge and Phil have been very friendly, but right in the middle of the games, Craig Whitney, the former bureau chief and now an executive with *The Times,* dropped into town for a visit, and things got more formal.

Kim, the American assistant, wanders in with a box of sour-cream pastry, more delicious than anything we buy in Little Italy.

"Where did you get these?" I ask in amazement.

"One of my girlfriends," Kim says. "She's a great shopper. She knows where all the private stuff is."

With the bureau informal again, I realize how much I feel at home in this outpost. I have a sudden fantasy of somebody back in New York asking me to stay on a few more weeks, a few months, to help with the workload. The old dream of being a foreign correspondent.

Then I ask myself: How street-smart would I be on a cold January night, having to size up somebody on a dark corner, to decide if I could trust him well enough to go to his apartment for a talk, or accept a document from him, or just believe what he tells me? Or would I get myself set up in no time?

Would I be able to pick up the complicated Russian verbs? Would I be able to remain stable in this isolated post? Could I handle the cold winters? Could I sound knowledgeable enough to please the home office and not sound like a fool in print?

I have such great respect for reporters like Serge and Phil and Felicity that I do not automatically assume I would be as good as they are. Ever since I gave up being a national correspondent, I have tried to bury this curious side of me, the restless, ambitious part of me. On this lovely afternoon in Moscow, the old dream kicks in again, the dream of being someplace new—learning, hustling, trying, failing, improving.

I file my column, thank Kim for the pastry, wish Serge good luck in his next post, and walk down the stairs and out past the sentry box. Even on this beautiful afternoon, the Russian guard stays in his little guardhouse. I turn and wave to him. What the hell.

"Do svidaniya," I say. Good-bye, Moscow.

LENINGRAD, JULY 23

I am pounding my fist on the counter and cursing at a ticket agent from Aeroflot. I am not particularly proud of my behavior, but I know it is the only way I will get out of Leningrad tonight.

It started to go bad when we flew here Monday night. My Goodwill Games pass did not seem to matter much anymore. Our hotel was under repair, scaffolding outside the window, dust everywhere, mosquitoes in the room.

On Tuesday we paid the six-dollar tourist fee to beat the line at the Hermitage, knowing this might be the one day in our lives to see the treasures. After five glorious, calf-numbing hours, we stumbled back to our hotel, where dinner was a horrow show and the mosquitoes kept us awake all night.

This morning we asked Intourist to find us a hotel with hot water and no mosquitoes, and they sent us to a modern hotel at the edge of the city, but it was a dump, ten years old and falling apart, like many new structures in the Soviet Union. After looking at four dismal rooms, we realized we had loved the Soviet Union, but now it was time to head west.

A civil young Intourist agent made a few phone calls, smiled,· and said it was all set—the last flight of the day, Finnair to Helsinki, Lufthansa to Frankfurt. We gave her our last few packages of pantyhose, and she smiled graciously.

On the way to the airport, our cabbie kept talking to us over his shoulder, driving too fast. Suddenly, a truck stopped dead in our lane, and our cabbie tried to swerve out of the way. We could feel the scraping of metal upon metal, centimeters from serious injury, but the cabbie shrugged and kept rolling.

At the airport, for the first time in nearly three weeks we ran into the bureaucratic dumbness that some visitors to the Soviet Union had warned us about. After making us wait an hour, the agent gave us a blank look about rewriting our business-class ticket. After another hour of haggling, I found a Finnish agent from Finnair, who came out from his office and told the Soviet agent how to handle the ticket, but that only made her sulk even more. She asked me to step aside while she took care of other customers, but I refused.

Turning to the American executives, the Swiss businessmen, the Italian travelers, I apologized in English.

"I'm sorry," I said, "but I'm not giving up my place until these people fix my ticket."

I was convinced the agent was doing it on purpose, perhaps because she did not fully understand the coding on my business ticket, perhaps because she was mad at the Finnish official, perhaps because she did not like my face, perhaps because it was her nature. When I asked for a supervisor, the sullen agent said she was in charge. Please to be patient.

I could see Marianne standing behind me, starting to cry.

"We're not getting out of here," she said.

I began to feel like Baryshnikov and Hines in the movie *White Nights,* trying to escape the KGB agents in a desperate chase. I knew we had exactly one chance at catching the last flight today.

When I was preparing for this trip, I read in several places that Russia has a thousand-year tradition of bullying. Everybody has a boss, right up to the czar, right up to Stalin, and deep down inside, everybody expects to be browbeaten by somebody. I pulled out my badge from the

Goodwill Games, I pulled out my *New York Times* identification, I pulled out my New York Police Department press badge, I pulled out my Baseball Writers of America card. I cursed and I threatened and I pounded the ledge with my fist. I did everything but take off my shoe and pound it on the desk.

After the good two weeks in Moscow, I hate to seem like a spoiled American journalist, but I see only one way out tonight. I remember my friend Roy Larsen from the *Chicago Sun-Times* berating an inept official from the Vatican who could not produce the Pope's speech hours after it had been delivered. Sometimes there is only one way a journalist can get results—to use righteous anger like a weapon. I use language from my schoolyard basketball days in Queens, I use some French, I use some Spanish, I use whatever I know. I am McEnroe cursing the umpire at center court, I am Connors grabbing his crotch at the camera, I am every bad little American boy that ever was.

"My tickets are business class," I shout, pointing my finger at the agent. "Fix it! Get it right! You!"

The agent seems rattled, but she suddenly remembers how to rewrite a business ticket. We have exactly five minutes to catch the plane when the customs man says we are overweight by forty kilos. I am sure we are entitled to extra weight in business class, but I have no recourse but to whip out my American Express card and contribute $150 to the socialist cause.

We run down the gangway. The doors close behind us on an immaculate Finnair jet. The chic stewardesses pass out tasty snacks on china dishes. We are in the West. I happen to know a Sheraton at the airport in Frankfurt where there will be a huge double bed and thick towels and, oh, yes, baseball on the U.S. Army television channel, too.

Hines and Baryshnikov lean back in their plush Finnair seats and take a deep breath. Hines and Baryshnikov are heading west. Gonna find Lenny Dykstra and Mookie Wilson.

CARDIFF, WALES, JULY 26

This morning we were drinking tea in the living room, watching the lambs grazing on the hillside, with the rugged Brecon Beacons jutting into the clouds to the south.

"Well, shall we go to the baseball game?" Alastair asked, jingling his car keys.

"Alastair, there are no baseball games in Wales," we said.

"Sun's out," Alastair said, shooing us into the car.

Alastair Mackintosh, who used to live across the street from us in Port Washington, says we bring the sun with us, which is why he invites us every summer.

No matter where he is posted by British Airways, Alastair comes home to Breconshire, just north of the dormant coal region, surrounded by sheep farms and narrow lanes and pubs with surprisingly good food, not far from Roman gold mines and Norman market towns, tiny chapels and monasteries. Sometimes he takes us up in his glider, searching for the perfect wave above the stark Welsh hills.

Wales is where we go to get away, the place in the world I feel most comfortable aside from my regular Port Washington–New York axis. It feels like home, the Welsh people sturdy and familiar, less rigid and distant than the English across the border ("Foreigners," Alastair calls the English). Wales reminds me of the self-sufficient rural America that *Life* magazine used to champion in my childhood right after World War II, that I later found only in ruined, somewhat sinister parody in Appalachia many years later.

As our Russian experience crumbled in the final hours in Leningrad, we knew if we could get to Alastair's house, everything would be all right. As we caught flights from Leningrad to Helsinki to Frankfurt to London, I caught up on the baseball scores in the *International Herald Tribune*, but I did not expect to see a ball game in Wales.

Alastair drives down from the mountains to the capital, where he seeks out a lovely urban park, surrounded by genteel red-brick buildings. In the distance, we spot two teams in bright shorts and jerseys, with a cluster of wives and other spectators behind a few benches.

"Soccer? Cricket? Rugby?"

Then I spot a man swinging a wooden bat at underhanded pitches. I count nine fielders in a 360-degree circle around the pitcher, with four posts stuck in the ground. The ball is fair in any point of the compass, which explains the players chasing the ball through moving cars and people walking their dogs.

We introduce ourselves to William Barrett, a headmaster by profession and a volunteer official of the Welsh baseball league, who tells me Jane Austen mentioned baseball in *Northanger Abbey,* written in 1792, forty-seven years before Abner Doubleday allegedly invented baseball in Cooperstown, New York.

"Our players are mostly dockworkers who pay a pound a game for the rights to the field," Barrett says. "We used to get thousands of people out for the game, but there are too many other diversions now. But we're proud of our programs for young boys and girls."

Midway through the game, I find myself watching the hurler for the Llanrumney team, a burly redhead with a droopy moustache and an athlete's bulk. His best pitch is a spinning, rising fastball straight at the chin, as intimidating as a major-league brushback pitch.

After a lifetime of watching games, part fan, part writer, I still enjoy watching athletes strut and swagger, still enjoy how they play their games. Is it hero worship or envy or another form of the art appreciation that also lures people to ballet and theater? Even on holiday in Wales, my ultimate haven, I cannot resist getting interested in a game, in a new athlete.

"Do you think I could talk to the pitcher?" I ask Barrett.

While Llanrumney is batting, Barrett calls over John Smith, the burly pitcher who reminds me of coal miners back in eastern Kentucky. Smith has hurled for Wales against an English team from Merseyside in thirteen straight international matches.

"I don't make anything from baseball," Smith says, "but it's a nice feeling when the youngsters come up to you and say, 'Don't you play for Wales?' "

As we chat about pitching, I realize Smith knows as much about his mechanics and his limitations, about the hopes and fears of the hitters, as does another aging hurler from America.

I ask. John Smith has never heard of Tom Seaver.

"I'm thirty-four now, getting on in years," Smith says, "and I don't throw as hard as I used to. But the beauty of this game is that you learn to get them out other ways. I'm trying to place my fielders more now. Let them get the batters out for me."

I write all this down, enjoying the interview with yet another "old pro," and then Smith excuses himself to buzz a few fastballs at the batters' chins. William Barrett tells stories of the legendary Fred Fish, who once hit eleven homers in twelve times up, the immortal Tommy Denning, the Irish immigrant Paddy Hennessey, and the American sailors from *The Manley,* who demonstrated the Yankee game during World War II.

The game is over; Llanrumney wins again. I wave good-bye to our new pals, as Alastair heads for our tour of the coal fields of the Rondda Valley. I'm on holiday in Wales, and the office does not know where I am. No deadlines, no change of plans, no telephones. I am also one column ahead.

AUGUST

LONDON, AUGUST 3

The Chicago Bears and Dallas Cowboys are in town for an exhibition at Wembley Stadium, flexing their muscles and nearly dislodging tits-and-ass from the front pages of the tabloids. A beer company is sponsoring a league, with leftover American quarterbacks teaching the game to the locals. In Regent Park yesterday, we saw several teams practicing. People hold Super Bowl parties and form fan clubs for National Football League teams.

It is definitely hypocritical of me, showing interest in a football game in London when I do my best to avoid going to New Jersey for the Jets and Giants. I don't mind admitting it, football's biggest value to me is to justify a few days in London, or a week in a warm place for the Super Bowl.

Our real reason for coming to London is the theater—that is to say, the National Theatre, three theaters on the south end of the Waterloo Bridge doing everything from Shakespeare to avant-garde. When most Americans talk about the theater in London, they mean *Cats* and *Starlight Express* in the West End, but for us the National Theatre is the home of dreams and language.

In past visits here, we have seen a wickedly funny *Double Dealer*, written by Congreve centuries ago, and Gogol's sarcastic *Inspector General*. Last year we saw Ian McKellan die three different ways in a week —throwing himself under a train in Chekhov's *Wild Honey*, machine-gunned for his pride in Shakespeare's *Coriolanus*, and stabbed in a haunting *Dutchess of Malfi* by Jacobean playwright John Webster.

As soon as we arrive in London, Marianne rushes to the National Theatre, buying tickets for as many matinees and evenings as she can arrange. Tickets in hand, we romp like children through the open-air bookstalls, bargain with lithograph vendors, visit the art galleries at the Royal Festival Hall, drink shandy—lemon soda and bitters—on a bench, and watch the tour boats go past. At six we eat dinner in the cafeteria or the formal restaurant upstairs, and then we stop in the lobby and enjoy the live jazz or classical music. At intermission, we rush out for coffee on the patio and watch the boats glide by on the river, lights flickering in the milky dusk. This is our Disneyland, our Club Med, our Yellowstone National Park.

To validate our pilgrimage to the National Theatre, I am writing a column about England's fascination with Refrigerator Perry.

Tonight a crowd of 82,699 surges from the underground in a driving rain to watch the midsummer exhibition. On the same pitch where England beat West Germany for the World Cup in 1966, Walter Payton and Jim McMahon play a few downs, enough to fulfill the contract, and then a horde of anonymous brutes take turns wallowing in the mud. The promoters have lined up the Super Bowl champions and the outfit that calls itself America's Team, but the Brits know when they are being shortchanged. As the Bears slog out an unimaginative 17–6 victory, the fans chant, "Bo-ring, bo-ring."

I interview a few fans, describe the local cheerleaders and the attempt at hamburgers, and I write a column about the ultimate degradation of British civility. If they like football so much, I write, maybe we can work out a trade. We'll give them the National Football League. All I want in return is the National Theatre.

PORT WASHINGTON, AUGUST 25

Some people think August is "the pits of the world," as the mad Irish poet J. P. McEnroe once called something else. Old Reliable, Dave Anderson, always takes August off, and doesn't come back until the National Football League starts playing real games.

Usually Dave is right, but this August has been enjoyable ever since I got back. As a correspondent in Mexico and Russia this summer, I felt it was important to avoid the cheap jokes and stereotypes that American journalists can invoke—Montezuma's revenge, grim Kremlin robots.

But soon I was back in the middle of the tabloid wars, the Mets in first place, Giants fans insisting they will settle for nothing less than the Super Bowl this year, George Steinbrenner always good for a few laughs, and now Junior McEnroe coming back from his honeymoon to give us some lunacy at the U.S. Open. This is the summer doldrums?

As soon as the jet lag wore off, I went up to Yankee Stadium, where I quickly realized I hardly knew a soul. A quick check of the roster showed the Yankees had changed ten of twenty-four players since I had visited the old fortress on Opening Day. Several coaches had also been disappeared, as they say in Latin America.

A year or two ago, I might have launched into a sermon about the instability of working for the Yankees, but this time I wrote a short story about Rip Van Winkle returning from a summer in Mexico and Moscow and finding everything topsy-turvy in Yankee Stadium.

When Rip discovers a plaque to Billy Martin in the center-field pantheon of Popes and Hall-of-Famers, Rip tries to place a call to Mr. Steinbrenner.

"Which Mr. Steinbrenner do you want?" a voice asks.

"There are two?" Rip asks.

"George and Hank, father and son," the voice says.

Rip silently replaces the telephone in its cradle and tiptoes out of the press room. One Mr. Steinbrenner is more than enough for him. He peers into the manager's room, wondering whom he will see in there. Yogi Berra? Alvin Dark? Bucky Harris? Judge Crater? Amazed to discover Lou Piniella has lasted four months, Rip then blunders around the locker room, discovering that coaches and players have vanished in his absence.

From the Ripper column, I moved to a column about the return of Lee Mazzilli, the handsome Brooklyn boy who used to bring Saturday Night Fever to Shea Stadium when the Mets were bad. Mazzilli has been brought back to replace George Foster, who was released after claiming the Mets were prejudiced against black players. I pointed out that the Mets have never had many black players, but that Foster's reasoning and timing were terrible, since he had been benched in favor of Kevin Mitchell, a young black player.

Mostly, I wanted to have some fun with the return of Mazzilli. I used a few quotes from the delighted player, but most of the column was about the aging teeny-boppers who have haunted Frank Cashen, the general manager of the Mets. Cashen had once told me, over a beer at the World Series, how the female fans used to spot him on the number 7 elevated train, shrieking, "Leee! You traded Leee!"

Met fans can be vulgar and unruly, but they have endowed that franchise with amazing goodwill and energy since the team was dropped on New York's doorstep in 1962. The literate Cashen knows all about Greek choruses, and he wanted to appease the Furies before the championship series.

I called the column "Exorcising the Demons." The last paragraph went:

> As Mazzilli bounced onto the field, a few waved and asked for autographs, and if one listened closely he could hear a few shrieks of 'Leee!' cutting through the sound of the jets from LaGuardia. That shrill wail on the summer breeze never sounded better to Lee Mazzilli. It sounded pretty good to Frank Cashen, too, because it meant that no matter what happens to the Mets for the rest of the season, the spell of the furies is no longer on his back.

I was enjoying being back home, able to tease and twit the usual suspects. Hitters say there are times when they can see the ball clearly, when their feet are dug in just right at the plate, when their hands can flick the outside pitch to the opposite field, or pull the fastball over the fence. Columnists, like athletes, have their slumps and their hot streaks. In five years of writing a column, there have been weeks at a stretch when I did not like a thing I wrote, when I was merely interviewing athletes and printing their words and my reactions. Then I would wake up one morning and the ball seemed as large as a grapefruit again.

The other day, George Steinbrenner did it again. The man keeps retiring the numbers of Yankee heroes, twelve at latest count. I wrote, "There is no quarrel with the first ten selections, but the enshrinement of Rizzuto last summer and of Martin last week, both current Yankee broadcasters, gives the impression of pushing tradition to cover up the chaos of their daily operation."

I predicted that Steinbrenner would keep on retiring numbers until only Jim Bouton's Number 56 remained. Bouton is a pariah to the Yankees because his classic book, *Ball Four,* dared suggest that ballplayers drink, curse, and fool around on the road. He has never been invited back for Old-Timers' Day, and never will be.

This milking of tradition is just another facet of the bad taste of George Steinbrenner, God's gift to columnists. But give George credit: He got me through the August doldrums, right up to my favorite two weeks of the year.

FLUSHING, AUGUST 29

When I was covering religion, I used to treat myself to two tickets for the entire U.S. Open. I would either take vacation, or, if there was not much news that day, slip over to Forest Hills and check with the office from a pay phone.

"What's all that cheering?" an editor might ask.

"A revival meeting," I might reply.

Actually, it was the mob goading Nasty or Little Jimbo into some new level of juvenile delinquency. One year I went to twelve day sessions out of thirteen, which I realized was a bit compulsive. I would go with my tennis partners or somebody from my family, observe the players and muse about what I might write if I were covering, a major sign I had not lost my enthusiasm for sports.

Now that I'm back in sports, the Open is still my favorite two weeks of the year—tennis in the afternoon, baseball a few nights at Shea, no bridges to cross, no Bronx, no New Jersey, everything coming true for the Mets, the Dodgers in town this weekend, Welch and Mary Ellen around, Gary Carter itching to come back from his injury, fans booing Darryl Strawberry. And Junior McEnroe coming back from his honeymoon. For these two weeks, I never second-guess myself for coming back to sports.

It is surely a sign of my bourgeois middle age, but I feel more at home at the Open than at any other sports event, even with its obnoxious trappings, the crass sponsors and the joyless agents, the spoiled players and the indulgent suburbanites in their designer tennis clothes.

I love tennis because even a middle-aged hacker can sit in the stands and try to learn something from the professionals. How come I hit one backhand straight and flub the next one straight in the air? I love tennis because of the intense personal competition, boxing without brains being scrambled. I love tennis because I have friends at the Port Washington Tennis Academy, where Harry Hopman used to teach, where McEnroe was developed, where Tracy Austin still hangs out. And I love the U.S. Open because it is a bazaar, a fiesta of bright flags and pretty women and many languages and skillful athletes, just twenty-five minutes from my house.

The Open is a tricky event for a columnist because we assign two of our best writers, Pete Alfano to cover mostly the men and Roy Johnson to cover mostly the women. Both are good reporters with growing writing styles, who could easily be columnists. At a few sports, I feel compelled to back up with quotes from the locker room, the drama on the field, the color of the event, the broad significance, but at the Open I always know Pete and Roy will capture the total feel. This challenges me to reach another level, something different, something personal.

Another reason I enjoy the Open is the international writing crew, a floating crap game of Americans and Europeans, nearly as many women as men. It is the only sports event that feels like a social occasion, lots of laughing in the press box, reunions with old friends like Rino Tommasi from Milan, Alex Martinez Roig from Barcelona, Alexander Timar from Agence France Presse, Nora McCabe of Toronto, and the scandalous Gianni Clerici of Milan, who once wrote of a female tennis player that she was in such great condition, she felt like a new woman.

Only in a tennis press box does newlywed Bud Collins introduce you to his bride, Mary Lou, a teacher who reads hardcover books while waiting for her husband to write his column. Every year Collins, aka Collini, organizes a doubles tournament for the press—the U.S. Hopeless—with teams named Assholes, Preverts, Coprophiliacs, Pompini, Culatoni, Spagnole, Khybers, Maricons, Pédés, and Fags. One year the prizes were given out by a model known as Miss Herpes.

Between tennis games and hugs from old friends, we manage to get some work done. Last week the editors stopped worrying about whether I might favor Martina, and they asked me to write an appreciation of the last days of Chris Evert and her old beau, Jimmy Connors.

In a long telephone conversation, Chris talked more about Jimmy than about herself. She was engaged to Connors back in 1974, and she has spoken well of him ever since. I recalled that Harry Hopman, with his interest in horse-playing, was always disappointed that Chris and Jimbo did not have a child, just for the bloodlines.

"One of the reasons New Yorkers love Jimmy so much is because he goes out there fighting," Chris said the other day. "New Yorkers are pretty basic people, and they love the way he was living his life out there on the court."

Chris did not sound very confident about her own game, minimizing an inflamed knee and saying she was not as resilient as she used to be.

"It was always that I could reach back and find some way to get up for a match," she said. "Now, it's how I feel that day."

My sentimental tribute to Jimbo and Chris ran the Sunday before the Open, with a cute photograph of the two of them clowning around during a doubles match in 1983. They definitely used to bring out the romantic side in each other.

Once the tournament began, I would concentrate on the male players, particularly J. P. McEnroe, Jr.—George Steinbrenner in short pants— God's gift to tennis writers. Junior got married the other day to Tatum O'Neal, the actress, who is about to have their baby. He tried to come back for the Open, but he just didn't have it, losing to Paul Annacone in the first round.

A year or two ago, I would have written a descriptive column, going heavily with quotes from McEnroe about his painful day on center court. A glorified sidebar, maybe. But recently I've been having fun with other voices, the way I did in my Rizzuto column last year or my Larouche fantasy this spring, or my Rip Van Winkle persona a few weeks ago.

My voice for the McEnroe column was a young, egomaniacal yuppie from Manhattan, with a fancy apartment and fancy foreign car, taking a day off to visit the Open, perhaps a little high on something.

In my lead, I imagined my yuppie stepping from his million-dollar apartment to head for the Open: "What a bummer. Go out for the morning paper and step over two bag ladies and three bums and one screaming maniac. They should ship 'em all out of town and leave New York to us civilized New Yorkers."

My yuppie read in the paper that McEnroe said New Yorkers boo him because they see themselves in McEnroe. My yuppie did not agree with that:

"That baby? That twirp? Ranting and raving out there on the tennis court? Who's he kidding? He's not anything like a real New Yorker. He's got it totally backwards. We boo him because he doesn't have enough class for the Big Apple."

Creating this character is my comment on the new breed of moneyed dandies who live in glitzy apartment buildings, who drive foreign cars, but it was also a way of twitting McEnroe, who is certainly not like anybody else in my hometown. Oh, no. He just looks like my youngest brother, Chris, and he talks like my middle brother, Pete. Your basic wise-ass New Yorker.

On Wednesday morning, my sister Janet called and said Don Imus had nominated my McEnroe column for the Pulitzer Prize during his morning radio show.

For my Friday column, I wrote about the doubleheader in Flushing over the weekend—tennis and the Mets, night and day. The city officials have been urging everybody to take the subway or the railroad instead of driving to Shea Stadium and the Tennis Center, but I predicted some people would not get the word and would be caught in a dreadful traffic jam.

"But just remember as you sit in traffic," I wrote. "Somehow, it is all John McEnroe's fault."

Was it prophecy or just picking on Junior? This morning I arrived at the Open and was greeted by an apparition in plaid Bermuda shorts, purple sport shirt, and topsiders. It was Bud Collins, the Mister Sociability of the tennis circuit. (Who will ever forget Chris Evert, coming off the court at Wimbledon after a loss to Martina in the finals, and spotting the garish Collini with his NBC crew? "Nice pants, Bud," Chris intoned with dry irony.)

"Nice traffic report, Vecsey," Collins announced today in his Boston accent.

Collini scoffed, but McEnroe and his doubles partner, Peter Fleming, missed all the warnings about gridlock in Flushing, and showed up late for their doubles match. When Junior was informed that he and Fleming had to forfeit the match, he roared out of the parking lot—and back into traffic. That will teach him to not read the papers.

A few days later, I received a note from Clara G. Agin, which began, "Dear George: I take the privilege of addressing you so informally as your senior homeroom teacher at Jamaica High School long years ago. Don't flatter yourself! I still hold you up to my grandsons as an example of how a young gentleman does not behave."

She went on to list a number of disreputable acts in her classroom, and she said she particularly enjoyed the McEnroe column: "From your articles I take it you are now a husband, father and father-in-law and are qualified to recognize a brat when you see one!" I was tempted to write back that it must have been another George Vecsey in her classroom, but maturity won out, and I sent her a thank-you note.

SEPTEMBER

FLUSHING, SEPTEMBER 7

I find myself melancholy on this last day of the U.S. Open. Brigadoon is fading into the mists for another hundred years—or at least the next fifty weeks. But there is a perfect angle for the last day of the tournament: All four finalists are from Czechoslovakia.

Because of the rain earlier in the weekend, the women's final is being played today instead of its usual Saturday. Martina Navratilova from Revnice is playing Helena Sukova from Prague, and Ivan Lendl from Ostrava is playing Miloslav Mecir from Prievidza. Instead of playing "The Star-Spangled Banner," will they play "Má Vlast"?

Poor Czechoslovakia. Ever since I spent eleven days there working on Martina's book, whenever I hear the horns and the cymbals and the drums of Smetana's patriotic "Má Vlast" ("My Country"), I think of the statues and the castles and the bridges of Prague, the lost princes of Bohemia walking through the narrow streets, wearing blue jeans.

It was the most psychologically depressed country I have visited, worse than Mexico with its fallen peso but its Indian stoicism, certainly worse than Russia with its stultifying system but triumphant sense of homeland. Czechoslovakia was an occupied country, facing the next thousand years with a broken heart.

Yet somehow this tiny northern country with few indoor courts has produced four finalists in the U.S. Open, something not even the host nation has ever done. For poor Czechoslovakia, with missiles planted in its fields and mountains, supervised by its "guests" from the East, this success in tennis is tempered by reality. Martina is now an American from Forth Worth. Lendl lives in Connecticut, with an application for American citizenship. And Hana Mandlikova, who did not reach the finals, is rumored to be considering Australian citizenship. I'll write more about Czechoslovakia than tennis today.

I passed up Bud Collins's annual press tournament in order to be fresh for the two finals. The U.S. Hopeless is always a fitting way to end the Open. The male reporters are allowed to shower in the men's locker room, mostly deserted on the final day.

A couple of years ago, a few of us noticed John McEnroe in one room, glowering at us, while Jimmy Connors, in another room, also glowered at us, both making sure they never made eye contact with each other. The hostility of the two male finalists was a far cry from Chris and Martina, who once shared bagels during a long men's semifinal match while waiting to play each other in the finals.

When I arrive at the Open, I look for Malcolm Moran from *The Times* and Karla Hudecek, his journalist-wife, in the stands. Karla is wearing a red skirt and white sweater with blue trim.

"I thought it was appropriate to wear the Czech colors," says Karla, who has visited her relatives in Czechoslovakia.

Because the two finals could last three hours or six hours, I need color for my early column. Karla's use of the national colors will come in handy, although I won't mention her by name.

Just before the women's final, I take a seat in the open press section, behind the service area. While Martina and Helena are playing a long second game, I notice Martina's contingent waiting anxiously behind the ushers' rope. I slip into the crowd and say hello to Judy Nelson, Martina's best friend, and Aja Zanova, the former championship figure skater, who helped make Martina feel at home in New York. They look anxious at arriving late for Martina's match.

"We got caught in traffic," Aja says. "We forgot about the baseball game."

I feel a nudge in my ribs, and I turn to see Jana. Since I saw Jana in Dallas in February, she has left Czechoslovakia to move to Bonn, where she has a boyfriend. Her skin color and her expression look better than the last time.

"Everything is good," Jana says.

When the third game is over, they rush to their seats at courtside to give Martina the visible encouragement she needs. Some reporters have made cruel jokes about Martina always having Team Navratilova, things they would never say about Chris or Jimbo or Junior. These reporters do not think of what Martina gave up when she left Czechoslovakia at the age of seventeen, and how she has tried to recreate a feeling of family, a sense of community, for herself.

I go back to my seat to watch Martina play Sukova. When I was working on our book, I'll admit, I used to have to control my nervous twitches during Martina's matches, which is why Abe Rosenthal was exactly right in forbidding us to collaborate on books with people we cover. But now that the book has come and gone, I don't twitch at Martina's matches. She outlasted Steffi Graf in the semifinals, but she and everybody else knows that Steffi will be back.

If I were writing a column about Martina today, I would focus on the old relationship between her and Helena: Martina's grandmother once beat Helena's grandmother in a tennis match in Czechoslovakia, and Helena's mother, Vera, who died of brain cancer several years ago, had been Martina's coach when Martina defected. Today Martina defeats Vera's shy, willowy daughter, 6–3, 6–2, but during the postmatch interviews, no reporters seem interested in this history. Maybe they didn't read the book.

After listening to the interviews, I find a quiet corner of the press room and write an early column about the Czech presence here. I use a lot of material from the men's semifinals yesterday, when Mecir loyally explained the Czechoslovak success in tennis: "You don't have to be rich to play." The big, graceful Mecir (known as *Il Gattone*, the Big Cat, on the tour) says he would prefer being home fishing rather than seeing the sights of the West.

After Lendl wins in straight sets, I rush over to the interview room and listen to Lendl sound more and more like a capitalist from Greenwich than a recent Czechoslovak soldier. Told that Mecir prefers the European clay circuit so he can rush home to play for his army team, Lendl says sardonically, "That's one way to look at it."

Under other circumstances, I might have written an entire sub column about the life and times of Ivan Lendl, once thought to be a "choker," but now the champion in his new home. But I have written enough about Lendl's dour Eastern European psyche, and would rather stay with the overview about the Czechoslovak presence here today. The lights are on in the press box overlooking the emptied center court, but there is no sociability now. Everybody has deadlines; everybody has planes to catch. I decide not to say good-bye to anybody. The party's over.

I pack up my machine and trudge through the corridors of the tennis center, sticky and smelly from two weeks of beer and soda, expensive garbage. I walk past the outer courts, now dark, where only a few days ago the best players in the world were playing in bright sunlight. In the darkened dirt parking lot, I squish through the muck of thirteen days of traffic, feeling an immense sadness. The Open is over for another year. The boys and girls have gone away.

PHILADELPHIA, SEPTEMBER 12

There is not going to be a real pennant race this September, not with the Mets leading by twenty-two games with twenty-three games left to play. All the hopes of the last few years, all the building, all the trades, have worked out exactly as Frank Cashen and the Met fans had hoped.

For Met fans, this is the Brooklyn Dodgers' famed Next Year, but I kind of miss a pennant race, which is almost always better than the World Series itself. The World Series is a television event, a hot ticket for privileged people, a ritual for the hordes of sportswriters, a reward for two teams already feeling like champions.

Since there is not going to be a race, the next best thing is to pack an overnight bag and take the train to Philadelphia—for a whiff of chilly September air, a team on the road trying to wrap up a title.

I learned to savor a pennant race in 1964, when the wounded Phillies dissipated a six-and-a-half game lead with two weeks to go. I was one of a dozen reporters who arrived in St. Louis on the last Monday of the season and headed out to old Busch Stadium. The dugouts were jammed with rookies from the minor leagues, veterans picked up in late-season deals, players in warm-up jackets sipping coffee from paper cups, players nervously cupping cigarettes in the palms of their hands.

The collapse of the Phillies, the daily cruelty of a season that had lasted two weeks too long, was what baseball was all about. This was why I had gone into the business.

The Cardinal manager was Johnny Keane, wrinkled and kindly, Colonel Potter in *M*A*S*H* before Harry Morgan created the role. Keane had nearly been fired earlier in the season, but now finding himself on the brink of first place, he surveyed the reporters as we clumped into the ballpark, our old portables in our hands.

"Boys, I know why you're here," Keane rasped. "And I'm glad to see you."

We spent that week in St. Louis watching the Phillies lose three straight times in ghastly fashion. On the night the Cardinals swept into first place, Keane was talking to us in his office when a back door flew open. It was ancient Branch Rickey, the great baseball innovator, the man who had signed Jackie Robinson and was now an adviser to the Cardinal ownership. Rickey had been maneuvering to get Keane fired in midseason. Like Banquo's ghost, Rickey suddenly materialized, his famous beetle brows quivering.

"Johnny Keane, you're a gosh-dang good manager," Rickey exclaimed, before vanishing through the back door. That was a pennant race.

On the final weekend of the season, Casey Stengel's dismal Mets came to town and had a wonderful time terrorizing the Cardinals, until arm-weary Bob Gibson saved the pennant on the last Sunday of the season. Asked why he had stayed with Gibson, who had been maligned by earlier managers, Johnny Keane said simply, "I had a commitment to his heart." That was a pennant race.

Then we stayed for the first two games of the World Series, and I sent flowers to Marianne on our anniversary, October 1. That's what most of our anniversaries have been like—flowers from the road.

She practically shooed me out the door this morning: "Time for a little road trip." About five o'clock, I took the subway out to the ballpark to catch the Mets as they arrived. One of the most wonderful things about baseball is the amount you can learn, funny stories or bits of intrigue, just from hanging around the clubhouse and the field.

As the Mets started to limber up before batting practice, Keith Hernandez surveyed the Mets fans parading through the stands here, making more noise than the Phillies fans.

"They're everywhere," he said. "They're crazy."

As Hernandez talked about the Mets' wonderful season, radio reporters scurried to insert their microphones into the pack, heaving themselves over the top like linebackers making a late tackle. I kept waiting for Hernandez to shove the microphones out of his face and snap, "Get the fuck out of here," which he has been known to do, but he kept talking.

"To me, the most disappointing thing would be to win the division and not win the World Series," Hernandez said. "That would hurt." ·

Even Davey Johnson opened up a little bit, giving an impromptu state-of-the-team address from the top step of the dugout. In his three years as the Mets' manager, I have not been able to warm up to Johnson, and vice versa, to be sure. I think he is a fine manager, good for his players, but I find him unnecessarily suspicious, particularly for somebody so bright, so educated.

His former teammates on the Baltimore Orioles used to call him Dum-Dum, because he asked so many questions. Now, he sometimes glares at journalists who ask questions. Tonight, however, Johnson talked quite a bit about his managing moves over the season, and it was enjoyable listening to the turns of an active mind.

"This team has nothing to be ashamed of," Johnson said. "They deserve a lot of credit. You go six months, you win your division, you've taken the biggest step. I don't ever want to lose, but if you lose, don't hang your heads."

He was stating what I learned more than two decades ago—winning your race is the most important thing in baseball. Winning the Championship Series and the World Series is a crap shoot.

I was hoping the Mets would clinch tonight so I could write my Sunday column about all they had accomplished. Then I envisioned my Monday column about clinching celebrations.

Pouring champagne in the clubhouse used to be a reasonably spontaneous celebration, but it has deteriorated into a drunken ritual for the benefit of sportscasters who squeeze into crowded clubhouses to be doused with champagne so they can look like one of the gang on the eleven o'clock news. They practically take numbered tickets, like in the meat market.

To prepare for the champagne column, I spent a few innings talking with Tim McCarver, who told me about Joe Hoerner cutting some tendons on his middle finger when a champagne bottle exploded during the Cardinals' celebration in 1967. He also told me about how he warned Keith Carpenter, the former owner of the Phillies, to wear old clothes to the ritual dousing in 1976.

"After the game, I was in my uniform, and I was running around pouring champagne, and I spotted Keith," McCarver said in his engaging Memphis squawk. "Just as I was about to pour champagne on him, I realized: *He* was wearing *my* good clothes."

"Did you stop spraying him?" I asked.

"Didn't matter," McCarver said. "Somebody else had gotten him first."

After a few innings with McCarver, I had enough anecdotes for a column about celebrations. But the Mets lost, 6–3, when Mike Schmidt crushed a three-run homer off Dwight Gooden. My overnight trip has turned into a weekend. As the saying goes, "That's baseball."

PHILADELPHIA, SEPTEMBER 13

When the Mets lost last night, I decided it was an extension of Koppett's Law. The Renaissance philosopher and *Times* sports-department veteran Leonardo da Koppett once postulated that in the postseason baseball championships, whatever will inconvenience the greatest number of people will inevitably occur.

But later I decided that an extra night in Philadelphia is not hard duty. I haven't been alone on the road since the first week in Mexico, the weather is gorgeous, and staying at the Barclay Hotel in Rittenhouse Square, away from the Mets and the fans, makes me feel like an individual.

I woke up this morning and wrote my Sunday column about all the blue-and-orange-clad Mets fans loose in the Broad Street subway last night. After talking to the faithful, I realized they will not be satisfied with anything less than winning the World Series—Catch-86, I called it in my headline. I included last night's conversations with Hernandez and Johnson, phrasing the column so that if the Mets won tonight, I could include the clinching in the later editions.

By eleven o'clock I was finished and filed, which meant I had six hours totally to myself on a perfect crisp Saturday. I decided to take a long walk, starting at the Judy Chicago exhibition at the Philadelphia Art Alliance.

Marianne and I have a theory that the most attractive strangers we see are often in art museums and at concerts. Walking through an exhibit, with a whole afternoon to myself, reminded me of my early years on the road, walking through new cities, meeting people, late hours, good restaurants.

I was a young man who missed his wife and babies, who barreled home from the airport at seventy miles an hour so I could paint a room or take the kids to the park. I was also a young man who got lonely on the road.

Harold Rosenthal, the acerbic old hand with the *Herald Tribune,* once discovered a sentence in a sociology book: "The incidence of immorality is highest among transient workers." He translated it for the rest of us: "It means the road will make a bum of the best of them."

Well, it could. I liked to think I was not interested in hanging around bars late at night, but covering baseball, you could hardly avoid it. That's where all your friends were. Mostly I would have a drink or two and listen to Casey Stengel, or argue with other reporters, all of them male in those days.

Whether more from morality or timidity—I have never figured out the exact proportions—I was somewhat shocked by life on the road, at first. Couldn't believe the apparent ease with which some ballplayers found women. Even a few reporters seemed to have groupies. I'll never forget one of my first charter flights with a New York team and hearing one reporter say to another one, "Just think, in two hours we'll be getting laid."

There was one bar in St. Louis, in the funky neighborhood behind the Chase Hotel, where nurses dropped in after the four-to-midnight shift. Having beers with nurses gave me a lasting appreciation of their earthy humor, their toughness. They were something like ballplayers, something like us, but a bit more valuable to society.

That was the highlight of my social life on the road in the sixties. My theory, then and now, is that marriage is a pretty intimate business; I can't imagine how people find the time and energy for all their adventures. And at what cost of respect and loyalty and love?

I would admit that life became more complex when I began meeting activists and lawyers, teachers and journalists, women with wonderful Tennessee and Kentucky accents, but I was lucky to keep in mind that my wife was the most attractive, most interesting woman I knew.

Then and now, I opt for pleasures like a long walk through quiet streets, watching a wedding party being photographed in Rittenhouse Square, eating a Chinese meal and reading the local papers, returning to the square and reading a hundred pages of Garrison Keillor. The afternoon went too fast.

Tonight a crew from a New York television station cost the Mets their clinching party. In town to film their newscaster being doused with champagne, the technicians started slapping palms and laughing out loud as the Mets went ahead, 3–0—strictly against press-box etiquette, strictly against the laws of nature. The gods turned against these loud and foolish New Yorkers, helping Philadelphia rally for a 6–5 victory.

The Mets were testy and bored after the game. I didn't tell them the television crew had jinxed them.

PHILADELPHIA, SEPTEMBER 14

"Guess what?" Marianne said when I called this morning.

One thing a journalist learns is that life continues while he is on the road. I once got a "guess-what" call at four in the morning in Oakland to find out Marianne had just decided to buy a house. Laura used to play her best basketball games when I was out of town. David changed schools while I was at the Super Bowl. In 1963, while I was at the baseball All-Star Game, Marianne had an emergency appendectomy and I had to rush home—from Cleveland. Nobody believed my excuse.

This morning I played straight man: "You got a show at the Whitney."

"No, stupid, we have a puppy."

Long silence. As "guess-what" news goes, this one ranked somewhere between relatives coming for a visit and the plumbing falling apart.

"David wanted a pet," Marianne said. "We went to the North Shore Animal League to look at birds, and somebody brought in this sweet cocker spaniel. David took one look at her and fell in love."

I grunted through the rest of the conversation. With David in his senior year, we are free to take off spontaneously, to take advantage of my job. We do not need a dog. I could not help but think that if the Mets had won Friday night, I could have rushed home and avoided this "guess-what."

"You'll love her," Marianne said.

I continued to fume about the dog as I reported back to the ballpark. The cellophane covers were still draped over the Met lockers, in case of a champagne celebration, but I knew the Mets were going to lose. I had to scratch out a column about the Mets having to clinch it in the Land of the White Rat. The office suggested I follow the Mets to St. Louis, but I have to get home and see about this business of the dog.

PORT WASHINGTON, SEPTEMBER 16

The three of us—David, puppy, and I—watched the horror show last night as Roger McDowell walked in the winning run in the thirteenth inning and Gary Carter hit into either eleven or twelve double plays, I lost track. This means I will have to write another clinching column when the Mets come home. Enough already.

The only good thing about last night's game was sitting on the couch with my son and my puppy. She is two and a half years old, with soft, curly black hair, and still thinks she's a baby.

"We got her for you," Marianne said. "For when David goes to college."

FLUSHING, SEPTEMBER 18

When the Mets won the World Series in 1969, I wrote about the fans as part of the Woodstock Nation, playing "This Land Is Your Land, This Land Is My Land" on Joan Payson's lawn instead of Max Yasgur's farm.

I even had my picture taken on the ravaged field, like a road-show version of Edward R. Murrow during the Blitz. That photograph of me, the Sixties Kid, with my press pass stuck in the breast pocket of a gaudy sports jacket and a silk bandanna around my neck and long hair flopping down the back of my head, is on the back jacket of *Joy in Mudville*, the book I wrote about the Mets' improbable championship.

I was very young then, just turned thirty, the barrier between trustworthiness and senility, according to the code of the Yippies, and I reflected my youth in the opening paragraphs of my book:

"They spilled over the barricades like extras in a Genghis Khan movie, all hot-eyed and eager for plunder. The Mets had just won the 1969 World Series, and the fans wanted to take home a talisman piece of Shea Stadium, to secure good fortune for the rest of their lives. . . . "

Seventeen years later, there is not enough hair left to hang down toward my shoulders, and I haven't worn a silk scarf since the sixties went away. Once again I have watched fans rampage at the ballpark, only this time I am muttering things like "animals" and "cretins" and "hooligans."

Something has changed. I am more than willing to concede my values are different from what they were seventeen years ago, but I also think the mood in the stands has changed since 1969, from hip and spontaneous to aggressive and hostile. Maybe it's my age talking, maybe I have secretly joined the Reaganites, the law-and-order people, but I was not enthused last night when the Mets clinched their division title by beating the Cubs, and the fans poured onto the field even before the final out.

I could barely reflect those feelings as I touched up my early column on how exciting it had been to have a bit of pennant-race nervousness. When the Mets won, I put on a new lead: "It's safe to look now, faint hearts. The Mets have survived the desperate hours."

But after I filed my new lead on deadline, I watched hundreds of fans deliberately gouge and pry at the sod, and anything else they could get their hands on. I had the feeling the barbarians had somehow slipped through the portals of civilization.

My feelings brought me back to Shea on this sunny, quiet morning, to watch Pete Flynn, a red-haired man with a strong Irish accent, try to repair the scarred turf. His ground crew is cutting patches of sod to match the gaps in the grass caused by the fingernails and screwdrivers and garden tools of the mob.

Last night's vandals were maybe only 6,000 out of the 47,823 paying fans, but there were enough gristle-bellied, full-grown, hell-for-violence adult males not only to do damage to the sod, which was bad enough, but also to menace the players. As the Mets tried to work their way to safety, the fans jumped into the dugout, landing on the players' backs, walloping them and gripping them in bear hugs.

Coming back to the ballpark today, I keep hearing little bits of horror stories about what the players had to endure. One fan landed smack on Rick Aguilera, sending him sprawling to the ground. Another fan tried to pull the glove right off Hernandez's supple hand. Yet another fan pulled the mask off Gary Carter's head, with Carter trying to hold on to it. Suppose the intruder had twisted Carter's neck, or gouged his eyes?

The players, arriving slowly and tentatively after their own revels last night, are in no mood to jar their aching heads with deep speculation about fans. But Frank Cashen, the general manager, is roaming the field, poking the tips of his shoes into the gaps in the turf, using words like *incensed* and *disgusted*.

Cashen tries to put a distance on the riot by saying, "I didn't see many of our season-ticket holders out there," but I think that is ducking the issue. In recent years, I have spent a lot of time outside the press box, sitting with David or just walking around the ballpark, and it is my opinion that the mood has grown increasingly savage.

As somebody who still feels the sixties were "my decade," I can't help but feel something has gone wrong from the emotions and political beliefs of the sixties. The people who clawed at the turf in October of 1969 seemed childlike, good-natured, innocent. I remember how a few fans sent me pictures they had taken of themselves on the grass, and wrote me letters about how they had carefully transplanted the bit of sod into their own lawns. Admittedly, some of them were zonked on marijuana, but what are the new rioters ingesting—Sterno?

To sit in the stands these days is to encounter willful aggression, people who have no responsibility to anybody around them. They bring loud radios, they stand up, they curse, they pick on fans wearing the colors of another team, and inevitably there is a fight.

I meet plenty of knowledgeable, loyal fans, who keep score and trade information and argue in a jocular vein, but my vision of fans these days is of a brawling, profane mob—"Them," in the disdainful, Joyce Carol Oates sense of the word.

Part of the problem is that a third of any baseball crowd seems drunk from the beer sold on the premises. The clubs say they are trying to cut down on consumption, but I cannot expect baseball to be serious about cutting back on beer sales when the beer companies are the major sponsors of baseball, when giant beer signs glow down like icons on the stupefied mob.

The televised beer commercials do their part to encourage rowdiness by suggesting that life is more fun with alcohol in your system. If you drink enough of the sponsor's beer, you'll be magically transported to clean, well-lighted bars, where you can trade jokes with Mickey Mantle and Billy Martin. Let me give you a little camping tip: If you see them in a bar, look for the nearest exit, and don't turn your back on the seedy-looking guy with the mustache.

With all these beer commercials, every man a Butkus, it's no wonder the fans think they belong on the field, celebrating with the players. What do you do about fans? Can't live with 'em, can't live without 'em.

I remember wringing my hands over the use of police dogs and horses during the final innings of the 1980 World Series in Philadelphia, but at least the fans refrained from tearing up the stadium and endangering the players. What's next, moats and barbed wire, like in those grim, rudimentary soccer stadiums of Europe and Latin America?

After Pete Flynn's crew does the best it can, I sit in the sunny stands and watch the second-string Mets pick their way gingerly over the loose turf and the crevices, and then I write a column with the headline: THE MARK OF THE FANS.

For Sunday, I am finally going to use all those good Tim McCarver anecdotes about clubhouse dousings. People are talking about the sight last night of the Met players slurring their words and staggering around in strange costumes.

I don't expect the players to know better, and I don't expect television executives to know better, but I would expect the club owners and Peter Ueberroth to be sensitive about the image of players staggering around drunk, pouring champagne on broadcasters—especially in light of the drug issue surrounding the sport.

For Monday, I'll write about the proud plunderers who tried to rip off Hernandez's glove and managed to pull Carter's mask right off his head. I've already got the headline—MUGGING OUR HEROES.

In 1987, Ueberroth recommended to club officials to limit the celebration to one bottle of champagne per man, and to keep it away from the television cameras. Andy MacPhail of the Minnesota Twins and Al Rosen of the San Francisco Giants were particularly good about limiting the drinking.

PORT WASHINGTON, SEPTEMBER 27

We were standing around the batting cage the other night, talking about life, when Joe Klein of *New York* magazine came up with the idea of the month:

"You know what Steinbrenner ought to do?" Klein asked. Then he answered, "He ought to sell the Yankees to Donald Trump."

It made such perfect sense. Instead of being run by Quarters Steinbrenner from a pay phone, the Yankees would be run by Young Donald from Queens. I don't think it will happen, because the Yankees are George's primary sense of identification. He must hector them and disrupt them in the middle of a pennant race to satisfy his own need to be dissatisfied, his own need to fail.

Whether or not George will sell, I gave credit to Joe Klein for the idea, and wrote that things just haven't been the same since the United States Football League lost its court decision and folded this summer. All Donald does now is build buildings.

One of the side benefits of the sports column is that I can write about the broad issues—Ed Koch putting in his perfunctory inning at the ballpark, or the scandals in the city government, or the vans with Jersey license plates running red lights in midtown, or a builder like Young Donald who wants to construct Brasilia on the West Side—all the things that make my hometown so much fun.

Donald really hasn't been absent. The man has become a mythic figure in New York, battling George for the back page and Ed Koch for the front page of Rupert Murdoch's paper.

When I go to sleep at night, I thank the Lord for individual owners like George and Donald and Ted Turner. In my old age, I would much rather write about a megalomaniac who bought a team because he was bored building ships or skyscrapers than write about an athlete who can run fast.

Using the new tax laws as my reason for selling the Yankees, I wrote, "I can see it all now: A few minutes before New Year, the atrium and Ivana Trump all aglitter, Donald and George emerge from the mists of the fountain and proclaim that the Yankees have been sold and Don Mattingly and Dave Righetti have been signed to career contracts."

My headline was: ABOUT MISSING DONALD. It was a sort of a love poem to him and Ivana, to come back, all was forgiven.

A few weeks later, I received a fancy embossed piece of stationery. On it was written: "Dear George: I miss you, too. Donald."

NEW YORK, SEPTEMBER 30

For several months it has been apparent that the middle three games of the National League championships would be held in New York, the city with more Jews than any other city in the world. With all that notice, Peter Ueberroth and his television advisers scheduled the fourth game on Sunday night and the fifth on Monday afternoon, while Jews will be observing Yom Kippur, the Day of Atonement.

Jews never expect the world to stop cold while they fast and attend temple. One game during Yom Kippur would have been understandable: two are unconscionable. As a Christian whose life has been shaped by Jewish friends, by Judaism, I found myself incensed that Ueberroth and his television advisers would disregard Jewish fans.

I thought about the Jewish homes where I was welcomed as a child, thought of the new friends who made us feel at home in Louisville, thought about the seders at Wolfe and Jacky Kelman's house, thought of all the bar mitzvahs I've attended, the lovely Jewish girl I dated in college, smiled at the memory of introducing Marianne to her first Jewish mother, visualized the eclectic kosher salons at Miriam and Rachel Rabinowicz's apartment, and I felt a surge of protective anger at baseball's callousness.

Jewish fans can only write letters and threaten to cancel ticket subscriptions. I get to write a column.

What really angered me is that baseball did not have enough faith in its own product to go head-to-head with a Cleveland-Pittsburgh *Monday Night Football* game that is meaningless in most of the country.

Baseball has been obeying television for decades, more slavishly as the prices went up. Bowie Kuhn went so far as to sit out of doors without a topcoat in nasty weather during one Series, presumably to make the point for the television camera that baseball in late October wasn't so terrible. Of course, he was wearing long johns underneath.

The decision to play two games during Yom Kippur could have been avoided by Ueberroth, a capable and persuasive man who has taken enlightened stands like trying to share the huge Olympic profits with sports federations of Third World nations.

A friend of mine who worked around Ueberroth told me how Peter liked to spring little Olympic quizzes on his assistants. One day in front of several aides, a man said, "All right, Peter, let's try one on you. Who won the 1964 marathon?" The next morning, Ueberroth called the man into his office and said, "If you ever pull that on me again, your ass is gone." You wouldn't want to cross Peter, my friend said.

It makes sense to me that Ueberroth might have political ambitions or want to move on as chief executive officer for a major firm. He earned this national forum by his success in Los Angeles. I just wish he showed more feel for the game, and for the city where he is based. Why make it hard for Jewish Mets fans to follow their team?

In my column for tomorrow, I predict a deluge, a biblical flood, for October 12, lasting twenty-four hours, washing out both games until Yom Kippur is over. The editors ordered a cartoon of Shea Stadium looking for all the world like Noah's Ark, floating off into Flushing Bay. What's the sense in being an old religion reporter if you can't invoke a little Old Testament prophecy?

Ueberroth decided to serve only one term, and his replacement was A. Bartlett Giamatti, the former president of Yale University, who knows the game better than Ueberroth and certainly has no less flair for power.

OCTOBER

PORT WASHINGTON, OCTOBER 1

In an analgesic haze a few years ago, I thought I heard my dentist say something very weird. When the gas wore off, I said, "You know, Dr. Karter, I could have sworn you said I need braces."

He said it was not my imagination, that my teeth were so crooked and overlapped that he could not repair them much longer.

"Braces are an affectation of the newly rich and the middle-aged," I told him. "You might just as well find me with a hairpiece squatting on the top of my head like a lost muskrat, with gold chains around my neck, my shirt unbuttoned to my navel, and dating young girls. I'm not the type."

Today, on our twenty-sixth wedding anniversary, I am sporting the glittering smile of a preadolescent. I can recall being cruel to friends of mine who had braces back in the fifth grade. Tinsel Teeth. Metal Mouth. Railroad Tracks. I probably would never have agreed to wear braces if I had not gone through the Meadows while working on Bob Welch's book. Five years later, I was able to concede that I probably did dislike the sight of my crooked teeth, that I probably avoided showing emotions that would require an open mouth.

This morning Dr. Michael Diamond installed a track on my upper teeth, twisting them in new directions. When I left, his wife, Dina, handed me a bottle of champagne. Somehow she knew it is our twenty-sixth anniversary.

Tonight Joe and Elizabeth Vecchione took us out to celebrate the anniversary. The braces could handle pasta, fish, even salad. It's going to be fine. The Mets clinched the pennant so early that, for one of the rare times in my career, I am home on our anniversary.

HOUSTON, OCTOBER 7

These are not just the 1986 Mets and Astros meeting for the National League pennant. These are the descendants of the old Mets and Colt 45's, who were born in the same expansion year of 1962.

I was a kid reporter, traveling for the first time, being eaten alive by mosquitoes in a rickety place called Colt Stadium, while the Mets were being eaten alive by the Colts.

My first column for this series is going to be about mosquitoes rather than ball games. I talked on the phone with Rusty Staub, who was a teenager on the old Colts, and he told me how they used to keep cans of insect repellent in the dugout.

"Everybody talks about their size," Staub said. "Sure, they were huge, but size was not the problem. Quantity—that was the problem."

When I get to the Dome for the workout today, Tim McCarver is helpful once again, recalling how mosquitoes used to get into the famous postgame spread of food in the visitors' clubhouse.

Rocky Swoboda, now working on television, tells me about the insect legends he encountered his first trip to Houston: "They said the mosquitoes in the old ballpark used to pick cats right off the ground and fly away with them."

I go searching in the Astros' clubhouse for Jim (Doc) Ewell, the peppery trainer emeritus, who is glad to talk about the heat and the humidity in the old ballpark.

"Jocko Conlan, the umpire, used to sit in his underwear outside the umpires' room," Ewell says. "A couple of times, he swore he wasn't going to go out there on the field, it was so hot. I had to go in there and talk to him."

Damn, I love baseball. People stand around and tell you stories. All you have to do is remember them and put them in order: "By now, the mosquitoes in the old Colt Stadium have reached epic proportions—as big as hawks, as big as pterodactyls, as big as the Concorde itself. . . . "

HOUSTON, OCTOBER 8

As long as the Mets are in postseason play, I will write every day, no problem in a pennant race. I wanted to do something about the peculiar angst of the Houston fan. This team has been beating the Mets regularly since the two of them were formed in the same expansion draft, but Houston has never won a pennant, while the Mets have won two. Dick Schaap is doing a piece for ABC from Grif's, a popular sports bar, and I tagged along.

"Houston is tired of excuses," pronounced Michael Griffin, a Boston Irishman who wound up running a bar for sports maniacs here. Grif explains that Houston has a losing complex to match that of Red Sox fans or Cubs fans or any other kind of fan. They expect to lose, somehow.

The fans in Grif's also told me that Houston's sense of sports inferiority was made worse by the economic depression here, and also by the explosion of the Challenger in January, which killed seven astronauts, including Judith Resnick and Ellison Onizuka, who were honorary regulars at Grif's.

"Judith once entered our Guinness drinking contest, and Ellison was a judge in our Irish stew contest," Grif said. "Jeeze, we watched that thing on television right here. What a mess."

As he talked, my old instincts as a national reporter took over. The blue *New York Times* vending boxes in every city are a reminder that we are becoming more and more a national newspaper, that my columns should not be aimed merely at New York readers, but for all mobile, well-educated modern Americans. A column about Houston fans resenting New York will strike a responsive chord in Cleveland or Seattle.

The charter busloads from Grif's must have been pleasantly shocked when Mike Scott struck out fourteen Mets tonight in a 1–0 victory over Dwight Gooden. The Mets, and particularly Gary Carter, put themselves at a disadvantage by complaining about Scott scuffing the balls. The Mets have now fully established that they are spooked by Scott. Meanwhile, the Houston fans have established that they are spooked by the town's losing history. The Red Sox and Angels are playing in the other league. Sounds like a great October for complexes.

HOUSTON, OCTOBER 10

The Mets beat the Astros to tie the series last night—a few hours ago, actually. It is still dark as I drive Vic Ziegel and Maury Allen to the airport to catch our dawn flight. We've known each other since the early sixties, when both of them covered baseball for the *Post*. Vic was my tour guide on the road, always up on where *Beat the Devil* was showing, or where Clancy Hayes was playing Dixieland. Now, Vic is the sports editor of the *Daily News,* and Maury still works for the *Post* and writes books, and we have our projects and our families, and we rarely spend time together. For an hour in the car, we chat easily, like in the old days.

At the airport, I pick up a free copy of *USA Today* to consult their colored weather map about my prediction of a mammoth rainstorm in New York on Sunday night, to punish baseball for scheduling two games on Yom Kippur. Rain. They are talking rain.

NEW YORK, OCTOBER 11

My daughter Corinna called me this evening and told me a story. She and her husband, Rolf Gilstein, had tickets for today's game in broad daylight—Baseball Like It Oughta Be, as the sign says outside Shea Stadium.

The crowd was sweet and subdued because of the noon starting time, with almost nobody tanked up the way they are at night games. With the Mets behind, 5–4, in the ninth inning, Rolf—the cellist with the Laurentian String Quartet at Sarah Lawrence College—had to leave for a concert.

"We were walking out behind the pullpen, where all the limousines are parked," Corinna told me, "and we heard the crowd cheering. I asked the driver of a limousine if I could watch on the color TV in the backseat, and he said sure. I saw the Mets had a runner on base.

"Rolf was standing right behind the Mets bullpen. You couldn't see the field because of the fence. Then Rolf heard a cheer and he looked up and he saw the ball floating through space, getting bigger and bigger, just floating up there. It kept coming closer and closer, and then it went over the fence. It was Lenny Dykstra's home run.

"We ran to our car and drove out of there while the crowd was still cheering. Rolf got to his concert on time. Wasn't it exciting?"

FLUSHING, OCTOBER 12

My prediction of rain was not perfect. Under cold and gloomy skies, the Mets play and lose the fourth game as thousands of Met fans fast and observe Yom Kippur. After visiting the locker rooms and making a few changes in my column, I leave Shea at 12:30 A.M., and it is drizzling.

PORT WASHINGTON, OCTOBER 13

"You win," Joe Vecchione says over the telephone. "Take the day off."

It has been pouring all day, and the Mets finally postpone the three o'clock game on Yom Kippur. That means Jewish fans can go to temple, break their fast, and spend an evening with their families before getting back to the Mets tomorrow.

I remember Sandy Koufax deciding not to pitch on Yom Kippur during the 1965 World Series, but rain postponed a game in Minnesota, allowing Koufax to pitch in turn. The next day, a bunch of reporters from New York asked Koufax how he felt about not missing his turn.

"Please don't print this," he said, glancing at the familiar faces.

Then, looking at the skies like an ancient prophet or a Catskill comedian, or both, Koufax said, "God knows."

God knew. Day off today.

FLUSHING, OCTOBER 14

Gloating in print about the rain-out sounded a little too Murdochian for me, but I do have a fantasy of spotting Ueberroth and the league presidents and the network bosses, fixing them with an Old Testament stare, and saying, "Watch it!"

The rain tapers off, and Nolan Ryan faces Dwight Gooden in the fifth game, which is so vital because the Astros have Mike Scott looming ahead for the seventh game, if necessary. It is seventeen years to the day that Ryan relieved Gary Gentry in the third game of the World Series, right in this ballpark, and put the Mets ahead to stay. Now, Ryan is the leading strikeout pitcher of all time, a man from the sixties opposing a superstar of the nineties.

Starting in mist, finishing in sunlight, Ryan pitches nine of the most compelling innings you will ever see, striking out twelve Mets, giving up two hits, one of them a home run in the fifth inning by Darryl Strawberry.

Because of Ryan's tender elbow, the Astros usually limit him to 100 pitches, but today he gives them 134. The Astros bat for Ryan in the tenth, and they lose the game in the twelfth on Gary Carter's ground single up the middle. By that time, I am already putting together an ode to Nolan Ryan, who has been so brave, so good, that even the rambunctious Mets fans don't chant anything particularly ugly at him.

After the game, we surround Ryan in his locker. His voice is flat as the Texas landscape, but he does not back off in his disappointment over umpire Jim Brocklander calling the Astros' Craig Reynolds out at first base while a runner was crossing the plate in the second inning.

On television, Reynolds seemed obviously safe. Some people will use this as a justification for using instant replay, but baseball can live with human error now and then.

"Yogi says the team that gets the breaks will win it," Ryan says. "Well, if he calls it right, we're out of here in nine."

Somebody tells Ryan that he seemed to hobble a bit after a hard slide in the fifth inning, but Ryan shrugs it off.

"Just jammed it," he says. "No problem."

I rush upstairs with second-edition quotes from a man who pitched two marvelous games in Shea exactly seventeen years apart. He is so nonchalant about the ankle that I make no mention of it in my tribute to his durability.

The next day we learn that Ryan has gone for X rays. He pitched the last five innings on a badly swollen ankle.

HOUSTON, OCTOBER 15

Interesting tableau at LaGuardia Airport while we are checking in with Continental. A thief tries to run away with a camera of a Houston television crew, but he cannot go too far with forty pounds of equipment in his arms. He abandons the camera and escapes through a crowd, and the Houston television people get back on line, muttering about my hometown. What else can go wrong for Houston today?

The flight arrives on time to a crisp fall day in Houston. I rent a car and drive directly to the Astrodome. It is the last I will see of sunlight, because I have to go indoors and bang out yet another first-edition column before anything happens.

After three flights between New York and Houston, I feel numb. I wonder how the players feel, the Astros facing elimination, the Mets knowing they had better win today, or else face Mike Scott tomorrow. I don't guess they think about us being in the same line of work, but there is pressure on a sports columnist every day. Respond to events. Take control. Be at your best. Few hours of sleep. Fly at dawn. Back to work.

Ever since Scott won the fourth game on Sunday, I knew there would be a sixth game in Houston, an early-edition column, one team facing elimination. I have been saving material about how difficult it has always been for the Mets to win in Houston, going back to the first year when they played in mosquito-infested Colt Stadium. The themes of a week ago are still working.

My lead is, "This was always a tough town for the Mets . . . " and I resurrect the memory of Casey Stengel, awake for twenty-four hours after a long game and an overnight flight, finally getting to the Houston hotel at dawn in 1962 and rasping, "If any of the writers come looking for me, tell them I'm being embalmed." A quarter of a century later, we are still writing about Casey. He is still a framework for things that happen to the Mets.

Two hours later, Casey's embalming line seems as pertinent as on the muggy morning he uttered it. The Mets are trailing, 3–0, going into the ninth inning and Mike Scott looming ahead like a nightmare.

A few minutes before six o'clock deadline, I dash out a new lead about this still being a tough town for the Mets. While I am sending my substitute lead, Ira Berkow rushes downstairs to be close to the Astros' dressing room when the game is over.

Bing-bing-bing. Lenny Dykstra hits a drive that falls in for a triple. The Mets score three runs to tie the score. My sub lead is useless for this edition. Ira comes trooping up the stairs, and we settle down for extra innings.

In the fourteenth, the Mets score a run. Ira rushes downstairs. I bang out a lead about the Mets finally conquering the Houston jinx. In the bottom of the inning, Billy Hatcher hits a homer off the foul pole in left field and dances backward down the first-base line. Ira does not dance backward up the stairs to the press box.

Sixteenth inning. The Mets go ahead again with three runs. Ira runs downstairs, but I'm linked to my word processor, watching Jesse Orosco fritter away two-thirds of his lead. Will this be a classic collapse by the Mets? It could go either way. But Jesse finally gets the last out on a strikeout, and the Mets have won the pennant. Ira does not have to climb any more stairs.

I rush down to the Mets clubhouse, and watch them spray champagne at each other. Once lubricated, some of the pitchers start sliding on the clubhouse floor, bumping heads like otters playing in the mud.

For my second-edition column, I have decided to zero in on Jesse Orosco, never a very enchanting interview but the central figure in the sixteenth inning today. After nearly letting the game get away, Jesse would much rather drink champagne than sum up the inner torments of his psyche, but a mob of reporters surrounds Jesse, and he is forced to make sense.

"You looked nervous on the tube," somebody says.

"I wasn't nervous," he says, "but I was starting to chill out."

"What did Carter and Hernandez tell you on the mound in the sixteenth?"

" 'Shoot, get somebody out,' " Orosco recalls. "Shoot, I'd blown one lead, I wasn't about to blow another one."

That's about as deep as it ever gets with Orosco, who begins to fidget, wanting to stop talking and start drinking. I talk to Carter and Hernandez to fill out the dialogue on the mound, and then I rush upstairs to write for the second edition.

I save some of the theme from the first edition, how Houston was always a tough town. I keep Casey's embalming remark. Always keep Casey, at the expense of almost anything else. My last paragraph is: "It stayed that way for twenty-four years, but the Mets may finally have embalmed the curse of Houston, by a margin as slender as what is left of Jesse Orosco's fingernails."

NEW YORK, OCTOBER 18

A few days ago, we were contemplating a Houston-California World Series, a Sunbelt World Series, a payoff for two expansion teams that have never won a pennant. Instead, by the annual crap shoot of the so-called Championship Series of baseball, we have a New York-Boston World Series, a tale of two cities.

No other team has as many fans in New York as the Boston Red Sox. In my worlds of publishing and newspapers and entertainment, many of the best and the brightest are outright flaming Red Sox fans. I can think of my old pal Jonathan Schwartz spending hours in a parked car on the Upper West Side, while dinner grows cold, listening to the Red Sox on the radio because reception is not good in his apartment. I can think of my first agent, Philip Spitzer, flying up to Fenway for Opening Day every year. I can think of my current agent, Esther Newberg, taking her life in her hands to sit among Yankee fans during crucial series in Yankee Stadium. I can see Sydney Schanberg and Jim Clarity escorting

Dith Pran to a Red Sox game in Yankee Stadium. When the Red Sox come to New York, the IQ level in Yankee Stadium goes up an average of ten points.

There could not be a better team as honorable opposition for the Mets, and not just for the ease of commuting, either. Fenway Park (along with its venerable cousin in Chicago, Wrigley Field) has long been a magic hub, a place of pilgrimage, for baseball fans, for baseball writers.

The first time I visited Fenway was in 1962, barely two years out of college and traveling with the Yankees for *Newsday.* The first night I walked into the oddly shaped ballpark, painted then as now in battleship green, I was hooked on the Fenway mystique, particularly after I heard Mickey Mantle admit he didn't understand the Harvard kids when they yelled things at him from the center-field bleachers. Maybe they were speaking Latin.

The next sunny May morning, I walked all over Boston until I reached Harvard Square in Cambridge. I called friends of mine at the med school and the law school, but they were busy studying for exams. I felt so lucky to be out of school, to have no more exams, no more classes. I was out working, doing something I liked, getting paid, with freedom to wander all over greater Boston during the daytime.

I realized I had achieved my ambition from junior high school, when I watched the elevated trains gambol back and forth across the Flushing skies. Call it claustrophobia, call it impatience, call it creativity, I had made a private vow to do anything, anything, to never get tied down to daily routine. By the time I was twenty-three, I had managed to shake loose in the middle of the day while my friends were still tied down to school regulations. I felt younger and older, at the same time. I had a job; they were students. I was married; they were single. I liked my life then, and—confessions of an aging sportswriter—for all my complaining, I still do.

Of course, my friends are doctors and lawyers and judges, while I am still squeezing into clubhouses and still being grumbled at by managers and still scrambling to file stories on deadlines in the middle of the night, but I am also living out my youthful fantasy—and as my friends often remind me, their fantasies, too.

The World Series was at the center of my childhood fantasies, the games all played in daylight, rushing out of school at three o'clock to hear Old Reliable Tommy Henrich crush a home run off Don New-combe, raking leaves in the backyard, listening to Cookie Lavagetto break up Bill Bevens's no-hitter with two outs in the ninth, Yogi Berra frolicking in left field in the early October haze in Yankee Stadium, and when my father started coming up with tickets for me, the sight of the limousines parked outside the stadium, the men in camel's hair coats and brimmed hats, the smell of cigars in the early October warmth.

Now baseball and television have cheapened the long season by mak-ing four good teams slug it out in two league championship series for the privilege of playing in the World Series. And they have throttled the last glimpse of sunshine by turning the World Series into a prime-time event, lit artificially, played at strange hours to accommodate television in America's four time zones.

The chill was already settling in when we staggered back from Hous-ton and attended the pre-Series workout in Shea Stadium yesterday afternoon. Winter had sent its calling card; reporters stuck hands in their pockets when they were not taking notes, players wore thick club jackets around the batting cage.

Many of us crowded around Don Baylor, the venerable slugger who used to be with the Yankees but could not stomach the George-and-Billy Follies. (He once heaved a garbage can around the Yankee club-house when Martin was brought back as manager—a symbolic gesture if ever there was one.)

Baylor is one of the grown-ups of his business. As a teenage football star, he once helped integrate his high school in Austin, Texas, and the conservative baseball establishment regards him as a future manager or executive. Since coming over to the Red Sox, Baylor has loosened up this introverted club, starting up a kangaroo court, fining teammates for missing signs or wearing loud shirts, the way his old Baltimore team-mates used to do.

Baylor drove in ninety-four runs this season and hit a clutch homer to keep the Red Sox alive in the dramatic fifth game of the league cham-pionships. Now, the Red Sox will be forced to go without him in as many as four games because of baseball's schizophrenic approach to the des-ignated-hitter rule.

I hate the designated-hitter rule of the American League even though it keeps aging players like Baylor in the game. It makes for dull baseball, because managers don't have to think about using a pinch hitter for their pitcher, and therefore don't make other strategic moves, defensive changes, the old double switch, hiding a relief pitcher in the batting order, all the slow-motion details that make baseball the best spectator sport of all.

The difference can catch up to you. In the 1981 World Series, Bob Lemon could not resist the unusual opportunity to send up a pinch hitter for Tommy John in the bottom of the fourth inning. The Yankee bullpen blew the game and the Series. Playing under "real baseball rules," Good Old Lem just wasn't prepared for the decision.

The strange thing was, Lemon had been the epitome of the hitting pitcher, a converted outfielder who had batted .232 with 37 homers and was often used as a pinch hitter. One of the more sublime delights of baseball is watching Warren Spahn or Don Drysdale or Bob Gibson or Bob Lemon just busting to get up there and take his rips.

My pal Bob Welch brags more about the home run he hit off Mario Soto to win a 1–0 game than he does about his pitching. Welchie can win a game for himself with a good bunt or an alert dash around the bases. One of the old strengths of baseball was requiring players to go both ways, offense and defense, rather than be like football with its nickel backs and third-down tight ends and other such anonyms.

Starting in 1976, baseball used the designated hitter in even-year World Series, and allowed pitchers to bat in odd-number years. However, this year they changed the rule, allowing the designated hitter in American League parks and allowing pitchers to hit in the National League parks. This means the Mets will be able to use extra hitters in Boston, but Don Baylor will have to sit down in New York.

During yesterday's workout, we asked Baylor what he thought about being mostly an observer in Shea Stadium.

"I'll be a cheerleader. I just want to do whatever I can to help the club," Baylor said, making it sound legitimate.

The Red Sox don't miss Baylor tonight, as they beat the Mets, 1–0, on an error at second base by Tim Teufel, but my Sunday column predicts they will be hurt by his absence in New York before this series is over.

* * *

I'm convinced that the more flexible brand of National League ball helped the Dodgers overcome injuries and stun the Athletics in the 1988 World Series. Tom Lasorda was able to play mix-and-match with his lineup, while the American League team seemed more calcified, less able to respond when its sluggers stopped slugging.

FLUSHING, OCTOBER 19

The attendant punches my World Series credential and hands me a carton of cold fried chicken and gooey macaroni salad. I give her two dollars and say, "Thanks, miss." In the crowded press room, reporters from all over the country are standing up and eating with their hands. Welcome to the big time.

Out of personal preference, I have brought fruit salad from home. Pete, the guard at the press-room door, who was always considerate of my father, accepts my boxed lunch and stashes it behind a desk.

Question in journalistic ethics, class: Have we been bought off by major-league baseball for the price of a boxed fried-chicken supper?

A few days ago, Denis Hamill, a news columnist for *New York Newsday,* made fun of reporters eating their boxed meals at Shea Stadium and crowding into the locker rooms after the game. Hamill's column did not raise the question of whether we had any options.

The intrepid journalist discovered that the Mets' catering service charges roughly $5,000 to feed 450 people.

"If Harry M. Stevens gave that much money to a cop from the 77th Precinct, he would be working in the kitchen at Attica," Hamill pronounced, adding, "For those who do take the free lunch, this is known as gluttony and it adds to the image that a free press means having a license to freeload."

We have been paying five dollars for the hot meal at Yankee Stadium in recent years, and I tip a couple of dollars per meal at any ballpark. I have a reasonably comfortable conscience on press-room meals, but I was offended and also embarrassed for *Newsday,* one of the first papers to turn down gifts and free travel, that Hamill wrote this column.

Feeding 450 people before a postseason game is a thoughtful gesture to working stiffs who have no other realistic way to eat during an eight-to-ten-hour day. Journalists don't have the time to stand on line with civilians at the hot-dog stands, and it's not easy to pack a brown-bag supper along with our computers, portable telephones, and books—particularly when you're staying in a hotel room.

Hamill also seemed aghast at the turf war between television's camera-wielding truth squads and the crazed guerrillas from the press in the clubhouse after the game. And he hasn't seen me curse into the microphone when a broadcaster tries to interrupt an interview, a tactic I learned from Dick Young.

We know what we are. Undignified, maybe. Unprofessional, no. I've chased lawyers outside courthouses, run through city streets pursuing reluctant celebrities, even had Terence Cardinal Cooke perform a mighty 180-degree turn in a narrow hotel corridor, cassock flowing, rather than answer a few questions. That's what reporters do, scurry after a story, sometimes not even knowing what it might be.

Nobody ever said journalism was a totally dignified career. If it were, they would pay us more money, give us better working conditions, and the business would then attract yuppies rather than masochists.

We come back from big sports events with ballpoint-pen marks on our clothing, and we learn never to wear good shoes because they get scarred by other people's feet. We crowd into clubhouses for the same reason Hamill hangs around police stations—it is where the action is.

The World Series becomes more of a media zoo every year, with every paper from Canada to Panama sending somebody for an individual slice of news and mood. Lately, baseball has been trying to limit access to the clubhouses, which forces colleagues from large papers like mine to grovel among ourselves for the precious little badges. The World Series is hardly the sweet, sunny coda to the season that it used to be. It is now a dark, cold, often gloomy marathon last act tacked on to a historic opera.

Tonight the gloom is all on the Mets' side, as the visitors win their second straight, 9–3. I wrote a column on Ron Darling preparing to pitch the fourth game near his family home in Worcester, Mass. During tonight's long game, my colleagues reinforce themselves from the boxed suppers, muttering about the damp October night and the impossible deadlines with eight-thirty starting times. Fucking baseball. Fucking Ueberroth. Fucking television. Fucking Mets. Fucking city. Fucking paper. Has baseball bought our loyalty for a piece of stringy fried chicken? Tell Denis Hamill it doesn't look that way.

BOSTON, OCTOBER 21

Tonight I watched Dave Anderson scoop the world, particularly me, his fellow columnist.

I was in a mellow mood, having driven up with Marianne yesterday, checked into a hotel with a view of the Charles River and Harvard, had a long lunch with our pal Gregory, and visited the Museum of Fine Arts at dusk. From the windows of the museum, as darkness fell, you could see the lights of the ballpark shining through the thick trees, calling, "Come to work, come to work."

The lights shimmered as I walked through the Back Bay Fens, giving me the magical feeling I would rather be here than anywhere else in the world at this moment.

The Mets seemed grim at the end of batting practice, with Ray Knight still seething over being benched for Sunday's game. Other Mets seemed intent, cornered, at finding themselves two games down.

At the end of batting practice, we were shooed off the field, and I tracked down our seats in the auxiliary press box. The World Series has become such a media swarm in the past generation that the major papers place one or two people in the main press box, while the rest of us are stuck in obscure corners. In this tiny old park, I expected to be watching the game from behind the bleachers, but I was stunned to discover that the Red Sox management has done a totally admirable thing, putting the auxiliary press section in regular seats between home and first, about twenty rows back, a better view than any of us get from any press box.

It's a different game up close. I was sitting with Al Campanis next to the visiting dugout in Shea Stadium a few years back, and I suddenly became aware of a young reliever breaking off magnificent pitches, with spin and speed.

"Chief, who in the world is that?" I asked.

"Oh, it's a kid Tommy's getting ready for his first start," Al said. "His name is Hershiser." In the press box, he was still just a long name with Roman numerals, but from up close, you could see Orel Hershiser IV was going to be one terrific pitcher.

From my point of view tonight, there was only one thing wrong with the seats the Red Sox handed us: Team *Times* was posted in the very first row, directly behind the paying customers, the fans, civilians. We happened to be near a group of good young fans, aggressive, knowledgeable, and talkative, who knew each other from the regular season.

Fully psyched for another Red Sox victory, they were also bright enough to be aware of a couple of hundred reporters right behind them. Boston people already talk out of the side of their mouths, but these fans twitched their mouths even further, until they were talking out of the back of their heads. They knew their baseball. They loved their Red Sox. And they wanted to give us some local character.

On both sides of me, I could see Malcolm Moran and Ira Berkow and Arthur Pincus perking up at the funny remarks of these Red Sox rooters. Dave, in his own cool way, was enjoying them, too. I appreciated the fans' existence, but I was in such a mellow mood that I wanted a one-way window between me and them. I did not want a meaningful relationship with them.

"Don't encourage them," I hissed at Arthur and Ira, as if these fans were squirrels or pigeons looking for a free lunch.

The Red Sox let the Mets get back into the Series by fumbling the ball, throwing to the wrong base, bumbling around the bases, just like the Red Sox of old. Twice Jim Rice came up with two runners on base, and both times he made out.

"Way ta hit in duh clutch, Rice," one of the fans shouted.

They cocked their heads to see if anybody was listening, and they caught Arthur Pincus grinning. By midway through the game, we knew their names, their hometowns, the names of their wives, girlfriends, and children. I rolled my eyes in disdain.

During the seventh-inning stretch, Dave asked, "Hey, just out of curiosity, who normally sits in these seats?"

"Right where you're sitting, normally there's a nice old guy, ninety-three years old," one fan said. "Comes to almost every game. Saw Babe Ruth pitch. Great old guy, real sharp."

He pronounced it "shahp," of course.

Dave did not change expression.

"Was he able to buy a ticket tonight?" Dave asked.

"I don't see him right now," the fan said, "but I tell you what. I'll meet you here tomorrow an hour before game time, and I'll introduce you to him. Name is Morrissey. He's good for a couple o' yarns."

He pronounced it "yahns," of course.

Dave sat down again, an angelic smile on his face.

"Got your early column, huh, Dave?" Arthur asked.

"Saw Babe Ruth pitch, huh, Dave?" Malcolm asked.

"It's like Red used to say," said Ira Berkow. "God will provide."

I forced a smile. I still did not have an early column for the next day.

"Guess we know why Dave has a Pulitzer Prize," I said.

BOSTON, OCTOBER 22

While Dave walked out of Fenway with his Babe Ruth column guaranteed last night, I hustled for a column on Dwight Gooden. Before the Mets' win, Bill Robinson told me he expected a superlative game from Gooden tomorrow because of the drubbing Gooden received last Sunday.

"Dwight does not like being humiliated," Robby said, but I could not tell how much of that was wishful thinking. Gooden's record "slipped" to seventeen victories, down from twenty-four, and he began having a series of "episodes"—the mysterious sprained ankle, the dubious excuse for being late for a spring-training game, the squabble with a rental-agency clerk.

The young man must carry his team and his reputation on his shoulders, knowing that everybody is watching, everybody wants something from him.

I have never been one to claim that print reporters are guidance counselors or big brothers. In fact, we're snoops and nags. But I also think the young man would have been better off facing reality, including tabloid frenzy, rather than being shielded so strongly by the Mets.

Last night I wanted to talk to Gooden about his start in the fifth game. I walked over to him in the crowded clubhouse where the Mets players were wolfing down their postgame meal: chicken, pasta, and salad on paper plates. I always feel uncomfortable interrupting athletes who are trying to gulp down their first meal since lunch, but this is how I earn my living.

The ancient visiting clubhouse, where Lou Gehrig and Joe DiMaggio dressed, was jammed with reporters wearing fall clothes. The air was thick with sweat and wool and tomato sauce as I stood next to Gooden.

"Got a few minutes?" I asked.

"Later," he said, not looking up. "Eatin'."

Well, that was reasonable—curt, but reasonable. Most athletes create their own invisible shields, if they want them, but Gooden has been issued his by the Mets.

When he was finished eating, he circled around to the shower room, avoiding the growing knot of reporters waiting by his locker. I used to operate on the theory that a man must always return to his pants in a locker room, but that belief was shaken in the Knicks' clubhouse a few years back when Ray Williams had the clubhouse attendant bring his pants to him in the shower room so Ray could beat a retreat out the back door.

Gooden eventually reclaimed his pants, which gave us a few minutes to ask questions. (Yes, he puts them on one leg at a time, like everybody else.) We asked Gooden how he had felt losing at Shea last Sunday, and he said, "You always hate to get beat, but especially at home. This is your ballpark, your turf."

We tried to get him to talk about his start tomorrow in the fifth game, but he seemed vague and disinterested. I filled out my notebook with opinions from Robinson and Mel Stottlemyre, the pitching coach, and Darryl Strawberry, Gooden's best friend on the team, and then I left the park.

This morning I sat down and wrote a column about a star pitcher trying to rebound from a bad outing in his first World Series game. Then I went back to Fenway and watched Ron Darling tie the Series with another gritty pitching performance. Long after the column was in print, I realized that Gooden had not given me any confidence to sustain Bill Robinson's quote as the headline of my column: "DWIGHT WANTS THE BALL."

BOSTON, OCTOBER 23

For my early column, I have criticized the eight-thirty starting time throughout this Series. I know television has purchased the Olympic movement, the World Series, the Super Bowl, but I resent the paying fans becoming a studio audience, and young fans in New York and New England having to fight off heavy eyelids to watch their home teams play. My theme will hold up throughout the night, giving me the chance to watch this game.

From our excellent seats, we can see that Gooden does not have it. He used to blow away the best hitters with his fastball and his self-confidence. It was all just a game. But from this close, I can see for myself that Gooden's fastball no longer seems to rise from the strike zone, his curve no longer breaks sharply into the strike zone. He struggles, he procrastinates, he stares at the catcher, he turns halfway from home plate, he rubs up the ball. Gooden may want the ball; he doesn't necessarily want to throw it.

The Red Sox' Bruce Hurst, however, has found his best rhythm of his career at the best possible moment. He is tall and bulky and ungainly, but he seems to control the ball after it has left his hand. He could be employing a long-handled paint roller, or turning the spit on a hog barbecue, or digging for clams with a long rake.

Gooden looks funereal as he trudges off the mound in the fifth inning, no doubt feeling he has let the Mets down. The confident young man of 1985 has vanished. Where did he go?

After Hurst strikes out Len Dykstra to end the game, I pay a visit to a makeshift interview room under the stands beyond third base. While reporters and television crews jostle for position—the old western feud of the sheepherders and the cattleherders in modern life—Rice fixes a baleful stare on all of us. Finally, he tells us to shut up so he and Hurst can get it over with. His own sour mood seems worse than that of the crazed reporters and electronic people. Doesn't Rice know his team is ahead?

Nobody is saying anything, so I decide I don't need any of this artificial press conference. I slip out the side door and find myself on the warning track in shallow left field. The quickest way out is to turn right toward home plate, but the lights are still lit, and the stadium is empty, and the grass is lush and green, so I decide to take a midnight stroll.

In all the years I have been coming to Fenway Park, I have never paid a visit to the wall. On this misty, magical night of hope and redemption, I have the freedom to take a left turn on the warning track, to gaze up at the slots and crannies and protuberances that make the scoreboard an extra factor in any game. I tap the wall, feel it with my fingers, imagine watching a white ball soaring at me, having to judge whether to try to catch it on the fly or run forward to field the rebound.

Surrounded by the empty green ballpark, I continue my walk past the right-field bleachers where David and I once sat on a nasty spring afternoon and watched a game-ending homer by Fred Lynn soar magically into our section. I have been a fan in this ballpark, not just a weary reporter with a computer hanging from his shoulder. I peer over the five-foot wall at the bullpen, at the litter of coffee cups and sunflower-seed shells.

I make the turn in right field, hearing the crunch of the red clay under my feet. Camera crews are still shooting in front of the Red Sox' dugout, the hair-spray gang intoning its final messages to sleepy America—"one game from destiny"; "Beantown is cooking tonight"—and then I pass onto Jersey Street.

Out here the fans are still scuffling through a soggy mass of newspapers and beer bottles, arms linked, singing, chanting. I cross the bridge over the Mass Pike, where truck drivers are blasting on their air horns, and I turn into the teeming squalor of Kenmore Square. Young people have climbed onto a traffic stanchion and are cheering, "Go, Sox," and "We're Number One."

My usual Zenlike avoidance of fans is tempered by realizing this is Boston, this is Fenway Park, this is one of my favorite places in all of sports. These fans are only one game away from winning the World Series. They seem so very happy.

PROVINCETOWN, OCTOBER 24

We have come to get away from the World Series for a few hours, and we have succeeded gloriously. The man in the red dress sashaying down the main street, the last scarlet tanager of summer, gave no hint of being emotionally involved in the Series. The waitress who brought me the biggest, freshest plate of fried clams in the world was not wearing a Red Sox cap.

But we heard enough of the tortured New England baseball psyche this morning as we drove away from Cambridge. Alert young men and women were running along the Charles, muscular rowers were out in their shells, but Mickey the Fan and Ernie the Fan and Vinnie the Fan and Freddie the Fan were busy on the talk radio.

Until I turned on the radio, I had been quite comfortable with the Red Sox winning the World Series. The Mets had a great year, but they were lucky to escape Mike Scott and a seventh game in Houston; now they must beat the Red Sox twice in New York. However, there are thousands—maybe millions—of people in New England who think the Mets can do it.

Just a few hours after the euphoria in Kenmore Square, the fans have turned regarding those two games in Shea Stadium. These poor numb souls have seen too many horrors in their lifetime—Country Slaughter scoring from first with the winning run in the 1946 World Series, Jim Lonborg running out of gas in the 1967 Series, Darrell Johnson batting for the pitcher in the seventh game in 1975, Bucky Dent hitting a home run off Mike Torrez in the play-off in 1978. As I fiddled with the dial this morning, I could hear these sad sacks fearing the worst:

Get that Buckner outta there. The guy's got guts, but he can hardly move. That Evans only hits in 9–1 games. Clemens hasn't had it for a month. Same old Sawx. Let Baylor start instead of Buckner. The Sawx will never take the extra base; some day it's gonna kill 'em. Spike Owen is an idiot; where did they get him? The Can will blow it in the seventh game. We'd better hope for rain on Sunday, so they can go with Hurst in the seventh game. Same old Sawx.

The way I hear it, these people are assuming Clemens is going to lose on Saturday, forcing Boston to use the emotional Oil Can Boyd on Sunday. They are one game ahead in the World Series, and they are rooting for rain. I wonder if the Red Sox players are listening to this stirring vote of confidence as they pack their bags and head to Flushing.

FLUSHING, OCTOBER 25

For my Sunday column, I wrote about the fan in Fenway Park who carried the banner: I AM A CALVINIST. THE RED SOX ARE PREDESTINED TO WIN, but I also wrote about the fearful callers on the talk radio shows in Boston yesterday. In the special tense of an early column that will be read after people know the result, I questioned whether the Red Sox could ever safely feel predestined to victory.

"New Yorkers like to feel we know all about suffering, and of course we do, with our loonies loose on the street and vans running red lights and public officials dividing the loot out in Queens, but there is no one great focus of civic suffering that unites us the way the Red Sox unite Boston."

I wasn't foolish enough to predict a Met victory, but I toyed with the theme of all the terrible things that have happened to the Red Sox since their last World Championship in 1918.

"It is a region starving for redemption, carrying around a scarlet letter 'B' for Bucky Dent," I wrote.

Based on my early column, I filed two postgame leads in my portable word processor, one for the Red Sox winning, one for the Mets winning. When the game ended, I would push a button, either way.

After that, I went through the motions until game time. I brought some fruit salad from home, and gave my Denis Hamill Memorial Boxed

Lunch to Pete the guard. I brought my usual esoteric reading matter, *The Nation* and *Christian Century,* to keep my head on straight before the game. Then Joe Vecchione lugged out some first-edition sports sections from the office.

"High-paid copy boy," Joe called himself, before holding a staff meeting in the press room.

As the Red Sox took a 2–0 lead, I found myself not caring which team won or lost. As a writer, I have enjoyed the Mets since the first April of 1962 and I was there when they won the World Series in their eighth season. Sitting in the stands, David and I suffered the dreadful old Mets of the late seventies, and I have been watching Frank Cashen and Davey Johnson create order out of chaos over the last few years. But as a journalist, the best story I could imagine was the tortured Red Sox winning the World Series after sixty-eight years. I was quite comfortable with that.

The Mets tied the score. I was comfortable with that. The Red Sox went ahead, 3–2. Good story. Gary Carter tied it again in the eighth with a line-drive sacrifice fly to left field. Great game.

In the top of the tenth, the Stadium grew silent, winter in the air, as the Red Sox scored two runs. I had no feeling of mourning for the team I had watched as a fan in my decade away from sports. I took out my machine and added a few details about predestination, and all the ghosts of Red Sox past being exorcised. After the top of the tenth inning, I filed the sub lead to the copy desk with a note on the top: "Hold for orders." You bet.

Not far from the main press box, out behind first base, a bunch of us from New York had managed to appropriate a vacant radio booth—Vic Ziegel, Jack Lang, and Mike Lupica from the *Daily News,* Joe Gergen from *Newsday,* and Dave Anderson.

With two outs, and our leads all mentally stored, we watched in fascination as Gary Carter stroked a single to left and Kevin Mitchell singled to center and Ray Knight singled to center to make the score 5–4. Would I live with the Red Sox holding off the Mets' rally? I checked my loyalties. Go with the story. We looked at each other sideways, nobody rooting, nobody really predicting the Mets could do any more, but a few of us uttering "holy shit" as Mookie Wilson came up to the plate.

William Hayward Wilson is one of my favorite Mets, an absolute prince of a man, smart and sweet and honest, but too often have I seen him "hacking away," in his vernacular, at bad pitches for me to think he would save the game.

The pitch from Bob Stanley was so bad, however, that Wilson leaped out of the way. Our radio booth was close enough to home that we could see Wilson's little dance, ankles elevated, body elongated, as the ball flashed underneath him, toward the backstop. In our little booth, several of us shrieked as Mitchell ran home with the tying run. We did not shriek for happiness, but for the journalistic thrill of being where the action was.

We had a good view of the Red Sox dugout, and we could see the players, in their dark blue jackets and their red lettering, retreating down the steps, like nuclear-plant employees backing away from a radioactive spill. The Red Sox dugout was Chernobyl.

With the entire stadium vibrating, Mookie Wilson hit a dribbler down the first-base line, toward us, toward the injured first baseman, Buckner. We watched him hobble toward the line and plant his damaged ankles. Then we could see the ball, a little computer cursor of white, squirt through his gnarled feet, while Knight raced around third base and scored. The game was over, the Mets had won, and six seasoned reporters looked at each other and screamed—not a scream of joy, just a scream of witness. Then some of us dived for our machines, and others raced for the clubhouses.

Because of *The Times*'s deadline, I had no time to interview anybody. Forget my Chipmunk roots. This column had to come from my head. I remembered that my early column had included the worst fears of the Red Sox fans on those talk radio shows on Friday: "Get Buckner outta there; the poor guy's got guts, but he can't move."

It wasn't that I had known. The Boston fans had known. Those poor souls with their gargling accents and their premonition of doom, they had woken up on Friday morning with a 3–2 lead and they had called up their favorite sports talk show and verbalized their worst fears that the Red Sox would blow it. All I had done was listen to them, and have the presence of mind to remember it for an early column about the curse of the Red Sox.

With the one o'clock final deadline less than an hour away, I plugged in my machine and started pounding away: "The special agony of the

Boston Red Sox continues for at least another day—or maybe another sixty-eight years.

"The collective pain of this franchise and the fans of New England was extended in excruciating and ghastly fashion early this morning. . . ."

I wrote five paragraphs in that vein, giving my eyewitness view of the strange event, and then I picked up all the predestination stuff, the italicized fears of the fans, and then I rewrote my final paragraph, saying the Sox "have only a few hours to recover . . ."

I had thought a Red Sox championship would be the best story of this Series. Shows how much imagination I have.

PORT WASHINGTON, OCTOBER 26

It is safe to say that everywhere in New York today, people are discussing where they were when Mookie's grounder played croquet with Buckner's legs. It is going to be one of those historical landmarks, like where you were when the lights went out during the great blackout, where you were during Pearl Harbor, where you were when Bobby Thomson hit the home run.

Some people couldn't stand to see the Mets lose, and pulled the covers over their heads and went into a protective sleep, like a hibernation. I heard of one man who switched on the VCR and went to sleep, woke up this morning and heard the words "seventh game" on the radio, and went tearing down to the VCR to see how it happened.

David just got home in time to see Mookie's mystical levitation and subsequent poltergeist ground ball. He had been performing an errand of mercy at my alma mater, Jamaica High School, one of my few enduring loyalties, the stately Gothic building on the glacial hill near Grand Central Parkway, a few miles from Shea Stadium.

I cannot drive past Jamaica without envisioning the earnest, positive boys with their crew cuts and the girls with their ponytails of the middle fifties, sure they were going to get into Harvard and medical school, have large families, and send their children to Jamaica High School. I was a chubby fullback on the soccer team, a marginal student, a sports columnist for the school paper, poorly dressed, socially inept, totally in awe of dozens and dozens of my classmates, often too willing to play the clown for them.

Last night in the girls' gymnasium, they were holding the thirtieth anniversary reunion of my class of 1956, and they were giving me an award as the class alumnus of the year. If I could have thought of an excuse to the duck the game, I might have tried it, but my conscience said the sports columnist from *The Times* ought to be at Shea Stadium, not Jamaica High School. Walter Schwartz, now my lawyer and the municipal judge of Ardsley, New York, then my editor on the Jamaica High *Hilltopper*—I still call him "Chief"—even volunteered to cover the game in my place.

Instead, I sent David to represent me at Jamaica.

"How did your thank-you speech go?" I ask him this morning.

"All right," he says. "I said, 'I've always heard a lot about Jamaica High, because my father's always driving us past it. Now I'm finally here, and I'm missing the Met game. I know my father appreciates the honor. Thank you very much.' It didn't really matter what I said, because everybody was listening to the game on Walkmans."

David got home in time to see Mookie's historic time at bat. We kill a few hours talking about one wild pitch and one wiggly grounder. Baseball. Now it's noon, time for another column, the weather is damp and threatening, and I am hoping for a rain-out.

I know Dave Anderson is writing about the Mets, how Davey Johnson took a gamble last night in removing Strawberry from the game in one of Johnson's National League–strategy lineup switches after Straw made the last out of the eighth inning. The move looked bad when Rick Aguilera gave up two runs in the tenth, but it worked out all right as Mitchell hit a single batting for Aguilera. Still, Strawberry was furious last night.

Because Dave is focusing on the tensions between Johnson and Strawberry, I will question John McNamara's wisdom in not removing Buckner when the Sox had a two-run lead in the tenth. It is not a blatant second-guess in my mind, because several of us discussed it in the press booth going into the bottom of the tenth. I also was in print with my Boston fans bleating about Buckner's legs.

Asked about it last night, McNamara said, "Normally with Buckner, we pinch-run for him. We didn't have to tonight, and he has very good hands."

This is the kind of basic, informed second-guess that makes baseball the best sport for fans and writers—and so hard on managers. There is no tyranny of the running clock, no football crapola about having to see the game films. Try as they might, baseball managers cannot convince writers or fans that all the information is not available. We all know everything. It's just a matter of making the right decision. McNamara went with his aching first baseman and paid the price.

Shortly after I file my column, the game is called off. We all need a day of rest—the players, the fans, the writers, Buckner's legs, and all the demons pursuing the Red Sox in this cold, clammy October.

FLUSHING, OCTOBER 27

The longer this Series goes, the more fascinated I am by the sixty-eight years since the Red Sox won a World Series, by all the terrible things that have happened to them since Harry Frazee sold Babe Ruth after the 1919 season.

Never having based my life upon intuitions or jinxes, I nevertheless love the image of the Red Sox as a haunted house of seven gables, the current generation suffering because of sins committed in the past. How literary, how New England, how Melville, how Hawthorne.

Yesterday's rainout would seem to have helped the Red Sox more than the Mets because it allows McNamara to bypass Oil Can Boyd in favor of Hurst, who has beaten the Mets twice already. But Hurst will be pitching with only three days of rest, and I can just hear the Red Sox fans on the talk shows yammering about Lonborg being tired in 1967 and Darrell Johnson switching pitchers in 1975. I am too heavily into predestination to stop now.

For my early column, I quote McNamara saying, "I don't know nothin' about history," and then I gave a healthy dosage of history since Babe Ruth was traded:

"The players don't deal with concepts like The Curse of Babe Ruth, but who is to say the whiff of failure has not settled into the steel, the earth, the wood and the very ozone of Fenway Park?"

Before filing the column, I include two alternative leads, one for each team winning, reviving all the past October horrors.

If the Red Sox were to lose, I wrote: "Enos Slaughter ran all the way home again last night. Jim Lonborg's arm was still tired on two days' rest. Joe Morgan slapped a hit off Jim Burton. Bucky Dent's fly ball once again soared over the left-field fence."

In case they won, I turned it around: "Enos Slaughter was thrown out at home last night. Jim Lonborg's arm bounced back on two days' rest. Jim Burton struck out Joe Morgan. Mike Torrez blew away Bucky Dent."

Either way, I'm protected. Then I drive to the ballpark. I don't feel like chatting with colleagues or players I've seen nearly every day for three weeks. I put on my headset and listen to The Band. I just want to see who wins. Do it. Write it.

From the radio booth behind first base, we watch Ron Darling give up three runs. He has been so gallant in the autumn tension, but now he is tired. Sid Fernandez comes into the game in the fourth inning and picks up where he left off Thursday night, giving the Red Sox heat. One imagines fans in Somerville and Nahant muttering, "Cripes, who is dis guy?" Maybe they are even muttering it in the third-base dugout. Ten days ago, I predicted the Red Sox would miss their right-handed designated hitter, Don Baylor, before this thing is over. Baylor remains in the dugout, while Fernandez mows down the eight other regulars.

All writers, if they are honest, will admit to wanting their theme, their subject, to be involved in the outcome. If you sit in the press box, you will hear writers talking about "my man." They are not rooting for players or teams, they are rooting for their own perspicacity. Since I have chosen the Curse of Babe Ruth, I await its influence with professional neutrality.

Just like Darling, Hurst falters in his third Series game, giving up three runs in the sixth inning to tie the game. He departs in the seventh, and Ray Knight greets hapless Calvin Schiraldi with a home run to put the Mets ahead. They score twice more, as Shea Stadium goes crazy.

The Red Sox make it 6–5 in the eighth, but the Mets score twice more, including a slashed fake-bunt single up the middle by Jesse Orosco.

The only trace of Casey Stengel is his Number 37 painted on the outfield wall, but, damn, the Old Man would have loved seeing Orosco perform what Casey used to call "the butcher boy."

Casey used to give seminars, slashing invisible grounders past invisible infielders, asking the Socratic question, "Why wouldn't ya wanna . . . ?" One day he was demonstrating the butcher boy to a bunch of writers and he noticed a player was actually listening to him. It was not a Met, however. It was Maury Wills of the Dodgers.

Shea Stadium is rocking for Orosco's butcher boy, but the Mets and their fans are not my story. I am writing predestination from a chilly, spectral New England angle. Late in the game, I jump in the press elevator and follow the tunnel to the left to the visiting clubhouse.

When the game ends on the field, we watch the Red Sox clump past us, a few seeming surprised to see our grubby army camped in the cellar. The door closes. Ten minutes later, it opens, and we squeeze through, display our Series credentials.

Most of the Red Sox are clustered in the trainer's room, which is off-limits to the press, and others are in the showers and the lavatories, also off-limits. But Bob Stanley, the historic figure who pitched to Mookie Wilson in the sixth game and was wild again tonight, is sitting on a huge trunk in the center of the room. Already unpopular with the Red Sox fans, Stanley knows he is going to hear about it all winter, every time he goes out for a haircut or to buy a loaf of bread.

A few lockers down, Calvin Schiraldi sits in his uniform, his head down. A dozen of us form a circle around him, silently waiting for him to acknowledge us or snap, "Get the fuck away from me," which, in this circumstance, I could understand. But Schiraldi looks up and starts answering the questions.

This is his third disastrous game of the postseason. He let a game get away against California in the league series, and now he has helped lose these two games in New York. He is a tall, ungainly college boy from Texas, with dark, moist eyes, bright enough to know he has secured himself a place in Boston's antihistory.

"Responsible? I blew two games," Schiraldi says. "I was the one who let the runners score. Will I get over it? I guess. At this time, I don't know how."

A few of us pry at him a little more. His voice is low and soft, and he does not look up, but he musters no viciousness toward us. My notepad is filled with quotes, my next deadline is approaching, but I am fascinated with people who lose with grace.

There is a lull in the questions. People don't know what to say, but we look at the dark, tousled hair and anguished eyes of this young man, and we are too absorbed to leave. I lean down and say in the most sympathetic tone possible, "Calvin, George Vecsey, from *The New York Times*. Just out of curiosity, what makes you sit here and answer our questions? A lot of your teammates are in the trainer's room. How come you're sitting here?"

He does not look up, but he answers softly, "You've got a job to do. I've got a job to do. This is part of your job. It's part of mine."

I am not always this gracious in moments of stress, when somebody sticks me in a bad hotel or tries to tell me what to think. I am old enough to be the father of many of these players. As a parent, I would hope my children would be as gracious as this young man is.

"Thanks for being here," I say softly, before rushing for the press elevator.

Back upstairs, I file a sub column, giving thanks for the marvel of electronic reproduction, which allows me to use some of the Curse of Babe Ruth material from the early editions without having to retype it. It is late at night, but I can finally be definitive about the fabled curse. I used the lead that starts: "Enos Slaughter ran all the way home again last night," and then I heighten it with another paragraph: "All the ghosts and demons and curses of the past sixty-eight years continued to haunt the Boston Red Sox last night. . . ."

Near the bottom, I increase the gloomy New England litany of October horrors: "Schiraldi had not been born in 1946 when Slaughter went into motion. . . . But now this young man with the long eyelashes is a Red Sox for the ages, part of the sixty-eight heartbreaking years, and counting."

I file my third column of the night, the stadium still buzzing. The guards have done a good job to keep the fans from destroying the stadium, but thousands of fans still prance in the stands. Some of the

Mets return to the field, frolicking on the mound, their gaits noticeably less balanced than in the desperate innings a couple of hours earlier. Near the dugout, a few television crews with glaring lights continue to interview any players who can still stand up.

In the press box behind home plate, dozens of reporters are still pounding away. I pack my books and equipment while waiting for the editors in New York to read my copy. I know we will be talking about these thirteen games all winter, for years to come. I know, right now, these have been some of the best weeks of my career. This is why I decided to come back to sports—not to witness something like this, but to write about it.

NOVEMBER

NEW YORK, NOVEMBER 2

It is barely daylight on Sunday morning, but grim-looking runners are already scampering on the streets of Manhattan, tuning their bodies for the rigors ahead of them.

This is one of my favorite days of the year, the New York City Marathon, when the recreational athlete becomes the true star, when firemen and lawyers, teachers and homemakers, run 26 miles and 385 yards through my hometown.

Covering the Marathon is a form of hero worship. Every fall I train for the local five-mile Thanksgiving race—speed drills and distance workouts, stretching exercises and carbohydrate loads—but I cannot conceive of running a marathon.

We have a rooting interest, too. Corinna's husband, Rolf Gilstein, is flying in from Columbus, Ohio, where his quartet performed in recital last night. Corinna is meeting him at Newark and rushing to the starting point on Staten Island. The word is that her wiry, energetic Norwegian-Canadian husband has the flu.

I once met a rabbi who claimed he had run every day for ten years. Even when sick? Particularly when sick, he said. Made sense to me. Whenever I come back from my modest runs, Marianne asks, "Are you in control again?" As long as you keep moving, nothing bad can catch you.

We meet at the Stage Delicatessen, Ira Berkow and Joey Goldstein and I. Marathon Day is Thanksgiving, New Year's Eve, Chanukah, and his birthday for the world's greatest sports publicist. Tomorrow there will be eight or ten stories, columns, sidebars in *The Times*—more because the paper has Marathon-mania than because of any overt selling job on Joey's part. He has left a million details in the hands of Dave Herscher, his assistant, while Joey takes Danish and coffee with two columnists from *The Times*. My column is going to be about Fred Lebow, the impresario of the Marathon, installing mandatory testing at this race.

Herscher, slender and nervous, comes running into the Stage Delicatessen. Everybody wants extra credentials. The buses are leaving in five minutes. Lebow wants this. The writers want that. The waiter is quicker with one-liners than with the check. Ira and I smile at the confusion.

Outside in the street, hundreds of runners are scampering toward the flotilla of buses heading for the starting line. They are wearing scruffy warm-up clothes they will discard at the starting line. They look so healthy, so purposeful, that I feel guilty eating Danish in their presence.

Joey, dapper in a homburg and a topcoat, escorts us onto the press bus, making sure we are seated before the press caravan departs. The starting point on Staten Island is its usual hectic self. Lebow giving directions on the bullhorn. Loudspeaker announcements. Martial music. Men taking a quick, nervous pee in every corner. Women standing on line outside portable johns. I spot several friends, Bob Coddington from my old neighborhood, Eddie Coyle, an old pal who writes about running for the *Daily News*. I worry about whether Rolf's plane was on time, and whether he is well enough to run. Mayor Koch shows up. The cannon goes off. The world-class runners surge toward the bridge, followed by twenty-thousand dedicated loonies.

After watching the start, I am allowed into a staff van that barrels over the bridge and up the West Side of Manhattan. As happens every year, we fall behind our police escort, and the driver tries to go sixty miles an hour, lights blazing, horn honking, swerving and screeching on bald tires through Sunday-driver dunderheads, while we hunch down in the backseat, afraid the damaged springs will break our necks against the roof. The van deposits us inside the barricades at the Tavern on the Green, and I watch the race on television.

When Gianni Poli of Italy and Grete Waitz of Norway cross the finish line, I attach myself to Herscher, who escorts me to the drug-testing tent in the woods. There Dr. Ronald D. Grossman of Hopewell, New Jersey, explains how the testing works: The first three runners, male and female, plus two selected men and two selected women, must urinate into a jar, observed by volunteer medical personnel.

"Some East European athletes used to carry clean urine in a tube attached to their arm," Dr. Grossman says. "When they went after the race, you couldn't tell it was coming from a tube. The new rules say you have to lower your pants to the knees, and your shirt to the chest level."

I keep going round and round about how I feel about mandatory drug testing. Sometimes I think it is an invasion of privacy, particularly when there is no known cause for testing. Other times I am tired of finding out later that athletes were using steroids or stimulants in a major sports event. I am put off by the idea of urinating into a bottle with somebody watching, but the runners will gladly trade privacy for five-figure prizes.

When my interviewing is over, I stick around to watch the average runners plodding in at three and a half hours, four hours. Men with bellies, women with white hair, people with odd gaits and terrible form, but all of them pushing to the finish line. I admire them all, with their chosen costumes, their self-expression, their dreamy looks, the hugs and kisses, the spittle dried around their mouths, the salt deposits on their bodies, the smell of sweat, the rustle of tinfoil capes, the roses provided to the women finishers, the family reunions, the laughs and the stories as the runners start to revive. They are not world-class athletes, but they have done something I will never do.

After three o'clock, I tear myself away from the sweaty reunions and I walk down to the *Times* office, twenty blocks, my exercise for the day. With deadline approaching, I call Corinna and Rolf at their apartment.

"Rolf's plane was on time," she says. "He had a fever of over one hundred. I told him, 'Rolf, you're crazy, I'm driving you home right now,' but he insisted. I drove to within a quarter mile of the starting line and dropped him off. Then I met him in Central Park. He finished in three and a half hours, and you know what? His fever was gone. Those Norskies are tough."

I'm starting to feel I missed my column. Testing for drugs depresses me. I should have written about Rolf and some of the other crazies, my heroes, but it's too late now.

VANCOUVER, NOVEMBER 6

I am out here in paradise on the most perilous assignment since James Gordon Bennett, Jr., of the *New York Herald* dispatched Henry Morton Stanley to deepest Africa to find the missing explorer Dr. David Livingstone.

My assignment: to track down the mysterious Barry Beck.

Back in New York, Beck is regarded as elusive as J. D. Salinger or Howard Hughes or Greta Garbo. He was the captain of the Rangers hockey team, yet he closed up his apartment on the swinging East Side and disappeared into the wilds of British Columbia.

Was it because Bubba despised the grim young coach Ted Sator? Was Bubba bothered by his injured shoulder? The fans think Beck is weird to leave the excitement of New York. Hockey writers suspect he is disturbed to give up half a million dollars. And the Rangers think he is crazy to leave the action of hockey—and for what?

We have picked up rumors that Bubba had legal trouble, drug trouble, medical trouble, love trouble, all kinds of trouble. He has added to his mystique by refusing to talk.

I have been chosen for this epic adventure because Joe Vecchione, whose wife, Elizabeth, is from Newfoundland, knows my daughter married a man from Victoria. That means I can speak Canadian, eh?

I have another edge in this manhunt because a few years ago I wrote a column about Beck's maturity from a former juvenile delinquent to captain of the Rangers. Ever since, Barry has always greeted me with a handshake and a smile, the way athletes do when you have written something complimentary about them, when they learn to trust you a little. No big scoops, nothing extra, just an honest look or a helpful tone of voice.

The advantage is compounded by my friendship with Bubba's agent, Rob Ingraham, one of the nicest people we know. We met when Rob was managing Jonathan Boyer, the first American to ride in the Tour de France. After one race ended on a mountaintop in the Pyrenees, I went for a hike and caught Rob singing to a herd of goats. We've been pals ever since.

"Bubba's fixing up a house overlooking the water," Rob told me.

"He's had it. I don't think he'll talk to anybody, but I know he likes you."

Rob advised Bubba how to manage money, how to handle New York, how to act with the press—what every agent should do, but most don't.

A few days later, Rob called back and said, "Bubba doesn't understand all the fuss, but if you think it's worth coming out to Vancouver, he'd be glad to see you."

My office was giving me a few days in the most beautiful city in North America to hang out with a friend. I jumped on the first plane I could catch. This morning I ran six miles in Stanley Park, with waves breaking on the rocks, cold water lashing my legs, the scent of pine trees and salt air driving me on. How could Bubba leave New York for this?

The poor confused man pulls up at the hotel at noon in a pickup truck. I forget my prepared line: "Dr. Livingstone, I presume?" Smile lines replace the deep frowns on his rugged face every spring when the Rangers are eliminated from the play-offs.

There are bags of cement under my feet. Most of his boyhood friends work in construction trades now.

"We help each other when we need a job done," he says. "Bring in a bunch of beers and go to work."

We cross the bridge to North Vancouver, and head west. I notice that Bubba's hair is dark brown again. In New York, he sometimes had his thick hair done in reddish tones, with punk-rock waves to it. He's back to basics now.

He maneuvers the pickup over the twisting mountain roads, turns down a steep driveway, and we get out. A Staffordshire bull-terrier puppy named Dino comes romping up to him. We walk onto a wooden deck overlooking the inland sea, slate-gray water merging with the mountains in the distance, huge ferryboats gliding in and out of Horseshoe Bay.

"I came home for the World's Fair this summer and found this place," Beck says. "That's when I made up my mind to stay home."

Bubba lifts up the cover to the outdoor hot tub, and steam emerges. He finds me a spare bathing suit, and we jump in the tub, the better to conduct our interview.

I point to the livid scar on Bubba's damaged left shoulder, the injury that held him to twenty-five games last year.

"The injury was my downfall," he says, meaning it gave him time to think about his own mortality as a player. "I always said I'd retire at thirty. Well, I'm twenty-nine now. They say every dog year is worth seven human years, and I put in nine years of hockey, plus living in New York, the fast life. That makes me an old man. It's time I should retire."

It is starting to get dark. The ferryboats glow like vertical sky-scrapers as they glide back and forth in the dark.

"I'd never been out here during the season," he says. "It's beautiful. Plus, I'm getting to know my parents better, seeing my friends. It's like being a teenager again."

I think of the crowds in Madison Square Garden chanting curses at the players, the pack of reporters jamming into the clubhouse after the game, the executives from Gulf and Western slipping around the corridors with sleek smiles on their faces, the derelicts on the street, the high-rises blocking the sun, the garbage in the streets. How can Bubba give all that up?

"There are rumors you had some kind of problem in New York and had to leave town," I say.

Beck shrugs. He says it would not be fair to collect a paycheck if his heart was not in playing for Ted Sator. But he adds that he would not come back this season even if Sator were replaced.

After my six-mile run this morning, my muscles are happy with the tub. I lean back against the cedar slats, feeling very unprofessional. *The Times* has sent me all the way out here, so I must ask some more questions.

"You must be independently wealthy to give up your contract," I say.

"If I need money, I'll chop wood, work with my hands, whatever it takes," he says.

"In New York, they think you're crazy," I say.

"I went home," Barry Beck says. "Found other things to do. Didn't need the money. Got busy. Simple."

"Too bad," I say. "Too bad."

In the fall of 1987, long after Sator had been dismissed, Bubba came back to the Rangers, looking terrific, eager to play hockey again. He hurt his shoulder almost right away, and went home to Vancouver for good.

NEW YORK, NOVEMBER 13

Corinna has given up her job in a literary agency to work in the Hartford bureau of the Associated Press. My little daughter who has worked and studied in France, who is aggressive enough to make it on Wall Street, smart enough to make it in law school, personable enough to make it in business, wants to be a reporter. Where did we go wrong?

Like Tevye in *Fiddler on the Roof,* who laments having five daughters, I cry out, "One yuppie, that's all I asked from a merciful God—one of my three children to wear business clothes, work in a pleasant office, do something that society rewards with a lot of money, like selling stocks or defending multinationals, so the kid could support us in our old age."

But Laura is doing well as a copy editor in Albany, David just sold a second article to *The Times,* and now Corinna is going back to the AP. When she worked in the home office in New York a year ago, the old-timers showed her my father's old desk. Pop helped a lot of people get their first jobs, but computers have changed things since the middle fifties. There seem to be fewer hands-on jobs for young people.

The *Daily News* in the middle fifties was a Parris Island for copy boys (there were, of course, no copy girls). You would be walking through the composing room and hear the words "Look out, college boy," and you knew you had exactly two seconds to jump out of the way of a heavy metal dolly moving about as fast and as menacingly as a New York taxi. Odd-looking bookies on company time hunched over the sports wires, muttering and sighing if you tried to strip the copy.

Charlie Hoerter, the evil-eyed sports editor, would ingest a large container of draft beer after the first edition and lurch around the department, firing people. The first time Charlie fired me, I started to pack up and go home, figuring that was it, I was going to have to become a lawyer or a teacher, but the older hands told me Charlie would never remember the next day, and, of course, they were right.

Before the computer age, I got a chance to distribute copy and look over shoulders and carry metal engravings and glance at page proofs while I was bringing them up from the composing room, things young people don't do today. I considered myself a veteran by the time I went to Hofstra College, and I was damned if I was going to spend my own money taking journalism courses. I was surly to journalism teachers I encountered, assuming they were failed newspaper people who couldn't get a job. I was a punk.

Loading up on psychology, history, English, foreign-language, and drama courses, I sat alongside talented people like Lainie Levine, now Lainie Kazan, the performer, and Joel Oliansky, the Emmy Award–winning writer. When I was a freshman, friends told me about a drama major who was excused from gym and ROTC. Not only that, he wore a beard, unheard of in the fifties. His name was Francis Ford Coppola, and he still has the beard.

Working full time at *Newsday* as a college senior, my future apparently assured, I became a fervent student for the first time in my life. Jack Mann was saying we did not have to write sports like the majority of writers on the city papers, who made each game sound as complicated as the Battle of Austerlitz, who filled columns with "wily managers" and "affable backstops." You might not have the talent, but at least you could be inspired by Shakespeare, Dickens, Tennessee Williams, Flannery O'Connor, Robert Herrick. "Corinna's Going A-Maying." We wound up naming our second daughter after a poem I read in college.

After I spent a decade as a sports reporter, Gene Roberts, for mystical reasons he never explained, recruited me to be *The Times*'s Appalachian correspondent, based in Louisville. When I found myself puzzled by terms like *grand jury, indictment, q-head, talker, libel,* and *slander,* I began to think there were a few things I might have learned in a journalism class, after all.

Now that I am back in sports, that world is far more complex than in my first tour of duty, with drug stories, contract stories, franchise and municipal stories, international politics. Nowadays, I advise young people to take at least a few of the most general journalism courses, backed up with courses in political science, law, economics, science, and a foreign language, of course. I am hardly fluent in Spanish and French, but I am amazed how few American journalists can say even a few words in any foreign language. It's almost a national phobia.

More and more younger reporters—at *The Times,* at least—have studied and worked in other complex fields. The days are long gone where newsrooms were full of glib, restless people, getting by on idealism or nerve or sheer writing ability. It's an age of specialization.

How do you get the first job? My father got jobs for me when copyboy jobs were more plentiful. Both Laura and Corinna have gotten more help from friends and college contacts than from their father.

When I talk to journalism classes, I always say: Consider your options; think about law, advertising, business, publishing, teaching, public relations; there are not many good jobs in the newspaper business.

And when an ambitious clerk at *The Times* asks how he or she can get ahead, I usually say, "Get the hell out of here. Go someplace where they'll let you write." *The Times* has been getting better about trying to develop young people, but it is very hard to get the right kind of experience at big papers. Young people need clips. Six months of good clips at a local paper and you're halfway to a better job.

I never advised my children to enter a limited profession with dreadful hours and grubby surroundings, for the privilege of making half or a third what their yuppie classmates will be making.

"Am I doing the right thing?" Corinna asks.

I remember Pope John Paul II in Mexico in 1979, addressing the journalists, urging us not to think of journalism as just a job "but as a vocation." Listening to the Pope, I realized I have always thought of journalism as partially a service, partially a way to create and express some form of truth—not exactly a nun in El Salvador, but not exactly a yuppie, either. Sometimes you actually make things better for people; sometimes you're just happy reading your own words in print. I can't imagine what else I would have done in life if I had not been a journalist.

How can I answer my own daughter? I want to lament, just like Tevye, until I think how proud my father would be to see two Vecsey girls in the business. Tevye had a word for that, too. Tradition.

After two more career changes, Corinna scored in the ninety-ninth percentile in her Law School Aptitude Tests, and was planning a law career "on the side of the good guys," as she put it.

BOSTON, NOVEMBER 21

David and I flew up on a misty morning to look over a few colleges. His first visit was Boston University, where they gave a highly organized tour of the huge campus. Our next appointment is at Northeastern, an hour from now.

"Let's walk past Fenway Park," I say.

We walk past the cafeterias and the convenience stores, turning left, over the Mass Pike.

"The last time I was here, everybody was happy," I say, remembering the hordes lurching happily back to Kenmore Square after Hurst beat the Mets in the fifth game. How could those poor devils know what was in store?

We find ourselves behind the left-field wall, the screen just hanging there, waiting to snag a home run next April.

"That's where Carter's second homer went," David says, motioning toward the warehouses.

The first time I took David to Fenway, we left New York before dawn, in time for the Patriots' Day game at ten. A few years after that, David saw a Red Sox old-timer make a running catch in left field. (TED WILLIAMS: GOOD FIELD, NO HIT was my headline.) When David was ten, Jim Rice autographed David's second-baseman's glove, now a tiny wrinkled relic in his closet.

Now, David is seventeen, a published writer. For the past year, he has been telling stories about running into the Mets in Port Washington —serving Ed Hearn and Sid Fernandez as a busboy at Louie's restaurant.

Journalism has a tradition of amiable raconteurs who can charm a barful of pals but, as Jack Mann puts it, "can't write a note to the milkman." I told David to write it. Between a Mets game and David Letterman, he banged out a thousand words, and sold it to *The Times*'s Long Island section. A month later, he sold another article, on Halloween.

The damn kid has no idea how many people are out there, calling, inquiring, reporting, writing, revising, polishing, scheming to get their first article published.

David is also my best male friend, the one I watch baseball games and Steve Martin movies with. It's beginning to dawn on me that he is actually going away to college.

We start walking along Jersey Street, toward right field.

"That's where Lenny's ball went," he said.

Lenny. The household hero. Ever since David discovered the out-fielder with the serial-killer smirk, Len Dykstra has been David's alter ego, the energetic little boy who turns up in the major leagues.

As we follow the trajectory of Lenny's home run, we have flashbacks of the dreadful predicament of the Mets, going into the third game.

"Lose two at home," David says.

"Slip off to Boston," I respond.

"Don't take a workout."

"Stay away from the wall."

"Sleep. Eat. Rest."

"Read the papers."

"Oil Can Boyd."

"Gonna master the Mets."

"Lenny bats leadoff."

"Comes out of the dugout. Sees the right-field stands. Big deal."

"Babe Ruth. Ted Williams. Carl Yastrzemski. Big stinking deal."

We are into it now. We can see Lenny spitting and smirking, deep in his own fantasy world, wondering what the fuss was all about, leading off the third game of the Series. Then we can see Dykstra's ball flying toward the right-field stands, sending a message to the Red Sox, sending a message to the fans, sending a message to the Mets.

"Hey, these guys aren't so tough," David says, for Lenny.

"Fuck Babe Ruth," I say, echoing the ultimate Japanese insult during the war.

"Big deal, five hundred twenty-one home runs for Ted Williams. Who needs the wall?"

We are chortling now, looking down at the sidewalk to see if the Greater Boston Historical Society has gotten around to including this historic moment on the footpath for tourists. This is where Cotton Mather preached his fire-and-brimstone sermons. This is where Paul Revere warned that the Redcoats were coming. This is where Len Dykstra's home run took off into the night.

"No memorial for Lenny," David says.

"No blue lines. No footprints. No class," I decide.

We both bemoan the long wait until the next home run next spring. I think about all the columns I could find in Boston, in case David decides to go to school here.

"Are we going in the right direction?" David asks.

"More or less."

In 1987, David dashed off an essay about no longer enjoying sledding on the local hill—"Old at Seventeen." He mailed it to the "About Men" editor at The New York Times Magazine, *and they called back and said they were using it. Only later did somebody inquire, "By the way, are you related to our Mr. Vecsey?" We liked that part. He did it on his own.*

DECEMBER

NEW YORK, DECEMBER 1

Hubie Brown was fired as coach of the Knicks this morning. I wasn't surprised, after hearing the boos from New York fans who have not forgotten the beautiful championship teams of the early seventies.

Some writers, including my brother and me, have been pointing out that Hubie robbed his players of their initiative by calling his rigid plays from the sidelines, and that Hubie has never blamed himself for anything, but I couldn't pull the trigger on Hubie.

I guess that's why people should read a couple of papers every day. Some columnists have a soft spot for Bobby Knight, or Vince Lombardi, or Woody Hayes, or Caligula. What can I say? I've liked Hubie in some weird way since the first time I met him, in March of 1980.

Just back in sports, I was assigned to write a profile of the coach of the Atlanta Hawks. Not knowing Hubie Brown from Buster Brown, I wandered into the gym at Morehouse College in Atlanta just in time to hear a coach screaming, "You fucking fuck! You were garbage when I found you, and you'll be garbage when you're gone."

That was Hubie, yelling at John Drew, his best player.

Later at lunch, I told Hubie I had never heard a coach vilify one of his players in an open workout like that. Hubie didn't back down, saying some of his players were "garbage" and would be "back on the street" before long.

He was more prophetic than he might have known. A few months later, one of his former players, Terry Furlow, died in an auto accident with traces of drugs in his system. A current player, Eddie Johnson, got into drug problems, although they were treated as a psychological problem and chemical imbalance. And Drew, the player Hubie called "garbage," was later banned from the league for drug problems.

This morning when I heard Hubie had been fired, I remembered his preoccupation with the street, and I went back to my notes from our first interview. I am a compulsive saver, with two shelves of notepads dating back to 1970.

My collection came in handy in the early seventies when a lawyer for a coal company accused me of misquoting him about the responsibility for the collapse of a West Virginia dam that killed over a hundred people. After I produced my notepad, with the key phrases scribbled in legible longhand, the lawyers for the survivors won millions of dollars in damages. I haven't thrown away a notepad since.

Sure enough, my Hubie Brown folder contained several good articles by other people, as well as my typed notes from our luncheon in 1980 —Hubie comparing his wastrel players to his father, who had taken a job as a janitor to support his family after being laid off on the New Jersey docks.

"This is the land of Mary Poppins, the land of make-believe," Hubie had told me in Atlanta. "When their little world evaporates, there's only ten percent of them ready for the real world. I tell them, 'Avoid the street,' but, hey, it's the same for me, Jack. I'm only half a step from the street."

I wasn't lulled into thinking Hubie was a benign saint. Maybe it was Hubie's vocabulary that impressed me. I always thought Jack Mann and Bob Waters at *Newsday* had the best drill-sergeant vocabularies I ever heard, but Hubie is right up there. A man who calls people "fucking fucks" can't be all bad—even if he does it in coaching clinics, with nuns in the front row.

In New York, Hubie could not conceal his scorn for Dave De-Busschere, the general manager, or the Gulf and Western officials, or most of his players, or most of the press. I knew Hubie was cultivating me by answering my questions without the sarcasm he gave the beat reporters. When I left the clubhouse, Hubie would give me one of his depressed little smiles and say in his rasping voice, "Hey, thanks, you've been good to us."

I can deal with that form of patronization. But what Hubie could not know, what I only realized recently, was that Hubie reminds me of friends I grew up with, hard-working Irish-Americans with swagger up front and insecurities underneath, arrogant one moment, bitterly funny the next. In some tribal way, I found myself liking him.

When Bernard King's knee fell apart and Bill Cartwright's foot wouldn't heal, I refused to blame Hubie for that. I pointed out that Patrick Ewing might not be a total savior, that the Knicks' front office had made some dreadful trades, and I reminded people that Hubie had done some excellent coaching wherever he had been.

After the Knicks lost last Saturday, I wrote, "If it keeps up, the boos will lodge in the rafters, like a perpetual ringing in the ears—not exactly the sounds Gulf and Western has in mind for this entertainment center."

Actually, I have more problems with Gulf and Western than I did with Hubie Brown. I am realistic enough to know that corporate ownership is the wave of the future. There is no point being too nostalgic for the Horace Stonehams and Calvin Griffiths, the old walruses who made trades autonomously in the middle of the night after a drink or seven, but there was something honest and rudimentary about them.

When Gulf and Western absorbed the Knicks, it still had Michael Burke and Sonny Werblin, sports executives who at least understood the mentality of the New York fan. After them came Jack Krumpe, and who could tell what he really knew or thought or felt? Behind him were other striped suits in the corporate box seats, people with no background in sports, people you never met, people who won't answer telephone calls, protected by glib public-relations men you never met, either. After he was fired, DeBusschere said every small decision had to be kicked upstairs to executives who might be in Japan or London closing a movie deal.

Gulf and Western is not having a good year. Every couple of weeks it holds a press conference for a new Ranger or Knick official. The new president of the Garden is Richard Evans, who previously revived Radio City Music Hall. Evans is a westerner without much feel for New York or sports, but he seems bright and positive, reminding me of some chief executive officers I've met. If Evans cannot guide Gulf and Western out of this morass, the corporation should get out of the sports business.

NEW YORK, DECEMBER 8

My friends in the sports department have been impressed at sighting Max Frankel in the sports department a couple of times since he was appointed executive editor on October 11. I spotted him at one of the World Series games at Shea Stadium, and apparently he is a serious fan.

When I heard about Frankel's appointment, I remembered a dinner of national correspondents in New Orleans early in 1972. Frankel was boning up to cover Nixon's trip to China, and between courses he would study a Chinese-English dictionary on his lap. His work from China, including the lovely image of citizens sweeping snow from the streets with brooms made of small branches, would win a Pulitzer Prize.

It's going to be different for us under Frankel. Abe Rosenthal, his predecessor, and Arthur Gelb were supportive about sending me back to sports, treating me as a valued Roman centurion posted in distant Gaul. Frankel actually knows this terrain.

Abe is going to be writing a column twice a week. His last few years have been tense, and some people are glad to see him move away, but I have prospered under him, and have seen the warm and wise side of him. Abe once took a trip through Appalachia with some of the national reporters, and we stayed up nights sipping beer. He was as savagely incisive in a cabin in a Kentucky state park as he was in the five o'clock news briefing.

"What do you see yourself doing in five years?" Abe asked casually.

"Oh, maybe working in the Paris bureau," I said.

"George, there are two kinds of foreign correspondents," Abe said. "The kind who want to work somewhere—and the kind who want to live somewhere. Both are fine. They're just different."

I knew what he meant. I wanted to live in Paris, not be a foreign correspondent covering revolutions out of a suitcase. His quick remark helped clarify my career decisions. And he made me a sports columnist ten years later.

It's pretty clear Frankel has the same kind of journalistic judgment. In one of the early meetings, Frankel said he wants the sports columnists to write more of our opinions, not just locker-room features. The phrase he used was "kick ass."

* * *

Max reads the sports section—carefully. I learned this early in 1987, when I dropped into his office for a visit, and he said one columnist should have covered the American Conference championship rather than both covering the Giants' championship game, because The Times *is becoming more of a national newspaper. Referring to a column I had written four months earlier, Frankel said I could have taken a stronger stand about the Navy allowing Napoleon McCallum to join the Los Angeles Raiders on weekends while on active duty. That kind of empowerment from the top is what every sports columnist loves to hear.*

Later in 1987, Dave Anderson and I were assigned three columns instead of four per week, and Ira Berkow was included in the regular rotation—a welcome break for me as well as for Times *readers. The paper also nominated my 1986 columns for the Pulitzer Prize.*

PORT WASHINGTON, DECEMBER 14

Dave Anderson called at eleven-thirty this morning. Old Reliable was at Giants Stadium for a football game.

"Hey, babe, I don't know if you already heard, but Dwight Gooden was arrested in Tampa last night. He got into some kind of trouble with the police and they arrested him. The radio said there was a fight. Just thought you'd want to know. No charge."

I had been sitting around listening to WNCN and stretching for a run, but obviously Gooden had not been big enough news to interrupt Delius. When I'm home, I don't listen to the news stations unless I'm specifically keeping an eye on a story. Trouble usually finds you. I had already written a column about a hockey player with a consecutive-game streak, but Gooden takes precedence. Just slightly.

I called the office at noon and let them know I was doing a Gooden column. Arthur Pincus, who runs the office on weekends, had Leslie Chambliss, my pal from Alabama, read me the wire-service reports, and keep me informed about what Bob Thomas, a former cityside reporter, was picking up over the phone.

The first reports said Gooden was picked up late last night by officers in Tampa and that he got into a scuffle and was charged with a third-degree felony. The officers claimed they had stopped Gooden because his Mercedes-Benz was weaving back and forth in traffic. The police said Gooden got out of his car and began cursing the officer, refusing to turn over his license and accusing the police of harassment.

Early reports said all the officers were white and all five people arrested were black, and Gooden's lawyer suggested racial prejudice had been involved in the police action. Gooden apparently had bruises and cuts but nothing serious. The results of a blood test have not yet been determined.

After an hour of phone calls and checking the reports, I still could not be sure what Gooden had been doing in his car, and how he got into a brawl with police.

I was a news reporter long enough to know the tensions in any encounter with the police, particularly on the highways after dark. I knew there was a possibility the police had overreacted, making the situation worse with brutal tactics.

I flashed back to 1972, when I was sent from Louisville to Baton Rouge to cover a disturbance involving a Moslem splinter group. A Louisiana trooper stopped me at a barricade and leveled a shotgun at me and ordered me to produce identification. I told him I was not going to put my hand inside my jacket, not with him pointing that shotgun at me. He would probably have been even more aggressive and jittery if I were black—and that's my point. Blacks have learned to survive by not taking unnecessary chances.

I've been to Tampa, and I've been around the South a lot, and I think the days of every white police officer behaving like Rod Steiger in the movie *In the Heat of the Night* are long gone. The police in Tampa may be shadowing Gooden, for good reasons or not, but I strongly doubt they want any kind of violent confrontation with Tampa's leading sports celebrity. Police have enough aggravation without that.

Before writing a word today, I pulled out my Dwight Gooden folder, crammed with twenty-five articles.

In January he had sprained an ankle and was going around on

crutches. After the Mets received an anonymous phone call, he told several different stories about how it happened.

In March he was fined by the Mets for missing a spring exhibition and claiming he had been in a traffic accident, which apparently was not true.

In April he and his girlfriend and his sister became involved in an argument at a car-rental counter in New York, which included his sister throwing a cup of soda at the agent.

In October, after two poor World Series performances, he missed the Mets' victory parade the morning after they won the championship. The Mets gave several explanations, starting with oversleeping and escalating to his being sick from too much beer.

In November Gooden confirmed that one woman had given birth to his son, and that his wedding to another woman had been postponed. At the same time, he responded to rumors of drug abuse by telling reporters he had requested random drug tests "as often as they want, and they can be forever."

We've been picking up rumors that the Tampa police have been watching him closely, but we couldn't come up with enough to write anything.

The people at the Meadows sometimes went overboard in seeing chemical abuse in nearly every human flaw, but the relentless counselors and the street-wise patients taught me to look for signs of trouble —lateness, temper, fights, excuses, denial.

If Gooden were attending a therapy session at the Meadows, the counselors and patients would flatly accuse him of having some problem. From a thousand miles away, and with only a few hours to write, I could not overlook the possibility that Gooden had been a victim of racist brutality by the police. Combining my instincts as an old news reporter in the South and my experience at the Meadows with Gooden's problems of the past year, I made the judgment that whatever happened Saturday night was compounded by some lack of control on Gooden's part.

As I started writing, I already had the headline in mind. I used to resent *The Times*'s policy of letting the sports columnists write their own headlines, a flashback on my part to some claustrophobic winters on the *Newsday* copy desk many years earlier. However, I soon learned that writing (or suggesting) my own headline was an added creative challenge. Often I could bring in an obscure reference, or make one more wordplay that fit in with the theme of the column.

Today, I did not exactly know how I was going to frame the column, but I could see the words OUT OF THE STRIKE ZONE at the top of the column. I began by recounting the several versions of the scuffle. Then I wrote:

"The police have too many reasons to be edgy these days; too many addicts and lunatics and Rambos and Dukes of Hazzards on the loose. The thing to do with an armed police officer is to say 'Yes, sir' until you can get to a well-lighted station house and call your lawyer."

It was clear in my mind that I was writing about the century-old wisdom of blacks learning to survive in the United States, that they must always remain in control, for self-preservation. Then I began to worry in print about Dwight Gooden, the individual, the young man with the averted eyes and the swallowed voice of last October. My final paragraph said:

"People who have been able to get near Dwight Gooden say he is a nice young man. It is time for his family, his friends, his representatives and his employers to make a list of his problems in the past year and tell him he's having trouble finding the strike zone, on the mound and in real life."

Since my name will be on that column in the morning, I don't want to be wrong, or sound stupid. But even more important than my reputation is that a man's life could be on the line. I am still thinking about my column when I go to sleep.

PORT WASHINGTON, DECEMBER 21

The news just broke that Dwight Gooden's blood tested at a level of .111—above the legal level of .1 for driving an automobile in Florida. He says he had a drink or two just before being stopped. Most people who drink used to believe that a drink or two could not affect driving, but some people are affected more than others.

The word about the blood test made me a bit more comfortable about having suggested Gooden was out of control last Saturday night. But I'm never totally satisfied with my columns, particularly on a sensitive issue like this one, and I've been questioning whether I made my points clearly.

The reaction began Monday morning, when I got a call from Barry Gray of WMCA, who has been doing a solid radio talk show for many years. I tried to stress that my column had been concerned about Gooden, and then several black listeners called up to tell how they are often stopped by New York police just because they drive nice cars.

"The cops think I'm a drug dealer because I drive a Trans-Am," said a reasonable-sounding man. "White people don't know what that's like. They could have stopped Gooden just because he was driving a Mercedes."

I am not about to tell any black person what life is like for him or her in America. I did bring up Gooden's other problems for the past year, and said I was concerned Gooden did not have a total grip on his life.

On Tuesday, I got a call from a friend of mine, a black woman who used to sit near me in *The Times* city room. She told me how she and some other black journalists around town keep in touch about the way the press handles stories like the Gooden situation.

"I know your head is on straight," my friend told me. "But some of my friends want to know if you know more than you wrote. They think you were pretty hard on him."

"I don't have any evidence, just rumors," I said, not willing to say we had been checking out some things for the past year. "My real concern is that Gooden didn't handle it well when he was pulled over. I thought I was giving him advice on how to protect himself."

"You don't know what it's like," she said. "My son is just going into adolescence. He hangs around with kids of all different races in the city. If they go into a store, he is the one the guards stop. He is the one they follow. They make a judgment just by the color of his skin. Look, I came along during the civil-rights era. I remember being stopped by cops in California just because I was a black woman out with white people. I don't think it's changed all that much. How do you really know what happened down in Tampa?"

I had to admit that I was reacting as a columnist, using my instincts and all available information. Since I wrote my first column, Dudley Clendinen, our Atlanta correspondent, interviewed a white passerby who said the police were "beating" several of the men in Gooden's group. But the police maintain Gooden and his friends were belligerent.

After my first column—and before news of the positive blood test— I received over twenty letters, almost all critical of me for wondering if Gooden had been in total control that night. A few letters had the smug tone of northern white liberals quick to charge *The Times* with racism, whose vision of the South seemed stuck a quarter of a century earlier.

Met fans who wrote tended to say that Gooden seems like a nice young man. I even got a letter from a white journalist friend who said Gooden once had been polite in turning down his autograph request— therefore, Gooden must have been polite to the police, too. I am going to write a note to my friend saying he sounds more like a fan than a journalist.

The letters from blacks dealt more with their personal experiences, being stopped by police, why they had left the South many years ago. Several readers demanded to know why I brought up the fact of Gooden having a son born out of wedlock. What did that have to do with anything? I saw Gooden's tangled personal life as just another sign of lack of control.

Blacks have every right, and historical evidence, to be skeptical of anything white people say about them.

After the news of the blood test, I wrote another column for tomorrow with the headline: GOODEN CASE: ANOTHER LOOK.

I raised the concerns black people have about being stopped by police in America, and I quoted my black journalist friend, anonymously, to remind people how much blacks fear the police. I also talked to a colleague who had lost a child to a drunken driver, and I said Gooden had been lucky he did not kill anybody while driving around with alcohol in his system.

Then I criticized the mostly white New York Met fans who, as far as I could see, wanted to believe Gooden was a victim of prejudice.

"Of course, they're on his side," I wrote. "He's Doctor K. He's a meal ticket for more pennants."

I wrote that even if beer was involved, and nothing illegal, that alcohol abuse is just as serious as drug abuse. "But beer is baseball's leading sponsor; let us not expect to hear from the Commissioner on this one."

I concluded that Gooden's family and friends should sensitize him about operating a car under any kind of stimulus.

"Gooden's problem could have had more to do with being black in America than being over the limit behind the steering wheel. Either can be dangerous. A mixture could be extra lethal."

In the past, some of the most famous sports journalists celebrated drinking as a life-style, praised Babe Ruth or Mickey Mantle for hitting home runs on a hangover induced at Toots Shor's "watering hole." These days, columnists like Mike Lupica and Steve Jacobson write with great wisdom and concern about drugs and alcohol abuse.

We just can't glorify the old habits of drinking anymore. I'm not against drinking, and will drink a glass of wine or amaretto from time to time. Bob Welch does not campaign to shut down every bar, and in fact he hangs out in his favorite place in every town, where the bartenders loyally keep his glass filled with soda. Bob says it is his problem that he cannot afford to touch a drop, not somebody else's, and I go along with that.

But when a young athlete shows some of the danger signals of being out of control, and then is caught with excessive alcohol in his system, I take it seriously enough to write about it. The old days of fun and games are over. I'm sorry some readers think I'm a racist for raising these questions. I thought I was raising concerns about Dwight Gooden's life.

When Dwight Gooden tested positive for cocaine three months later, I was neither surprised nor glad. It just seemed to confirm my fears that he might be headed in that direction. He spent a month in the Smithers Center for Alcoholism and Drug Treatment in New York and went back to work, under the supervision of Dr. Alan Lans, a gentle and patient psychiatrist at the Smithers Center. For that season, Gooden still seemed like the withdrawn young man of previous years, and he gave me (and Dr. Lans) reason for concern by still drinking a beer on occasion, something recovering drug patients are advised not to do. (The first danger signal that Lawrence Taylor of the New York Giants still had a cocaine problem in 1988 was that he was drinking beer.)

In the spring of 1988, Peter Richmond of the Miami Herald *told me, "You're not going to believe this, but the best interview in the Mets clubhouse is Dwight Gooden. He is very nice, very articulate, very together." I would not call Gooden the best interview on the Mets, but Gooden seemed a different young man than he was a few years earlier. He made eye contact and he talked in paragraphs, not syllables. He was married, moved from Tampa and his old crowd, and seemingly in control of his life. The Mets no longer shielded him from the press. He was a grown-up.*

Having watched my own three children suddenly make judgments and connections they could not have made a year earlier, I felt paternally happy for Gooden, age twenty-three. In the same week, I had pleasant conversations with Darryl Strawberry, age twenty-six, and Patrick Ewing, age twenty-five. It made me realize that a white writer could not begin to imagine the pressures on young athletes, particularly the black ones, suddenly thrust into a world of huge crowds and agents and lawyers and demanding strangers, as well as notepads and microphones and cameras. I was so impressed with the maturity of Gooden, Ewing, and Strawberry, on and off the playing field, that I wrote a column about it.

PORT WASHINGTON, DECEMBER 24

A dozen of us are gathered for Christmas Eve when the phone rings.

"Joyeux Noël, Georges," Roby Oubron says.

"It's one-thirty in Paris," I say to Roby in French.

"We were watching midnight mass on television," Roby says. "We wanted to call you."

Roby is a former world champion in cyclocross, bicycle racing over rugged terrain. Later, he was a national cycling coach in France. He looks like Picasso in his late sixties, compact and vibrant, but kindlier.

We met when I covered the Tour de France in 1982, when Roby was working with Jonathan Boyer, the first American to ride in the Tour, and also with Bernard Hinault, the champion from Brittany. As Roby drove me from Bordeaux to the Pyrenees, if I had a question about the race, Roby would pull up alongside a cyclist on a narrow country road, lean out the window, and ask why the cyclist was making his move. It was like going to the World Series and sitting with Ted Williams next to the dugout.

One night over a bottle of red, Roby told us how he had taken shrapnel near the Rhine, and lay on the battlefield until an American soldier pulled him to safety.

"J' adore l'Amérique," Roby had said.

Later, I found out he had returned to Paris after his recuperation, pedaling around the city, directing members of the Resistance to safe houses. He was picked up by the Gestapo, but his spirited young wife shamed an old friend with ties to the Vichy government to arrange for Roby's release before the next train rolled eastward. According to family legend, Roby was furious for months that his wife had talked to the collaborationist.

Simone Oubron gets on the phone and chatters in French with Corinna. When Corinna lived in Paris for a year, Simone would invite her for dinner once a week. You know, the cold, unemotional French who dislike Americans.

While I listen to Corinna catch up on the news, I think about how different my life is because I am a journalist. We are surrounded by family and a few close friends at Christmas, but much of our life is scattered around the world, with the unique friends here and there who answer our deepest needs for friendship.

In Paris, there are Roby and Simone and their grandson, David. One of Marianne's best friends lives in Boston. Her closest friend from childhood is moving to Egypt. In Orange County, California, I have an adopted Greek grandmother named Mamma Tulla, who calls me "my boy." There are "homes" in Wales and Dallas, Mexico and Los Angeles, London and Canada, where we are welcome.

Our friends are athletes and writers, businesspeople and public officials, artists and musicians, people who tend to live on the edge, in competition with others, in competition with themselves.

The longer I stay in this job, the more my home becomes a retreat for me, a pleasant base, but our support system, our adventures, our challenges, stretch for thousands of miles. I am reminded of it not only by the telephone call from Paris but from my annual "Postcards" column.

I began the column at the end of 1982—a way of thanking "the good folks in the last hard town we met," as Tom T. Hall put it in his song title. Many people tell me they look forward to it at the end of each year.

When I started going through the clips from 1986, I was aware of the trail of tragedy through the year—Flo Hyman, the volleyball star, dying suddenly in January; Kevin Stockton dying suddenly while I was working with his dad in Mexico; Milton Richman, that proud columnist from United Press International who died in June; Dick Howser diagnosed for brain cancer; Len Bias and Don Rogers, athletes I had covered, dead from drugs.

My second reaction was how many of the columns that meant the most to me were about blacks—Charles Boston in Mississippi, Spud Webb's family at the Soul Market in Dallas, David Robinson of Navy and Mouse McFadden of Cleveland State during the basketball tournament, finding myself homesick after chatting with the black boxers at the Goodwill Games, and ending the year with the two controversial columns about Dwight Gooden. To cover sports is to touch upon being black in America.

Another thing I realized from my clips was that the Mets' series with the Astros and the Red Sox in October were thirteen of the best baseball games of my life. The road trips, the late hours, the bizarre games, made me remember how much I love baseball, how much of my job revolves around that sport.

"All these winter sports are merely the parsley on the plate of life; the real nourishment will return in late February," I wrote at the end of my "Postcards" column.

In these last dark days of 1986, I think of the Moscow bureau, lights burning late at night, good journalists writing about a republic in ferment. I think about the faces in the Moscow metro, the people who looked like me and my family. I remember my fantasy in the last hours in Moscow—being asked to stay on to help cover all the hot stories. Moscow does not go away. Neither do the baseball game in Wales, the park in Mexico, the raucous press section in Boston, the friends awaiting our next visit to Paris.

When Marianne and I were young, we thought we would grow older surrounded by family and neighbors, church on Sunday, office friendships, and neighborhood parties. Instead, we live for the big story, the next trip, the reunions, the telephone call on Christmas Eve from the Eleventh Arrondissement.

PHOENIX, DECEMBER 31

In the last hours of 1986, I am back with the people with the blue cat's-paws painted on their faces. Penn State is playing Miami in the Fiesta Bowl for the national championship on Friday night, and it seemed like the place to be.

Exactly a year later, we still have our morality plays handed to us. The Miami team has given us our bad guys by showing up for public events wearing the latest fashion, combat fatigues, and acting truculent. Joe Paterno's team is always the favorite in the bowl-game version of pro wrestling. Wish I could feel that strongly about it.

It's been 364 days since I woke up in Miami and went for a run wearing my BRASIL T-shirt. I celebrate the end of the year by finding a public park and, wearing my Goodwill Games T-shirt with the Cyrillic writing on it, I jog my two and a half miles before the sun sinks below the mountains.

The reporters in the press room look younger than ever, talking excitedly about the game and finding a good restaurant on New Year's Eve, but I'm forty-seven and a half, and my stated goal is to be asleep by midnight. I don't do New Year's Eve.

Journalism is a young person's business, for the same reason soldiers will storm a beach at the age of nineteen but think twice about it at twenty. When I reached my middle thirties, if an editor told me to go out and cover something, I found myself interviewing the editor to discover the history behind the assignment. As a columnist, or a specialist in any field, you start saying to yourself, "Ah, it's been done before."

In sports, the players are always the same age, while I am becoming a balding columnist with a gray beard, a jacket, and a tie. I've got kids the same age as the athletes, but sometimes that helps me appreciate players like hapless Calvin Schiraldi of the Red Sox, sitting in front of his locker after losing the World Series.

When I started, Schiraldi would have seemed like a middle-aged player, but now he seems like a kid. Either way, I was glad it was me in that locker room that night, bringing my perspective, my vision, my questions, my words, to the job.

In some ways, I am still the little boy going to his first game with his father. Outdoors in the daytime. No classes. I have made the jump, I have broken out of the routine, but the leap demands two things— performance and energy.

Will I know if I lose it as a columnist? I have seen too many other journalists need a kick in the pants, a change of scene, or become obsolescent. A sports columnist ought to ask himself every day whether people are going around saying, "Poor old Vecsey, stuck in a rut, writing the same old stuff."

Being in Moscow made me want to push myself one more time, in a new assignment, in some foreign place, to take a chance, to risk failing. But a columnist risks failing four times a week. Maybe this is the way to do it—the football games as trade-off for the possibility of another World Series like 1986, balancing days when the column doesn't come easily against the trip to Seoul for the 1988 Summer Olympics, the World Cup in Italy in 1990, the Summer Olympics in Barcelona in 1992. Always someplace else. Permanent hookey.

I've been training to cover those events since my father took me to Ebbets Field forty years ago and Dixie Walker hit a home run over the screen. Something will happen tomorrow, and somebody will be there to describe it. Might as well be me.

INDEX

ABOUT THE AUTHOR

GEORGE VECSEY is a sports columnist for *The New York Times* who previously covered the Appalachian region, religion, metropolitan news and sports for *The Times,* and also worked for *Newsday.*

Born and raised in Queens, New York, he currently lives in Port Washington, Long Island, with his wife, Marianne Graham Vecsey, an artist. They have three children.

Among his books are: *One Sunset a Week: The Story of a Coal Miner; Joy in Mudville; Martina* (with Martina Navratilova); *Five O'Clock Comes Early: A Young Man's Battle with Alcoholism* (with Bob Welch); and *Coal Miner's Daughter* (with Loretta Lynn), later turned into a popular movie.

WOOD-
SONG

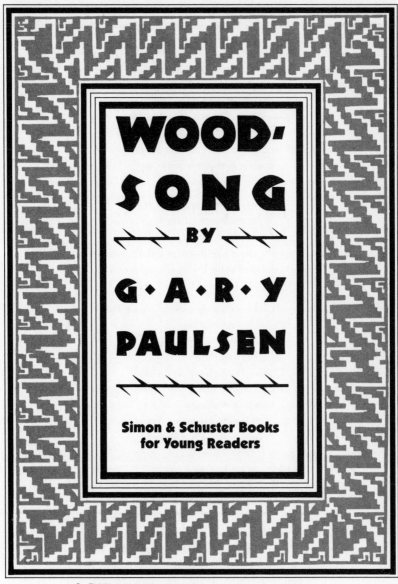

WOOD-
SONG

BY

G·A·R·Y

PAULSEN

Simon & Schuster Books
for Young Readers

LOIEDERMAN MIDDLE SCHOOL
MEDIA CENTER

SIMON & SCHUSTER BOOKS FOR YOUNG READERS
An imprint of Simon & Schuster Children's Publishing Division
1230 Avenue of the Americas
New York, New York 10020

BOOK DESIGN BY FRITZ METSCH

TYPOGRAPHY BY COM COM

The text of this book is set in Avanta.

The illustrations are rendered in pen-and-ink and reproduced in line.

Printed and bound in the United States of America

16 15 14 13 12 11

Library of Congress Cataloging-in-Publication Data
Paulsen, Gary.
Woodson / by Gary Paulsen.
p. cm.
Illustrated by Ruth Wright Paulsen.
Summary: For a rugged outdoor man and his family, life in northern
Minnesota is an adventure involving wolves, deer, and sled dogs.
Includes an account of the author's first Iditarod,
a dogsled race across Alaska.
ISBN 0-02-770221-9
1. Outdoor life—Minnesota—Juvenile literature.   2. Dogsledding—
Minnesota—Juvenile literature.   3. Sled dogs—Minnesota—Juvenile
literature.   4. Minnesota—Social life and customs—Juvenile
literature.   5. Paulsen, Gary—Homes and huants—Minnesota—Juvenile
literature.   6. Minnesota—Biography—Juvenile literature.
7. Iditarod Train Sled Dog Race, Alaska.   [1. Outdoor life—
Minnesota.   2. Sled dogs.   3. Sled dog racing.   4. Paulsen, Gary.]
1. Paulsen, Ruth Wright, ill.   II. Title.   F610P38 1990
796.5'092—dc20   89-70835   CIP   AC

This book is dedicated to Cookie,
who died on September 10, 1989.

"Her soul is on the raven's wing. . . ."

MAP OF THE IDITAROD

1. Anchorage
2. Eagle River
3. Settler's Bay
4. Rainy Pass
5. The Gorge
6. Rhone River
7. The Burn
8. Nikolai
9. McGrath
10. Iditarod
11. Shageluk
12. Yukon River
13. Kaltag
14. Unalakleet
15. Shaktolik
16. Norton Sound
17. Koyuk
18. Elim
19. Nome
20. Bering Sea
21. Arctic Ocean
22. Pacific Ocean
23. Mt. McKinley (Denali)
24. Alaska Range
25. Kuskokwim Mountains
26. Brooks Range
27. Fairbanks
28. Siberia (USSR)
29. Canada

RUNNING

· 1 ·

I UNDERSTOOD almost nothing about the woods until it was nearly too late. And that is strange because my ignorance was based on knowledge.

Most of my life it seems I've been in the forest or on the sea. Most of my time, sleeping and waking, has been spent outside, in close contact with what we now call the environment, what my uncles used to call, simply, "the woods."

We hunted. Small and large game. We hunted and killed and though I think now that it is wrong to hunt and kill, at the time I did not think this and I spent virtually all my time hunting.

And learned nothing.

Perhaps the greatest paradox about understanding "the woods" is that so many who enjoy it, or seem to enjoy it, spend most of their time trying to kill parts of it.

Yet, it was a hunter, a wild one, and an act of almost

1

unbelievable violence that led me to try to understand all of it, and to try to learn from it without destroying it.

I lived in innocence for a long time. I believed in the fairy-tale version of the forest until I was close to forty years old.

Gulled by Disney and others, I believed Bambi always got out of the fire. Nothing ever really got hurt. Though I hunted and killed it was always somehow clean and removed from reality. I killed yet thought that every story had a happy ending.

Until a December morning . . .

I was running a dog team around the side of a large lake, just starting out on my trapline. It was early winter and the ice on the lake wasn't thick enough to support the sled and team or I would have gone across the middle. There was a rough trail around the edge of the lake and I was running a fresh eight-dog team so the small loop, which added five or so miles, presented no great difficulty.

It was a grandly beautiful winter morning. The temperature was perhaps ten below, with a bright sun that shone through ice crystals in the air so that everything seemed to sparkle. The dogs were working evenly, the gangline up through the middle of them thrumming with the rhythm it has when they are working in perfect tandem. We skirted the lake, which lay below and to the right. To the left and rising higher were willows and brush, which made something like a wall next to the trail.

The dogs were still running at a lope, though we had come over seven miles, and I was full of them; my life was full of them. We were, as it happens sometimes, dancing with winter. I could not help smiling, just smiling idiotically at the grandness of it. Part of the chant of an ancient Navajo prayer rolled through my mind:

> *Beauty above me*
> *Beauty below me*
> *Beauty before me . . .*

That is how I felt then and frequently still feel when I am running dogs. I was in and of beauty and at that precise moment a doe, a white-tailed deer, exploded out of some willows on the left side of the team, heading down the bank toward the lake.

The snow alongside the trail was about two feet deep and powdery and it followed her in a white shower that covered everything. She literally flew over the lead dog who was a big, white, wolfy-looking male named Dollar. He was so surprised that he dropped, ducked, for part of an instant, then rose—almost like a rock skipping on the trail—and continued running. We were moving so fast and the deer was moving so fast that within a second or two we were several yards past where it had happened and yet everything seemed suspended in slow motion.

Above all, in the deer, was the stink of fear. Even in that split part of a second, it could be smelled. It could be seen. The doe's eyes were so wide they seemed to come out of her head. Her mouth was jacked open and her tongue hung out to the side. Her jaw and neck were covered with spit, and she stunk of fear.

Dogs smell fear at once but I have not always been able to, even when I was afraid. There is something coppery about it, a metallic smell mixed with the smell of urine and feces, when something, when somebody, is afraid. No, not just afraid but ripped with fear, and it was on the doe.

The smell excited the dogs and they began to run faster, although continuing down the trail; I turned to look back from the sled and saw why the doe was frightened.

Wolves.

They bounded over the trail after the doe even as I watched. These were not the large timber wolves but the smaller northern brush wolves, perhaps weighing forty or fifty pounds each, about as large as most of my team. I think they are called northern coyotes.

Except that they act as wolves. They pack and have pack social structures like timber wolves, and hunt in packs like timber wolves.

And they were hunting the doe.

There were seven of them and not one looked down the trail to see me as they jumped across the sled tracks after the deer. They were so intent on her, and the smell of her, that I might as well not have existed.

And they were gaining on her.

4

I stood on the brakes to stop the sled and set the snow-hook to hold the dogs and turned. The dogs immediately swung down off the trail toward the lake, trying to get at the wolves and deer. The snowhook came loose and we began to slide down the lake bank. I jerked the hook from the snow and hooked it on a small poplar and that held us.

The doe, in horror now, and knowing what was coming, left the bank of the lake and bounded out onto the bad ice. Her tail was fully erect, a white flash as she tried to reach out and get speed, but the ice was too thin.

Too thin for all the weight of her on the small, pointed hooves and she went through and down in a huge spray of shattered ice and water.

She was up instantly, clambering and working to get back up on top of the ice next to the hole. Through sheer effort in her panic she made it.

But it slowed her too much.

In those few moments of going through the ice and getting out she lost her lead on the wolves and they were on her.

On her.

In all my time in the woods, in the wondrous dance of it, I have many times seen predators fail. As a matter of fact, they usually fail. I once saw a beaver come out of a hole on the ice near his lodge in the middle of winter and stand off four wolves. He sustained one small bite on his tail and inflicted terrible damage with his teeth on the wolves, killing one and wounding the other three. I have seen rabbits outwit foxes and watched red squirrels tease martens and get away with it, but this time it was not to be.

I had never seen wolves kill a large animal and indeed have not seen it since. It was horrible and I was not prepared for it. I thought I had great knowledge of how everything in the woods worked. I had hunted and trapped and I had been in the army and seen and done some awful things, but I was still not mentally prepared for the killing.

Largely because of Disney and posed "natural" wildlife films and television programs I had preconceived ideas about wolves, about what wolves should be and do. They never really spoke to the killing.

Spoke to the blood.

In films they would go to the edge of it, and then show the carcass being eaten. In books they always seemed to describe it clinically and technically.

And it is neither clinical nor technical.

There is horror in it.

Wolves do not kill "clean." (If there can be such a thing.) It is a slow, ripping, terrible death for the prey and only those who have not seen it will argue for that silly business about the prey actually selecting itself.

Two wolves held the doe by the nose, held her head down to the ice, and the other wolves took turns tearing at her rear end, pulling and jerking and tearing, until they were inside of her, pulling out parts of her and all this time she was still on her feet, still alive.

I did not have a gun or I think I would have used it. I was having some trouble with the dogs as the blood smell excited the wolf in them. They wanted to be at the kill. They were jerking and pulling on the gangline so hard I thought it would break, and I stumbled down in the deep snow along the lake bank and held them—one bit me on the hand—but I could not stop looking.

It was all in silence.

She was still on her feet though they had the guts out of her now, pulled back on the ice, eating and pulling, and I wanted it to end, wanted it to be over for her.

And she sank.

She somehow did not die then and still does not die in my mind. She just sinks. Over and over I can see her sinking as they pull at her. When I could stand it no longer, when I was sick with it and hated all wolves for the horror of it, I yelled.

"Leave her . . ."

And I think I cursed as well but it didn't matter. When I yelled it was as if a film had stopped. The wolves somehow had not known I was there. They had been so intent on killing, on the smell of it, that they had not seen me or the dogs and the sound of my voice stopped them.

But it did not frighten them.

The doe was down now, spread and down and steaming out the rear, and all the wolves stopped dead and turned to look at me and the dogs.

Just that. Look.

And I knew that it was wrong for me to have yelled, that I was interrupting something I did not understand, some ancient thing I did not know any more than I knew what it was like to live in the Ice Age.

They stopped and studied me.

One of them, I think a male because he was larger than the others, raised on his hind legs to see better over some low willows in front of me and when he raised—standing like a man—the morning sun caught his head and I could see that it was completely covered in blood.

Steaming with it. He'd been inside her and he was soaked with blood and the snow all around the back of the doe was soaked with blood, a great red apron of blood. He stood for two, three seconds, staring at me and through me, knowing me, and I began to understand some of it then.

I began to understand that they are not wrong or right— they just are.

Wolves don't know they are wolves.

That's a name we have put on them, something we have done. I do not know how wolves think of themselves, nor does anybody, but I did know and still know that it was wrong to think they should be the way I wanted them to be.

And with that thought, with that small understanding, came the desire to learn, to know more not just about wolves but about all things in the woods. All the animals, all the dances . . .

And it started with blood.

· 2 ·

CONSIDERING the enormous effect dogs have had on my life, I came to them late and in an odd-enough way.

I was forty years old and living in poverty when I first became involved with sled dogs. Writing is a strange way to make a living, and I had sold many books by the time I was forty but was not making enough money to live on. I worked construction, ran heavy equipment, tracked satellites, taught—did many things to support life—and by the time I was forty I was working very hard and had become almost completely broke, living with my wife and son in a small cabin in northern Minnesota with no plumbing, no electricity, and no real prospects.

And so to dogs.

The state of Minnesota was having a rough time with beavers. They had more or less run amuck and were damming up rivers and flooding highways, filling pastures, even beginning to invade the cities. I had trapped a bit when I was a boy, and to make some money I decided to trap for the state—the state paid a small bounty and the pelt brought a similar small amount of money.

It was a one-man operation, and not very successful because I ran it on foot—or on a pair of skis when the snow came—and I rarely got over a twenty-mile trapline. (There was also the difficulty that I had trouble even then with trapping and killing; I was not good at it because I did not really want to do it.)

Some friends heard of my trapping and gave me four older dogs—they were Storm, Yogi, Obeah, and Columbia—and a broken sled—the siderails were broken and needed replacement—and so I was into dogs.

But of course I was not. I did not know how to run them, or be run by them. I did not even know how to harness them or hook them properly to the gangline that pulled the sled when they were harnessed.

But I fixed the sled and tried to harness them and that first time I did not know about, well, anything. The dogs more or less wandered around the yard without leaving and I thought it was madness to even try to use them when the only way they would leave the yard was for me to drag them.

After a time I stopped and sat on a stump and watched them and tried to think of a way to make them run. Finally I decided you couldn't make them, you had to let them.

One of the dogs, Obeah, seemed to be trying to look ahead, and I thought he might want to pull the others. Lead them. So I put him in front and it worked. We left the yard and ran on a trail through the woods and I thought all the Yukon King thoughts there are.

I was running a team in the north and they were out there ahead of me and it was beautiful. . . .

And I knew nothing.

I was so ignorant, so steeped in not knowing, that I did not even know what I didn't know. I didn't know what questions to ask, or how to ask them, and I would not begin to learn until Storm taught me.

His blood taught me.

There will be more about running dogs later, and more about Storm, but for the moment it is enough to know that when I started I thought I knew what I was doing. The dogs moved for me. I expanded the trapline to nearly sixty miles over the next three months. By the middle of hard winter I thought I was Sergeant Preston—a Mountie on a radio show I had listened to as a child.

By this time I had three more dogs—a seven-dog work team—and a tent. Obeah had evolved into something I thought was a good leader. I think this was largely because he looked like a sled dog should look—like a Sergeant Preston kind of sled dog. He was large and wolf-like, with a thick gray mane and a tail that curled over his back. He was standoffish. He did not want to be petted. Now and again he would lift his lip at me, and twice he bit me on the leg. Obeah always wanted to fight other males and I thought—mistakenly—that all of this was proper behavior for a sled dog.

At least the Yukon King type of sled dog I had always dreamed about.

I wasn't trapping very much and I was running a long distance—it took three days to run the sixty-mile line. But I confined my running to the daylight. I did not know about using a head lamp, did not know that the dogs ran better at night. I would run during the day, work on my trap sets, then pitch a tent and camp at night and harness up and run the next day, and there was great beauty in that.

Sleeping with them. I would fix the tent and arrange my sleeping bag and pad and then put the dogs around me in a circle just outside the firelight. On truly cold nights, when it dropped to ten or fifteen below, I would bring several of the dogs into the tent and pack them around the bag tightly and fall asleep with them breathing around me, with their hearts beating against me through the bag, with their souls in the tent with me. They also felt the warmth and would move in closer against the bag, jamming into the sides. On one very cold night—it must have been thirty or thirty-five below—I awakened in the morning with dogs all around me and three of them curled up on top of me; a living blanket.

With all this closeness, with all the running, with the dance of the dogs, I thought I knew them and with that thought—with that attitude—I wasn't learning anything.

I just ran the line, took a beaver now and then, and pretended somewhere in my mind that I was Sergeant Preston and had a whole team of Kings out in front of me.

Until Storm taught me.

There came a night, finally, when I was about twenty

miles from home and it was very cold—close to forty below—and rather than spend the night out camping, I decided to run in the dark and go on home.

Running sled dogs is much like sailing a boat on the ocean. Distances are almost critically relative. Sailing a hundred miles with the wind might take twelve or fourteen hours, depending on wind strength, boat, and sailor. To turn around and sail the same hundred miles against the wind, and especially if there is a current against you, might take one, even two weeks. Indeed, sometimes it simply can't be done. Ever.

Dogs are much the same. Twenty miles with a work team traveling seven miles an hour—which is about average—would seem to take about three hours. And sometimes does. But an inch of new snow to slow the sled, or an extra heavy load to slow it still more, perhaps a head wind to cap it, and the dogs can only make three or four miles an hour. Suddenly the trip—the same twenty miles—becomes a five-, six-, or even seven-hour run. And on a seven-hour run with a heavy load it is necessary to stop and rest the dogs, let them sleep for a couple of hours and feed them, so that adds still more.

All of these things were against me. A run I thought would take three hours was in reality going to take me closer to nine hours, all in the dark and intense cold, in new snow and what turned out to be hilly country, with a sled that weighed close to five hundred pounds, fully loaded.

It became one of the longest nights of my life.

I did not understand at that time that you should feed the

dogs straight raw meat and fat. It is the same as putting gasoline in an engine. Some people actually told me that meat was bad for them and to only feed them dry dog food. I had a sack of dog food with me and fed that to them when I stopped to camp.

All wrong. All of it wrong. What I did not know then is not only should the dogs be fed meat and fat, but they most decidedly should not be fed dry dog food when they are going to work hard or be stressed at all. The bits of ground corn used as a base for the dog food are worthless and largely indigestible. And they are very sharp. When a working dog's stomach tightens, as it does when he pulls, the corn becomes like tiny little knives that cut and tear at the insides of his intestines. . . .

I knew none of this.

And so to Storm.

Storm was an almost classic sled dog. He looked much like a brindle wolf, with beautifully slanted eyes. He had a great reach to his front legs and a thick mane and straight back. In many ways he was still very primitive, but he liked people a great deal and would lean against your leg to be petted.

He pulled.

Of course they all pull. It is genetic, so old a code or command that it has become part of what sled dogs are; the fiber of their very being. When they are six months old you harness them and they pull. There is no training necessary. It just is.

But some of them pull better than others. Storm pulled from somewhere within himself, from some primitive core so strong that he could not not pull, even if he wanted to.

He was also what is known as an "honest" dog. Some dogs pull and when they get tired they slack off but they keep enough pull on the harness tug so it appears they are working while they are really resting. When they have rested for a quarter mile or so they go back to work. It's not bad; it's very much one of those they-know-you-know-they-know situations and part of running dogs. But some dogs, and Storm was one of them, pull hard all the time, even when they are tired. These are called "honest" dogs and are keyed to running somehow more than other dogs.

So into this night, in my ignorance, we started to run; into what I thought would be a three- or four-hour easy run we started.

And it was not so bad at first.

Part of it showed me new beauty. There was a full moon and when we first started the night run we went across a lake, a beautiful, long lake, in the moonlight. The moonlight off the snow in the cold air was so bright and flat white you could have read a book, and the dogs worked wonderfully in the cold. At the end of the lake there was a large hill. The base of the hill was heavily forested and the trail wound through the trees.

As the dogs moved through the dark shadows of the forest and climbed the hill we went through some strange kind of temperature inversion, and just as they came back out into the moonlight, into the flat-white light at the top of the hill, the steam from their collective breath came up and over their backs and hid them.

15

When dogs run they are silent. Only in the movies do they rattle and bark while they are running. So in silence, all in silence except for the gentle whuffing of their breath and the slight jingle of their harness snaps, I was pulled over the top of the open hill in the moonlight by a steam ghost.

It was heart-stoppingly beautiful.

And that was part of that run.

We ran down from the hill through some country that a tornado had ripped and torn. For six or seven miles the trail wound through the wreckage of downed trees and broken limbs.

It was hard going, with the new snow, and frequently having to stop and chop through downed trees with an axe, then hump the sled over them; hacking and swearing and pushing, the dogs slamming and jerking and pulling until finally we got through and were in calm forest again, winding through thick spruce trees. In and out of dappled moonlight and beauty. The sweat was freezing on the outside of my clothes as it steamed out so I had to stop and scrape it off with a stick and suddenly, for no reason that I knew, Storm sprayed blood.

In the moonlight I could not tell that it was blood, but only something dark that sprayed out of his rear end. Storm was directly in front of the sled in the wheel position (a term that dates back to stagecoaches) and it covered the front end of the sled and the sides of the trail; a sudden dark liquid.

I stopped the sled and tied it off to a tree. I thought he had developed diarrhea—which was bad enough—and I ran up to his side.

He stood normally, slamming into the harness to get the sled moving. The temperature had dropped still more and the dogs all wanted to run. They work to the cold—the colder the better.

The smell was wrong.

As I kneeled next to him near the stain in the snow, the smell was wrong for what I thought it was. I lit a match and was horrified to see blood.

Storm was spraying bright red blood out his rear end. Blood covered the sled and the trail. I had never, never seen this, known this before; had never hurt a dog before.

And now this.

All the dogs were screaming—high-pitched deafening screams because they were impatient and wanted to run, knowing they were heading in the direction of home.

Storm ignored me and kept screaming and lunging to go as if nothing were wrong.

And each time he lunged blood squirted.

I became frantic. In my life blood meant something bad; something fiercely bad. Blood was an end. I didn't know what to do. I stood next to him and did not know what to do.

Doctor, I thought—I need to get him to a doctor before he dies. And without any more pulling. I had to ease him down and get him to a doctor. That's all I could think.

I unhooked him from the gangline and carried him, lunging and screaming, to the sled. I tied him in the basket of the sled with a short piece of line to his collar. Then I stood on the runners and let the team loose.

We didn't make fifty yards before Storm went absolutely insane. When he looked ahead in the darkness and saw that other dogs were pulling while he was riding on the sled he went mad. He flopped and ripped and tore at the sled, at the rope holding him by the collar, at me—at the world— until he had worked himself off to the side of the sled and was pulling there, pulling with the rope on his collar, pulling so his neck was warped back around.

I stopped and put him back on the sled and tried to start again but it was no good. He immediately fought to get down again, screamed for it, and when he got down he began to pull with his neck.

I tried a longer rope, tried to let him trot along in back, and that did not work either. He simply ran up alongside until the rope caught, then began to pull, his neck wrapped around to the side.

They do not really know harness. When Captain Cook first saw Eskimos and their dogs in Alaska they did not have harnesses. The dogs pulled from crude collars. Storm didn't care that he wasn't hooked in a harness. The collar would do fine.

He pulled the way they have always pulled.

And there it was. I could not stop because I thought if I waited too long to get him to a doctor he would bleed to death. I could not get him to ride the sled because if I did the exertion of his slamming around trying to get back out and pull made him bleed all the more. I could not get him to trot easily along in back.

Finally, in a kind of mad worry, I took off his harness and

let him run free, thinking he might just follow us as we made our way through the darkness.

Instead he immediately ran up and around the sled and into his old position. He tried to pull even though he wasn't hooked to anything. And I thought for a moment that might work—at least he didn't have the weight of the sled to pull. But he bled anyway, and seemed to work hard anyway, and seemed to be pulling hard anyway. Because he wasn't hooked to anything, whenever there was some unevenness in the trail he would lunge ahead and trip and nearly fall. When he stumbled, the sled almost ran over him—which almost certainly would have killed him. At last I knew that I could do nothing but what he wanted to do.

Let him pull.

It was a terrible thing to learn on that night because of his blood. Blood was so important to me, meant so much to me, and here it was, leaving him and I thought his life was leaving him. Finally done, I put the harness back on him and hooked him up and made the run through the night thinking that I was allowing him to die.

Seven more hours we ran. I stopped along the way to snack the dogs on dry food and bits of meat. They ate the snow. And Storm pulled.

Across two rivers and several lakes and through some sharp hills in the moonlight we ran and Storm pulled and I waited for him to end, hating myself for doing the only thing I thought I could do.

But it was nothing to him.

To Storm it was all as nothing. The blood, the anxiety I

felt, the horror of it meant as little to Storm as the blood from the deer on the snow had meant to the wolves. It was part of his life and if he could obey the one drive, the drive to be in the team and pull, then nothing else mattered.

And he did not die. Later, when he was very old, Storm would teach me about death, but not that night. That night he ran and we ran until just before dawn I could see the glow from the Coleman lamp coming through the windows of the cabin across the swamp near our home. He never once faltered, and did not falter for six more years, never stopped pulling. I took the dogs out of harness and rubbed their shoulders and marveled at Storm, who stood with his tail wagging, not bleeding any longer. I put them on their chains so they could get at the fresh straw in their houses to make soft beds and realized that I had learned something again that night. I had learned that I knew absolutely nothing— the same lesson I learned from the wolves and the doe— knew nothing about animals, understood nothing about the drives that make them work, knew nothing.

And I also learned—as with the wolves and the doe—that I wanted to know more, wanted to know everything there was to know about dogs and the woods and running with a team.

But I had one more important lesson to learn first, and it would also be in blood.

COLD can be very strange. Not the cold felt running from the house to the bus or the car to the store; not the chill in the air on a fall morning, but deep cold.

Serious cold.

Forty, fifty, even sixty below zero—actual temperature, not windchill—seems to change everything. Steel becomes brittle and breaks, shatters; breath taken straight into the throat will freeze the lining and burst blood vessels; eyes exposed too long will freeze; fingers and toes freeze, turn black, and break off. These are all known, normal parts of intense cold.

But it changes beauty as well. Things are steeped in a new clarity, a clear focus. Sound seems to ring and the very air seems to be filled with diamonds when ice crystals form.

On a river in Alaska while training I once saw a place where a whirlpool had frozen into a cone, open at the bottom like a beautiful trap waiting to suck the whole team down. When I stopped to look at it, with the water roaring through at the bottom, the dogs became nervous and stared down into the center as if mystified and were very glad when we moved on.

After a time I stopped trapping. That change—as with many changes—occurred because of the dogs. As mentioned, I had hunted when I was young, trapping and killing many animals. I never thought it wrong until the dogs came. And then it was a simple thing, almost a silly thing, that caused the change.

Columbia had a sense of humor and I saw it.

In the summer the dogs live in the kennel area, each dog with his own house, on a chain that allows him to move in a circle. They can only run with the wheeled carts on cool nights, and sometimes they get bored being tied up. To alleviate the boredom we give the dogs large beef bones to chew and play with. They get a new bone every other day or so. These bones are the center of much contention—we call them Bone Wars. Sometimes dogs clear across the kennel will hold their bones up in the air, look at each other, raise their hair, and start growling at each other, posturing and bragging about their bones.

But not Columbia.

Usually Columbia just chewed on his bone until the meat was gone. Then he buried it and waited for the next bone. I never saw him fight or get involved in Bone Wars and I always thought him a simple—perhaps a better word would be primitive—dog, basic and very wolf-like, until one day when I was sitting in the kennel.

I had a notebook and I was sitting on the side of Cookie's roof, writing—the dogs are good company for working—when I happened to notice Columbia doing something strange.

He was sitting quietly on the outside edge of his circle, at the maximum length of his chain. With one paw he was pushing his bone—which still had a small bit of meat on it—out and away from him, toward the next circle.

Next to Columbia was a dog named Olaf. While Columbia was relatively passive, Olaf was very aggressive. Olaf always wanted to fight and he spent much time arguing over bones, females, the weather—anything and everything that caught his fancy. He was much scarred from fighting, with notched ears and lines on his muzzle, but he was a very good dog—strong and honest—and we liked him.

Being next to Columbia, Olaf had tried many times to get him to argue or bluster but Columbia always ignored him.

Until this morning.

Carefully, slowly, Columbia pushed the bone toward Olaf's circle.

And of all the things that Olaf was—tough, strong, honest—he wasn't smart. As they say, some are smarter than others, and some are still not so smart, and then there was Olaf. It wouldn't be fair to call Olaf dumb—dogs don't measure those things like people—but even in the dog world he would not be known as a whip. Kind of a big bully who was also a bit of a doofus.

When he saw Columbia pushing the bone toward him, he began to reach for it. Straining against his chain, turning and trying to get farther and farther, he reached as far as he could with the middle toe on his right front foot, the claw going out as far as possible.

But not quite far enough. Columbia had measured it to the millimeter. He slowly pushed the bone until it was so close that Olaf's claw—with Olaf straining so hard his eyes bulged—just barely touched it.

Columbia sat back and watched Olaf straining and pushing and fighting and when this had gone on for a long time—many minutes—and Olaf was still straining for all he was worth, Columbia leaned back and laughed.

"Heh, heh, heh . . ."

Then Columbia walked away.

And I could not kill or trap any longer.

It happened almost that fast. I had seen dogs with compassion for each other and their young, and with anger and joy and hate and love but this humor went into me more than the other things.

It was so complicated.

To make the joke up in his mind, the joke with the bone and the bully, and then set out to do it, carefully and quietly, to do it, then laugh and walk away—all of it was so complicated, so complex, that it triggered a chain reaction in my mind.

If Columbia could do that, I thought, if a dog could do that, then a wolf could do that. If a wolf could do that, then a deer could do that. If a deer could do that, then a beaver, and a squirrel, and a bird, and, and, and . . .

And I quit trapping then.

It was wrong for me to kill.

But I had this problem. I had gone over some kind of line with the dogs, gone back into some primitive state of exaltation that I wanted to study. I wanted to run them and learn from them. But it seemed to be wasteful (the word *immature* also comes to mind) to just run them. I thought I had to have a trapline to justify running the dogs, so I kept the line.

But I did not trap. I ran the country, and camped and learned from the dogs and studied where I would have trapped if I were going to trap. I took many imaginary beaver and muskrat but I did no more sets and killed no more animals. I will not kill anymore.

Yet the line existed. Somehow in my mind—and until writing this I have never told another person about this—the line still existed and when I had "trapped" in one area I would extend the line to "trap" in another, as is proper when you actually trap. Somehow the phony trapping gave me a purpose for running the dogs, and would until I began to train them for the Iditarod, a dogsled race across Alaska, which I had read about in *Alaska* magazine.

But it was on one of these "trapping" runs that I got my third lesson, or awakening.

There was a point where an old logging trail went through a small, sharp-sided gully—a tiny canyon. The trail came down one wall of the gully—a drop of fifty or so feet—then scooted across a frozen stream and up the other side. It might have been a game trail that was slightly widened, or an old foot trail that had not caved in. Whatever it was, I came onto it in the middle of January. The dogs were very excited. New trails always get them tuned up and they were fairly smoking as we came to the edge of the gully.

I did not know it was there and had been letting them run, not riding the sled brake to slow them, and we virtually shot off the edge.

The dogs stayed on the trail but I immediately lost all control and went flying out into space with the sled. As I did, I kicked sideways and caught my knee on a sharp snag, felt the wood enter under the kneecap and tear it loose.

I may have screamed then.

The dogs ran out on the ice of the stream but I fell onto it. As these things often seem to happen, the disaster snow-balled.

The trail crossed the stream directly at the top of a small, frozen waterfall with about a twenty-foot drop. Later I saw the beauty of it, the falling lobes of blue ice that had grown as the water froze and refroze, layering on itself. . . .

But at the time I saw nothing. I hit the ice of the stream bed like dropped meat, bounced once, then slithered over the edge of the waterfall and dropped another twenty feet onto the frozen pond below, landing on the torn and separated kneecap.

I have been injured several times running dogs—cracked ribs, a broken left leg, a broken left wrist, various parts frozen or cut or bitten while trying to stop fights—but nothing ever felt like landing on that knee.

I don't think I passed out so much as my brain simply exploded.

Again, I'm relatively certain I must have screamed or grunted, and then I wasn't aware of much for two, perhaps three minutes as I squirmed around trying to regain some part of my mind.

When things settled down to something I could control, I opened my eyes and saw that my snow pants and the jeans beneath were ripped in a jagged line for about a foot. Blood was welling out of the tear, soaking the cloth and the ice underneath the wound.

Shock and pain came in waves and I had to close my eyes several times. All of this was in minutes that seemed like hours and I realized that I was in serious trouble. Contrary to popular belief, dog teams generally do not stop and wait for a musher who falls off. They keep going, often for many miles.

Lying there on the ice I knew I could not walk. I didn't think I could stand without some kind of crutch, but I knew I couldn't walk. I was a good twenty miles from home, at least eight or nine miles from any kind of farm or dwelling.

It may as well have been ten thousand miles.

There was some self-pity creeping in, and not a little chagrin at being stupid enough to just let them run when I didn't know the country. I was trying to skootch myself up to the bank of the gully to get into a more comfortable position when I heard a sound over my head.

I looked up and there was Obeah looking over the top of the waterfall, down at me.

I couldn't at first believe it.

He whined a couple of times, moved back and forth as if he might be going to drag the team over the edge, then disappeared from view. I heard some more whining and growling, then a scrabbling sound, and was amazed to see that he had taken the team back up the side of the gully and dragged them past the waterfall to get on the gully wall just over me.

They were in a horrible tangle but he dragged them along the top until he was well below the waterfall, where he scrambled down the bank with the team almost literally falling on him. They dragged the sled up the frozen stream bed to where I was lying.

On the scramble down the bank Obeah had taken them through a thick stand of cockleburs. Great clumps of burrs wadded between their ears and down their backs.

He pulled them up to me, concern in his eyes and making a soft whine, and I reached into his ruff and pulled his head down and hugged him and was never so happy to see anybody probably in my life. Then I felt something and looked down to see one of the other dogs—named Duberry—licking the wound in my leg.

She was not licking with the excitement that prey blood would cause, but with the gentle licking that she would use when cleaning a pup, a wound lick.

I brushed her head away, fearing infection, but she persisted. After a moment I lay back and let her clean it, still holding onto Obeah's ruff, holding onto a friend.

And later I dragged myself around and untangled them and unloaded part of the sled and crawled in and tied my leg down. We made it home that way, with me sitting in the sled; and later when my leg was sewed up and healing and I was sitting in my cabin with the leg propped up on pillows by the wood stove; later when all the pain was gone and I had all the time I needed to think of it . . . later I thought of the dogs.

How they came back to help me, perhaps to save me. I knew that somewhere in the dogs, in their humor and the way they thought, they had great, old knowledge; they had something we had lost.

And the dogs could teach me.

· 4 ·

THE adventure really begins in differences—the great differences between people and animals, between the way we live now and the way we once lived, between the Mall and the Woods.

Primarily the difference between people and animals is that people use fire. People create fire, and animals don't. Oh, there are minor things—like cars and planes and all the other inventions we seem to have come up with. But in a wild state, the real difference is that we use controlled fire.

And it was in the business of fire that I came to the first of many amazements inside the woods.

It started with a campfire.

I was on a hundred-mile run in deep winter with new dogs—pups, really, just over a year old. I had gone beyond the trapping stage and was training new dogs for a possible attempt on the Iditarod. The pups had lived in kennels, mostly. They had only been on short training runs so that almost everything they saw on this run was new to them. They had to learn to understand as they ran.

A cow in a field was a marvel and had to be investigated; it took me half an hour to get untangled from the fence. A ruffed grouse that flew down the trail ahead of us had to be chased. A red squirrel took the whole team off the trail into the woods, piling into deep drifts and leaving us all upside down and packed with snow.

It was, in short, a day full of wonders for them and when night came and it was time to stop—you can really only do about twenty miles a day with young dogs—we found a soft little clearing in the spruce trees. I made beds for them and when they were fed and settled, or as settled as young dogs can get, I made a fire hole in the snow in the center of the clearing, next to the sled, and started a small fire with some dead popple. It was not a cold night so the fire was very small, just enough to melt some snow and make tea. The flames didn't get over a foot high—but the effect was immediate and dramatic.

The dogs went crazy with fear. They lunged against their chains, slamming and screaming. I went to them and petted them and soothed them and at length they accepted the fire. I put their frozen blocks of meat around the edges of the flames to soften, and fed them warm meat. Then they sat and stared at the flames, the whole ring of them.

Of course they had never seen fire, or flame, in the kennel—it was all completely new to them. But the mystery was why they would automatically fear it. They had seen many new things that day, and they didn't fear anything but the fire.

And when they were over the fear of it, they were fascinated with it. I stretched my foam pad and sleeping bag out in the sled to settle in for the night. This is a complicated process. The felt liners for my shoepacs had to be taken off and put down inside the bag so my body heat could dry them for the next day. My parka had to be turned inside out so all the sweat from the day could freeze and be scraped off in the morning. Any wet clothing had to be flattened and worked down into the bag to dry as well. While I was doing all this in the light from my head lamp, I let the fire die down.

Just as I started to slide into the bag one of the dogs started to sing. It was the sad song.

They have many songs and I don't know them all. There is a happy song they sing when the moon is full on the snow and they are fed and there is a rain song, which is melancholy—they don't like rain very much—and there is a song they sing when you have been with them in the kennel and start to walk away, a come-back-and-don't-go-away sad song.

That was the song one dog had started to sing. When I turned to look at him he was staring where the fire had died down into a cup in the snow, and in a moment the rest of them had picked up the song and were wailing and moaning for the lost fire, all staring where the flames had been.

In an hour they had gone from some coded, genetic fear of fire, to understanding fire, to missing it when it went away.

Cave people must have gone through this same process. I wondered how long it had taken us to understand and know fire. The pups had done it in an hour and I thought as I pulled the mummy bag up over my head and went to sleep how smart they were or perhaps how smart we weren't and thought we were.

Sometimes when they run it is not believable. And even when the run is done and obviously happened it is still not believable.

On a run once when it was the perfect temperature for running, twenty below—cold enough for the dogs to run cool, but not so bitterly cold as to freeze anything exposed—I thought I would just let them go and see what they wanted to do. I wouldn't say a word, wouldn't do anything but stand on the back of the sled—unless a bootie or a quick snack was needed. I'd let them run at an easy lope. I thought I would let them go until they wanted to stop and then only run that way from then on, and they ran to some primitive instinct, coursed and ran for seventeen hours without letup.

One hundred and seventy-five miles.

And they didn't pant, weren't tired, could have done it again. I nearly froze—just a piece of meat on the back of the sled—but they ran and ran in a kind of glory and even now I can't quite believe it.

The second incident with fire was much the same—something from another world, another time. It happened, but is not quite believable.

We had run long in a day—a hundred and fifty miles— with an adult team in good shape. The terrain had been rough, with many moguls (mounds of snow) that made the sled bounce in the trail. I had taken a beating all day and I was whipped. I made beds and fed the dogs and built up a large fire. It had been a classic run but I was ready for sleep. It was nearly thirty below when I crawled into the sleeping bag.

I was just going to sleep, with my eyes heavy and the warmth from the fire in my face, when the dogs started an incredible uproar.

I opened my eyes and there was a deer standing right across the fire from me.

A doe. Fairly large—more than a year old—standing rigid, staring at me straight on in the face across the fire. She was absolutely petrified with terror.

At first I thought she had somehow stupidly blundered into the camp and run past the dogs to the fire.

But she hung there, staring at me, her ears rotating with the noise of the dogs around her. She did not run and still did not run and I thought she must be a medicine doe sent to me; a spirit doe come in a dream to tell me something.

Then I saw the others.

Out, perhaps thirty yards or more beyond the camp area, but close enough for the fire to shine in their eyes—the others. The wolves. There was a pack of brush wolves and they had been chasing her. I couldn't tell the number, maybe five or six; they kept moving in agitation and it was hard to pin them down, but they were clearly reluctant to let her go, although they were also clearly afraid of me and being close to me. Unlike timber wolves, brush wolves are not endangered, not protected, and are trapped heavily. We are most definitely the enemy, and they worried at seeing me.

And when I saw them I looked back at the doe and could see that she was blown. Her mouth hung open and spit smeared down both sides with some blood in it. They must have been close to getting her when she ran to the camp.

And the fire.

She must have smelled her death to make the decision she made. To run through the circle of dogs, toward the fire and the man was a mad gamble—a gamble that I wasn't a deer hunter, that the dogs weren't loose or they would have been on her like the wolves, that somehow it would be better here.

All those choices to make at a dead, frantic run with wolves pulling at her.

This time it had worked.

I sat up, half raised, afraid to move fast lest she panic and run back into the wolves. I had more wood next to the sled and I slowly put a couple of pieces on the fire and leaned back again. The wolves were very nervous now and they moved away when I put the wood on the fire, but the doe stayed nearby for a long time, so long that some of the dogs actually went back to lying down and sleeping.

She didn't relax. Her body was locked in fear and ready to fly at the slightest wrong move, but she stayed and watched me, watched the fire until the wolves were well gone and her sides were no longer heaving with hard breathing. She kept her eye on me, her ears on the dogs. Her nostrils flared as she smelled me and the fire and when she was ready—perhaps in half an hour but it seemed like much more—she wheeled, flashed her white tail at me, and disappeared.

The dogs exploded into noise again when she ran away, then we settled back to watching the fire until sleep took us. I would have thought it all a dream except that her tracks and the tracks of the wolves were there in the morning.

Fear comes in many forms but perhaps the worst scare is the one that isn't anticipated; the one that isn't really known about until it's there. A sudden fear. The unexpected.

And again, fire played a role in it.

We have bear trouble. Because we feed processed meat to the dogs there is always the smell of meat over the kennel. In the summer it can be a bit high because the dogs like to "save" their food sometimes for a day or two or four—burying it to dig up later. We live on the edge of wilderness and consequently the meat smell brings any number of visitors from the woods.

Skunks abound, and foxes and coyotes and wolves and weasels—all predators. We once had an eagle live over the kennel for more than a week, scavenging from the dogs, and a crazy group of ravens has pretty much taken over the puppy pen. Ravens are protected by the state and they seem to know it. When I walk toward the puppy pen with the buckets of meat it's a toss-up to see who gets it—the pups or the birds. They have actually pecked the puppies away from the food pans until they have gone through and taken what they want.

Spring, when the bears come, is the worst. They have been in hibernation through the winter, and they are hungry beyond caution. The meat smell draws them like flies, and we frequently have two or three around the kennel at the same time. Typically they do not bother us much—although my wife had a bear chase her from the garden to the house one morning—but they do bother the dogs.

They are so big and strong that the dogs fear them, and the bears trade on this fear to get their food. It's common to see them scare a dog into his house and take his food. Twice we have had dogs killed by rough bear swats that broke their necks—and the bears took their food.

We have evolved an uneasy peace with them but there is the problem of familiarity. The first time you see a bear in the kennel it is a novelty, but when the same ones are there day after day, you wind up naming some of them (old Notch-Ear, Billy-Jo, etc.) There gets to be a too relaxed attitude. We started to treat them like pets.

A major mistake.

There was a large male around the kennel for a week or so. He had a white streak across his head which I guessed was a wound scar from some hunter—bear hunting is allowed here. He wasn't all that bad so we didn't mind him.

He would frighten the dogs and take their hidden stashes now and then, but he didn't harm them and we became accustomed to him hanging around. We called him Scarhead and now and again we would joke about him as if he were one of the yard animals.

At this time we had three cats, forty-two dogs, fifteen or twenty chickens, eight ducks, nineteen large white geese, a few banty hens—one called Hawk which will come up again later in the book—ten fryers which we'd raised from chicks and couldn't (as my wife put it) "snuff and eat," and six woods-wise goats.

The bears, strangely, didn't bother any of the yard animals. There must have been a rule, or some order to the way they lived because they would hit the kennel and steal from the dogs but leave the chickens and goats and other yard stock completely alone—although you would have had a hard time convincing the goats of this fact. The goats spent a great deal of time with their back hair up, whuffing and blowing snot at the bears—and at the dogs who would *gladly* have eaten them. The goats never really believed in the truce.

There is not a dump or landfill to take our trash to and so we separate it—organic, inorganic—and deal with it ourselves. We burn the paper in a screened enclosure and it is fairly efficient, but it's impossible to get all the food particles off wrapping paper, so when it's burned the food particles burn with it.

And give off a burnt food smell.

And nothing draws bears like burning food. It must be that they have learned to understand human dumps—where they spend a great deal of time foraging. And they learn amazingly fast. In Alaska, for instance, the bears already know that the sound of a moose hunter's gun means there will be a fresh gut pile when the hunter cleans the moose. They come at a run when they hear the shot. It's often a close race to see if the hunter will get to the moose before the bears take it away. . . .

Because we're on the south edge of the wilderness area we try to wait until there is a northerly breeze before we burn so the food smell will carry south, but it doesn't always help. Sometimes bears, wolves, and other predators are already south, working the sheep farms down where it is more settled—they take a terrible toll of sheep—and we catch them on the way back through.

That's what happened one July morning.

Scarhead had been gone for two or three days and the breeze was right, so I went to burn the trash. I fired it off and went back into the house for a moment—not more than two minutes. When I came back out Scarhead was in the burn area. His tracks (directly through the tomatoes in the garden) showed he'd come from the south.

He was having a grand time. The fire didn't bother him. He was trying to reach a paw in around the edges of flame to get at whatever smelled so good. He had torn things apart quite a bit—ripped one side off the burn enclosure—and I was having a bad day and it made me mad.

I was standing across the burning fire from him and without thinking—because I was so used to him—I picked up a stick, threw it at him, and yelled, "Get out of here."

I have made many mistakes in my life, and will probably make many more, but I hope never to throw a stick at a bear again.

In one rolling motion—the muscles seemed to move within the skin so fast that I couldn't take half a breath—he turned and came for me. Close. I could smell his breath and see the red around the sides of his eyes. Close on me he stopped and raised on his back legs and hung over me, his forelegs and paws hanging down, weaving back and forth gently as he took his time and decided whether or not to tear my head off.

I could not move, would not have time to react. I knew I had nothing to say about it. One blow would break my neck. Whether I lived or died depended on him, on his thinking, on his ideas about me—whether I was worth the bother or not.

I did not think then.

Looking back on it I don't remember having one coherent thought when it was happening. All I knew was terrible menace. His eyes looked very small as he studied me. He looked down on me for what seemed hours. I did not move, did not breathe, did not think or do anything.

And he lowered.

Perhaps I was not worth the trouble. He lowered slowly and turned back to the trash and I walked backward halfway to the house and then ran—anger growing now—and took the rifle from the gun rack by the door and came back out.

He was still there, rummaging through the trash. I worked the bolt and fed a cartridge in and aimed at the place where you kill bears and began to squeeze. In raw anger, I began to take up the four pounds of pull necessary to send death into him.

And stopped.

Kill him for what?

That thought crept in.

Kill him for what?

For not killing me? For letting me know it is wrong to throw sticks at four-hundred-pound bears? For not hurting me, for not killing me, I should kill him? I lowered the rifle and ejected the shell and put the gun away. I hope Scarhead is still alive. For what he taught me, I hope he lives long and is very happy because I learned then—looking up at him while he made up his mind whether or not to end me—that when it is all boiled down I am nothing more and nothing less than any other animal in the woods.

· 5 ·

WE burn wood to heat the house and we have a wood-burning, old-time kitchen stove. There is probably nothing that makes me feel quite as warm as coming in on a cold winter morning, leaning over the kitchen stove to warm my hands, and smelling rich pine woodsmoke and fresh bread baking in the oven.

The cats love the wood stove, too. They spend most of the winter either pressed against the side of it or sleeping beneath it. We had a neighbor—an old bachelor—who let the chickens into his house. They would roost on the stove each night to stay warm as the fire died down. It made an unholy mess—chickens cannot be housebroken—and when he fired the stove up and it cooked the chicken stuff the smell would drive you out, but he seemed to like it and the chickens provided company for him.

We don't let the animals in, except for house dogs (we have three loose little terrier kind of things) and, of course, the cats, but the chickens have discovered that the chimney conducts heat as well as smoke out of the house. It's usual in the winter to go out in the morning and see chickens on the roof, flocked around the chimney warming themselves. (They have a perfectly good, insulated coop but we let them run because it makes the eggs taste better, and they prefer the chimney to the coop.)

One of them is a banty hen we call Hawk, and since she is at least partially a creature of the woods it might be proper to tell about her here.

Banties—my wife says—are mean, small chickens you can never get rid of. They can indeed be mean, but they are wonderfully self-sufficient and fun to have around even if it takes about thirty of their small eggs to make a decent omelet. They are forever setting on nests hatching out chicks, brooding and clucking and attacking anything that comes close. Mother love takes on whole new meaning when you cross a banty hen taking care of fifteen or twenty chicks. I have seen grown men run when they get attacked by this small chicken.

I was running a team in the late spring—we pull a wheeled cart with a platform on the back (rather like a sled with wheels) when there is no snow. We were on a county road near thick forest when we came on a dead ruffed grouse. She probably got hit by a car while gathering gravel for her gizzard; grouse come out to the road each evening and get stones to help grind up the seeds and berries they eat and are frequently hit by cars. The dogs had her in an instant before I could stop them and she was gone—feathers floating in the air. As we started on our way, I happened to glance into the low brush and saw her nest. I tied the dogs off so they wouldn't run—again, I had some pups in the team and they were insane, especially after finding the grouse—and I went to the nest.

There were fourteen eggs cuddled in the soft grass and leaves. They looked so forlorn that I picked them up and carried them in my cap rather than leaving them for some passing skunk. I'm not sure what I expected to do with them. My wife is an artist and I thought perhaps she might want them for a still life, but when I got home with the dogs—the eggs somehow unbroken, cradled in my pack bouncing on the rig—I saw Hawk sitting on her clutch of eggs.

So I popped the grouse eggs under her—she pecked my hand bloody for the effort—just to see what would happen.

My wife later said that I unleashed a summer of terror on us when I put the eggs under Hawk.

The eggs hatched out. Every single grouse egg, along with her own ten eggs, hatched out and she adopted them. The baby grouse—and there isn't anything cuter than a grouse chick—bonded with Hawk and thought she was their mother.

Within days of hatching she had the whole brood coursing the yard looking for bugs or bits of grain that we threw to them. If they saw a grasshopper the whole mob would take after it.

Hawk was a protective mother and the chicks, both grouse and chicken, grew fast and well.

That's when things got out of hand.

The grouse chicks didn't know they were supposed to be chickens. Except for short distances banty chickens can't fly well, because they have been bred to be too heavy for their wings. But the grouse rapidly grew into adolescents with good wing feathers. They were soon flying all over the yard—whipping from tree to tree or up to the roof.

Hawk would watch them and call to them and at first they came, gathering under her wings for protection—even when they were so large they would lift her up off the ground when they all piled under her.

When the grouse chicks grew enough to ignore Hawk, it made her furious to lose control. The young grouse flew away from her up into the trees even when she ordered them to come to her, and her anger made her fluff up and stomp around. She took it out on all of us.

Next to the house was the woodpile. It was as high as the roof of the house—we use wood for cooking and heating so it becomes a major pile—and Hawk took to sitting on top of the woodpile, watching the yard and her chicks to protect them no matter how far they ranged.

Nothing dared move in the yard.

The first time I noticed it was when Russel—our fat old tom cat—was goobering around in the yard. He made the mistake of crouching and pretending to stalk one of the chicks. The frightened chick made one small distress peep and that's all it took.

I was standing in the driveway facing the woodpile and saw Hawk launch herself like a speckled red missile. She hit Russel in the back of the head so hard cat hair flew out in a circle. Then she hung on and rode him out of the yard, raking his sides like a professional bull rider.

That first attack opened the door for her and she began to rule the yard with an iron hand from the top of the woodpile. She watched like a hawk (hence her name) and woe unto anybody or anything that stepped too close to her chicks. Since as the chicks grew they scattered all over the place, and since there were over twenty of them, it was impossible to not be near one of her chicks. The yard became a war zone.

Images:

My wife carrying laundry to the line and going to her knees as Hawk catches her in the back of the head; Hawk flying off to the right clutching a pair of shorts in her claws.

Quincy, our smallest terrier, keeping a low profile as he tries to sneak across the yard and get to the relative safety of the lilacs near the driveway; Quincy flopping end over end as Hawk nails him in the back of the head like a feathered cannonball.

My son—six-foot-two—coming back from the mailbox with an armload of mail, getting smashed full in the face just as he steps over the battery-powered electric fence we use to keep the goats out of the yard; paper and envelopes flying through the air as his legs hit the wires.

Fred, our obese half-lab yard dog, crouching down with all his hair up and very many teeth showing, facing Hawk who has her neck feathers ruffled out and her beak down as they get ready for head-to-head battle. Hawk winning.

A fox drawn by the meat smell from the kennel but pulled into the yard by the chicks; the fox grabbing a chick and getting hit so hard by Hawk coming from the top of the woodpile that I could see spit fly as the chick was blown out of his mouth.

And finally, my wife coming into the house; tomatoes she'd been carrying from the garden crushed all over her shirt, her hair a mess around the bicycle helmet she'd started to wear for protection around the yard, and anger in her eye.

"The Hawk," she said, grabbing a towel and wiping herself off, "strikes again."

The grouse grew up and most of them went back to the wild. As they left, Hawk mellowed.

But the people and animals who lived through the episode still tiptoe across the yard when Hawk is sitting on the woodpile.

·**6**·

MYSTERIES.

Sometimes things happen in the woods that are not supposed to happen, mysterious things that make the hair go up on your neck, unexplainable, out-of-place things.

I was sitting by a brush pile one fall morning—we'd been hunting mushrooms and I had the team and small cart tied up some distance away—when a chipmunk came out on a log at the base of the brush pile and chukkered at me. Chipmunks are very tame, and it's common to have them eat out of your hand. I was eating a cookie so I leaned forward and held it out and the chipmunk would come toward me a couple of inches, then go back, then forward and back, getting closer to the cookie piece in my fingers all the time. Suddenly a red squirrel—not much larger than the chipmunk—jumped down from the top of the brush pile, ran out on the log, and attacked the chipmunk.

For a part of a second I thought she was fighting for the right to get the cookie, but I was wrong. In half a moment she turned the chipmunk over, grabbed him by the throat, killed him, then dragged the chipmunk back down the length of the log to a shadowed place at the edge of the brush pile and began to eat him.

It was so fast, so brutal, that I hadn't had time to move, and it was completely without reason. Red squirrels are not carnivorous—they eat the insides of pine cones. They most decidedly do not attack and eat chipmunks. Ever.

I wanted it not to be. I wanted the cute little chipmunk to still be sitting on the log coming for the piece of cookie in my hand, wanted the red squirrel to be sitting on a limb holding a pine nut in her hand, turning it and nibbling.

Not sitting back in the shadows pulling the guts out of a chipmunk.

I have never seen it before or since. One moment of stark, staggering violence for no reason, with no sense—there and gone—but I will always be able to see the squirrel looking at me over her kill, nose and front chisel teeth and muzzle dripping blood.

There are night ghosts.

Some people say that we can understand all things if we can know them, but there came a dark night in the fall when I thought that was wrong, and so did the dogs.

We had been running all morning and were tired; some

of the dogs were young and could not sustain a long run. So we stopped in the middle of the afternoon when they seemed to want to rest. I made a fire, set up a gentle, peaceful camp, and went to sleep for four hours.

It hadn't snowed yet so we had been running with a three-wheel cart, which meant we had to run on logging roads and open areas. I had been hard pressed to find new country to run in to keep the young dogs from becoming bored and this logging trail was one we hadn't run. It had been rough going, with a lot of ruts and mud and the cart was a mess so I spent some time fixing it after I awakened, carving off the dried mud. The end result was we didn't get going again until close to one in the morning. This did not pose a problem except that as soon as I hooked the dogs up and got them lined out—I was running an eight-dog team— my head lamp went out. I replaced the bulb and tried a new battery, but that didn't help—the internal wiring was bad. I thought briefly of sleeping again until daylight but the dogs were slamming into the harnesses, screaming to run, so I shrugged and jumped on the rig and untied it. Certainly, I thought, running without a head lamp would not be the worst thing I had ever done.

Immediately we blew into the darkness and the ride was madness. Without a lamp I could not tell when the rig was going to hit a rut or a puddle. It was cloudy and fairly warm—close to fifty—and had rained the night before. Without the moon or even starlight I had no idea where the puddles were until they splashed me—largely in the face— so I was soon dripping wet. Coupled with that, tree limbs

I couldn't see hit at me as we passed, almost tearing me off the back of the rig. Inside an hour I wasn't sure if I was up, down, or sideways.

And the dogs stopped.

They weren't tired, not even a little, judging by the way they had been ripping through the night, but they stopped dead.

I had just taken a limb in the face and was temporarily blinded. All I knew was that they had stopped suddenly and that I had to jam down on the brakes to keep from running over them. It took me a couple of seconds to clear my eyes and when I did, I saw the light.

In the first seconds I thought it was another person coming toward me. The light had an eerie green-yellow glow. It was quite bright and filled a whole part of the dark night ahead, down the trail. It seemed to be moving. I was in deep woods and couldn't think what a person would be doing there—there are no other teams where I train—but I was glad to see the light.

At first.

Then I realized the light was strange. It glowed and ebbed and seemed to fill too much space to be a regular light source. It was low to the ground, and wide.

I was still not frightened, and would probably not have become frightened except that the dogs suddenly started to sing.

I have already talked about some of their songs. Rain songs and first-snow songs and meat songs and come-back-and-stay-with-us songs and even puppy-training songs, but I had heard this song only once, when an old dog had died in the kennel. It was a death song.

And that frightened me.

They all sat. I could see them quite well in the glow from the light—the soft glow, the green glow, the ghost glow. It crept into my thinking without my knowing it: the ghost glow. Against my wishes I started thinking of all the things in my life that had scared me.

Ghosts and goblins and dark nights and snakes under the bed and sounds I didn't know and bodies I had found and graveyards under covered pale moons and death, death, death . . .

And they sang and sang. The cold song in the strange light. For a time I could do nothing but stand on the back of the wheeled rig and stare at the light with old, dusty terror.

But curiosity was stronger. My legs moved without my wanting them to move and my body followed them, alongside the team in the dark, holding to each dog like a security blanket until I reached the next one, moving closer to the light until I was at the front and there were no more dogs to hold.

The light had gotten brighter, seemed to pulse and flood back and forth, but I still could not see the source. I took another step, then another, trying to look around the corner, deeply feeling the distance from the dogs, the aloneness.

Two more steps, then one more, leaning to see around the corner and at last I saw it and when I did it was worse.

It was a form. Not human. A large, standing form glowing

in the dark. The light came from within it, a cold-glowing green light with yellow edges that diffused the shape, making it change and grow as I watched.

I felt my heart slam up into my throat.

I couldn't move. I stared at the upright form and was sure it was a ghost, a being from the dead sent for me. I could not move and might not have ever moved except that the dogs had followed me, pulling the rig quietly until they were around my legs, peering ahead, and I looked down at them and had to laugh.

They were caught in the green light, curved around my legs staring at the standing form, ears cocked and heads turned sideways while they studied it. I took another short step forward and they all followed me, then another, and they stayed with me until we were right next to the form.

It was a stump.

A six-foot-tall, old rotten stump with the bark knocked off, glowing in the dark with a bright green glow. Impossible. I stood there with the dogs around my legs, smelling the stump and touching it with their noses. I found out later that it glowed because it had sucked phosphorus from the ground up into the wood and held the light from day all night.

But that was later. There in the night I did not know this. Touching the stump, and feeling the cold light, I could not quite get rid of the fear until a black-and-white dog named Fonzie came up, smelled the stump, snorted, and peed on it.

So much for ghosts.

In new snow there can be no secrets, no mysteries. Everything leaves tracks. It is possible to see where the owl took the mouse when it tried to run across the snow in the night; the perfect pattern of the owl's wing feathers hitting the powder-snow as the bird dropped on the mouse is there.

You can see the intricate necklace-pattern of tracks made by a hunting ermine as it looks for mice, going down into the under-snow cities the mice have in the swamp grass during the winter, then exploding out the top again with the kill, and down again for another one.

The tracks are always there, and they always tell the truth.

But once I came on a clearing about forty feet across. Dead in the middle of the clearing a fox had taken a grouse. On cold winter nights and days grouse make small caves in the snow to keep from freezing and if they are caught in the caves they can be taken. It is easy to find the holes they make when they plummet into the snow but very hard to catch them off guard because when they hear the sound of someone or something coming through the snow, they explode up and out in a white cloud.

But a fox had taken one in its cave and eaten it. The feathers were there. The tracks of the kill were there.

But there were no tracks leading out to the center of the clearing, no fox tracks around the grouse cave. Nothing. No tracks leaving, no tracks coming.

I tied the dogs off to a tree and took the snowshoes from

the sled and spent the better part of an hour trying to work it out, moving around in the new snow. There were no fox tracks anywhere in the neighborhood. I moved out in larger and larger circles and could find no fox tracks, no sign that a fox had come from anywhere or gone anywhere. The more I looked the less I could find. There could not have been a fox, simply could not have been one and yet there was.

Somehow.

One fox. One grouse. In the middle of the clearing and nowhere else on earth. A quick death, a handful of feathers, then nothing.

Cedar waxwings—small cardinal-like birds that are largely gray—come in the first part of spring. You'd think that over the thousands, perhaps millions, of years they have been migrating they would have worked it out to arrive in the north country at the right time, but they always come early, while there is still snow and no real food for them.

When we see them coming in small flocks, we put out suet for them. They hit the kennels and steal meat but they would rather have berries and seeds.

High-bush cranberries taste—according to my grandmother—like somebody's old socks. Perhaps they aren't that bad, but they do smell awful when they're cooked and it takes a lot of sugar to make high-bush cranberry jelly worth eating. Maybe because of the way they taste the berries are rarely eaten by game early in the fall when they come ripe.

They freeze and hang, beautifully red and luscious-looking, for the whole winter—the color truly is wonderful against the snow. The grouse start to eat them as the winter wears on and they care less about the taste.

The berries are still there in the spring, still frozen, and I happened to be sitting near a high-bush cranberry stand when a flock of cedar waxwings arrived one spring afternoon and that is where I saw another mystery that haunts me.

I had always thought of birds as not terribly intelligent—although Hawk did much to change my mind. I never thought of them as counting, or paying much attention to each other.

But the cedar waxwings didn't just descend on the tree willy-nilly. There was great order as they settled in rows on limbs, eight or ten birds in each row. Then the bird closest to the berries in each row would take a berry carefully and hold it out to the bird next to him in his beak. That bird would take the berry and turn and pass it on to the next, who would take it and turn and give it to the next, and so on until the bird at the end got the berry.

Then the first bird would take another berry and pass it on, and so on, until each bird in the line was holding a berry. When each bird was holding a berry they all faced front and ate them, working the pulp off until they had the meat and spitting out the center pit.

Then they would start over. My wife says it's because they hate the taste of the berries and pass them on hoping to get a sweeter one, and of course there aren't any—they're all sour.

But she's just guessing and I still do not know why they do it.

The doe was something that I could not believe, even when I saw it. . . .

It happened on a night run. It had been cold, but not deep cold—between twenty and thirty below at night—and very still. I was thinking of summer because my feet were cold. My toes have been frostbitten and they get cold easily. Thinking of summer, or Jamaica, or the inside of a red stove helps.

I was thinking specifically of two summer incidents involving deer—one indescribably sweet and the other funny in a painful way.

Both times, I had been fishing in a canoe. There is something about canoes; they do not cause fear. It is possible to paddle gently up to many wild animals and they simply stand and watch—this same thing happens often with dog teams. The silence is probably the cause, but there is grace to a canoe—or a dog team, or a sailboat (which whales allow close to them)—a gentle elegance that seems to fit much more into nature than the roar of an outboard or snowmobile. (Perhaps for that reason in many states it is illegal to hunt from a canoe—deemed unfair—and the same law should apply to dog teams.)

One early summer we had friends visiting us from the city. I took the man and his four-year-old son out in the canoe to work some crappie beds. This morning the crappies were best in close to shore and we caught seven or eight good ones by hanging right on the edge of the lily pads and casting out to the deeper side. The water was very shallow where the canoe floated—not over a foot deep—and the man and I were busy fishing while the young boy, who couldn't cast yet, was having more fun hanging a lure over the shallow side and watching the dozens of small sunfish come to it and nibble.

It was so still the water looked plated with the sky, and absolutely quiet except for a loon that let go once in a while before diving with the high, keening wail and whoop that is so wonderfully soft and melancholy. I was just working my lure in close to the boat when I heard the boy giggle quietly, and I turned to see him reaching out to touch a fawn.

She was new, maybe two, three weeks old, still red with the camouflage spots. She walked out into the water slowly, one careful step at a time, and stretched her nose to touch the finger the boy was holding out, as if they were old friends. It was very deliberate, a youngster meeting another youngster, and I was afraid to breathe lest the moment be broken. I looked up quickly to signal the father but he was seeing it already—his eyes were shining with it—and the moment hung in silence, a moment so incredible in all the moments there are that it seemed magic, staged.

When they had touched, the fawn turned and walked slowly back up into the hazel brush, where I could now see the mother, frantic with worry, trying to get her baby to come back, and then it was done.

Silence, for a long time. Even the small boy was silent.

Finally I coughed. "It's all part of Disneyland of the North," I said. "The fawn comes out on a rail and you touch it and it goes back. . . ."

But it was not a time for jokes and I let it fall. We just sat for a time, watching the hazel brush where the fawn and mother had disappeared, and I had one long, intense moment of gratitude that is still going on, gratitude that I have seen such a thing.

The second time I was canoeing down a flat, winding river that cuts through the woods like a sluggish snake. I had gear in the canoe for a week and I was trying to catch a muskie so I could let it go. (I do not understand why I was doing this either—I have never caught a muskie so I could let it go, though I have tried for several thousand casts, and have to a large degree stopped trying to catch a muskie so I can let it go. It seemed almost a vision quest for a time but it's fading now as I get older and the muskie I didn't catch gets bigger while the muskie I did catch—none—gets smaller.)

It was an incredibly hot day. A late August sun seemed to boil the river and the deerflies and horseflies were not to be believed. I have never seen them worse—it must have been a peak in their cycle. They formed a thick cloud around the canoe so that at times it was impossible to even see the bank. They all bit hard and the blood-smell from the bites brought more of them. They drank repellent like Kool-Aid, licked it off and took more. I tried lighting a smudge in a tin can in the middle of the canoe as I paddled—which worked for mosquitoes—but it didn't bother the flies at all.

They just kept eating and soon my exposed arms and face and hands were bloody.

By accident I discovered a partial solution. The canoe slipped into the shade, under some overhanging cedars, and as if by design some of the flies moved away, back out into the sun to fly along and wait for me to come out again.

In this manner I moved down the river, grabbing shade close in when I could. I was sliding under a leaning cedar when suddenly there was a tremendous crashing sound to my right. I hardly had time to turn when a doe launched herself from the thick brush on the bank in a magnificent arc that carried her out and up, higher than my head, to crash into the shallow water near the bank.

Even in the split second of the event I could see the flies. They were horrendous—a thick mass of them on her head, a swarm trailing back like a comet's tail as she flew through the air. Flies packed into her ears, into her eyes. Flies to drive her mad, insane, temporarily blind.

She had no idea I was there. She landed so close she drenched me with water but in her mad run she'd left the bank blind, wanting only to get in the water and away from the maddening flies.

She jammed her head underwater and slammed it viciously back and forth in a swirling motion then raised it. She snapped it out of the water and was looking straight into my eyes from a distance of four or five feet.

Everything—breath, heart, everything—was absolutely still. Even the flies seemed to stop.

I have never seen such anger, such defiance compressed in a single moment. The flies had taken her beyond control and when she saw me her eyes opened wide in surprise, then seemed to narrow in cold rage. She didn't care that I was man—the enemy—didn't care that I was there, that she was only an arm's reach away. She didn't care about anything right then except the flies. Her eyes, her manner, all things about her for that moment seemed to say: Mess with me and you're a dead man.

Raw, irritated, frustrated, ripping anger.

I didn't move and in that very short time she realized what I was, blew out of the water in a fountain of spray and bottom mud, and was gone.

I thought of her now on the cold night, remembered the wonderfully hot sun cooking down on my back as I paddled. Even the flies seemed to be from the warmth somehow. Musing, lost in the scene, I did not notice that the dogs were slowing and had stopped until my stomach rammed into the handlebar of the sled.

"Pick it up," I said, which usually snapped them into motion, but this time they didn't move. The leader whined in unease and the two wheel dogs—the dogs pulling directly in front of the sled—turned and tried to climb back onto the sled. With their motion several of the other dogs began to growl and I felt the nervousness come back from the dogs and into me.

They'd acted this way before, usually when they'd run into a moose in the dark. We had been attacked by moose on a few occasions and it was not something I wished to do again. Moose are large, and essentially insane with an almost pathological hatred of the dogs, the sled, the musher, trees, trains, cars, and everything else as near as I can figure. When they come at you it's like getting run over by a Buick with legs.

I wished I was some other place.

The nervousness of the team increased and I knew I would have to deal with it, so I set the snowhook and walked up alongside the dogs, flashing my head lamp ahead, trying to see around the slight curve to the lead dog.

He was stopped in the middle of the trail with all his hair up, his lips bared, growling low in his throat.

Ahead of him, slightly to the side of the trail, stood a doe.

She was absolutely still, looking straight ahead over the dog.

None of this made sense. Number one, a deer would not stand so still that close—four, five feet—to a dog. Number two, the dog would not normally have hesitated. He would have been on the deer, or tried to get at her, and all the other dogs would join in. You never moved so fast on a run as when a deer jumped out in front of the team and bolted down the trail. They fairly flew trying to catch it.

And here all of them were whimpering and cowering, spooked by one doe.

Who was standing absolutely still.

And I was getting spooked by her.

She stood staring across the dogs as if they weren't there.

I pushed the dogs sideways on the trail and made my way slowly to the front, closer to the deer.

There weren't three feet between her and the lead dog, who was still whining.

And still she did not move.

Finally I stood so close I could touch her. The light from my head lamp hit her eyes. They were fogged, fogged with death; I could see that she was dead. Standing dead in the night wind next to the trail, guarding the winter night.

She had frozen solid, on her feet, exactly as if she were alive—perfectly still and upright. It could not be yet was; I looked for many things in my mind to explain it. A sudden heart attack, freak paralysis . . . I tried to think of all the possibilities but it still did not make sense and we could not stay.

I could not bring myself to go closer to her, and when I pulled the leader forward and lined him out on the trail and pulled the hook, the team shot past the dead doe without looking up, staring at the ground, not barking or lunging to get at her but moving as fast as possible.

Moving away from that place.

· 7 ·

WE have had and been owned by many dogs since we started to run them. We borrowed many initially because we did not have dogs and they came and went, ran for us awhile, then belonged to someone else. They were loved while they were with us and missed when they left, whatever the reason. Indeed, at the time of this writing we have forty-one dogs, counting the joyful madness we call the puppy pen, and each dog has taught us much.

There is this dog named Fred who has lived with us for going on nine years. When he first came to live with us he made several sled dogs pregnant and so we had him altered. He is loose and moves freely through the kennel, stealing food as he goes. The upshot is that between the operation and the uncontrolled eating Fred has become enormously fat. His weight-for-size should be about forty pounds—and that would be a shade heavy.

Fred came to weigh over a hundred and thirty pounds. He was so heavy his legs sometimes collapsed under him, so we put him on a diet and that is when I began to see and understand temper in dogs.

It was not easy to place restrictions on Fred. He was smarter than us. As soon as we started the extreme weight-loss regimen, Fred began showing up with bits and pieces of food he'd buried all around the yard and kennel over the past year. We took that away, and began taking the food the sled dogs had buried as well, because Fred was stealing from them. Fred still had more—food that he had hidden in the barn—and when we took even that away he began to steal tomatoes and potatoes from the garden. Finally, when we fenced the garden and forced him to go on two-mile walks by dragging him on a leash, Fred began to lose weight.

At the same time he lost his temper. Always a well-minded dog, he stopped coming when we called. He quit his normal watchdog duties—he'd always been a good barker if somebody drove up—and took to sitting in the yard, staring at the house.

Then he bit me.

Fred had never been one to bite although he could be very single-minded in his thinking. One unforgettable incident with the electric fence illustrates his persistence. When we first put the wire in, it was just high enough to catch his tail, which he carried curled up. In due course he clipped the wire and the jolt put him down. In a flash of rage and with a mighty, bellering growl Fred turned on the wire and bit it. And was promptly knocked off his feet. Again—before I could stop him—he bit the wire and again he was knocked down. On the third try he backed off and thought about it. I figured he was done, until he sat up and hit the wire running. Once more it hammered him, but his momentum carried the day and he broke the wire.

Whereupon he stood, wet on it, and walked away growling. (Indeed, he still growls at the wire when he walks by.) He sticks to a thing, but he isn't vicious.

Yet he bit me.

He studied the house, figured I was the reason for his discomfort, waited until I was walking across the yard, and lifted my kneecap as deftly as a surgeon.

It put me on my hands and knees and he moved off a few feet and sat, watching me, panting quietly.

I got the message and we fed him—small amounts, still almost starvation, but something—and Fred returned to his former cheerful self. Although I limped past him cautiously for several months, he never popped me again, but I learned to watch the dogs for signs of irritability and temper.

Different dogs of course have different tempers. Some are more short-tempered than others, but on one occasion I had a whole team mad at me.

It made for a wild ride.

The thing is, it started gently enough. My leader was a sweet dog named Cookie and I had six dogs, all cheerful. It was on the trapline. I had checked several sets and the weather had turned sour. By late afternoon there was a full storm blowing snow so hard it was impossible to see where we were going.

The dogs always know direction but this was before I learned to trust them—learned to understand that lead dogs know more than the person on the sled. Afraid I would get lost in the storm, I challenged every decision. If Cookie wanted to go left, I wanted to go right, if she wanted to go right, I wanted to go left or straight ahead.

Each time she persisted, overriding my commands, I scolded her for fighting me, and each time I would find later that she was right.

Still I did not learn and I continued to challenge them, often causing the team to get tangled. In time they grew sick of my idiocy. When I went up to pull them over, floundering in the deep snow, they ignored me, tried to shrug away my hand. Still trying to be partially polite, they let me know I was being a *putz,* and still I persisted.

Finally I went too far.

We were running along the top edge of a long ridge, higher and higher. The wind was tearing at us. I had my head buried in my parka hood and couldn't even see the front end of the team.

But I was sure I knew the ridge, knew where we were, felt that I had been there before.

I was absolutely, dead wrong.

The team went slower and slower until they were walking, lugging up the middle of the ridge and—perhaps after a quarter of a mile—they stopped. I yelled at them to turn right ("Gee" is the command for right, "Haw" for left). I knew where we were now—was sure of it—but Cookie tried to turn them left, down a long, shallow incline.

I became furious at their mutiny, swore, yelled at the team, then stomped forward, grabbed Cookie by the back of her harness and half-pulled, half-threw her off to the right.

She vanished in the driving snow and wind, moving angrily in the direction I had thrown her. The team followed her, and I jumped on the sled as it went by.

For one or two seconds it was all right. I stood on the brake and held the sled back and we slithered down the hill.

Then it all blew apart. With a great lurch I felt the sled fly out into empty space and drop beneath me. I barely had time to fall backward and go into a tuck before I hit the side of a nearly vertical incline and began to tumble.

I flapped and rolled for what seemed like hours, end over end. I heard the dogs falling beneath me, the sled rolling over and over, and all the gear and food being tossed out, crashing around me.

With a resounding thump the whole pile—sled, dogs, gear, and me, upside down—plummeted into a heap in the bottom of what seemed to be a deep gully.

It was impossible for a moment to understand what had happened. There was not a place where I ended and the dogs and junk began. One dog—named Lad—had his nose jammed squarely in my mouth, another was in my armpit. The sled was on top of me, and if you'd asked me my name I couldn't have told you.

Cookie had knowingly taken the team over the edge of a sharp drop. It was something she never would have done on her own, but I had pushed and griped and hollered too much and she thought it time to give me a lesson.

If I wanted to be stupid, if I persisted in being stupid, if I just couldn't resist being stupid, then she figured I had it coming and she wouldn't hold me back.

It was a good lesson.

But it wasn't over yet. I stood and shook the snow out of my clothes—it was actually packed in my ears—and tipped the sled upright. It took me fifteen minutes to find all the gear and repack the sled and the dogs watched me quietly the whole time.

When the sled was loaded I set to work on the dogs. They were an unholy mess, tangled so badly the gangline was in knots.

The dogs were . . . strange. While I worked to untangle them, it was almost as if I weren't there, as if a robot were working on them. They were pleasant enough, but they did not make eye contact with me. They looked straight ahead while I untangled them. They almost, but not quite, ignored me. Even the dogs that would normally be jumping all over me held back.

It was eerie, quiet even with the wind blowing over the top of the gully. But after a moment I dismissed it as all in my head and went back to the sled.

I pulled the snowhook and stood on the runners.

And the whole team lay down.

They did not drop instantly. But each and every dog, as if by a silent command from Cookie, dug a bit and made a bed and lay down in the snow and went to sleep. I tried every way I knew to get them to run. Fed them, begged them, bit their ears, but they completely ignored me. I wasn't even there.

They didn't get up for eighteen hours.

I had gone over the line.

In the storm, in the pushing and yelling and driving, I had passed the point where they would accept me, run for me, pull for me, and they told me there in that gully. In that wild place they told me so that I would understand that they were the team, they were all of it, and if I ignored them or treated them wrong I would know it.

Finally I pulled out my sleeping bag and made a camp of sorts and heated some tea and dozed and drank tea and thought of how it is to be stupid.

And later, when they felt I'd had enough—late the next day while I was still in the sleeping bag—Cookie stood and shook the snow off. The rest of the dogs did the same, shook and marked the snow. I got out of the bag and fed them and packed and stood on the sled and they pulled up and out of the gully like a runaway train. They pulled up and into the sun and loped all the way home in great joy and glee; joy they were happy to share with me.

Unless I grew stupid again.

It is always possible to learn from dogs and in fact the longer I'm with them the more I understand how little I know. But there was one dog who taught me the most. Just one dog.

Storm.

First dog.

He has already been spoken of once here when he taught

me about heart and the will to pull. But there was more to him, so much more that he in truth could take a whole book.

Joy, loyalty, toughness, peacefulness—all of these were part of Storm. Lessons about life and, finally, lessons about death came from him.

He had a bear's ears. He was brindle colored and built like a truck, and his ears were rounded when we got him so that they looked like bear cub ears. They gave him a comical look when he was young that somehow hung onto him even when he grew old. He had a sense of humor to match his ears, and when he grew truly old he somehow resembled George Burns.

At peak, he was a mighty dog. He pulled like a machine. Until we retired him and used him only for training puppies, until we let him loose to enjoy his age, he pulled, his back over in the power curve so that nothing could stop the sled.

In his fourth or fifth year as a puller he started doing tricks. First he would play jokes on the dog pulling next to him. On long runs he would become bored and when we least expected it he would reach across the gangline and snort wind into the ear of the dog next to him. I ran him with many different dogs and he did it to all of them—chuckling when the dog jumped and shook his or her head—but I never saw a single dog get mad at him for it. Oh, there was once a dog named Fonzie who nearly took his head off, but Fonzie wasn't really mad at him so much as surprised. Fonzie once nailed me through the wrist for waking him up too suddenly when he was sleeping. I'd reached down and touched him before whispering his name.

Small jokes. Gentle jokes, Storm played. He took to hiding things from me. At first I couldn't understand where things were going. I would put a bootie down while working on a dog and it would disappear. I lost a small ladle I used for watering each dog, a cloth glove liner I took off while working on a dog's feet, a roll of tape, and finally, a hat.

He was so clever.

When I lost the hat it was a hot day and I had taken the hat off while I worked on a dog's harness. The dog was just ahead of Storm and when I kneeled to work on the harness—he'd chewed almost through the side of it while running—I put the hat down on the snow near Storm.

Or thought I had. When I had changed the dog's harness I turned and the hat was gone. I looked around, moved the dogs, looked under them, then shrugged. At first I was sure I'd put the hat down, then, when I couldn't find it, I became less sure and at last I thought perhaps I had left it at home or dropped it somewhere on the run.

Storm sat quietly, looking ahead down the trail, not showing anything at all.

I went back to the sled, reached down to disengage the hook and when I did, the dogs exploded forward. I was not quite on the sled when they took off so I was knocked slightly off balance. I leaned over to the right to regain myself, and when I did I accidentally dragged the hook through the snow.

And pulled up my hat.

It had been buried off to the side of the trail in the snow, buried neatly with the snow smoothed over the top so that

72

it was completely hidden. Had the snowhook not scraped down four or five inches I never would have found it.

I stopped the sled and set the hook once more. While knocking the snow out of the hat and putting it back on my head I studied where it had happened.

Right next to Storm.

He had taken the hat, quickly dug a hole, buried the hat and smoothed the snow over it, then gone back to sitting, staring ahead, looking completely innocent.

When I stopped the sled and picked up the hat he looked back, saw me put the hat on my head, and—I swear— smiled. Then he shook his head once and went back to work, pulling.

Along with the jokes, Storm had scale eyes. He watched as the sled was loaded, carefully calculated the weight of each item, and let his disapproval be known if it went too far.

One winter a friend gave us a parlor stove with nickel trim. It was not an enormous stove, but it had some weight to it and some bulk. This friend lived twelve miles away— twelve miles over two fair hills followed by about eight miles on an old, abandoned railroad grade. We needed the stove badly (our old barrel stove had started to burn through) so I took off with the team to pick it up. I left early in the morning because I wanted to get back that same day. It had snowed four or five inches, so the dogs would have to break trail. By the time we had done the hills and the railroad grade, pushing in new snow all the time, they were ready for a rest. I ran them the last two miles to where the stove was and unhooked their tugs so they could rest while I had coffee.

We stopped for an hour at least, the dogs sleeping quietly. When it was time to go my friend and I carried the stove outside and put it in the sled. The dogs didn't move.

Except for Storm.

He raised his head, opened one eye, did a perfect double take—both eyes opening wide—and sat up. He had been facing the front. Now he turned around to face the sled—so he was facing away from the direction we had to travel when we left—and watched us load the sled.

It took some time as the stove barely fit on the sled and had to be jiggled and shuffled around to get it down between the side rails.

Through it all Storm sat and watched us, his face a study in interest. He did not get up, but sat on his back end and when I was done and ready to go I hooked all the dogs back in harness—which involved hooking the tugs to the rear ties on their harnesses. The dogs knew this meant we were going to head home so they got up and started slamming against the tugs, trying to get the sled to move.

All of them, that is, but Storm.

Storm sat backward, the tug hooked up but hanging down. The other dogs were screaming to run, but Storm sat and stared at the stove.

Not at me, not at the sled, but at the stove itself. Then he raised his lips, bared his teeth, and growled at the stove.

When he was finished growling he snorted twice, stood, turned away from the stove, and started to pull. But each time we stopped at the tops of the hills to let the dogs catch their breath after pulling the sled and stove up the steep incline, Storm turned and growled at the stove.

The enemy.

The weight on the sled.

I do not know how many miles Storm and I ran together. Eight, ten, perhaps twelve thousand miles. He was one of the first dogs and taught me the most and as we worked together he came to know me better than perhaps even my own family. He could look once at my shoulders and tell how I was feeling, tell how far we were to run, how fast we had to run—knew it all.

When I started to run long, moved from running a work team, a trapline team, to training for the Iditarod, Storm took it in stride, changed the pace down to the long trot, matched what was needed, and settled in for the long haul.

He did get bored, however, and one day while we were running a long run he started doing a thing that would stay with him—with us—until the end. We had gone forty or fifty miles on a calm, even day with no bad wind. The temperature was a perfect ten below zero. The sun was bright, everything was moving well, and the dogs had settled into the rhythm that could take them a hundred or a thousand miles.

And Storm got bored.

At a curve in the trail a small branch came out over the

path we were running and as Storm passed beneath the limb he jumped up and grabbed it, broke a short piece off—about a foot long—and kept it in his mouth.

All day.

And into the night. He ran, carrying the stick like a toy, and when we stopped to feed or rest he would put the stick down, eat, then pick it up again. He would put the stick down carefully in front of him, or across his paws, and sleep, and when he awakened he would pick up the stick and it soon became a thing between us, the stick.

He would show it to me, making a contact, a connection between us, each time we stopped. I would pet him on top of the head and take the stick from him—he would emit a low, gentle growl when I took the stick. I'd "examine" it closely, nod and seem to approve of it, and hand it back to him.

Each day we ran he would pick a different stick. And each time I would have to approve of it, and after a time, after weeks and months, I realized that he was using the sticks as a way to communicate with me, to tell me that everything was all right, that I was doing the right thing.

Once when I pushed them too hard during a pre-Iditarod race—when I thought it was important to compete and win (a feeling that didn't last long)—I walked up to Storm and as I came close to him he pointedly dropped the stick. I picked it up and held it out but he wouldn't take it. He turned his face away. I put the stick against his lips and tried to make him take it, but he let it fall to the ground. When I realized what he was doing, I stopped and fed and rested the team, sat on the sled and thought about what I was doing wrong. After four hours or so of sitting—watching other teams pass me—I fed them another snack, got ready to go, and was gratified to see Storm pick up the stick. From that time forward I looked for the stick always, knew when I saw it out to the sides of his head that I was doing the right thing. And it was always there.

Through storms and cold weather, on the long runs, the long, long runs where there isn't an end to it, where only the sled and the winter around the sled and the wind are there, Storm had the stick to tell me it was right, all things were right.

And it came to Storm to grow old. Eight, nine, then ten years and he slowed. He trained many pups and, finally, he retired and stopped pulling. We tried to make him a pet and move him into the house, as we often do when dogs retire, but he didn't want that, didn't want to leave the kennel. He rattled around in the house and kept trying to walk out through the windows and glass doors, so we let him outside and kept his food dish full and left him untied.

For a year Storm was the old man in the kennel. He sat in the sun and played with the pups and watched the team leave and come back and always he had a stick. He would hold the stick when I came out to the kennel to harness and when I returned from a run.

And another year passed and he grew blind and his thinking changed so that he was not always aware but still he was happy. He sat by his house and when he heard my steps coming, he would hold his stick out for me. Sometimes I would go to his house and sit next to it in the sun and he would lay his head in my lap with the stick in his mouth and I would think of things I had forgotten about; young things and old things, long runs and short runs, puppies and cold and wind, northern lights and firelight against snow, the creaking sound of an old-fashioned lashed sled moving beneath me, and the joy, the raw-cold joy of going again and again inside the diamond that is northern winter, and all with Storm.

And there came a time when it was supposed to end. Storm failed and began to wander aimlessly through the kennel, bouncing off other dogs' houses, and I knew it would not be long until he faced east as so many of them did when they died. I wanted to leave him loose for that, so he could find the right place.

But we had some new dogs and some of them were aggressive and insecure and wanted to fight all the time. They would even almost fight old Storm when he came too close to their circles, though it was very rare for young dogs to attack older, more respected ones. I did not want Storm to end that way, in violence, so when I went on a trip one fall day I left Storm tied to his chain.

It was a temporary thing, just until I got back, but while I was gone it came on Storm to end and in the final time of his life he somehow got the chain wrapped around his doghouse so he could not face east, could not do it properly.

I saw where he had struggled and torn at the ground with his old claws to get around, to face east as so many animals do if there is time in the end but he could not. He could not tear the chain out of the ground, could not wear it around, could not move the house, could not face the east and end it right.

And it was my fault. I should have known that this was the day he would end, should have felt that he was going to die. I should have known to let him loose, even if there was a risk of a fight. After all, it would be natural for him to fight—they love to fight.

But I did not.

It was my fault and when death came and Storm could not face east he knew that I would be upset. Storm knew I would feel bad, and he did the only thing he could do.

When I came back the next day I went to the kennel and there was silence until I came close and then the dogs went into the death song, which sounds much like the rain song, and I knew then Storm was gone. Knew before I saw him, knew before I even arrived at the kennel. It is a low song, that stays low and does not go into the keening whine that means excitement and I felt all the sadness that comes with the end of a life and went to take his body from the kennel and bury him.

I found him next to his house. He had jammed into the side, trying to get around to the east. The earth was torn beneath him, the chain held his head north.

But he didn't blame me.

I will always blame myself, but Storm did not blame me.

His last act, his last thought, was for me. Storm lay dead and in his mouth was a stick, the stick.

Our stick.

· **8** ·

THE wind seemed to scream as we cut through the night. It had been a cold week—fifty-three below one night, forty-five below the next two, and never rising above twenty below with wild wind out of the northwest the whole time.

Somehow, we had gotten caught out in the worst part of the weather. The true cold had found us eighty miles out. I was not dressed for deep cold and I worried about the dogs. Two of them had frostbitten ears. As I treated them with ointment I decided to hole up until the weather eased a bit—I thought overnight.

I rigged a snow shelter and made a lean-to with a tarp and dug snow caves for the dogs and we holed up to wait until the worst of the cold had passed. We had some dog food and about twenty pounds of fat for the dogs and I had one lovely, lovely can of Chef Boyardee ravioli.

We hunkered in for the duration.

I lasted a day looking at the ravioli, drinking hot "tea" (I had one tea bag which I used over and over). Hunger set in and I used two small pieces of the dogs' fat and mixed it with half the ravioli for a stew.

It tasted wonderful and I ate it, waited another half a day and ate the rest, and it wasn't so bad.

The wind roared but the dogs were covered—I fed them twice and re-covered them—and it could have gone on. I had plenty of wood for fire and the wind was away from me.

But on the morning of the third day I became violently ill. I thought it might be the flu, when I could still think, or food poisoning from the pieces of fat. Then it didn't matter.

I went into a high fever and delirium. I began to hallucinate and while hallucinating somebody arrived (a man I did not know) and he "helped" me harness my team.

The wind was still bad and the dogs did not want to leave their warm snow caves but my helper gave a hand. He was a short man, thick through the middle with curved, sloping, strong shoulders and a great confidence and knowledge of dogs. He shook the dogs out of the snow and made them stand in the wind and twice looked at me and smiled. His face was flat and oval and his eyes were gentle. He signaled me to go, motioning with his hands to move the team, to get the dogs to run. I caught the sled as it went by and I think I tried to wave at him as we left in the dark.

I know looking back on it that it was a hallucination. I can sit and think of it and know that, but it was still real.

I don't remember that whole run. It was a series of night-

mares, of dreams mixed with reality, of scenes and movements and pictures.

I tried to ride on the back of the sled but I was too sick
and kept falling. Fumbling in the dark and cold and wind,
I used some rope to tie myself to the sled and still fell many,
many times. Each time the dogs would stop and let me get
back on the sled. When it was finally too much and I
couldn't stand, I crawled into the sled and wrapped myself
in my sleeping bag—which the man had helped me pack—
and let the dogs have me.

I could not sleep, but kept going in and out of consciousness. Once when I felt that we were stopped I looked up,
out of the bag, and the man—the same man who had helped
me leave the clearing, the Eskimo man—was pulling my
lead dog out of a drift that had blown in over the trail.
Again, when the dogs were straightened out and moving he
waved to me as the sled passed close to him. I waved back
and reached for him but could not touch him as the sled
moved rapidly away.

Through that long night we ran. It was very hard going
for the dogs, fighting the wind and the snow, and I couldn't
help them, lying half dead in the sled. Many times they were
stopped, hung up in deep snow or trying to fight their way
through large drifts, and each time I raised in the sled and
saw the man in the parka with the wolf-fur trim around the
hood grab the leader by the back of the harness and help
him through the bad part.

Once I became sick and leaned over the side of the sled
and was violently ill and the dogs turned and came back to

eat it, which made me sicker. They were an awful mess, tangled and piled on each other and fighting over the vomit. I was so weak that I could not stand. One of them was a large dog named—of all things—Clarence and he loved to fight. Of course many of them do, but Clarence was so large and strong that when he fought he could do serious damage and he jumped on another dog named Yogi and started to kill him. He had Yogi by the throat and I could do nothing.

And the man was there again. The man with no name was there and he smiled peacefully and quietly and untangled the dogs with his gentle competence and pulled them out straight and got them going again, then stood back as we went by and I tried once more to touch him but could not.

And again.

We came to a place in the dark wind where the trail was gone. There had been a trail there when we went out but a logging crew had gone through with a skidder and the blade had taken the trail down to bare ice. It was a steep downhill grade and I was not on the back of the sled where I could use the brakes. The sled began to creep up on the dogs and as it did, it lost steering and turned sideways and rolled over. I was dumped into the side of a pine tree with gear and dog food, and the dogs balled up again in a horrible pile at the bottom of the hill. I couldn't see them well in the dark and tried to crawl to them but everything was blurred and the man came again, the friend.

He lined the dogs out and put the gear back in the sled and set the snowhook so they couldn't run until he'd helped me back into the sled. Then he pulled the hook and put it into the sled and I waved once more and thanked him. He ignored me and called to the dogs with a short sound, a word that sounded like an explosion in his mouth: "Httcha!"

And the dogs took off again, running for him, and I went into the sleep-unconsciousness once more.

Somewhere there was a lake with bad ice and the front end of the team picked their way across it and somewhere we ran down a creek bed on the ice and there was open water and the dogs worked around it. I saw these things as if in a dream. We bounced off many trees and I hit my head several times and was sick again—though the dogs kept going this time—and finally I remembered and saw nothing until I felt the sled was stopped, stopped dead. I opened my eyes and saw that we were in the kennel and the dogs were rolling and scratching at their harnesses, waiting to be let out so they could shake their legs and sleep in their houses. My wife came out and helped me—I was staggering and not being effective at putting them away—and I tried to tell her about the man, my new friend, but it came out all confused. So I stopped and thought I would tell her later but I didn't, somehow, and did not speak of him or see the man, my new friend, again for a long time.

Until I had trained in Minnesota and gone north into Alaska to run in the Iditarod and hit a place called the Burn.

It is, of course, madness—a kind of channeled, focused madness.

The Iditarod.

The idea is that the musher will take a team and go from downtown Anchorage to downtown Nome, some eleven hundred plus miles across the Alaskan wilderness, over mountain ranges, up the Yukon River, out to the coast of the Bering Sea, and up along the coast and across parts of the sea ice to Nome.

That is the idea.

And on the face of it, with the world the way it is now, with planes and computers and cars with brains and comfort-controlled environments and every single whim catered to by technology—with all of that, all that we have become—it doesn't somehow seem possible to do something so basic and elemental. It is such a massive undertaking, such a logistical complication to train a team and take them up to Alaska and run the race. The only way to do it is to break it down to simple, small units of time.

The first run took seventeen days and fourteen hours and it can be remembered best in days.

THE RACE

· DAY 1 ·

OUT of Anchorage. Just madness. There is no sleep the night before, two nights before, trying to get everything ready, no sleep or rest. The food is all shipped to twenty checkpoints across the state, the dogs are trucked into downtown Anchorage to the staging area on Fourth Street where there is—ridiculously—no snow and they must bring it in. Because the snow is shallow the sleds cut through to bare asphalt, so there is no steering, no real control. The dogs are insane to run. We pull number thirty-two—about the middle of a seventy-team race—and the dogs get to stand and watch thirty-one teams go out ahead of them. Out and down four blocks to turn sharp right and head out of the downtown section. Thirty-one teams to watch and then they take us into the chutes and the dogs know it is our time. They lunge and tear and pull and scream until they count us down and we are released. Some new dogs, some old. Cookie is there, and Storm and Fonzie and Columbia and Yogi from the work team, and new dogs that I almost don't know yet.

Forward. They blow out of the chutes so hard that my arms are jerked nearly out of the sockets and I cannot believe they are the same fifteen dogs I have trained, have run so many times before. I am as nothing on the rear of the sled, nothing. We pound the four blocks in a heartbeat. I know we cannot make the turn and we don't. The dogs sweep around, there is a moment when there seems to be control and then I roll, over and over, but hang onto the sled somehow and slide out of downtown Anchorage on my face, dragging on the back of the sled like garbage.

Only the sled and the dogs on the team matter, so little is known of other teams until much later, after the first three days. Some do not make it out of Anchorage. One musher breaks an arm, another a shoulder—three, five blocks out and they must scratch.

And that is the worst.

To scratch. Before the race it is spoken of as a disease. I am a leper, I will scratch—it is the same. Many will, but nobody wants to. Everyone wants to finish.

I regain control of the team, get back upright on the runners, and somehow get out of Anchorage. It is still not real, a dream. Finally, out of the chutes, really, really starting to run the Iditarod. The dream. The run. The Run.

And it's all phony. The show start in Anchorage is done for television, and to give Anchorage publicity. Teams can't truly go from Anchorage to Nome because the freeway system coming into Anchorage blocks the trail. The whole first start, the madness of it, the chutes, all of it has to be done over. Thirty miles out of town is the suburb of Eagle River where the dogs are put in trucks and taken eleven miles to Settler's Bay where the true race starts.

More chutes. More slamming and screaming and waiting for the front teams to leave and again, madness. The dogs blow out of the starting chutes and scramble for speed and this time it is into the bush, directly into the wilderness, but this sham start and restart has taken all day, and so the race truly starts at the end of the day.

Close to dark.

With the darkness comes chaos. The teams will not rest this first night—they are too excited and must be allowed to run until they settle in—so the darkness brings a particular insanity of passing teams and tangles and moose.

Moose.

My team stops dead in the dark and I go up to investigate the reason and find my leader (some run two leaders but I favor one), a sweet but simple dog named Wilson. I am trying to get him to lead so I can save Cookie for later, and I find him with his head between the back legs of a moose, frozen with terror. The moose, a large cow, turns to look at me when my headlight comes across her, then turns away. I do not have a gun, do not know what to do.

"What the hell are you waiting for?" a voice demands suddenly from the rear as another team runs up on mine in the dark. "Why are you stopped?"

"There's a moose," I yell back lamely.

"Well, kick it in the butt and get moving or get out of the way. . . ."

I try, kicking the moose in the left flank, and to my amazement she jumps and moves slowly off the trail so we can pass. (Later in the race I will try this again and the second moose will jump on me instead of off the trail, making my life very interesting for about five seconds.)

And on. In the confusion, my leader gets lost and takes a wrong turn while I am looking down into the sled bag and we go forty, fifty miles in the wrong direction, up into some canyons where the trail gets narrower and narrower until it finally just stops.

I go up to the front of the team in the darkness and drag them around, realizing we are lost. My clothes have been ripped on tree limbs and my face is bleeding from cuts, and when I look back down the side of the mountain we have just climbed I see twenty-seven head lamps bobbing up the trail. Twenty-seven teams have taken our smell as the valid trail and are following us. Twenty-seven teams must be met head on in the narrow brush and passed and told to turn around.

It is a nightmare. The whole crazy night turning teams, stopping fights, yelling at dogs, and wading in armpit-deep snow until, finally, we are all back on the right trail, and at last just before dawn I can stand it no longer—three nights now without sleep—and I pull the team off on a narrow turnoff and sit on the sled to rest. To doze.

I was not there ten minutes, lying back with my eyes

closed, when I heard footsteps on the snow. An older man who is famous stood next to me in the darkness and smiled down and said:

"Would you like a chocolate chip cookie?"

Wonderfully, incredibly, miraculously he has somehow gotten two chocolate chip cookies through that mad night without breaking them. He handed me one and I sat up and poured tea from my thermos into my cup and his and we drank the tea and dunked the cookies and did not talk but just sat. I looked at my watch and found it was exactly twenty-four hours since we were in the staging area in downtown Anchorage waiting to get in the starting chute.

It is the end of the first day.

· DAY 2 ·

AT dawn we break into the open from thick, dark forest and are treated to a spectacular sight. The sun coming over our right rear lights up the entire Alaska Range across our front. There are no clouds and the mountains, McKinley on the right, tower over us in dazzling white enormity, filling the sky while the sun warms our backs and the dogs settle into running.

The madness of the night is gone. The front-end teams, the faster runners, have moved on and we (the dogs and I) are left to get down to the business of running better than a thousand miles.

It is a strange thing to do.

The dogs are magnificent. They are the true athletes of the Iditarod. The dogs continually cause wonder with their endurance, joy, and intelligence. But they have tremendous needs. They must be fed a snack every hour or so, and three or more hot meals a day. Their shoulders must be rubbed every hour and they must be allowed to shake the lactic acid buildup out of their joints each hour.

And their feet . . .

God, their feet. I am being pulled by fifteen dogs and that makes sixty feet to be taken care of; to be watched and rubbed with ointment and covered with booties if need be.

So much time will be spent on my knees that I have sewn half-inch foam pads into my pants at the knees to keep my legs from freezing when I kneel in the snow.

And in this business of running, this whole business of getting started and settling down to taking care of the dogs, in the tension and speed of the race I do not notice when we start climbing; beginning the long run up into the mountains. We move through the day up some frozen rivers and across some frozen lakes and when it gets dark again we come into the first of twenty checkpoints.

Noise and pandemonium. Dog teams coming and going, judges and spectators all around. Small planes landing on the ice and taking off. The dogs cannot rest because of the noise. I get my sacks of food and we head up the river a bit to be alone, but still they do not rest. They sit and watch other teams coming and going, watch the planes taking off over us.

Even in the dark, in the willows at the side of the river, it is crowded. A man with a team wanders in circles out in front of me, the dogs running around and around on the ice, jumping from one snowmobile trail to the next and circling back, confused by all the trails in the darkness.

Everybody is confused.

When it is clear the dogs will not rest, I hook up their tugs and we start off again. We luckily find the right trail and as we leave the checkpoint the man whose team was wandering follows us out.

That night passes again in confusion. Teams pass us, we pass other teams. I stop to rest the dogs again but they still will not sleep—won't, indeed, for two more nights—so I let them run. The snow is unbelievably deep. When I stop them and run up alongside the team at one point to work on their feet I mistakenly step off the trail and go in up to my armpits. I have to crawl out by grabbing at the dogs and using them for an anchor.

And my brain fries that second night.

Sleep deprivation catches me and I start hallucinating. We have been warned about that in briefings, along with frostbite, wind, whiteouts, wind, intense cold, and finally, wind. But nothing can prepare you for your first hallucinations in the race because they are not dreams, not something from sleep or delirium; the intensity of the race, the focused drive of it makes for a kind of exhaustion in the musher not found in training. The hallucinations seem to roar at you. They come while you are awake, come with your eyes open, and are completely real.

There is a small bit of snow that spurts up from each dog's foot as they run, a little white jet, and that turns in my mind to flame. I see my dogs all running in flame, their feet and lower legs on fire. Terrified, I set the snowhook and run up to put the fire out, lean down to pat the flames out and of course they disappear, are not there.

96

But the vision comes again and again until at last I some-how reconcile myself by thinking it is all right because the flames do not hurt the dogs. I am amazed that they can run in liquid fire and not feel pain or get injured.

The hallucinations do not go away. Indeed, they get more complicated. Often I nearly get lost by going up rivers that aren't there, following lights that do not exist.

At one point I have a man sitting on my sled. He is wearing a trench coat and a pair of horn-rimmed glasses and is holding a manila folder full of official-looking papers. As I watch he turns to look up at me—he is very distinct and I can see the wrinkles in the fabric of his coat, my own reflection in his glasses—he turns to look at me and begins to speak in a low voice about federal educational grants.

He is the most boring human being I have ever met—as dull as thick mud—and he goes on and on until at last I yell at him to shut up.

The dogs stop and look back at me and of course I am alone.

It is only in the night when the hallucinations are bad—between about eleven and four in the morning—and I will not learn how to truly control them for another day and a half.

The night drags on forever as the dogs keep trotting and I reel in and out of half-sleep on the back of the sled, but at long last it is dawn. There is cold now at dawn, deep cold. It is perhaps fifty below. And I come alongside a musher whose teeth are chattering—a bad sign—while he tries to get a fire going.

"Cold," he says, the word a benediction.

I nod from the closed tunnel of my parka hood and pull my team over to rest. They are at last ready to stop.

It is the end of day two.

· DAY 3 ·

WE must cross the Alaska Range.

Somebody before the race kept saying it was the highest mountain range in North America—which is true—and it takes all of this day climbing and another one climbing still more to get up into the peaks.

We pass through three more checkpoints, two of them villages with children running out to watch the teams come through. They are intensely curious and study each thing I do as I feed and take care of the dogs. One checkpoint is a trapper's cabin where we may stop but are not allowed inside the cabin.

My team is very slow, much slower than most other teams and I realize on this day that I will be very lucky to finish the race, let alone do well. Finishing is all I originally wanted, but the hot worm is always there—the thought that maybe your dogs are special and will prove themselves better

99

than Rick's or Susan's or any of the other front-end runners. It is a futile dream, a strange thought to have, but it is there nonetheless.

Until this third day.

The mountains, the climbing and climbing, have a way of establishing reality. As the team climbs into the peaks above timberline and comes out at the Rainy Pass checkpoint where there are thirty or so other teams stopping to feed and rest, I have entered into a state of almost idiotic bliss.

I am tired beyond belief. Beyond how it was in the army. Beyond anything I have known, I am tired. But the team is moving and seems healthy and everybody is eating and drinking and the scenery is so beautiful that it doesn't matter how far we're behind.

I am steeped in beauty. It is like going back ten, twelve thousand years, running over these mountains with a dog team. Like becoming a true human—a human before we became cluttered by civilization. Like going inside and becoming a cave painting.

We end the third day in the Rainy Pass checkpoint, resting. I sit on the sled and stare at the dogs while they sleep. My eyes close and when they open again—it seems a moment—four hours have passed.

Yogi is up, jerking around, wanting to fight, and I realize it is time to go.

· DAY 4 ·

OVER Rainy Pass and down through the gorge.

Everybody warned the rookies about the gorge, also known as "The Gut" and "The Chute."

It is a twenty-mile downhill run through a river gorge studded with boulders and you run on an ice ledge steeply down, weaving in and out of the boulders for the whole distance. The other mushers tell the rookies that it is easy to get in trouble in the gorge.

And it is.

In a moment of sheer stupidity, worried that I will lose my team, I tie my left arm to the sled. Seconds later I am knocked off the sled and as the dogs careen down through the gorge they loop out and around a boulder but the sled does not make it cleanly and hits the boulder and I am knocked off the runners and I cannot get up. I bounce, bang off boulders, swing back and forth like a piece of meat. I seem to do most of the gorge run on my back, whamming boulders with the top of my head.

Through a miracle or two my stupidity in tying myself to the sled does not kill me. A musher stopped at the end of the gorge fixing his broken sled grabs my team and pulls them to a stop as they pile into a small side ravine or I think it would have been worse.

Tattered, bleeding, ragged, and stunned I come out the end of the gorge to crash in the next checkpoint and spend the day recovering.

It is the end of day four.

· DAY 5 ·

AT Rhone River I take my twenty-four hour mandatory layover.

I sleep on the ground with the dogs near a small cabin that is the checkpoint and when I awaken it is about midmorning—I have about ten hours before I am due to leave—and I find that we are on a small island in a frozen river. It is the most beautiful spot I have ever seen.

The island is surrounded by mountains that shoot up to the sky. The peaks tower over the cabin, making it like a jewel in a giant, magnificent setting. I go to the back side of the island for water for the dogs and stand level with the bottom edge of a mountain that seems to go up forever, have to turn my head back and up to see the peak covered with snow.

It is like a cathedral. My head stops aching and the sharp

pain in my ribs goes down as I sit on a log and drink tea and let the beauty work into me for that whole day.

Rumors tear through the checkpoint like wildfire. One man is missing and feared dead. Two men are missing and feared dead. One woman was attacked by a moose and killed. Somebody was dragged to death coming down Rainy Pass in the gorge. None of the rumors are true, but they fly back and forth through the resting teams at the checkpoint, and I would be more worried by them except that I have been in the army and it has the same kind of rumor engine.

Late afternoon comes and the checker tells me I can go.

The dogs fairly hum with energy, having slept and rested for a full twenty-four hours. I stand on the sled and reach to release the snowhook but before I can they lunge and break the rope and I am gone out of the checkpoint, looking back at the snowhook as I leave.

It is the end of day five.

· DAY 6 ·

IN the dark we roar wildly through some trees that come so close to the trail the sled seems hardly to fit through. Twice I am knocked off the sled and scramble back on. Then we climb up a frozen riverbed and waterfall in the dark—the dogs jump up from boulder to boulder and I hang beneath the sled at one point with my feet out in open space—and suddenly we come out in the Burn.

We were warned about the Burn. It is a ninety-mile-wide stretch of broken country where a forest fire took everything out. For some reason there is often not very much snow in the Burn and this year is no exception. Just as it gets dark I look out across a vast expanse of rocks and dirt and dead grass and burned trees fallen across one another and no snow—not a flake—as far as I can see.

The dogs are still fresh, having slept a full day, and they don't care that there is no snow for the sled runners—it's all the same to them—and I have to run them. Inside half a mile I'm in trouble.

The dogs run beneath a burned tree and the sled jams. I cannot back them up so I take a small bow saw and cut through the tree, which allows the sled to escape. I barely grab on as it explodes forward.

To the next tree.

And the sled jams and I cut through the tree again; all through the dark night we slam from tree to tree with me dragging on my face half the time, bouncing off rocks and dirt while the dogs—resting each time I must cut a tree—stay fresh and powerful and lunging.

It is chaos.

I have not rested well and the hallucinations start about midnight and I have the same man in the trench coat on the sled for a time, talking to me about educational grants, until I tell him to shut up and leave and he becomes indignant.

I learn that night how powerful the hallucinations can be. In a rare moment when the sled is on smooth ground I come across a clearing and a dog team is stopped ahead of me.

All the dogs are asleep, spread out across the grass and one of the other mushers in the race is leaning over the empty sled with his fist raised.

"Get out of the sled or I'll kill you," he is saying and when I stop in back of him and ask him what is wrong he points down to the empty sled.

"It's this man. I've carried him over two hundred miles

and he won't help push up the hills. I'm sick of him. I'm going to leave him here in the Burn. . . ."

We talk for a bit and he relaxes and realizes he is hallucinating but as I leave I hear him say loudly again, "Get out of the sled. . . ."

And I think as we go that perhaps it is not real and I am hallucinating about a man having hallucinations and that in turn triggers the thought that perhaps all of it—the Burn, the race, the dogs, my life, all of it in the whole world is just a hallucination. My brain is running wild with this thought when the dogs stop and I look up and there is an enormous bull buffalo standing in front of my leader, smelling his head.

I stare at it for a long time. The man in the trench coat is back on my sled and the buffalo is standing there. My befuddled brain simply thinks it's another hallucination and I wait for it to disappear.

It doesn't.

I try to hush the man on the sled because I am worried he will anger the buffalo. I have never seen an angry buffalo, even in a hallucination, and do not want to start now. The buffalo seems as big as a house, but it slowly seeps into my thinking, like mud warming, that the dogs would not have stopped for my hallucination.

It is a real buffalo.

There is a herd of real buffalo in the Burn and this bull stands looking down on my leader—Wilson, who is very sweet and a wonderful dog but dumber than a walnut— smelling him.

I call the dogs up and they go around the bull and I am surprised when the man on the sled says nothing though we pass not four feet from the buffalo and could easily touch it. The buffalo does nothing to us, is very mellow.

I hear later that another musher fell asleep in the Burn next to his sled—his dogs were resting—and when he woke up the buffalo was standing over him, straddling him, smelling the breath as it came out of his nostrils.

Buffalo, he says when he tells of it—there is strangely no fear in his voice—have very bad breath.

The Burn, finally, becomes too much. I am going across a large clearing—several miles across—and it starts to snow and the wind kicks up until I cannot see the dogs, only the front end of the sled now and then, and I have no idea where the trail is supposed to be.

Wilson loses his way and begins to wander. Since there is no trail to follow he works around in a large circle to the right and heads off into the bush and I don't know anything of this until we come into a box canyon and cannot proceed any farther and I know we have lost the trail. We have run perhaps thirty or forty miles off the trail, and to compound the problem the wind and driving snow have quickly covered our tracks so we cannot easily find our way back and I cannot think, cannot begin to think. I sink down on my knees next to the sled in a kind of surrender, and when I look up, my friend is there.

The Eskimo man who helped me when I was sick is there and he takes Wilson by the back of his harness and drags the team around and I stand on the sled and we start.

I do not know where we are going but I have great confidence in the man with the curving shoulders and gentle smile and think that if we move slowly, just keep moving, he will not let me down.

Hours pass and each time I hesitate he shows up next to the team and waves me on. I keep going, against the wind and snow, until I look down and see sled tracks. They are filling fast so they must be very fresh. I call the dogs to increase speed and we run through the rest of the darkness and at dawn I see a cabin which signals the end of the Burn. I wish I could thank the man who saved me again but he is gone.

It is the end of day six.

· DAY 7 ·

IN and out of a checkpoint—a village named Nicolai. It is very crowded with snowmobiles roaring by and resting teams all around, so I don't stay. The wind stops and the sun comes out.

Everything again is steeped in beauty as I run down a river and over some large hills and we come around a corner in the brush, run up off the river and there is a bar.

In the middle of nowhere a man suddenly appears and asks me if I want a beer. I say no, I don't drink, and he gives me a soda instead. It tastes incredibly wonderful and I drink it down in one long swallow. While I am turned away he throws three more sodas in my sled.

It is a very nice thing to do except that I don't see him do it and leave the checkpoint without knowing the sodas are there. They settle down on top of my booties in the bootie sack and that night it gets forty or fifty below and the cans of soda freeze and burst. The next day it gets warm again; the sodas thaw and run into the cloth booties and refreeze in the cloth.

Later that day Wilson cuts his foot and I go to get a bootie for him and find they are frozen in soda slush. I thaw one in my armpit and put it on his foot and we start off.

Wilson smells the soda.

If it smells interesting, he thinks, it must taste good. Soon he is running on three legs sucking on his foot and that's the way I pass a team which is resting, with my leader running on three legs sucking a foot.

The musher just nods and watches Wilson run by.

We run all day on a beautiful trail, down some long, long hills into a checkpoint where a beautiful blond girl hands me a cup of hot chocolate. It is not possible for anything to taste as good as that hot chocolate tastes and I drink it slowly, trying to make it last.

I leave the checkpoint in the dark. The land has flattened into long hills like ocean swells and the wind has died down and the team runs well through the night while I stand on the back lost in hallucinations again. This time I see crowds of people cheering for me. Some of them are riding snowmobiles and some come out of cabins to wave and I can see their families inside the cabins sitting at tables and twice I have to move quickly on the sled to keep from being nudged by the snowmobiles when they come close to wave to me.

None of it real.

Dawn comes and we are in the interior of Alaska. So different, it is like another planet. No trees, only tundra and the long low hills and the jingle of the dogs' collars and the whuffing of their breath as they trot and we cover the miles, the long miles across the interior over to the Yukon River.

It is the end of day seven.

· DAY 8 ·

IT must be the same as going to the moon, crossing the interior of Alaska by dog team. After a time it seems the team isn't moving, that the country, the tundra, the endless grass and shallow snow are rolling by beneath us and we are standing still—so unchanging is the country.

Flat, gently rolling, it is stultifying. Running through the night to get to the cabin Wilson has started to do a new thing. He falls over.

When it first happened I was worried that something was wrong and ran forward to attend him. I put him on his feet and his tail wagged and he was all right and we took off.

In thirty yards he fell over again. Once more I put him on his feet and we set out.

Over he goes.

Finally I realize that the boredom is too much and he is falling asleep while running.

I pet him and sit next to him for a time but he won't sleep to rest. Only while we run. So he isn't tired, just bored, and once more we set off.

I watch him with my light and when his back starts to weave a bit I say softly, "Willy?"

And he awakens and is fine for forty or so yards. Then he does it again and I say it once more and through that long night every forty yards I say, "Willy?"

And it works. We keep moving and everybody stays happy. During the night I pass teams and they pass me. Finally, in the morning, the team stops at a small caved-in cabin. It is not a checkpoint, but a good place to rest the dogs. Inside the cabin a man I passed and who passed me later has a fire going in the stove. So I hang my clothes to dry and make tea. We are sitting and drinking when he asks me if I ran all night.

"Yeah."

"Twice somebody went past me in the dark," he said, "looking for somebody named Willy. I wonder who that was?"

I shrugged. "I have no idea . . ." This man had seen me running while Wilson sucked his foot. I thought there was no sense in making it even worse.

And that ended day eight.

· DAY 9 ·

WE pass through the ghost town of Iditarod, which is set up as a checkpoint. I pull the team up alongside the river to rest them under some overhanging willows. The dogs and I are sitting by a fire when a plane lands right next to me and a man gets out.

"Somebody told me you had big dogs," he says, looking at my team.

"I guess so. Big and slow."

"I have a female wolf in the plane and want to breed her to some big dogs. . . ."

I look at the plane more closely and sure enough, in the back seat is a wolf. She is huge—well over a hundred pounds—and has a muzzle on. I cannot believe this man has flown out here with a wolf sitting in back of him just to get her bred by my dogs.

"She's in season," he offers. "The only problem is she's killed three male dogs I've tried to breed her to. . . . "

"I'll pass," I say, and he shrugs amiably, jumps into the plane, and takes off. It is all so bizarre I think perhaps I dreamt it, but there are ski marks on the snow from the landing gear of the plane.

We leave again at night. There are some mean hills as we leave and they are dotted with gear dropped by rookies trying to get lighter. I see an extra pair of socks, some gloves, brass snaps, a Coleman stove, a good fur hat (which I try to grab but miss and don't want to stop for), several articles of undergarments. It seems a waste but I find later that people from the checkpoint will come out with snowmobiles and harvest the hills as they do each year.

Three days earlier one of my dogs had stopped eating any of the meats I had sent for the dogs—pork, lamb, beef, liver, and dry dog food. But she would eat the meat patties I had sent for myself, which had cheese and raisins and fat mixed in. So I gave her all my own food and consequently didn't have any food at the checkpoints. Other mushers had helped me some, but a major food chain had butter and a dry beverage powder at all the checkpoints as a promotional stunt. So when I left a checkpoint I'd take four or five pounds of butter with me. I was eating sticks of butter as I went across the interior to maintain energy.

As might be imagined I became truly sick of butter— don't like it much yet—and when I got to the Shageluk checkpoint I was glad to find that the children from the school had a huge pot of moose chili cooking in the council hall just for the mushers.

It tasted wonderful and I could not stop eating it. Like a wolf, I gorged—ate nineteen paper bowlfuls of chili.

I then start the run up the Yukon River and inside of four hours I thought I was going to die of gastric distress. At one point it became so bad that the team stopped and looked back at me in surprise.

End of day nine.

· DAY 10 ·

THE run up the Yukon River is horrific. A hundred and eighty miles straight north into the wind, up the middle of the great river that historically is a highway across Alaska. In the summer barges bring supplies up the river to the villages. Now snowmobiles whiz by frequently as people go from one village to the next to visit.

All the cold air in Alaska seems to settle into the Yukon Valley and in the night it hits like a hammerblow.

Forty, fifty below—and colder. Going up the middle of the river in the deep cold night is like going inside an iceberg.

I cannot stand the wind. I turn backward on the sled and hook my elbows and ride but it is still too cold. I put on all my extra clothes and it is still too cold. I feel the cold cutting through all the clothing. I go up to check the dogs but they are all right—no signs of frostbite—so we continue. There is nowhere to stop at any rate.

Just ice. Flat ice and wind. We fight north the whole day and through the night and stop to rest in the morning at dawn around in back of an island to get out of the wind.

The cursed, cutting, tearing, soul-cold wind.

I sit on the sled with my back to the wind and let the new sun warm my face and it is the end of day ten.

· DAY 11 ·

ANOTHER long day and into the night and the bone-chilling cold. This terrible night I get too cold. The cold is coming down on me like a death, and I must run to keep my body temperature up.

I run fifty paces and ride fifty and run fifty and ride fifty the whole night and the running brings my body heat back up. But I cannot get enough air through my two wool masks so I pull them down and breathe straight into my mouth. I get enough air then, but the cold raw air freezes the sides of my throat and blood vessels burst and my throat generates mucus and soon I am choking on it.

It is very hard to clear. I must stick a finger down my throat to help pull it out and when I throw it on the ice the wheel dogs turn around and eat it. This makes me throw up and they eat that as well and I spend the whole day and night running up the river hacking blood and mucus and vomiting and hallucinating.

When I approach the village that is the last checkpoint on the Yukon River I look up on some cliffs on the left side of the river and see a bunch of crosses. We have been told about the graveyard to the south of town and I feel the ghosts of all the dead in the graveyard welcoming me to the end of the river run. It is a warm feeling, a gentle calling. I nod to them and smile and turn off the river on the overland trail out to the Bering Sea.

It is the end of the river and the end of day eleven.

· DAY 12 ·

THERE is a change on this day, in the dogs and in me. We run down from the river out to the Bering Sea on a classic run. It is about zero or slightly above and there is sun and it is downhill for over ninety miles and the dogs run to my mind.

I have changed, have moved back in time, have entered an altered state, a primitive state. At one point there is a long uphill grade—over a mile—and I lope alongside the sled easily, lightly, pushing gently to help the dogs. My rhythm, my movement, is the same as the dogs. We have the same flow across the tundra and I know then we will finish.

We could run forever into the wind, across the short grass, run for all the time there has been and all the time there will be and I know it and the dogs know it.

We come out to the coast at an Eskimo village and one

of the villagers, an older man, takes me in for the night and feeds me with great gentleness and talks to me while I sit in his small house. When my eyes close and won't open he shows me a bed he has prepared for me.

As I go to sleep I see him walk by wearing only long underwear and he looks the same as the man who saved me in the Burn and earlier when I was sick. He has the same curved, strong shoulders and a quiet soft strength. When I awaken some hours later and check the dogs and get ready for the run up the coast he comes out to wish me well.

We run out of the village north with the sun coming up on our right, heading north again, the only direction, and it is the end of day twelve.

· DAY 13 ·

THERE is something about the ocean that affects me. It is open offshore, not frozen, and blue from the sky, and though it's about twenty below it is a soft cold and the dogs are full of it. They won't stop to rest, keep hitting the harnesses. One female named Blue starts shredding her harness with great glee as a joke each time I stop to feed or rest if I don't get her the food fast enough.

I am sitting in the fourth to the last checkpoint when the race ends. We still have two hundred or so miles to go, across part of the ice on Norton Sound, and it is completely over. They're having their banquets and the winner is being paid and there is cheering and I still have four days to go to finish.

And we do not care.

We run the hills easily. Letting the team do as they wish,

I simply stand on the back or push up the hills and do not care about winning or losing—only the dance counts.

The beauty is, as through the whole race, staggering. The hills which would once have put me off with their steepness are full of light and game. Clouds of ptarmigan rise like giant white snowflakes into a bright sun in front of the dogs— sometimes two, three hundred of them. And the strange arctic hares that stand on their back legs to see better are all over the place. They seem to be people, especially in the twilight as evening comes and the edges of hallucinations start. I keep thinking there are people standing in back of bushes to watch us pass.

Finally the dogs can stand it no longer and they take off from the trail, chasing one of the hares, and I get a thrilling ride down a long hill. The hare easily outdistances the dogs and they wheel back up the hill in a single, sweeping circle. They do not care that they failed to catch him.

The dogs fairly hum with energy as we slide gleefully down the final hills into the checkpoint just before we go out on the ice and it is the end of day thirteen.

⋅ DAY 14 ⋅

FROM Shaktolik we must cross Norton Sound. Depending on who is telling you it is apparently about sixty miles of sea ice. Horror stories abound about the Sound.

Rumors.

Somebody has gone through the ice and they found her team wandering alone.

Somebody else went insane and is making big circles out on the ice but nobody wants to stop him because he will be disqualified if he is given help.

Somebody was found dead on her sled.

Somebody was torn from his sled by the wind and the dogs blew thirty miles across the ice sideways and he didn't find them for two days.

Somebody was on a large cake of ice and it broke loose and headed out to sea. They are worried that she will not be found or may drift across the Bering Sea to Russia.

Somebody froze his eyeballs because he didn't blink enough and is blind but is finishing the race anyway.

Somebody froze his nose and it will have to be amputated.

All of the rumors are virtually unfounded but they rip through the area as they did at Rainy Pass and I leave the checkpoint at dawn to head across the ice with some doubt.

It is the end of day fourteen.

· DAY 15 ·

THE ice gives us a joy run.

The wind abates, the sun comes out, the trail across is flat—frozen seawater—and the dogs are well rested. We fly. I let them lope easily in a gentle canter for close to forty miles before they come down into a trot and when we stop to rest several of the dogs actually start playing like puppies, crouching down and bouncing toward each other.

The day passes in a kind of Gidget-goes-to-Nome happiness and when darkness comes I see the lights of the checkpoint across the flat ice and the dogs do as well and they start running towards them in the same easy lope.

Distances are very deceiving out on the ice however and we still probably have thirty or so miles to go. In a while it seems as if the lights will never get closer and the dogs break down into a fast trot that carries them all the way in.

As we enter the village a small boy leaps out of the

darkness and grabs the leaders by the back of their harnesses to lead them up to his house where I will spend the check-point time. It is a nice gesture but the dogs pile up on themselves, get tangled and turn inward. I am terrified they will begin fighting with the boy in the middle—children and even adults have died this way—and I run up to him and grab him by the back of his jacket and hold him up away from the dogs and ask him why he grabbed my team.

He smiles and says it is because he wants a team to stay at his house so he can learn about the dogs and sleds, and I am stunned that an Eskimo boy on the Bering Sea would have to ask someone from Minnesota about dogs.

I stay in his house and his family feeds me and they treat me with the same gentle courtesy the older man showed me earlier. I try to speak of the dogs but find that I cannot speak well, can only talk in grunts and single words, and have some trouble being with people. After a time I go back out with the dogs and sleep with them on the ice. I awaken at dawn just as a team pulls in. They look good, and fresh for just coming across the ice, and I am surprised to see the musher run forward with a little rubber duck and roll on the snow with his dogs, squeezing the squeaky toy for them and play-ing with them. They love the game and he keeps hiding the toy from them and they try to get it away from him.

Then he puts the duck away and dresses them in doggie sweaters so they can sleep warm and I leave the checkpoint in a kind of gladness that I had seen him; a gladness that I knew dogs and they knew me and that we had come together.

And it is the end of day fifteen.

· DAYS 16 AND 17 ·

TWO more checkpoints.

We run along the coast, along the edge of the ice with towering cliffs going up to our right. The ocean is breaking away the ice and finally there is nothing except water in front so we angle up into the country, across a mountain—dead over the top of it—and down across another bay on ice.

Here the wind is strong and blowing straight from the rear. The ice is sheer, flat, absolutely slick, and the wind blowing from the rear makes my body act as a sail. The sled blows forward and sideways and I must ride the break to keep from running up on the dogs all across the bay.

The dogs seem to smell Nome now. They have changed and know we are near the end and when we leave the last checkpoint but one and head out onto the beach—a forty-mile-long beach ending in Nome—they seem to have new purpose in their steps. It is perhaps all in my head, but then so much else is that it doesn't matter.

We run through the day along the edge of the beach, running on the ice itself because the wind has blown all the snow off the beach sand. As dark comes I can see the lights of the finish, of Nome, twenty or more miles ahead and when I realize what they are I stop the team.

I do not want to go in and finish the race.

I do not understand why, but I do not want to go in. I actually begin to walk up and take my leader and turn the dogs around and run back, back. . . .

There is no sense to it but somehow it is because the race is something that doesn't seem like it can be done. Not really. You can talk about it and plan for it and train for it but it is not something you can do.

The Run.

Even then, when you are making The Run it doesn't seem possible and while you are in it and crossing the Alaska Range at Rainy Pass and running through the Burn and across the interior; even when you think you are alone on the planet and then know that you are alone on the planet; even as you run out to the coast and up the coast and across Norton Sound and along the icy cliffs through all the glorious northern villages with names like Kaltag and Koyuk and Shaktolik and Unalakleet and Elim; and even when you see the lights of Nome and think you will easily finish, even then it is not something you can do.

Not something that can be done. And yet you do it and

then it becomes something you don't want to end—ever. You want the race, the exaltation, the joy and beauty of it to go on and on. . . .

And so I stopped them and thought of turning around and going back into the middle of the world, the place I had found in the center of the world where it was only the dogs and only me and I hung there for a time, with my hand on the leader's back and I think I would have turned them except that I heard a yell and it was my wife.

A man in Nome had brought her out on a small road in a jeep. They had seen me coming and seen me stop and her voice broke the spell.

I got on the sled again and let them run and they followed the ice along the beach until we hit the ramp where they launch boats and we ran up that onto Front Street and down the mile of bare asphalt to the arch, the finish line.

Cookie, the leader, stopped before the arch and I had to drag her beneath it to finish—she was afraid of the crowd of people. I turned and could not keep from crying as I hugged my wife and son and then the dogs, starting from front to back, hugging each dog until two mushers took them away to put them on beds and I turned to the mayor of Nome who was there to greet me and said the one thing I never thought I would ever say.

"We'll be back to run it again."

And I knew that it was true.

GARY PAULSEN's three Newbery Honor books, *Dogsong, Hatchet,* and *The Winter Room,* as well as *Sentries, Tracker,* and *Dancing Carl,* have made him one of today's most popular writers. Living in northern Minnesota with his wife, Ruth Wright Paulsen, and their son, Jim, he has steadily pursued his great interest in dogs and dogsledding, chronicled for the first time here.

DATE DUE